POWER BROKERS
KINGMAKERS & USURPERS THROUGHOUT HISTORY

POWER BROKERS

KINGMAKERS & USURPERS THROUGHOUT HISTORY

SEAL OF ROBERT BRUCE, KING OF SCOTS.

Rupert Matthews

Facts On File
Oxford · New York

POWER BROKERS
KINGMAKERS & USURPERS THROUGHOUT HISTORY

Copyright © 1989 by Facts On File Ltd

Facts On File, Ltd.   or   Facts On File, Inc.
Collins Street   460 Park Avenue South
Oxford OX4 1JX   New York NY 10016
United Kingdom   USA

British Library Cataloguing in Publication Data
Matthews, Rupert Oliver
    Power Brokers:
    Kingmakers and usurpers throughout history
    1. Heads of state & rulers, history.
    Biographies. Collections
    I. Title
    909
    ISBN 0-8160-2156-2

Library of Congress Cataloging-in-Publication Data
Matthews, Rupert,
    Power brokers: kingmakers and usurpers throughout history
Rupert O. Matthews.
        p. cm.
    Bibliography: p.
    Includes index.
    ISBN 0-8160-2156-2
    1. Adventure and adventures—Biography.   2. Kings and rulers—Biography.
    3. World history.   I. Title.
    CT9970.M38   1989
    920.02—dc20

Production consultant Anthony Wheaton, Exeter
Jacket design by Richards Typesetting and Design, Exeter
Composition by Exe Valley Dataset, Exeter
Printed by Bookcraft Ltd, Midsomer Norton
10 9 8 7 6 5 4 3 2 1
This book is printed on acid-free paper.

Endpaper illustration by courtesy of Mansell Collection

40993

CONTENTS

INTRODUCTION

'Under a helmet of terror the all powerful lord of the people sat over the land and gave lavish gifts. It was not safe, nor without terror, to look at the light of Erik's eye, when serpent keen, the eye of the all powerful shone with terrifying light.'

This description of Eric Bloodaxe, King of York and briefly King of Norway, written over one thousand years ago, sums up the supreme dominance and authority of those who wield power.

Often backed by frightening violence, Eric ruled his kingdom by pure force in his statecraft and use of naked aggression in the face of challenge. His enigmatic nickname 'Bloodaxe' epitomizes the violent nature of his reign. It is a pattern repeated throughout the ages across the world.

Readers of this book will most likely be surprised by the sheer number of kingmakers and usurpers here recorded—and indeed the familiarity of some of their names. Yet these are only the ones handed down to us by recorded history. Without doubt, there have been hundreds more on a national level, and probably thousands on a provincial level. The men, and in many cases women, who usurped power in illiterate societies left no written records for us to ponder over. Civilized leaders overrun by barbarian hordes, or ousted by mercilessly efficient coups were often systematically put to the sword. Neither they, nor their peers would have had time to record the events for the edification of later generations.

Likewise, for every man or woman who has succeeded in seizing a crown or seat of power by force, perhaps a hundred more paid the price of failure through imprisonment or execution. History is usually written by the winners of such struggles.

This therefore is a collection of the most interesting *known* usurpations, revealing that history's power brokers came in all shapes and sizes, beliefs and disbeliefs, welcome and unwelcome, and, of course, both sexes. There is, however, a well-established and identifiable pattern to the course of events.

The common rule seems to be that weak government leads to usurpation. A cruel tyrant will survive—and even sometimes be admired—for as long as he keeps out invaders and maintains a semblance of law and order. A well-intentioned but ineffectual leader of whom few are afraid will hardly last the blinking of an eye. History, and the victims of those chronicled in this book, attest to that fact.

The real differences between one usurper or kingmaker and the next are in motive and method. There is a host of ruthlessly ambitious characters spurred on by a lust for wealth, status and authority, but many others with quite different reasons for seeking power.

Brunhild the Frankish Queen who seized power on the death of her husband in 576, took control simply to exact revenge. Her husband and sister had both been murdered by the king of a neighbouring country. Brunhild knew that only the full resources of her own kingdom would enable her to strike back. Instead of retiring into widowhood, she seized the crown and led her Frankish warriors into a war which devastated northern France for over twenty years.

Such coups as that of Brunhild are motivated not by pursuit of power for its own sake, but by a desire for that which only power can give.

On the other hand, there are those who seize power to save their own skins. It was often routine in Eastern and Middle Eastern countries for the King or Caliph ascending to the throne to kill all his brothers, sisters and other immediate bloodline to avoid close-lineage challenge to his position. A popular, but younger, brother perhaps with the support of the military, might well have tried to kill the heir-apparent before the royal stranglers were sent by the heir to eliminate him.

A case in point was that of Macrinus, who became Roman Emperor through the murder of his predecessor in AD 217. Macrinus was a senior civil servant who suddenly came under suspicion of a treason of which he was entirely innocent. Knowing that the Emperor Caracalla would sentence him to death, Macrinus acted first. If it had not been for the false accusation, Macrinus may well have lived out his life quietly as a civil servant, and never aspired to the Imperial Purple.

Greed, power-lust, revenge, patriotism even—so the list of reasons for stepping forward from the ranks and ousting the person above goes fascinatingly on.

The length of success of the usurpation also varies considerably. Only too often, history records that the usurper is overthrown for the very same reasons—and often by the same methods—which brought him or her to power in the first instance. Very few kingmakers and even fewer usurpers are known to have retired to a peaceful or affluent old age . . .

In compiling this book, many decisions have needed to be taken regarding both dates and spellings. In some areas of the world, and during some eras of history, records are at best sketchy or imprecise. It is sometimes difficult to correlate these records to the standard Western method of dating events as Before Christ (BC) or Anno Domini (after the birth of Christ). Ancient China, for instance, used a system of dating based upon the reigns of Emperors, while Imperial Rome related its histories to the founding of the Temple of Jupiter. It is, therefore, inevitable that some dates are rather vague. Where uncertainty prevails, this has been pointed out in the text.

More difficult to resolve are the problems raised by the transliteration of names from other cultures and alphabets. Such names, be they transliterated into Roman script from Egyptian hieroglyphics, Chinese or Arabic, are usually done so on the basis of phonetics. In other words, they are written down as they sound.

However, the accepted English spellings of these names tend to change, as scholars discover more accurate methods of transliteration. I have endeavoured throughout to use the spelling which will be most familiar to the general reader. Where one particular version of a name has been in use for many years, I have tended to adopt it in preference to a more accurate, but perhaps less well known, form of the same name. As an example, the thirteenth-century Chinese Emperor Kublai Khan has been so known in the West for many generations. Recent scholars have preferred to spell his name Qubilai, although I have preferred the older and better-known version of the name to avoid confusion.

This book is an essentially chronological catalogue of success and disaster, virtue and greed, treachery and loyalty. Most of all, it is a warning to all of the high price of failure. Everyone with a grain of ambition to succeed should read on. The lesson to learn is simple: never forget to glance over your shoulder to see who's coming up behind you!

SNEFERU (fl. c. 2900 BC)

Usurped: Egyptian Crown circa 2930 BC
Social Origins: possibly Royal Prince

KHUFU (fl. c. 2875 BC)

Usurped: Egyptian Crown circa 2900 BC
Social Origins: Noble Family

No doubt there were many usurpations and assassinations carried out in the prehistoric world about which we know nothing. The ambitions and motives of the people involved in such attempts have been lost for lack of written records, and their achievements have vanished with the years. It is in the earliest years of the mighty Egyptian civilization that the first historically documented usurpation is to be found. Yet even here the details are confused. Historians are not certain whether it was Sneferu or his successor Khufu who carried out a forceful acquisition of power, perhaps they both did. Whatever the details the change was dramatic enough to cause future troubles.

In about 2900 BC Egypt was a wealthy and highly organized nation. The fertile lands of the Nile valley had been unified by Narmer some two centuries earlier who took the title of Pharaoh. Three dynasties of Pharaoh succeeded each other peacefully, but the Pharaohs of the Third Dynasty seem to have been unadventurous and inept rulers. Almost nothing is known of them. The Pharaohs were believed to be living gods, claiming descent from the sun god and representing that god on earth. Originally the Pharaoh alone was believed to enjoy an afterlife, though he could appoint servants to accompany him. The prestige of the Pharaoh as living god was immense, which makes the usurpation at the end of the Third Dynasty all the more remarkable.

Then in 2900 BC, or possibly 2530 BC, Sneferu became Pharaoh. Sneferu was a highly successful and ambitious warrior, defeating the uncivilized enemies of Egypt on all fronts, and driving them from Egyptian lands. Some historians count Sneferu as the first ruler of the mighty Fourth Dynasty. It is thought that he was a victorious general who became exasperated with the weak Third Dynasty Pharaohs and used his troops to seize power.

Others regard Sneferu's successor, known variously as Khufu and Cheops, as the usurper. The records are imprecise but indicate that Khufu was born the son of a minor noble and had no connection with the royal and divine family of the Pharaohs. Nonetheless, Khufu managed to assume the throne following the death of Sneferu. This act may have had something to do with the fact that Khufu was the lover of Sneferu's favourite wife. Some experts believe that the texts indicate that Khufu was a junior son of Sneferu.

Whether the usurpation was achieved by a victorious soldier or palace intrigue, the events surrounding the collapse of the Third Dynasty swept away the Sacred Pharaohs descended from Narmer and replaced them with a line of non-royal rulers. It was perhaps because of their dubious origins that the pharaohs of the Fourth Dynasty erected huge monuments celebrating their achievements and fame. The greatest of these monuments was the tomb of Khufu himself. This is the Great Pyramid of Giza which was designed to emphasize the immortality, and therefore the worthiness for divinity of its builder.

After ruling for some 150 years the Fourth Dynasty was overthrown by the priests of the sun god Ra. The High Priest of Ra became Pharaoh and re-established the divine nature of the Pharaoh.

— ♛ —

HATSHEPSUT (? [-] 1480 BC)
Usurped: Egyptian Crown 1498 BC
Social Origins: Royal Princess

The ancient Egyptians had a peculiar system whereby the title and powers of Pharaoh could pass through a woman, but could not be held by her. In effect the son or husband of a royal princess could become Pharaoh while she herself was excluded from the throne. In about 1500 BC one royal princess rebelled against this system and inaugurated one of the most remarkable reigns of ancient Egypt.

The great military Pharaoh Thutmose I died in 1501 BC, leaving a number of children by different wives. One son, Thutmose II, followed precedent by marrying a half-sister, named Hatshepsut, who was closer to the crown than himself, so enforcing his own position. Thutmose II allowed Hatshepsut a share of power and together they instituted important reforms of the government.

After just three years, Thutmose II died. Without him Hatshepsut had no claim to the throne at all. However, once having tasted power, she was determined not to lose it. Hatshepsut immediately married a second half-brother who was promoted to the throne as Thutmose III. Some inscriptions indicate that Thutmose III was a son of Hatshepsut, rather than her brother, but the habitual incestual relationships of the Pharaohs means that the one

Hatshepsut
A small 15th-century BC statue depicting Queen Hatshepsut as a sphinx. Hatshepsut was the first queen to rule Egypt, but no mechanism or artistic device existed to show female royal power. She was therefore usually shown, as here, with the long royal beard and in male poses traditionally associated with the power of the Pharaoh. (*Macdonald/Aldus*)

3

relationship need not exclude the other. The new Pharaoh was treated as little better than a prisoner. He lived in sumptuous palaces and great luxury, but could do nothing without his sister-wife's approval. Hatshepsut kept the reins of power firmly in her own grasp.

This sudden seizure of power by a woman was unprecedented in Egypt. The Egyptians were accustomed to being ruled by a man and probably felt uneasy at the idea of a woman ruler. To get round this Hatshepsut not only used Thutmose III as a front, she also insisted that statues and paintings of herself should show a man. Thus we have the extraordinary situation of a reigning queen being depicted with a beard and an absence of breasts.

So complete was Hatshepsut's seizure of power that she remained in total control of Egypt until her death in 1480 BC. Following his release Thutmose III vented his anger on Hatshepsut by desecrating her tomb and destroying all references to her name on temples and monuments built by her. He also abandoned her policy of peace and internal reform by launching a long, costly but ultimately successful war against the Assyrians and Hittites.

HOREMHEB (? [-] 1320 BC)

Usurped: Egyptian Crown 1348 BC
Social Origins: Army officer

When the boy king Tutankhamun became Pharaoh of Egypt in 1360 BC he chose two 'advisers' to run the country for him until he came of age. One was his elderly uncle Ay, the most senior civil servant in Egypt. The other was the ambitious young general of all the armies, Horemheb.

These men persuaded Tutankhamun to abandon the new religion of Aten, introduced by his predecessor, and return to the national religion of Amon. This move endeared the young Pharaoh to the powerful Amon priests. However, he refused to persecute the followers of Aten and did not restore the fabulous wealth of the Amon temples.

In 1352 BC Horemheb led the army into Syria to fight yet another campaign in the long-running conflict with the powerful Hittite Empire, centred in what is now modern Turkey. While Horemheb was away waging this gruelling desert war Tutankhamun died. Ay, who was on the spot, seized power. He officiated at the funeral of Tutankhamun, a duty reserved for the succeeding Pharaoh. Tutankhamun's widow, Ankhesenamun, was determined not to lose her rights as the only legitimate member of the royal family. She sent a secret message to the Hittite Emperor asking for a prince to marry her and help in re-establishing herself on the throne. It was at this point that Horemheb took a hand.

Horemheb knew he had lost supreme power to Ay, but youth was on his side and the aging Pharaoh would not live long. The succession of a Pharaoh who was the son of his bitterest enemy, on the other hand, would put Horemheb in a difficult position. He realized that a Hittite Pharaoh would dismiss him from command and probably order his execution. The subsequent murder of the Hittite prince, the proposed husband of Ankhesenamun, by 'robbers' was almost certainly the work of Horemheb.

Having taken such a bold step, Horemheb determined on reaching for the crown itself. While covering himself in glory and popular appeal, he ostentatiously worshipped Amon and discouraged the worship of Aten in his army. This policy was designed to bring him the support of both the priests and the people. The plan worked well. While outwardly loyal to Ay and his civil servants, Horemheb was working his way closer to the throne.

In 1348 it became clear that the elderly Ay was on his deathbed. Horemheb hurried to the scene with his best troops. Young Ankhesenamun, whom Ay had kept at court to give a pretence of legality to his rule, disappears from the written record at this point. Her fate is unknown, but it is likely that Horemheb ordered her death. When Ay died, Horemheb moved fast. He persuaded the priests to proclaim him Pharaoh and stifled opposition with his troops.

In the first few months of his reign, Horemheb ensured that there would be no opposition. All senior civil servants were ousted and replaced with officers loyal to the new Pharaoh. The priests were rewarded for their support by royal decrees which crushed the Aten religion. For the remaining 28 years of his life, Horemheb was careful to keep a tight control on the country. The priests were kept quiet by lavish gifts to the temples, but firmly barred from politics. The civil service, once loyal to Ay, was gradually filled with Horemheb's men. When he died in 1320 BC, Horemheb the usurper was able to pass on a stable kingdom to his famous successor Rameses I.

SAMUEL (fl. c. 1000 BC)

Kingmaker of Israel circa 1000 BC
Social Origins: Judge or Priest

By about 1000 BC the twelve tribes of Israel were firmly established in Canaan, roughly the area north and west of the Dead Sea. At this time the tribes were simply a loose confederation bound by a common religion. Around them lived several other tribes leading a similar way of life and having similar social structures. The tribes were ruled by priests called

Judges, of whom Samuel was the greatest and most famous. For many years Samuel supervised the nation, but as he grew older he wanted to hand control over to his sons.

The people of Israel were unhappy with Samuel's sons who used their positions to take bribes and acquire wealth. The Israelites demanded that Samuel choose a man to be king of all the tribes as they recognized the benefits of a unified royal government. At first Samuel did not want to take on the role of kingmaker. He pointed out the burden of taxation which a king would impose, but the people insisted that he choose a king.

Eventually Samuel chose a tall, powerfully-built young man named Saul to be king. Saul belonged to the smallest tribe, that of Benjamin. This fact helped to gain him acceptance for none of the larger, more powerful tribes, felt threatened. At first Saul proved to be a great warrior who defeated Israel's enemies and governed wisely.

However, Saul and Samuel soon fell out. On one occasion Saul offered a sacrifice to God when Samuel was not present, which angered the priest. Later God ordered Saul to destroy the Amalekites. Saul did so but brought some loot back to sacrifice at the temple. Samuel thought that God had meant Saul to destroy the property as well as the people. From that time on the two men refused to speak to each other.

Convinced that Saul was no longer fit to be king, Samuel decided to act as kingmaker once again. He travelled to Bethlehem and visited the family of Jesse. Samuel recognized Jesse's youngest son, named David, as the man fit to be king. The priest secretly anointed David king with holy oil and then left. Samuel died soon afterwards, but David eventually ousted Saul and became king, just as Samuel had intended.

SOLOMON (fl. c. 970 BC)

Usurped: Kingdom of Israel circa 974 BC
Social Origins: Royal Family

In about 974 BC David, King of Israel, then a small state on the fringes of the Egyptian Empire, lay on his deathbed. He had several wives and many children, most of whom lived in his household. The eldest surviving son was Adonijah and most people assumed that Adonijah would succeed David. While David was ill Adonijah acted as regent. He presided over royal feasts and commanded the army.

However, Adonijah had a younger half-brother named Solomon who was determined to become king. While Adonijah and all the officers of state were

6

at a banquet, Bathsheba, mother of Solomon, crept into David's bedroom. With the help of a prophet named Nathan and a priest called Zadok, Bathsheba persuaded David to name Solomon as his successor.

Having gained the precious royal endorsement, Solomon and Bathsheba acted quickly. Solomon mounted David's ceremonial mule and rode to Gihon. Zadok took a horn of holy oil from the Tabernacle and hurried down to Gihon. There Zadok and Nathan anointed Solomon as king. A procession was then organized back to Jerusalem, with Solomon leading as the Lord's anointed. Having gained both David's approval and holy oil, Solomon was king in theory. It remained to be seen if he could secure actual power.

When Adonijah heard the trumpets and pipes of the procession, he not unnaturally asked what was going on. When a messenger came back with the news that it was the coronation procession of Solomon fear spread through the banquet. Every man knew that death was the likely fate for those who supported the loser in such a succession dispute as this. Almost to a man the officials and army officers returned to their own homes to await the result. In fact, Adonijah had been caught by surprise and there was nobody he could trust in Jerusalem. He therefore fled to the Tabernacle and threw himself on the holy altar demanding sanctuary.

Now in firm control of the government, Solomon promised to spare Adonijah so long as he behaved himself. Adonijah trusted his half-brother and left the Tabernacle. However, Solomon knew that so long as his elder brother remained alive his own hold on the throne would remain insecure. He therefore took advantage of a minor incident to rid himself of this problem.

Adonijah asked permission to marry Abishag, a personal servant of the late king David. Solomon pretended to be angry declaring that if Adonijah wanted royal servants he would soon want the royal throne. Solomon chose to construe this as treason and had Adonijah killed on the spot. Friends of Adonijah swiftly followed him to the grave. The usurpation of Solomon was complete. Solomon ruled wisely and well for over forty years until his peaceful death in about 932 BC.

OMRI (fl. c. 880 BC)

Usurped: Kingdom of Israel circa 876 BC
Social Origins: Army Officer

Unlike many who seize power through force, Omri did so for the very best of motives; that of justice. In about the year 876 BC Israel was being ruled by

King Elah, son of the usurper Baasha, who had been on the throne just two years. Omri was, at this time, supreme commander of the army.

When war broke out with the Philistines, Omri led the army to besiege the town of Gibbethon. A small royal guard remained with King Elah in Tirzah under the command of Zimri, a chariot officer. Zimri, however, soon proved himself to be an ambitious and unscrupulous man. One night King Elah visited Arza, his steward, for a banquet and became overcome by drink. In the midst of the festivities and drunken jollity, Zimri burst in and stabbed Elah to death. Zimri then had himself proclaimed king.

The news of this usurpation was greeted with anger by the army at Gibbethon. Omri immediately abandoned the siege and led his troops back to Tirzah. When Zimri realised that his bid for power was being resisted by the army he took a drastic decision. He locked himself in the royal palace and set fire to the building. Perhaps he was determined to die as a king, even if he couldn't live as one. Omri led his troops into Tirzah but was immediately faced by the rebellion of a man named Tibni. The insurrection was soon put down and Omri went on to rule Israel for twelve years.

HAZAEL (fl. c. 860 BC)

Usurped: Kingdom of Syria circa 860 BC
Social Origins: Palace Official

In the 9th century BC the Middle East was covered by a patchwork of small states sandwiched between the established power of Egypt and the growing Assyrian Empire. One of the greatest of these states was Syria, which stretched from the Mediterranean to the headwaters of the Euphrates and had its capital at Damascus.

During the 860s and 870s BC King Benhadad of Syria was allied first to the kingdom of Israel and then to Judah, both small Jewish states, in the almost constant warfare which racked the area. In about 860 BC Benhadad caught an illness which confined him to bed. While he lay sick, Benhadad heard that the Israelite prophet Elisha had arrived in Damascus. Elisha's fame had spread to Syria and Benhadad decided to ask Elisha if the illness would prove fatal.

Benhadad ordered Hazael, one of the palace officials, to take a present to Elisha and ask about the chances of complete recovery. Hazael, accordingly, visited Elisha only to receive the enigmatic statement that the illness was not fatal, but that Benhadad would die anyway. Elisha then burst into tears. When Hazael asked what was wrong, Elisha replied that Hazael would do great harm to Israel once he had become King of Syria. Elisha may have been prompted to such manipulative predictions by the complex international situation at the time, but if so his motives are unclear.

Whatever Elisha's aims, his words had their effect. Hazael returned to Benhadad and told him that the disease was not fatal. Hazael then spent some time thinking. Next morning, convinced that Elisha's prophecy should come true, Hazael crept into Benhadad's room and suffocated him. Hazael then made himself king. As predicted by Elisha, Hazael fought several wars against Israel, but he then fell foul of the Assyrians and suffered a series of defeats.

— 👑 —

JEHU (fl. c. 840 BC)

Usurped: Kingdom of Israel circa 841 BC
Social Origins: Army Officer

In the mid-9th century BC Israel was one of two small Jewish kingdoms which existed in the Middle East. Israel had to cope with a web of foreign intrigue between itself, Judah, the other Jewish Kingdom, Jehoshaphat and various other kingdoms. In 841 BC King Joram of Israel, son of Ahab, was wounded in battle against the Syrians and travelled to Jezreel to recover. Joram's mother, the infamous Jezebel, and his nephew, King Ahaziah of Judah came to visit him. The army remained in the field at Ramoth under the command of its officers, one of whom was Jehu, who was famous for his furious chariot driving.

During his short reign Joram had failed to expel properly the worship of Baal, so angering the religious establishment of Israel. The prophet Elisha determined to stop this religious unorthodoxy. He sent a young prophet to the army encampment with a box of holy oil. The prophet took Jehu aside and on Elisha's orders anointed him King of Israel and told him to kill the entire family of Ahab. The prophet then fled, no doubt hoping to avoid the inevitable bloodshed which would follow his actions.

Jehu told the army he had been made king, gathered together a picked body of troops and set off to take power. Driving his chariot as furiously as usual, Jehu was recognized by a watchman on the walls of Jezreel. When Joram heard an army officer was approaching he dragged himself into a chariot and set out to greet him. Joram was accompanied by his nephew King Ahaziah of Judah.

When the three men met, Jehu began insulting King Joram for the sins of his family. Joram realised that Jehu intended murder and turned his chariot,

9

shouting a warning to his nephew. Seeing his victim escaping, Jehu drew his war-bow and sent an arrow plunging into Joram's back. The king collapsed, dying, in his chariot. Ahaziah turned his chariot in panic and galloped off at high speed. But Ahaziah did not flee fast enough, soldiers sent by Jehu overtook him at Gur. Though Ahaziah escaped he was badly wounded and died soon afterwards.

Jehu, meanwhile, urged his chariot horses up to full speed yet again and galloped into Jezreel. Seeing him coming, and recognizing that death was close, Jezebel calmly put on her make-up and restyled her hair. When Jehu arrived Jezebel taunted him by comparing him to the earlier usurper Zimri (see Omri above). Jehu angrily ordered Jezebel to be thrown to the ground, where he drove his chariot over her body.

Not content with this violent seizure of power, Jehu continued his bloody attempts to fulfil the instructions of Elisha. Ahab had left seventy children who were being brought up by various nobles and wealthy men. Jehu sent messages to these men demanding that they kill Ahab's children. If they did not, said Jehu, he would come and kill the children and their hosts himself. With the army to back him up, Jehu got what he wanted and soon seventy severed heads adorned the gates of Jezreel. Jehu then went on to murder all the priests of Baal he could find, together with the officials who had served Joram. Having effectively destroyed any opposition to his violent usurpation, Jehu settled down to ruling Israel. His descendants retained the crown for nearly a century, the longest-lasting dynasty in Israel's history.

ATHALIAH (fl. 840 BC)

Usurped: Kingdom of Judah 841 BC
Social Origins: Royal Family

In 841 BC King Ahaziah of Judah visited his uncle King Joram of Israel at Jezreel. During his visit Ahaziah had the misfortune to become involved in the bloody rebellion of Jehu and to be killed (see JEHU above). When news of Ahaziah's unexpected death reached the court his mother, Athaliah made a determined bid for power.

Athaliah ordered troops loyal to herself to kill every member of the royal family. She coolly waited while her children, grandchildren and cousins were butchered and then had herself declared Queen. Nobody dared oppose Athaliah, even though she was a pagan worshipper of Baal, and she ruled Judah with an firm hand.

However, Athaliah's plans were not carried out as completely as she wished. Her own sister, Jehosheba, found a baby son of Ahaziah before the soldiers did. She hid the infant Joash in her bedroom until the bloody slaughter was over.

For seven years Athaliah ruled Judah, but her devotion to Baal caused much unrest and friction. Eventually, the religious troubles came to a head. Jehoiada, priest of the Lord and husband of Jehosheba, brought the young prince Joash out of hiding and took him to the Temple. Jehoiada gathered together the chief army officers, who were discontented with the rule of Athaliah, and brought them to the Temple. Here Jehoiada crowned the boy Joash king and anointed him with holy oil.

At that moment Queen Athaliah arrived at the Temple. She took in the scene with one horrified glance. She saw the boy wearing the royal crown, the priest with the anointing oil and the hostile glares of the army officers. In a desperate attempt to summon help Queen Athaliah shouted 'Treason, Treason', but to no avail. Some of the army officers dragged her out of the Temple to the palace stables and killed her. Jehoiada then supervised the destruction of the Temple of Baal.

TIGLATH PILESER III (?–727 BC)

Usurped: Empire of Assyria 745 BC
Social Origins: Royal Family

After an initial burst of growth under Tiglath-Pileser I, the Assyrian Empire entered a period of stagnation. Under Adad-Nirari III (810–783 BC) the Empire expanded again as the army made great conquests and secured much loot and booty. However, after the death of Adad-Nirari, defeat followed defeat under inept leadership. It may have been this period of frustration which caused Tiglath-Pileser III to launch his bid for power.

Born under the name of Pul, Tiglath-Pileser III was the son of Adad-Nirari III who made a career for himself in the army, reaching high command during the reign of his brother Ashur-Nirari V. During these years victories were few and far between for the Assyrians. From his later actions it is clear that Pul realised the weaknesses of the Assyrian army. Perhaps he tried to institute reforms, but if so his attempts were thwarted.

In 745 BC Pul put some very carefully laid plans into operation. He murdered Ashur-Nirari V and ordered his troops to kill every single member of the Imperial family. Pul then assumed the name of Tiglath-Pileser III, possibly as an attempt to forge a link with past. Interestingly the Bible, one of the few contemporary, non-Assyrian accounts of these years, refers to Tiglath-Pileser III as Pul. Presumably the king's enemies were not impressed by the change of name.

Tiglath Pileser III
A relief of the great Assyrian warrior-king Tiglath Pileser III who is shown with the stylized beard and long hair of the Assyrian nobility. Large carvings such as this, brightly painted in naturalistic colours, adorned the walls of Assyrian palaces and temples. This example comes from Tiglath Pileser's own palace in Nimrud.
(*Michael Holford*)

With his new-found power as undisputed ruler of the Assyrian Empire, Tiglath-Pileser III instituted reforms almost as sweeping as his usurpation. As Emperor, Tiglath-Pileser was considered by his subjects to be a semi-divine representative of the gods. Tiglath-Pileser III could, therefore, count on his instructions being obeyed without question.

The entire nation was organized for war, the main purpose of the civilians being to provide recruits, pay and supplies for the army. Equipping his men with breastplates, helmets and iron weapons, Tiglath-Pileser brought the practices of seige warfare to a fine art. He built huge battering-rams and mobile towers with which to attack fortified cities. He also enlarged the swift chariot corps which dominated the open battlefield and won many wars for him.

The conquering army of the Assyrians became greatly feared. Tiglath-Pileser being intent on amassing as much loot and tribute as he possibly could. The summit of his career came in 729 BC when he took the incredibly wealthy city of Babylon and assumed the title King of Babylon. Two years later Tiglath-Pileser III died, but his successors continued his policy of raid and conquest for more than a century.

— ♛ —

PEKAH (fl. c. 740 BC)

Usurped: Kingdom of Israel 740 BC
Social Origins: Army Officer

By 740 BC, the Kingdom of Israel was under constant threat from nearby enemies. The growing might of the Assyrian Empire was pushing at Israel's borders from the east while a collection of smaller states to the north and south were waiting to take advantage of any weakness. These dangers may have provided the underlying reasons for the usurpation by Pekah.

King Menahem had been a strong and tough king, but he died in 742 leaving the throne to his son Pekahiah. Little is known of the new king, which may indicate that he achieved little of note. Within just two years a powerful faction within Israel had decided that Pekahiah was not up to the job of ruling such a troubled kingdom.

A group of palace officials and army leaders, headed by Pekah decided to remove Pekahiah from the throne. One night Pekah, together with fifty men, took control of the royal palace. Pekah strode into the room where Pekahiah was sleeping and killed him. The conspirators then acclaimed Pekah as king.

For some twenty years Pekah proved to be just the strong man that Isarael needed. He fought successfully against the neighbouring Kingdom of Judah and managed to keep the forces of the mighty Assyrian Empire at arm's length. But eventually the Assyrians launched a determined assault and crushed Pekah's army. The prestige of Pekah as a warrior king could not survive this defeat. He had come to power as a strong man able to defend Israel, but was now seen to be weak and unable to fulfil his task. In 720 BC Pekah was murdered.

HOSHEA (fl. c. 720 BC)

Usurped: Kingdom of Israel 720 BC
Social Origins: Unknown

Following a series of defeats in war King Pekah had become unpopular. Hoshea took advantage of this unpopularity to murder Pekah and seize the throne for himself. However, Hoshea found his newly-won throne to be beset by troubles. The Kingdom of Israel was sandwiched between the powerful empires of Assyria and Egypt. At first Hoshea paid tribute to the Assyrians, but after six years became discontented and plotted with Egypt. Shalmaneser of Assyria discovered the plot, captured Hoshea and threw him into prison. Hoshea is never heard of again.

SARGON II (?–705 BC)

Usurped: Empire of Assyria 722 BC
Social Origins: Army Officer

Little is known of the actual usurpation of Sargon II. Before 722 he was a powerful general who led Assyrian forces on several victorious campaigns. Suddenly, in 722 BC, the reigning Emperor, Sharru-kin, vanishes from history to be replaced by Sargon II. The lack of detail is due largely to the highly effective way in which Sargon II covered his crime.

A major feature of this campaign of presenting a façade of legitimacy was Sargon II's name itself. Sargon I was a great legendary figure in Assyria, perhaps occupying a position similar to the British King Arthur. Sargon I had lived about 2200 BC and was the first great ruler of the Semitic people, which included the ancestors of the Assyrians. Under Sargon the Semitics had poured out from the wilderness to conquer and settle in the fertile lands of Mesopotamia.

By identifying himself with this earlier king, and actually claiming direct descent through a largely fictional ancestry which included Tigleth Pileser III (see above), Sargon II was probably attempting to establish a legitimate claim to hide his illegal usurpation whilst indicating that he was determined upon a career of conquest.

In both these aims Sargon II was dramatically successful. His right to the throne was not questioned while he lived, and even today we do not know the details of his bid for power. In military affairs, Sargon II was equally triumphant. He conquered and destroyed the kingdoms of Israel and Cappodocia, and forced Judah and other kingdoms to surrender to him. His victorious armies reached the borders of Egypt before returning to the east. A rebellion in Babylon was put down with startling ruthlessness and Sargon II moved on to take the important regions of Merodachbaladan and Commagene. He died soon after these last successes.

GYGES (?–c. 685 BC)

Usurped: Kingdom of Lydia circa 680 BC
Social Origins: Shepherd

One of the most romantic usurpations of the ancient world was that of Gyges who replaced Candaules as King of Lydia. According to later accounts Gyges was a simple shepherd before his bid for power, but these humble origins may simply have been invented to add poignancy to what was already a highly dramatic event.

Whatever his background, Gyges was present when Candaules organized a great celebration for his wedding to a particularly beautiful young noblewoman. The young Gyges was completely overcome by the charms of the bride and impulsively dashed forwards. He dragged the bride from the celebrations and made off with her. This, not unnaturally, enraged Candaules who became determined to exact revenge. It was, however, Gyges who emerged successful, managing to murder Candaules and seize power for himself.

As king Gyges moved his capital to the city of Sardis and set about extending his domain, he managed to exert pressure on the Greek cities of the Ionian coast, forcing them to pay tribute. His domination was tempered by the fact that Gyges was a highly cultured man who admired Greek art and thought. He sent presents to the prestigious Oracle of Apollo at Delphi and adopted many Greek customs. Most notably Gyges encouraged trade by improving roads and harbours and by introducing a reliable coinage. Through this mercantile activity he became immensely rich and lived in luxury.

After some 35 years of relatively untroubled rule, Gyges was killed by invading barbarian Cimmerians from the northeast. However Gyges's dynasty survived, in the shape of his son Ardys, and went on to become one of the most cultured and wealthy of the ancient world. The proverbially rich Croesus was a later king of the dynasty.

AHMOSE II (?–526 BC)

Usurped: Pharaoh of Egypt 568 BC
Social Origins: Nobility

Having freed themselves of Assyrian rule in about 610 BC, the Egyptians entered a relatively quiet period in their long history. The Pharaohs of the 26th Dynasty followed each other in regular succession and concentrated on internal policies. In so doing they were enhancing Egypt, but may have laid the foundations of their own downfall.

The rulers of the 26th Dynasty encouraged trade and cultural exchanges with other nations, particularly with Greece. To the Pharaohs, their advisers, and many recent critics, this activity has been seen to be one of Egypt's greatest. There was a flowering of the arts, as a more cosmopolitan culture was attained, and a general growth of prosperity. But, to the average Egyptian of the day, and particularly the soldiers, there was little to admire about these activities. They appear to have been seen as an abandonment of tradition, a dangerous liaison with foreigners or, in modern terms, a sell-out. This feeling was only exacerbated when the Pharaohs refused to interfere decisively in the rise of the Persian Empire.

Eventually, the Egyptian troops of the last member of the 26th Dynasty, Pharaoh Apries, turned to a man named Ahmose, or Aahmes. Ahmose seems to have been famous for his admiration of Egyptian tradition and distrust of foreigners. The Egyptian core of the army rose in revolt and overthrew Apries. Ahmose was invested with the double crown of Egypt and immediately satisfied his supporters by taking up a conspicuously xenophobic stand. Ahmose was, however, astute enough to recognize the financial benefits of trading with the Greek world. He established Naukratis as a port for Greek merchants.

Ahmose promoted the interests of the army and began an aggressive policy towards the Persian Empire. This resulted in an invasion by Nebuchadrezzar II, which was beaten off with the aid of foreign alliances. In the later years of his long reign, Ahmose was faced by another Persian invasion under Cambyses. Again Ahmose formed foreign alliances, but these collapsed upon his death. The new Pharaoh Psammetichus III did not have time to forge new treaties before Cambyses attacked. Egypt was defeated and became part of the Persian Empire.

— ♛ —

NERGALSHAREZER (?-556 BC)

Usurped: Kingdom of Babylon 560 BC
Social Origins: Noble Family

In 612 BC an alliance of various small nations came together and, after a struggle of epic proportions, destroyed the mighty Assyrian Empire. The ancient city of Babylon reasserted its independence and spread its influence through much of the Middle East. The greatest king of Babylon was Nebuchadrezzar, who rebuilt the city in magnificent fashion and constructed the famous Hanging Gardens to remind his beloved wife of her mountain home.

Nebuchadrezzar was devoted to the violent conqueror god Marduk and named his son and heir Amel-Marduk in his honour. If Nebuchadrezzar expected his son to live up to the god's behaviour he was sadly mistaken. Amel-Marduk, sometimes known as Evil-Merodach, abandoned his father's visions of foreign conquest and magnificent building. Instead Amel-Marduk vented his passions for tyranny and cruelty on his own people.

After just two years the oppression and cruelty of Amel-Marduk had reached an unbearable crescendo. At this time Nergalsharezer, whose name is sometimes spelt Neriglissar, decided to take a hand. Nergalsharezer was a powerful nobleman who was married to Amel-Marduk's sister. As such he had easy access to the king, where others were kept at a distance by armed guards. Nergalsharezer used this privilege to approach Amel-Marduk and then killed him. Declaring he had acted to protect the public good, a common claim by usurpers, Nergalsharezer than seized the reins of power. His brief reign was notable for spectacular building projects and an absence of the cruelty which had marked that of Amel-Marduk.

— 👑 —

PEISISTRATUS (?-527 BC)

Usurped: Supreme power in Athens 560 BC
Social origins: Nobility

Around the year 600 BC the wealthy city-state Athens was in turmoil. The Greek citizens were divided into a number of *genos*, clan-like organizations which were a legacy from a more uncivilized past and which carried on violent feuds with each other. The ruling nobles were unable to control the situation which was made worse by large numbers of discontented peasants who had fallen into debt or slavery and by a growing merchant class which had wealth but lacked a political voice.

In desperation the Athenians asked a prominent citizen named Draco and later a second named Solon to draw up a new set of laws and political structure. Between them these men set up a rudimentary justice system to replace the feuds of the *genos* and a rather crude form of democracy in which every citizen had some degree of influence. These laws were probably finalized sometime in the 560s. While they defused the explosive internal pressures, the laws failed to solve the underlying problems. Debt continued to cripple the poorer classes while the nobles continued to pursue their bitter conflicts.

Meanwhile a cousin of Solon, named Peisistratus, had been leading the Athenian army in a protracted war against Megara. In about 561 BC Peisistratus returned to Athens and was appalled by the internal conflicts going on. Unlike his kinsman, Peisistratus had little regard for legality and consensus politics. He decided to sort out the mess by himself.

In 560 BC an assassination attempt was made on Peisistratus, or so he claimed. For protection Peisistratus persuaded the Athenians to allow him a bodyguard of trusted soldiers. This 'bodyguard' quickly assumed the proportions of a small army. Before the civil authorities realized what was happening, Peisistratus led his 'bodyguard' to the Acropolis, then the fortified heart of the city, and took it by force. Peisistratus ignored all constitutional processes. He issued orders from the Acropolis. If anybody argued, Peisistratus sent his troops to exert pressure. Several noblemen were forced into exile.

The new tyrant took the side of the peasants and introduced many laws to benefit the masses. He also helped the merchant classes by issuing trustworthy silver coins and building a war fleet to protect Athenian merchant ships. On two occasions the nobility expelled Peisistratus, but both times he returned and from 542 until his death in 527 he enjoyed unopposed power. By favouring the masses and business interests over those of the aristocrats, Peisistratus smashed the power of the nobility and the *genos*. Through his tyranny he was laying the foundations for future democracy.

After Peisistratus' death in 527 his sons Hippias and Hipparchus took power. Hipparchus was murdered in 514 whereupon the rule of Hippias became extremely repressive. In 510 the populace revolted with the aid of Spartan troops and expelled Hippias, reintroducing the democratic principles of Draco and Solon.

— 👑 —

CYRUS THE GREAT (c. 600–529 BC)

Usurped: Kingdom of Medes circa 550 BC
Social Origins: Obscure

The rise to power of Cyrus, called the Great by later generations, was one of the most spectacular in history. At birth he was a nobody, when he died he was the most powerful monarch in the world. Unfortunately the early stages of this remarkable career are shrouded in mystery. Historians are not even certain who Cyrus's parents were.

According to Cyrus himself, he was the son of the ruler of the Persian city of Anshan. This man may have been Cambyses who seems to have been a member of the ancient Anshan royal family and who was used as a local governor by Astyages, King of the Medes who had conquered Anshan some years earlier. Some early sources say that Cambyses was married to Mandane, only daughter of Astyages. This story may have been invented to give Cyrus's usurpation some degree of legitimacy. In fact the stories surrounding Cyrus's early days are so obscure that he may have originated almost anywhere from almost any family!

Whatever his beginnings, Cyrus was certainly governor of Anshan in 549 BC. In that year he revolted against the power of Astyages and led an army of Persians against the Medes. Cyrus fought his way into Ecbatana, the royal city of the Medes, and captured Astyages. Cyrus soon discovered that the Medes were glad to be rid of their king, and settled down to unite the Medes and Persians in a single kingdom.

By 546 BC Cyrus had completed his usurpation. He had made himself acceptable to both Medes and Persians and had imposed his authority on the lands previously controlled by Astyages. Then Cyrus turned his army upon foreign enemies. After carefully ensuring the neutrality of Egypt, Cyrus provoked King Croesus of Lydia into war. Cyrus may have been tempted by the fantastic wealth of Lydia. Croesus himself was lured to defeat due to his misintepretation of a prophecy by the Delphic Oracle. He sought advice on the route his army should take to be told 'If Croesus crosses the River Aly, he will destroy a great kingdom.' Croesus sent his army across the Aly, was severely defeated and so destroyed his own kingdom, not Cyrus's as he had hoped.

After this spectacular victory, Cyrus went on to conquer and subdue the Greek cities of Ionia, together with Syria, Judah, Phoenicia, the Chaldeans and the kingdoms bordering the northern steppes. It was during Cyrus's seige of Babylon in 539 BC that Belshazzar held his famous feast at which, according to the Bible, a disembodied hand appeared which wrote the fatal words 'Mene Mene Tekel Upharsin'. This message was interpreted by the Biblical hero Daniel to foretell the end of Babylon. The next day Cyrus took the city. In 529 BC, at the age of about 70, Cyrus was killed fighting a tribe of barbarians. He left to his son Cambyses the greatest empire in the world at that time.

GAUMATA (?-521 BC)
Usurped: Persian Empire 522 BC
Social Origins: Priest

The rebellion of Gaumata was as curious as it was shortlived, based as it was on a deception which could not be maintained. For some years after his accession as the ruler of the mighty Persian Empire, Cambyses governed the eastern provinces through his younger brother Smerdis. In 525 Cambyses ordered the execution of Smerdis, for reasons which are still unknown.

Immediately afterwards Cambyses led his armies against Egypt. At first he was successful, defeating and capturing the Pharaoh Psammetichus III within weeks. Later efforts to subdue southern Egypt and Ethiopia were less successful. These reverses forced Cambyses to remain in Egypt for three years. This long absence from his home territory was greatly resented by those nobles who had stayed at home. Gaumata, a high priest, noted the discontent and decide to take advantage of it.

Gaumata announced that he was Smerdis, claiming that he had somehow escaped death, and had returned to claim the empire. Gaumata gained a strong following from the officials and noblemen in Persia and was soon accepted as Emperor. When Cambyses heard of the pretender he hurriedly abandoned all thoughts of conquest in Ethiopia and led his army back across the Syrian desert to Persia. Before battle could be joined between the Emperor and the pretender Cambyses was accidentally killed, leaving Gaumata in sole control. His rule was far from secure, however, for a young nobleman named Darius was suspicious of the claims of 'Smerdis'.

In evaluating the claims of Gaumata to be Smerdis, it is important to remember that the only writings we have which relate to these events were written by command of Darius, and hardly likely to be an unbiased source.

DARIUS I (?–485 BC)

Usurped: Persian Empire October 521 BC
Social Origins: Royal Family

The death of Cambyses in 521 BC left the usurper Gaumata (see above), who claimed to be a dead prince named Smerdis, in command of the great Persian Empire. For some months Gaumata ruled the empire from the royal palace, but suspicions began to grow. It was soon noticed that 'Smerdis' stayed within the palace and refused audiences to members of the royal family and any nobleman who had been close to the real Smerdis. Soon noblemen began to ask themselves if 'Smerdis' was who he claimed to be.

One day in October a group of seven royal noblemen, including Darius, decided to take action. They gained admittance to the palace under some pretence. The seven men then demanded entrance to the royal presence. When permission was refused, the seven men drew concealed swords and fought their way into the throne room. As soon as they kicked the doors open, the men recognized the pretender for who he was and slew him.

The impetuous young men, alone with the imposter's body, were then faced with the problem of what to do next. Cambyses had left no heir and many nobles, including themselves, had an equally good claim to the throne. They decided to leave the decision in the lap of the gods and to acclaim the man whose horse neighed first. By a trick of horsemanship, Darius caused his horse to neigh before the others and so became King of Kings, the title used by rulers of the Persian Empire.

Several provinces, or satraps, instantly rebelled against the rule of Darius, but he put down all the insurrections within two years. Darius proved to be an enlightened ruler. He reorganized the administration of the empire, built roads, established a postal system and constructed a mighty navy. He built, among other things, the magnificent Palace of Persepolis and a canal linking the Nile with Suez. One of Darius's few attempts at foreign conquest, when he sent an army against the Greek cities, ended in disaster on the Plain of Marathon. He died peacefully in 485 BC.

ARCHELAUS (?–399 BC)

Usurped: Kingdom of Macedonia, 413 BC
Social Origins: Royal Family

In the late 5th century BC the northern Greek kingdom of Macedonia showed few signs of the future greatness it would achieve under Phillip II and Alexander the Great. The bulk of the population were agricultural peasants who were ruled by a nobility who spent most of their time breeding and racing horses or engaging in feuds. The country lay on the very fringes of civilization and its people were looked upon as uncouth barbarians by the more civilized Greeks.

As if to confirm this unflattering view of the Macedonians, Archelaus set about gaining the throne in a particularly simple, but brutal way. By birth he was a royal prince, but he had so many relatives that he stood little chance of inheriting the throne. Determined to let nothing stand in his way, Archelaus simply murdered all his relatives, even those who did not stand between him and royal power. As the only remaining member of the royal family, he then took the throne.

During his fourteen year reign, Archelaus introduced many aspects of Greek culture to Macedonia. He organized an efficient tax system and used the money to improve and train the Macedonian army. He was murdered by a favourite in 399 BC.

EVAGORUS (?–374 BC)

Usurped: Kingdom of Salamis 410 BC
Social Origins: Nobleman

In the late 5th century BC most of the island of Cyprus was controlled by the great Persian Empire. However, the Emperor Artaxerxes II found that his mighty state was in danger of breaking up. The power of the army was on the decline and several satraps, or local governors, were assuming powers which rightly belonged to the central government.

In 410 BC Evagorus, who seems to have been a local nobleman, took advantage of the confusion and disarray of the Empire. He seized power in the city of Salamis on the east coast of Cyprus and declared himself to be an independent king. The Persians were too busy with more important rebellions to put down Evagorus. Perhaps they thought that they could deal with such a small city state as Salamis at their leisure.

In 405 BC Egypt regained its independence from Persia. After a brief period of internal consolidation, the Egyptian Pharaoh Amyrtaeus embarked on a moderately aggressive foreign policy. He gave support and encouragement to Evagorus, perhaps hoping to divert Persian attention from himself. Evagorus, who already had an alliance with the Greek city state of Athens, was shrewd enough to use Egyptian support for his own purposes and not be drawn into a struggle between greater powers. For a brief period he was even allied with Persia against the Greek city Sparta.

Evagorus stored arms and equipment until 391 when, with the help of the new Pharaoh Achoris, he launched an attack on Persian possessions in Cyprus. In a remarkably swift campaign, Evagorus captured the entire island, throwing off the Persian yoke. Artaxerxes sent a fresh army to retake the island, but the struggle persisted for ten years. Evagorus fought such a cunning war that even though he was defeated in the field, the Persians failed to win a total victory. In 381 BC a peace was made which divided the island between Persia and Evagorus.

For the following seven years Evagorus ruled his island kingdom with wisdom and tact. He introduced many Greek influences and built a powerful navy. In 374 he was murdered by a courtier.

— 👑 —

DIONYSIUS THE ELDER (c. 432–367 BC)

Usurped: Supreme Power in Syracuse 405 BC
Social Origins: Army Officer

In the years around 700 BC Greek colonists founded many cities in Sicily and southern Italy. By the late 4th century BC the city of Syracuse had emerged as the most powerful city in Sicily. The power of this state was, however, contested not only by smaller Greek cities but also by the power of Carthage, the great maritime nation of North Africa.

In 409 BC the Carthaginians sent a large army to Sicily on the pretext of helping their ally, the city of Segesta. The Carthaginian army proceeded to beseige and capture several Sicilian cities. Realizing the threat to her power Syracuse declared war on Carthage. However, the Greek city suffered defeat after defeat. In 405 the Syracuse government appointed an army officer of lowly ancestry, Dionysius, as supreme army commander.

Before attacking the Carthaginians, Dionysius turned on his own government and overthrew it. Perhaps he did not want to suffer the fate of earlier

Syracusian generals who had been disgraced after military defeats. With the government firmly under his control, Dionysius marched against Carthage and was promptly defeated. Within a few weeks the Carthaginians were beseiging Syracuse, but an outbreak of disease forced their withdrawal. This respite seemed almost miraculous, and Dionysius used it to establish his power even more securely. For the following forty years Dionysius continued his war with Carthage. He achieved many successes, extending Syracusian rule to Corsica and southern Italy, but was never able to expel Carthaginian troops from Sicily.

One of the most famous acts of Dionysius has passed into everyday language as a proverbial instance of dangerous glory. At a great banquet one of his courtiers, named Damocles, praised Dionysius as the most powerful and happiest man on earth. Dionysius himself realized all too well the precarious nature of his dictatorship. He decided to teach Damocles a lesson. He invited Damocles to sit on the royal seat at the head of the table and to enjoy the finest foods and the attentions of the servants. Then Dionysius suspended a razor sharp sword over Damocles's head by a single hair. Damocles found himself unable to enjoy himself with the constant threat of death hanging over him. In this way Dionysius taught his court the deadly danger which constantly threatened the great and powerful. The Sword of Damocles has become proverbial.

— ♕ —

DION (408–353 BC)

Usurped: Tyranny of Syracuse 356 BC
Social Origins: Aristocratic Philisopher

After the death of Dionysius the Elder (see above) in 367 BC the government of Syracuse was taken over by his son, known as Dionysius the Younger. The young man had been educated by Dion, his uncle and a philosopher-follower of Plato. When Dionysius assumed supreme power the personalities of the two men clashed.

Dionysius intended to continue the pragmatic government policies of his father. Dion, however, was determined to use his influence on Dionysius. It was his intention to make the young ruler into the archetypal 'Philosopher-King' who, as envisaged by Plato, would be dedicated to Justice, the idea of the Good and also have a sublime understanding of the metaphysical realities of the ultimate truth. At every possible opportunity Dion pushed these views on his nephew and attempted to guide his actions.

Within only a few months Dionysius the Younger, perhaps under-standably, became tired of what he considered to be the idealistic prattlings of an old fogie. He banished Dion from Syracuse never to return. Dion retreated to Greece with his pride damaged and smarting from what he considered very unfair treatment.

For ten years Dion pursued his career as a philosopher, but he never forgave Dionysius. Despite the successful rule of his nephew, Dion remained convinced that he had been in the right and that Dionysius was acting incorrectly. In 365 Dion persuaded Greek rulers to lend him an army with which to return to Syracuse. If only he had the opportunity, thought Dion, he could establish a Philosopher-Kingship under his own enlightened leadership.

Dion landed in Syracuse and used his army to drive Dionysius into exile. The philosopher then set about reorganizing the state along Platonic lines. This involved imposing a rigid class system, taking all property into the ownership of the state, tough censorship and conscription. It soon became obvious to everybody, except Dion himself, that the system was too rigid and took no account of human nature.

Like many other idealists, however, Dion remained convinced that his system was correct. He refused to abandon his unworkable plans. After two years the people of Syracuse had had enough. They murdered Dion and tried to govern themselves. This experiment failed in its turn, so Dionysius the Younger returned to take the reins of power.

— 👑 —

BAGAOS (?–334 BC)
Kingmaker of Persia 338 BC
Social Origins: Courtier

Artaxerxes III came to the throne of the King of Kings, the Persian Empire, in 359 BC, but did not have a quiet reign. Frequent rebellions by satraps, the local governors, kept him busy with internal disorders and frittered away the power and wealth of the Empire. Artaxerxes III became concerned by the growing might of Macedon on the Empire's northwestern frontier. He attempted to give help to states being attacked by Macedon, but was not strong enough to intervene directly.

In the work of re-establishing central authority Artaxerxes was helped by his chief minister Bagaos. Much power was placed in the hands of Bagaos, but Bagaos seems to have been greedy for more. In 338 Bagaos used his position of trust to slip poison into the Emperor's food. With Artaxerxes out of the way, Bagaos held supreme power, but he did not wish to be emperor. Perhaps he realized the Persians would not tolerate the rule of a commoner, for he seems not to have been a member of the royal family. Instead Bagaos installed a young prince named Arses as a puppet emperor. Two years later Bagaos murdered Arses and chose a second prince, Codomanus, as the next emperor. But though Bagaos held great power, he was playing a dangerous game. It was a game which was to cost him his life when Codomanus rose against him and ruled in fact as well as in name (see Darius III below).

DARIUS III (?–330 BC)

Usurped: Persian Empire 336 BC
Social Origins: Royal Family

When Codomanus was appointed King of Kings by the palace official Bagaos (see above) he was under no illusions as to the extent of his power. Bagaos

Darius III
A depiction of Darius III in a Roman mosaic found at Pompeii, based on an earlier Greek-original. Darius is shown fleeing from Alexander the Great at the Battle of Issus in 333 BC. To the Greeks Darius represented the autocratic rule of the hated eastern monarchs who had earlier tried to subdue Greece. To his own subjects, however, Darius seems to have been a popular ruler for he was able to raise fresh armies after each defeat. (*Macdonald/Aldus*)

controlled the empire with an authority which was virtually unchallenged. Codomanus was not content to leave things as they stood. He had the examples of the murderous fate Bagaos had handed out to the previous emperors Artaxerxes and Arses and did not want to share it. Codomanus made contact with those officials who resented the rule of Bagaos and organized a palace coup. Bagaos was eliminated, allowing Codomanus to take supreme power as Darius III.

Unfortunately Darius III was unable to enjoy his power for long. In 334 BC Darius III had to face his greatest foe when Alexander the Great of Macedonia crossed the Hellespont, the modern Dardenelles, and invaded Asia Minor. The local Persian army was crushed at the Granicus River and Alexander marched south. Darius energetically gathered a mighty army and marched to Palestine to fight Alexander. The armies met at Issus and Darius III was heavily defeated, his family and equipment being captured.

At this crisis in his life Darius showed amazing energy. While Alexander marched south to Egypt, Darius III raced to Mesopotamia where he raised and organized a formidable army of chariots and infantry. In 331 BC this army was in turn defeated by the invader. Barely pausing from his flight after the battle, Darius raced to Ecbatana where he recruited and disciplined yet another army. Alexander arrived before preparations were complete and Darius was forced to flee eastwards to Bactria.

In Bactria, Darius was imprisoned and murdered by the Satrap Bessus who hoped to grab the throne of the Persian King of Kings. He was disappointed, however, when Alexander took it himself. Darius was buried by Alexander with full honours. His determined resistance had won the admiration of the conqueror.

OLYMPIAS (?–316 BC)

Usurped: Regency of Macedonia
Social Origins: Royal Family

In 359 BC Philip II came to the throne of the Kingdom of Macedonia in northern Greece. In the same year he married Olympias, daughter of the King of Epirus. In this way Philip allied himself with the most powerful kingdom to the southwest. At the time of the marriage, Olympias had little more than a fairly unimportant, if turbulent future to look forward to, Macedonia being a small kingdom on the edges of civilization. There was no way in which she or her father could have envisaged the importance of the marriage.

Philip spent two years defeating the northern barbarian tribes before turning on the civilized states of Greece. In 357 Philip attacked and defeated several minor Greek cities, alarming Athens, the dominant Greek state. The following year Philip smashed a league organized by Athens. In that same year Olympias gave birth to a boy who was named Alexander. Over the following twenty years Philip fought continuous wars to increase his power in Greece. In 338 the great Battle of Chaeronea gave him complete power.

Meanwhile, however, Philip had quarrelled with Olympias and banished her from court. At the height of his power Philip was unexpectedly stabbed to death by a nobleman. The assassin was killed by guards immediately afterwards. While it was known that the murderer had a well-known grudge against Philip it was widely rumoured that Olympias had encouraged him to kill the king. It would clearly have been better for Olympias if the king were her loving son rather than Philip, and her son Alexander did then come to the throne.

Whether or not Olympias was involved in the murder of Philip, she certainly played a leading part in the intrigues which many years later followed the death of Alexander. When Alexander the Great had departed on his epic journey of conquest he left a general named Antipater as regent. After news arrived of Alexander's death in 323 the Greek city states rose in revolt. Antipater put down the revolt after a hard fought war which culminated at the Battle of Crannon in 322. The following year he was declared regent of the entire empire.

Olympias was far from happy with this arrangement. Perhaps she hoped to act as regent for her simple-minded stepson Arrhidaeus. In 319 she overthrew the authority of Antipater, who then died a suspiciously convenient death. Three years later Antipater's son, Cassander, managed to capture Olympias and had her killed.

— 👑 —

ANTIPATER (?–319 BC)

Usurped: Power in Macedon 322 BC
Social Origins: Army Officer

The unexpectedly early death of Alexander the Great at the Persian city of Susa caught everybody by surprise. The great conqueror had not had time to make provision for a successor to his Empire which stretched from Egypt and Greece to the Indus River, and his only child by his queen Roxana was not yet born.

When he had left Macedonia on his career of conquest, Alexander had left a trusted general named Antipater as regent. When news reached him of

Alexander's death, Antipater continued to rule Macedonia. Officially, Antipater was acting as regent for Roxana's son, but in truth he gradually gathered power into his own hands. He even took it upon himself to name his successor. In 321 BC, Antipater was named as Regent of the whole empire by the other generals, though in reality the title carried little power. In 319 he was overthrown by Olympias, Alexander's mother.

CHANDRAGUPTA MAURYA (c. 346–297 BC)

Usurped: Kingdom of Magadha circa 321 BC
Social Origins: Illegitimate Royal Prince

One of the first truly great rulers of India was Chandragupta Maurya, who managed to unite much of the sub-continent and to expel foreign invaders. His success is all the more remarkable becuase of his humble, almost disgraceful origins.

Chandragupta was born in the kingdom of Magadha, on the lower Ganges, to a low-caste woman with whom one of the kings of the Nanda dynasty was having an affair. The stigma of illegitimacy was almost as great as that attached to his caste. In Hindu India the social castes were rigidly defined and embodied in religion. The modern name of the lowest caste is the 'untouchables' which sums up the attitude of high caste nobles to such people. In the society of the time, the circumstances of Chandragupta's birth could not be less auspicious. Some historians consider the tale of a royal father to be a spurious one put about by Chandragupta to lend some form of authority to his power bid.

However, the reign of Chandragupta's alleged father proved to be highly unpopular. This gave the young prince the chance to foment trouble. Within a few short months, Chandragupta had made contact with many malcontents and persuaded them to follow him. In a swift and well-planned revolt, Chandragupta overthrew his father and seized the throne for himself. Wishing to distance himself from the Nanda Dynasty, Chandragupta adopted his mother's name Maurya, as that of his family.

Having seized power, Chandragupta was not content to rest. Taking advantage of the confusion following the death of Alexander the Great, Chandragupta immediately attacked the garrisons and cities the Macedonians had left in the Indus Valley. This move precipitated years of war with Seleucus I, the Macedonian General who had taken over the eastern section of Alexander's empire. The war ended when Chandragupta married Seleucus's daughter and gained several satrapies, or districts, in return for military equipment.

Chandragupta then followed his maxim that 'any ruler bordering the kingdom is an enemy'. In a series of brilliant campaigns he conquered the whole of northern India, welding the various states together into a single empire. At the height of his power Chandragupta could place 600,000 men and 9,000 war elephants into the field.

Chandragupta ruled his new lands with stern authority. He always appeared in public in a golden palanquin and ate from gold dishes over five feet in diameter. His magnificent palace had columns covered in gold leaf and was surrounded by a vast park. The splendour was designed, in part, to overawe his subjects and impress them with the importance of their present ruler.

Clearly the mighty king lived in constant dread that someone might repeat his usurpation. He never slept in the same bed two nights in succession and refused to rest in the presence of others. He was continually guarded by several hundred armed women who were fanatically loyal. The precautions proved themselves effective, but could not protect the great emperor from himself. When, in 298 BC, his close friend and prophet Bhadrabahu died, Chandragupta died of grief. The empire he had forged survived for over a century, but then collapsed into the anarchy of tribal loyalties and personal ambition.

AGATHOCLES (361–289 BC)

Usurped: Government of Syracuse 317 BC
Social Origins: Potter

The rise to power of Agathocles has often been used as an example of the career of a criminal tyrant. His story was used by Machiavelli in his work *The Prince*, and has been used as a moral tale several times since. In fact the story not only illustrates the amoral tendencies of Agathocles, but also his great talents.

He was born the son of a potter in the Greek city of Syracuse on Sicily in about 361 BC and spent the early years of his life learning his father's trade. However, when he was old enough, Agathocles joined the state militia. His bravery and dash soon marked him out as a fine soldier and he gained rapid promotion. About this time he came to the notice of the fabulously wealthy Damas, who steered the career of the young soldier. Through Damas, Agathocles obtained increasingly high command. When Damas died, Agathocles promptly married his widow, which may indicate that an adulterous relationship had already existed. In this way Agathocles came into possession of Damas's wealth and soon after was able to call himself the richest man in Syracuse. With this newly acquired position, Agathocles took an active part in the Senate and other political offices of the Republic of Syracuse.

Around 319 BC Agathocles fell foul of political rivals and was exiled. However, he forced his way into the city in 317 BC at the head of a force of mercenaries. On the pretence of wishing to discuss political matters, Agathocles called a meeting of the Senate. When the supreme ruling body of Syracuse was gathered, Agathocles gave a signal and his mercenaries dashed forwards with drawn swords. Not a single senator escaped the room.

Having removed any possible opposition, Agathocles took over the government of the city. In 310 BC he saved Syracuse from an invasion by the North African power Carthage, and then went on to extend Syracusian control over the whole of Sicily. These foreign conquests, together with a vigorous internal policy made Agathocles a popular tyrant. Internal resistance was almost non-existent throughout his long reign of 36 years. In his later years, Agathocles led several successful expeditions to southern Italy where he imposed tributes and some degree of authority. He was planning another such campaign when, in 289 BC, he was murdered by being handed a poisoned toothpick.

Some time before his death, Agathocles had provided for democratic institutions to replace his tyranny. These measures came into force with his death. The mercenary troops, however, did not take kindly to their prompt dismissal by the new government. The soldiers seized the town of Messina and led an active career of piracy and banditry for several years.

— 👑 —

PTOLEMY SOTER (367–283 BC)

Usurped: Kingdom of Egypt 321 BC
Social Origins: Army Officer

The death of Alexander the Great in 323 BC left the mighty empire which he had conquered in the hands of the Macedonian army. A meeting was arranged between the leading generals, known collectively as the *diadochi*, in an attempt to agree on some form of government for the vast territories. It was agreed that Alexander's idiot nephew and his unborn child should jointly inherit the empire, under the regency of the general Perdiccas. The empire was to be divided between the generals for the purposes of everyday administration, Ptolemy being given the fabulously wealthy country of Egypt. It was an arrangement which was to lead to a great deal of trouble.

The first signs of discontent came in 321 when Perdiccas attempted to use his authority as regent to interfere in the governments being run by the *diadochi.* The generals resented the intrusions and formed a league against the regent. Perdiccas decided to attack Ptolemy in an attempt to impose his authority. Ptolemy struck first and defeated Perdiccas who was killed in the aftermath of battle. From this battle can be dated Ptolemy's usurpation of power. He no longer pretended to owe allegiance to a united Macedonian Empire, but went his own way.

While the other generals squabbled over territories and attempted to impose their rule on each other, Ptolemy stayed largely clear of such wars. He remained in Egypt firmly establishing his control. Ptolemy was astute enough to realize that as a newcomer he had to secure quickly the loyalty of his subjects. He noted the immense piety and conservatism of the native Egyptians and played them. He declared his devotion to native Egyptian deities, such as Amon and Isis. Moreover he secured the body of Alexander and had it buried at Alexandria. Some years earlier Alexander had been hailed by the priests of Amon as the son of the god. The elaborate burial served to emphasize the divine ancestry which Ptolemy claimed for himself in order to impress his new subjects.

Ptolemy did not completely ignore his Greek ancestry. He brought hundreds of Greeks to Egypt to reform the administration of his new lands, which had fallen into decay under the Persians, who had previously ruled Egypt. He established the famous Library of Alexandria, which was to become the seat of learning for the whole Greek world. In 305 Ptolemy threw off the last vestige of outside authority and further enforced his internal authority by assuming the ancient title of Pharaoh.

Knowing that he must secure his borders against foreign conquest, Ptolemy spent much time in warfare. He quickly seized strongholds in the desert to the west, blocking the raids of tribesmen. A mixture of friendship and threats secured Egypt's southern borders. The frontiers to the east proved more difficult to define and defend. It was here that Ptolemy faced his one-time comrades in Alexander's army. Long and bitter wars were fought across Palestine between Ptolemy and the other *diadochi*.

It was a detail in these struggles which caused the construction of one of the Seven Wonders of the World. The city of Rhodes was an ally of Ptolemy, principally because of the highly lucrative trade which Rhodian merchants carried on with Egypt. As an Egyptian ally, Rhodes became the target for attack by Antigonus, one of the *diadochi*. An army of 70,000 men and a fleet of 400 ships arrived at Rhodes in 305 BC and began the great siege of Rhodes. Eventually, the attackers were forced to withdraw. To celebrate this victory the Rhodians employed the sculptor Chares of Lindos to erect a suitable monument. The result was the famous Colossus of Rhodes, a bronze statue of the Sun God which stood 110 feet (33 metres) tall.

The border struggles, though inconclusive, had their desired effect. Ptolemy prevented any army from reaching Egypt and was able to enjoy the luxuries of his kingdom until his death at the age of 82. Ptolemy left the throne to his son, also named Ptolemy, who in turn left it to his son. In fact the Ptolemaic dynasty lasted for nearly three centuries before Egypt fell to Rome. This lengthy rule by a single family was far from quiet. Numerous patricidal feuds, murders and plots wracked the country and its rulers.

— 👑 —

SELEUCUS NICATOR (?–280 BC)

Usurped: Power in Babylonia
Social Origins: Army Officer

The usurpation of power carried out by Seleucus Nicator followed a pattern made familiar by other generals of Alexander the Great. Like them he followed Alexander on his long trail of conquest from Greece to India and back to Persia. He was present at the army council convened in 323 BC to organize the government of the Empire after Alexander's early death. Here he acquired the city of Babylon and surrounding territory.

In theory Seleucus was appointed to govern Babylonia on behalf of Alexander's unborn son and under the regency of the general Perdiccas. It soon became clear that Seleucus had some very different ideas as to his position. He began ignoring requests and instructions sent by Perdiccas and refused to send his share of tribute. In 321 BC Perdiccas attempted to impose his authority on Seleucus and the other *diadochi* by force. Seleucus supported his fellow generals, but his power base lay too far to the east for him to intervene directly. It was left for Perdiccas to be defeated by Ptolemy, who had seized power in Egypt. When a second regent died in 319 Seleucus gained in title what he already exercised in fact: independence. His usurpation of power was complete, but his troubles had only just begun.

In the division of power of 323 BC Alexander's secretary Eumenes of Cardia had been given extensive territories in what are today Turkey and Syria. However, the bureaucrat was never popular with the generals and in 320 BC Seleucus began to suspect him of treacherous dealings and secret murders. Seleucus formed an alliance with Antigonus, who held lands in western Asia Minor, against Eumenes. Victory came quickly to the allies, but Antigonus seized Eumenes's lands for himself.

Incensed by this treachery Seleucus formed a second alliance of generals against Antigonus and plunged into a bitter war which was to last 14 years. Eventually Antigonus was killed in battle and the victors could divide up his lands. Seleucus made sure that he received the largest share, taking the whole of the Near East for himself. After this epic struggle with Antigonus, Seleucus ruled his great kingdom in relative peace until he was assassinated in 281 BC.

Seleucus Nicator
A coin of Seleucus Nicator. In the ancient world coins were powerful instruments of propaganda. They were used not only by the majority of a ruler's subjects, but were passed in commerce to other lands. By depicting himself wearing a Macedonian helmet, Seleucus emphasized the military conquest which brought him his Babylonian kingdom. The lion skin tied around his neck links him to Hercules, the strong man of Greek myth. (*Michael Holford*)

The dynasty Seleucus had established remained in power until 65 BC when Pompey the Great took their lands for Rome.

URUKAGINA (fl. c. 2250 BC)

Usurped: Power in Lagash circa 2250 BC
Social Origins: Obscure

The city of Lagash, like most other Mesopotamian cities of this era had a slightly curious governmental system. In theory the King of the City was a god, and power was exercised on earth by the god's chosen deputy or *patesi*. For several generations after 2500 BC Lagash was ruled by a succession of powerful *patesi* who conquered nearby cities and maintained internal order.

Some time around 2350 BC, however, the *patesi* were replaced by a series of priests. Recorded in later inscriptions as being unusually greedy, the priests stripped the people of all power and concentrated the wealth of Lagash in their own hands. Magnificent temples and richly decorated priestly palaces were built, while the people of Lagash suffered heavy taxation and the nation's defences fell into disrepair.

The people and lesser officials of Lagash soon began to resent this ecclesiastical rule. Urukagina, an unimportant government administrator, used this resentment to launch himself into power. He took on the mantle of people's champion and forcibly wrested power from the priests. He then rewarded his followers by allowing non-priests once again to own land and he also took many legal privileges from the priesthood. Urukagina did not enjoy his power for long. The city of Umma attacked Lagesh and captured it. Urukagina is heard of no more after the fall of his city.

WU WANG (fl. c. 1100 BC)

Usurped: Empire of China circa 1100 BC
Social Origins: Prince

In about 1100 BC China was a rapidly expanding empire under the guidance of the Shang Dynasty. Originating on the floodplain of the Yellow River, Chinese culture was based around intensive agriculture and by 1500 BC had invented writing and had developed a complex governmental system. For centuries the Chinese were spreading to the north, south and west, taking their culture with them. On the fringes of this civilization many barbarian tribesmen violently resisted the expansion of the Chinese. It was these conditions which opened the way for Wu Wang to seize power.

Though the details of the usurpation remain unclear, it seems that Wu Wang was one of the officials whose task was to command the troops on the frontier and ensure the safety of Chinese settlers. The confused nature of border warfare and the lack of efficient transport combined to transform the frontier warlords into semi-independent rulers. Wu Wang was probably one of these, obeying the Shang Emperors when it suited him to do so.

Some time around 1100 BC—it is difficult to give accurate dates for this period in Chinese history—Wu Wang suddenly turned his troops from the frontier to aim a carefully-timed blow at the reigning Shang. For some years central Imperial government had been becoming inefficient and resented, particularly in the areas distant from the court. Wu Wang took advantage of this unpopularity to launch a bid for power. According to later sources, Wu Wang fought the Emperor in a great battle and killed him. Strangely, Wu Wang seemed uninterested in governing the whole empire. Instead he took immense booty for himself and parcelled the lands out to his family and friends. Soon after Wu Wang's death these new landowners declared themselves independent and China plunged into a long series of civil wars.

— 👑 —

ADJATASATRU (?–c. 460 BC)

Usurped: Kingdom of Magadha circa 490 BC
Social Origins: Royal Family

It was the usurper Adjatasatru who set the kingdom of Magadha on the road to the greatness which it would achieve some 150 years later when it came to rule almost the whole of India. At the time of Adjatasatru, Magadha was just one of several small kingdoms to the north of the Ganges Delta.

In about 490 BC (it is difficult to be exact about dates in this period of Indian history), Adjatasatru murdered his father, King Bimbisara. The reasons for the crime are obscure, but Adjatasatru immediately seized power. He then led the army on a series of campaigns during which he conquered a vast area of the north Ganges Plain together with the wealthy city of Benares. He died some time around 460 BC.

— 👑 —

HIANG-YU (?–202 BC)

Usurped: Chinese Empire 206 BC

Social Origins: Nobleman

For several centuries before 221 BC China was divided into a large number of small independent kingdoms which fought almost continuously against each other. Over the generations the northern kingdom of Tsin grew to be the largest and most powerful of these states. In 221 BC the youthful King Chung conquered the last of his rivals to become ruler of all China.

During his reign of 15 years Chung achieved a great deal. He stripped the nobles of their local power, making them dependent upon himself, and burnt all local law books in order to enforce an Empire-wide legal system. The Chinese script was invented almost entirely during this reign together with a system of weights and measures. In order to emphasize his achievements, Chung took the title of Chi Hwang-ti, meaning the First Powerful Emperor, by which name he is generally known today. When he died in 209 BC all his achievements seemed doomed to collapse, for he left no heir.

Hiang-Yu was, at this time, a general in the army. He took advantage of the confusion to advance his own plans. It seems that Hiang-Yu did not act out of a sense of responsibility to the Chinese people, but out of selfish ambition. The description of Hiang-Yu which has come down to us was written by his enemies, but he was said to be a tall, muscular man who enjoyed nothing more than bullying and causing pain.

In 206 BC, Hiang-Yu entered the capital city as the undisputed master of China. He immediately turned the city and its inhabitants over to his troops to pillage. It was his way of rewarding faithful followers, but was hardly designed to endear him to his new subjects. Hiang-Yu would soon suffer for his heartlessness, being overthrown by a fellow general named Liu Pang (see below) and committing suicide.

LIU PANG (?–195 BC)
also known as Han Kao Tsu

Usurped: Chinese Empire 202 BC

Social Origins: Peasant

Under the great Chinese ruler Chi Hwang-ti (see HIANG-YU above) Liu Pang was recruited into the army and rapidly rose to high command. He seems to have been an astute bargainer who gained promotion more because of intrigue than because of his military prowess. After the death of Chi Hwang-ti, Liu Pang joined in the conflict between rival army leaders for power. Liu Pang lost the struggle and fled westwards to take refuge in the mountains.

It soon became clear to Liu Pang that the rule of the brutal Hiang-Yu was far from popular. After waiting for what he judged to be the correct moment, he came down from his mountain retreat and gathered together an army of discontents. With this force, Liu Pang launched his second bid for power. In a matter of months he had defeated the forces loyal to Hiang-Yu. The defeated warlord committed suicide to avoid capture and public humiliation, leaving Liu Pang as undisputed master of all China.

As emperor Liu Pang continued the centralising work of Chi Hwang-ti. He became a firm adherent to Confucianism and did his best to put its theories into practice. This involved the employment of large numbers of educated, salaried civil servants to run the empire, all of whom had to pass an entrance examination. Confucian scholars placed emphasis on the study of history to examine the mistakes of previous rulers, loyalty, modesty and other virtues. By inculcating these values in government Liu Pang laid the foundations of Chinese government which have persisted to the present day. The Han Dynasty, which he founded, was rather more shortlived, though it was one of the longest early dynasties. The Han Dynasty survived until AD 196. Liu Pang is sometimes known as Kao-Tsu.

— 👑 —

LYSIMACHUS (c. 360–281 BC)

Usurped: Kingdom of Thrace 306 BC
Social Origins: Army officer

Lysimachus was one of the powerful generals, or *diadochi*, who struggled for power after the death of Alexander the Great. Unlike some of his colleagues, such as Antigonus and Perdiccas, Lysimachus was fairly unambitious. In his quiet way Lysimachus achieved more success than some, at least for a while.

At the conference of *diadochi* held in 323 BC, Lysimachus received the small but wealthy province of Thrace in northern Greece. In theory Lysimachus was supposed to rule Thrace on behalf of Alexander's infant heir. In common with the other *diadochi*, however, Lysimachus soon looked upon Thrace as his personel property. The change in attitude does not seem to have come as quickly to Lysimachus as to others. He remained happy with the title of governor for many years and only began calling himself King of Thrace in about 306 BC.

Lysimachus took little part in the struggles between his brother officers until 315 BC. In that year Antigonus declared his ambition of uniting all the Asian territories under his own rule. If Antigonus had succeeded it would have created an extremely powerful empire on Lysimachus's eastern frontier. Faced with this disturbing possibility, Lysimachus joined Seleucus and Ptolemy in a war against his former colleague Antigonus. After early defeats, the allies began to regain lost ground and it was at this time that Lysimachus assumed a royal title. Finally, in 301 BC Antigonus was defeated and killed.

For the following twenty years Lysimachus ruled Thrace in relative peace. He became involved in struggles in Greece, but nothing on the scale of the war with Antigonus. In 285 BC, however, Lysimachus came into conflict with Seleucus, by then ruler of most of the Asian territories of Alexander's empire. Lysimachus killed Agathocles, son of Seleucus, who then became intent on revenge.

In 281 BC the armies of the two ex-comrades met at Corus, now in modern Turkey. The Thracian troops were hopelessly outmatched and suffered a terrible defeat. Lysimachus himself was slain in the rout. Soon after this defeat Thrace suffered an even greater calamity when hordes of barbaric Gauls streamed down from the north and pillaged the country from end to end. The invaders were only turned back at Delphi, after which they invaded Asia Minor to found the Galitian nation.

PYRRHUS (318–272 BC)

Usurped: Kingdom of Epirus 300 BC
Social Origins: Royal Family

The energetic and adventurous Pyrrhus of Epirus passed a tempestuous career in the early 3rd century BC which greatly impressed his contemporaries and has caused his name to pass into everyday language.

He was born as a member of the dispossessed and impoverished royal family of Epirus. The royal heritage of the family had been stripped away during the wars which caused the rise of Macedonia under Philip II and Alexander the Great. Unlike the rest of his family, Pyrrhus was not content with the quiet, modest life of an exiled prince. This dashing and courageous young man decided to win back his inheritance and, if possible, extend it.

In 301 BC, at the tender age of 17, Pyrrhus travelled to Macedonia to join the army of Demetrius Poliorcetes, son of King Antigonus of Macedonia. Demetrius had earlier gained fame as the creator of the seige works at

Rhodes. No doubt Pyrrhus hoped to gain experience and favour under such a proven leader. If so, he was to be bitterly disappointed. At the Battle of Ipsus, Antigonus was killed and Demetrius fled. Pyrrhus was captured and sent to Egypt to live as a hostage at the court of Ptolemy Soter (see above).

Pyrrhus was far from dispirited. He took an active part in court life and soon attracted the attention of both the royal ladies and of Ptolemy himself. Within a year, Pyrrhus had married one of Ptolemy's daughters and had persuaded his new father-in-law to support his claim to Epirus. In 300 BC, Pyrrhus set sail from Egypt with a force of Ptolemy's soldiers to try to gain what he considered to be his inheritance. In a lightening campaign, Pyrrhus overthrew the existing government in Epirus and set himself up as an autocratic king.

For some years, Pyrrhus was pre-occupied with securing his hold on his kingdom. He recruited and trained a formidable army. He used his experiences at Ipsus and elsewhere to invent new tactics, largely based upon the use of war elephants and heavily armed infantry. His domestic policies were both popular and successful, which allowed Pyrrhus to demand and receive the undivided loyalty of his subjects.

In 288, with a fine army and secure at home, Pyrrhus felt ready for his first foreign adventure. He chose as his first adversary his one-time employer Demetrius Poliorcetes who by this time had returned to rule a part of northern Greece. In a swift campaign, Pyrrhus defeated Demetrius and took his lands. Three years later, Pyrrhus's relations with the Asian ruler Lysimachus deteriorated and Demetrius's son was able to reclaim all that his father had lost.

Pyrrhus returned home, but soon after received a cry for help from the Greek city of Tarentum which was being threatened by Rome. Pyrrhus leapt at the chance to help his fellow countrymen. He loaded his highly trained army and his elephants into a fleet and set sail for southern Italy. He landed in 280 BC and immediately defeated a Roman army at Heraclea. A year later he smashed a second Roman army at Asculum. This second battle was extremely close and vast numbers of Pyrrhus's troops were killed. Surveying the field, Pyrrhus turned to one of his generals and declared 'One more such victory and we are finished.' The phrase 'a Pyrrhic victory' has since passed into common usage.

After these inconclusive Italian campaigns, Pyrrhus sailed for Sicily, with equally undecisive results, before returning home in 274 BC. It is a mark of Pyrrhus's success as a usurper that his grip on the throne was strong enough for him to spend six years campaigning abroad without any trouble at home. In 272 BC Pyrrhus was killed in a night skirmish with Spartan troops.

— 👑 —

PHILETAERUS (?–263 BC)

Usurped: Power in Pergamum circa 279 BC
Social Origins: Government Official

In 281 BC Seleucus Nicator (see above) added the western part of what is now Turkey to his ever growing Asian empire. However, he had neither the time nor the resources to install efficient government before he died in 280 BC. Seleucus's son, Antiochus Soter, was preoccupied by raids carried out by Gauls from the north and campaigns by Ptolemy II Philadelphus in the south. It was in these confused conditions that Philetaerus took his chance.

The rule of Antiochus was insecure throughout Anatolia. Philetaerus had the extremely wealthy trading city of Pergamum under his authority. Realizing that central authority was weak, Philetaerus began ignoring Imperial commands and witheld payment of taxes in an increasingly flagrant manner. When no retribution came his way, Philetaerus declared his independence as King of Pergamum.

Philetaerus maintained his freedom until his death in 263 BC, when the city passed to his son Eumenes. In successive reigns the territories of Pergamum expanded greatly, as did the prosperity of the city. By 160 BC the library at Pergamum rivalled that at Alexandria, while the city's palaces and temples were a byword for magnificence. In 133 BC Attalus III of Pergamum left his kingdom to Rome in his will.

HIERO II (?–216 BC)

Usurped: Power in Syracuse, 270 BC
Social Origins: Soldier

Hiero was swept to power in Syracuse by the forces unleashed in Sicily as a result of warfare between the great powers of the Mediterranean. Hiero nearly lost his position when the international situation changed, but in fact managed to use events to strengthen himself. If it were not for the ambitions of others, Hiero might have spent his entire life as an undistinguished soldier.

In 278 BC Pyrrhus of Epirus (see above) abandoned his attempts to defeat Rome in Italy. Instead he crossed to Sicily and intervened in the seemingly interminable squabbles between the Greek city states of the island. At this time the Republic of Syracuse was the most powerful of these states and joined the league against Pyrrhus. However, the King of Epirus smashed the allied army with his customary speed and energy, and quickly overran most of the island.

Faced with disaster and possible destruction, Syracuse took the only course open to her. The republican government decided they needed a military dictator and chose Hiero for the task. He immediately disbanded the city militia and set about recruiting and training an entirely new army. This achieved a double purpose. First it gave him an efficient force with which to fight Pyhrrus. Secondly the reformation ensured that the army commanders owed their position to Heiro personally, rather than to the republican government.

The league against Pyrrhus was revived and expanded in 276 BC, with the help of Carthage, the powerful North African city. Hiero won several notable victories, which increased his popularity and power. It soon became clear that Hiero's position was unassailable and he had himself declared King of Syracuse and took supreme power into his own hands.

In 269 BC, Hiero attacked the great port of Messina, then being held by an unruly band of pirates. However, the Carthaginians captured Messina before Hiero's troops could arrive. The pirates called upon Rome to help them. Eager for an excuse to interfere in Sicily, the Romans squashed their principles about piracy and attacked the Carthaginians.

Hiero might have been expected to turn against Carthage after they had robbed him of Messina. Instead he flung his troops at the Roman army. Perhaps he preferred the devil he knew to the one he did not. If so, it was a tragic mistake. The Syracuse troops were soundly beaten. Hiero had to accept the lordship of Rome. His fortunes appeared to be at a low ebb.

However, Hiero was clever enough to turn even this to his advantage. He served Rome well, giving the impression of being an eager ally. When peace between Rome and Carthage gave Sicily to Rome as a province, Hiero claimed his reward for being a loyal vassal. While most of Sicily passed under the rule of Roman administrators, Syracuse retained a large degree of independence. Heiro kept his throne until his death in 216 BC, a remarkably long reign of 54 years. His astute behaviour upon taking power and during the war between Rome and Carthage had ensured his success and the survival of Syracuse.

— ♔ —

ARSACES (?–248 BC)

Usurped: Power in Persia circa 250 BC
Social Origins: Nomad Chieftain

The bid for power launched by Arsaces profoundly altered the balance of power in the ancient Middle East. It spelt the end of one empire, the birth of another and set in motion a series of events which would bring the two mightiest empires of the world into conflict on the bloody field of Carrhae.

Arsaces was born as the son of a Scythian chieftain some time around 280 BC. At this time the Scyths were a ferocious nation of nomads inhabiting the open plains to the east of the Caspian Sea. The tribesmen lived by herding horses and cattle in vast numbers and following their animals across the sparse grazing of the steppes. Their fighting skills and love of battle were proverbial. When a chieftain died his finest warriors were sacrificed, mounted on slaughtered horses and set to guard their leader's grave for eternity. These savage tribesmen owed a vague allegiance to the Seleucid Emperor Antiochus II who employed them as mercenaries.

Arsaces was not content with the modest amounts of gold which he and his men could earn as soldiers of fortune and he resented the interference of Antiochus II in Scythian affairs. Arsaces began to dream of freedom and to cast greedy eyes at the wealth of the empire as a whole. For some years Arsaces bided his time, looking for his chance to strike.

The moment came in 250 BC. The Parthians, a people living to the south of the Scyths who had similarly nomadic traditions, had for some years grown resentful of Seleucid rule. Arsaces managed to persuade the Parthians to make him their leader in a revolt against Antiochus II. Raising hordes of mounted warriors to his banner, Arsaces declared himself independent King of the Scyths and Parthians. His power became absolute between the Caspian and the Indian Ocean. Within just a few months the usurpation was complete and Arsaces could call himself king.

Antiochus gathered together a mighty army and marched into Parthia, but Arsaces died before battle was joined. His brother led the Parthians to an overwhelming victory, which gained them most of the Seleucid Empire. Over the following generations the Parthian Empire continued to grow until it reached the boundaries of the rapidly expanding Roman Empire.

In 53 BC the inevitable clash came when Crassus led a massive Roman army into Parthian territory. The forces of the two great empires clashed at Carrhae. The swirling masses of Parthian horsemen completely out-manouevred the Roman legionaries who were slaughtered in their thousands. The battle decided the fate of the Middle East for centuries. Rome never again attempted to invade its eastern neighbour. The horse warriors first led to success by Arsaces had achieved their greatest victory. Some authorities, it should be stated, maintain that 'Tiridates' was a title assumed by Arsaces upon becoming king and that the two men were one and the same.

— 👑 —

43

DIODOTUS THE YOUNGER (?–225 BC)

Usurped: Power in Bactria circa 245 BC
Social Origins: Provincial Governor

Diodotus is one of the few usurpers in history who really had very little choice whether or not to seize power. Many who have seized power have excused their actions on the grounds that they were forced to act in order to preserve order or to protect their nation. Diodotus, however, made efforts to avoid taking power, but eventually had to recognize the truth of his position.

The extensive conquests of Alexander the Great took Greek settlers and Greek culture to the furthest reaches of the known world. The most remote settlements were in Sogdiana and Bactria between the Aral Sea and the Himalayas. In the year 250 Diodotus the Elder was governor of these provinces for the Seleucid Emperor Antiochus II. The Empire appeared stable and Diodotus the Elder managed his provinces and their trade routes to China with dedication and skill.

But in 247 BC Antiochus II suffered a devastating defeat at the hands of the Parthians (see Arsaces above). A great swathe of territory from the Caspian Sea to the Straits of Hormuz was taken over by the Parthians, separating Sogdiana and Bactria from the territories remaining to Antiochus II. In 245 BC Diodotus the Elder died. With communications cut between the eastern provinces and Antiochus II, Diodotus the Younger, son of Diodotus the Elder, took over the reins of power. For some time Diodotus attempted to establish contact with Antiochus II, but this proved impossible. Finally, Diodotus declared himself king as Diodotus II and made peace with the Parthians. There was little else he could do.

In 220 BC Antiochus III inflicted a temporary defeat on the Parthians and accepted the homage of the then King of Bactria. But the eastern provinces never lost their independence. For many generations the inhabitants of Sogdiana and Bactria attempted to keep Greek culture alive in their remote lands. The later history of the kingdom has been lost, but coins and sculptures testify to its partial success. Eventually, however, the nation became swamped by the peoples around them and vanished from history.

Usurped: Pharaoh of Egypt 221 BC
Social Origins: Royal Family

The Egypt of the Ptolemies has been described as the most luxurious, most pleasurable and most dangerous kingdom of the ancient world of which to be ruler. The statement has much truth in it, and Ptolemy IV was largely responsible for the truth of the judgement.

Under Ptolemy I and II, Egypt had been thoroughly reformed from top to bottom of the social structure. For millennia the peasants had subsisted on the autumnal crop of grain. The Ptolemies constructed vast irrigation works, introduced new strains of wheat and developed a complex crop rotation system which allowed a harvest in the spring in addition to the traditional autumn. In effect this doubled grain production in Egypt without increasing the internal demand. The surplus crops were sold abroad and vast amounts of money poured into Egypt. A new harbour at Alexandria was built for the grain ships, and the famous Pharos, or lighthouse, was erected to guide ships into port.

A large proportion of these proceeds were payable to the Pharaoh. Before long the Ptolemies presided over the most magnificent court in the known world. Huge monuments were erected to glorify the Pharaohs. The library at Alexandria was stocked with every conceivable book and the arts flourished as never before. The stupendous wealth allowed the Pharaoh to do virtually as he liked. Egypt was fortunate that the first three Ptolemies chose to spend their wealth on worthwhile projects. Things would soon change.

In the 220s BC Pharaoh Ptolemy III Euergetes invaded the Asian Seleucid Empire, defeated the enemy and returned with vast amounts of loot. It may have been greed for this sudden wealth which prompted the Pharaoh's son, also named Ptolemy, to act. In 221 BC the young prince murdered his father and assumed power with ease. This usurpation was almost the only decisive act Ptolemy IV ever made.

Having become Pharaoh, Ptolemy IV quickly seized the vast wealth of his father and gave himself up to a life of debauchery and hedonism. Spending on port facilities and temples waned as the pleasures of the Pharaoh's court demanded increasing supplies of rare foods, exotic drinks and magnificent jewels. Soon after his accession Ptolemy IV married his sister Arsinoe, but quickly discarded her in favour of a mistress named Agathoclea. Ptolemy's philandering did not stop there. He satisfied his lusts with a collection of paramours, both male and female. Ptolemy even took Agathoclea's brother as one of his homosexual lovers.

Ptolemy IV prided himself as having an artistic soul. He commissioned plays, books and sculptures to adorn his court. On one occasion Ptolemy IV wrote a play. No doubt all those at court who knew what was good for them applauded it as a magnificent piece of literature. However the example was never repeated. Perhaps Ptolemy found writing too much of an effort!

Amid this round of licentious living, Ptolemy had little time for government. The running of affairs of state passed into the hands of ambitious favourites, such as Agathoclea. It seems that the only aspect of government with which Ptolemy IV concerned himself was that of securing his own rule. When Ptolemy IV suspected his uncle of plotting against the throne his execution was ordered. Ptolemy's own mother was murdered together with another of her sons when the finger of suspicion was pointed at them. Through such despotic behaviour Ptolemy remained on the throne until his death in 204 BC.

DEMETRIUS SOTER (?–150 BC)

Usurped: Seleucid Empire 162 BC
Social Origins: Royal Family

The bid for power by Demetrius Soter was remarkable for not only did he overcome opposition within his own empire, but also defied the growing power of Rome. His success was unfortunate for the Seleucid Empire for it marked the start of a bloody period of internal struggle which laid the Empire open to conquest by Rome.

In a war with Rome which ended in 188 BC, the Seleucid Empire was utterly defeated. Until this time the Seleucids had ruled most of modern Syria, Palestine, Iraq and neighbouring lands. A heavy indemnity was imposed on the Seleucids by Rome to prevent them from using their wealth to recruit a fresh army. In order to ensure payment Rome took Demetrius, a son of Seleucus IV, as a hostage. In 175 BC Seleucus died and the throne passed to his brother Antiochus IV Epiphanes. Demetrius, meanwhile, remained in Rome as a prisoner, albeit in extremely comfortable quarters.

In 164 BC Antiochus IV died and power was taken by his son Antiochus V. By this time the indemnity had been paid, but Rome held on to Demetrius as a bargaining counter in Middle East politics. Demetrius was not willing to be used in this way, he had his own plans. In 162 the Syrian prince made a daring escape from Rome and boarded a ship to Syria. When he landed, Demetrius rode for the Imperial palace. Here he brutally murdered Antiochus V, declaring that he had returned to claim the throne which was rightfully his.

Demetrius Soter proved himself to be a wise ruler. His action in removing the brutal satrap, or governor, Timarchus from Babylon earned him the

46

nickname of Soter, which means 'saviour'. He had, however, inherited a rebellion in Palestine from his predecessor. Rome used this as a means of attacking Demetrius Soter and strongly supported the Jewish rebels who were ultimately successful in their bid for independence.

By taking the throne by force, Demetrius Soter had shown the path for other violent insurrections by other members of the Royal family. In 150 BC Demetrius was killed in just such a bid for power. Thereafter the history of the Seleucids degenerated into a bitter struggle between the descendants of Demetrius and Antiochus IV. By 53 BC the empire had been drained to such an extent that a Roman army was able to depose the last emperor with hardly a struggle.

— ♛ —

JUGURTHA (?–104 BC)

Usurped: Kingdom of Numidia 111 BC
Social Origins: Royal Family

Jugurtha was born the grandson of Masinissa who had founded the Kingdom of Numidia in 202 BC when he united the desert tribes in alliance with Rome and helped to defeat his former ally Carthage. As payment for his treachery, Masinissa was given sovereignty over the lands of the Numidians along the North African coast, west of modern Tunis. Masinissa was succeeded by his son Micipsa who welcomed Roman merchants and settlers.

When Micipsa died in 118 BC, Jugurtha was fortunate enough to be in the critical place at the correct time. Jugurtha swiftly made himself regent for Micipsa's sons, Hiempsal and Adherbal. He then murdered Hiempsal and drove Adherbal into exile. Jugurtha then turned on the wealthy Roman community. He executed every Roman he could capture and confiscated their property. The Romans sent a punitive expedition to Africa, but Jugurtha bribed the Roman generals not to attack him.

Believing that bribery had proved itself to be as efficient a weapon of state as murder, Jugurtha went a step further. He sent massive bribes to Rome in order to induce members of the Senate to make peace on terms favourable to Numidia. The plan worked well and peace was conclued in 111 BC. Unfortunately for Jugurtha, the bribery was revealed two years later. Rome instantly sent out a large army to avenge the insult.

For two years Jugurtha managed to elude the Romans, but in 107 BC the great soldier Marius was given command of the Roman expedition. Jugurtha was unable to withstand the military genius of Marius and his fresh troops. Within a year Jugurtha was captured and taken to Rome. Here Jugurtha suffered the terrible fate of those who incurred the anger of Rome. He was dragged through the streets as part of the victory parade of Marius. Then the once proud king of Numidia was chained to the Capitol Hill and left there until he starved to death.

It was a consequence of the demands of the war with Jugurtha which forced the Roman senate to make a fateful decision. Until 107 BC the Roman army was made up of well-to-do citizens, mercenaries and allies. Such an army was loyal to the Senate and People of Rome. Marius, however, needed to raise troops quickly and did so by recruiting the poorer citizens of Rome. Relying on their commanders for pay and loot, the new legionaries owed their loyalty to the army, rather than to the state. It was this which was to enable later Roman generals to launch so many successful coups and usurpations.

PTOLEMY VII EUERGETES (?–116 BC)
Usurped: Pharaoh of Egypt 170 BC
Social Origins: Royal Family

In the early part of the 2nd century BC, the Ptolemies, Pharaohs of Egypt were forced to abandon their policy of employing only Greek soldiers when the supply of adventurous young men began to dry up. By the time Ptolemy VI came to the throne in 181 BC a large part of the army was composed of Egyptian troops, who were to prove themselves unreliable. Early in his reign Ptolemy VI married his sister Cleopatra II and had a son named Ptolemy Philopator.

In 170 BC Ptolemy VI became involved in a war with the powerful Seleucid Empire on his northeastern border. The Egyptian army was heavily defeated and Ptolemy VI captured. In Alexandria, Ptolemy VI's brother happily took advantage of his brother's misfortune to have himself declared Pharaoh as Ptolemy VII. Until this power bid the new Pharaoh had been generally known by the unflattering nickname of Physcon, which means 'The Fat'. Feeling that this sobriquet did not fit his new dignity, Ptolemy VII took the name of Euergetes, which means 'The Benefactor'. When his brother returned from imprisonment a few years later, Ptolemy VII fled to Cyrenaica where he maintained his independence.

After Ptolemy VI's death in 145, Ptolemy VII Euergetes, married his brother's widow, who was also his sister, Cleopatra II, and returned to take over power in Egypt. Following the birth of a son to Ptolemy VII Euergetes

Ptolemy VII
A relief of the 2nd century BC showing Ptolemy VII making an offering to Hathor. This goddess was one of the oldest in the Egyptian pantheon, being the daughter of the Sun god Ra and wife of the sky god Horus. By such conspicuous worship of the traditional gods of Egypt the Greek Ptolemies won the affection and loyalty of their subjects. (*Ronald Sheridan*)

and Cleopatra II, the royal couple murdered Ptolemy Philopator. The royal murderer returned to his sister-wife's bed with his hands still blood-stained from the deed.

This murder has complicated the history of the Ptolemies. Some historians count Philopator as Ptolemy VIII while others claim that he never reigned. If Ptolemy Philopator is counted as Ptolemy VIII then the ruler known as Ptolemy VIII Soter becomes Ptolemy IX Soter and so on until the final

Pharaoh becomes either Ptolemy XV Caesarion or Ptolemy XIV Caesarion. The history of the Ptolemaeic dynasty is confusing as well as bloody!

Ptolemy VII Euergetes's bloody career did not end with the murder of his nephew. Later in his reign he fell in love with a niece, known to history as Cleopatra III (see below). He promptly abandoned his queen Cleopatra II to live with his new love. When Cleopatra III presented her uncle-husband with a son, Ptolemy VII Euergetes decided on a new murder. He butchered his first son by Cleopatra II and sent the severed hands to Cleopatra II.

— ♔ —

CLEOPATRA III (?–90 BC)

Kingmaker of Egypt
Social Origins: Royal Family

When Cleopatra III first appears in history she is the beautiful and ambitious niece of Ptolemy VII Euergetes (see above), debauched Pharaoh of Egypt. Using her undoubted charms, Cleopatra lured Ptolemy VII Euergetes away from his sister-wife Cleopatra II. She thus established herself as the richest and most important woman in Egypt. It seems that she also established a degree of dominance over her uncle-lover's policy and governmental appointments.

Cleopatra III bore at least two sons to Ptolemy VII Euergetes, whereupon she persuaded the monarch to murder his son by Cleopatra II to ensure the succession of her own children. She could not, however, persuade Ptolemy VII to agree to the death of Cleopatra II, for whom he seems to have retained some affection.

When the Pharaoh died, he left power jointly to his two sons by Cleopatra III, Ptolemy VIII Soter II (see below) and Ptolemy IX Alexander. Cleopatra III was determined to keep power in her own hands. She largely excluded the two boys from power, but treated Ptolemy VIII Soter II as the senior of the two and ruled in his name. One of her first acts as queen regent was to order the murder of her old rival Cleopatra II.

When Ptolemy VIII Soter II attempted to exercise real power, Cleopatra III acted quickly. She called upon those palace officials loyal to her and staged a coup. The older Pharaoh fled for his life, leaving Cleopatra III in control. The jubilant queen set about establishing a government in the name of her younger son Ptolemy IX Alexander. In reality, of course, she kept power for herself.

However, while completing her plans and formulating a government, Cleopatra III failed to notice the truculence of her drunkard son. In a sudden and unexpected move Ptolemy IX Alexander murdered his mother and assumed the dignities and powers of Pharaoh for himself. Unfortunately, he could not tear himself away from alcoholic excess. It was said that when he was not dancing in drunken exhilaration, he needed to be supported by two friends slightly less intoxicated than himself.

PTOLEMY VIII SOTER II (?–80 BC)

Usurped: Pharaoh of Egypt 88 BC
Social Origins: Royal Family

Left the kingdom of Egypt jointly with his brother, Ptolemy IX Alexander, Ptolemy VIII Soter II fled from court when his formidable mother, Cleopatra III (see above), turned against him. For some years the drunkard Ptolemy IX Alexander remained on the throne. His interests were mainly confined to drinking and hosting large parties. His court became a byword for extravagance and licentious living. It was said of him that his subjects hated him for the oppressive taxes he levied, but he was loved by the court for his generosity and prodigality.

In 88 BC Ptolemy VIII Soter II returned to Alexandria and in a short struggle wrested power from his wastrel brother. It might have been hoped that he would attempt to stem the slide into decadence which had set in under his predecessors. But he had little time to achieve anything before he died in 80 BC.

PTOLEMY XI AULETES (?–51 BC)

Usurped: Pharaoh of Egypt 80 BC
Social Origins: Illegitimate Royal Prince

When Ptolemy VIII Soter II (see above) died in 80 BC, ultimate power in Egypt remained in the hands of his wife Berenice, though the throne passed to Ptolemy X Alexander II, a son of Ptolemy IX Alexander. The new Pharaoh used Roman legionaries to enforce his rule, and married Berenice to give an air of continuity. After a few months he thought that he was securely in power and murdered Berenice in a particularly unsavoury manner.

The people of Alexandria, whom Ptolemy X Alexander II had thought he had pacified with foreign troops, were angered by this barbarous treatment of their popular queen. Rioting broke out in the city, and rapidly escalated into a savage street battle between the citizens and the Pharaoh's troops. The struggle ended when the people broke into the palace and murdered the Pharaoh.

The killing left Egypt with a great problem. In his will Ptolemy X Alexander II had left Egypt to the Roman government which had placed him on the throne. However, a young illegitimate son of Ptolemy IX Soter II was in Alexandria at the time. He acted quickly, taking advantage of the facts that he was in Alexandria, and that the riotous populace detested the idea of Roman rule. He had himself crowned as Ptolemy XI Auletes, meaning 'the Flautist'. His sobriquet comes from the fact that he was a highly accomplished musician who played the flute for many hours.

Ptolemy XI Auletes knew that Rome would not allow the rich prize of Egypt to slip through its fingers so easily. He also realized that Egypt could not hope to match the military might of Rome. Instead he decided to use the one weapon Egypt did possess: money.

For some years Ptolemy XI Auletes managed to play off the various Roman generals and politicians against each other. But in 58 BC, the Pharaoh paid a state visit to Rome. Here he bribed on a truly massive scale. Even Rome had not seen such lavish and open corruption. The wealth of Egypt was poured into Rome in the hope of buying independence. It worked. The Senate of Rome passed a motion recognizing Ptolemy XI Auletes as Pharaoh and an ally of Rome.

Later in his life Ptolemy XI Auletes lost his throne to a palace coup led by his daughter Berenice II. He only regained power with the aid of Roman troops under the command of Pompey the Great. It seemed clear to all that Egypt had become little more than a Roman satellite.

— 👑 —

MITHRADATES III (?–54 BC)

Usurped: Parthian Empire 57 BC
Social origins: Royal Family

By the 60s BC Parthia had grown to be an immensely powerful state. The ferocious horse warriors from the Caspian had conquered or absorbed most of the Asian lands of Alexander the Great's empire. Their territories stretched from Armenia to the frontiers of India. The steady westward spread of Parthian power made it inevitable that there would come a clash with Rome. It was this which created the conditions in which Mithradates III rose to power.

In 66 BC the great Roman general Pompey was sent to what is today Turkey and the Middle East to pacify the eastern frontier of the Roman Empire. Pompey wished to use his troops to conquer large new territories to gain loot and fame to further his political career at home. Before he could gain his objectives, Pompey needed to be certain of Parthian neutrality. He therefore promised King Phraates III of Parthia extensive territories if he did not interfere.

By 63 BC Pompey had conquered Armenia, the Seleucid Empire and several other smaller states. He gave Phraates III some of the promised lands and then returned to Italy, leaving the Parthian King awaiting the remainder of the territory promised to him. For some months, Phraates III waited patiently. Then he became concerned as to why the territories had not been handed over, but were still garrisoned by Roman troops. He sent messages to Pompey and received conciliatory replies, but no land.

In Parthian court circles Phraates III was beginning to be seen as a weak, ineffective monarch. The failure to enforce his deal with Pompey only strengthened this impression. In a semi-barbaric warrior kingdom such as Parthia, weakness was a fault not tolerated in a ruler for long. In 57 BC the sons of Phraates III, including the young prince Mithradates, came to the conclusion that the government of the empire would be better in their own hands.

Mithradates seems to have been the leader of the conspiracy which followed. It was certainly he who sneaked up on his father and murdered him. He immediately claimed the throne as Mithradates III. The brutal act of patricide seems to have aroused the Parthian people and Mithradates III found himself faced with a difficult task subduing his own kingdom.

Ironically Mithradates III called upon Rome to help him. He received large amounts of aid from the Roman Governor of Syria. Perhaps the Romans wanted to install a client on the throne of a neighbour as dangerous as Parthia. For a short time Mithradates was able to cling on to his violently-won and perilously-governed nation. But he fell victim to his enemies after just three years in power.

ORODES I (?–37 BC)

Usurped: Kingdom of Parthia 54 BC
Social Origins: Royal Family

Like that of his brother Mithradates III (see above), the usurpation and rule of Orodes I was dominated by family feuds and the relations of the powerful Parthian Empire, which ruled lands in and around modern Iran, with Rome.

Orodes had joined Mithradates III in the plot which led to the murder of their father Phraates III, but soon after fell out with his brother.

Both men wanted power for themselves, and resented having to share it with each other. Mithradates's friendship with the Romans was resented by Orodes, who may have become the leader of a nationalist opposition. In 54 BC Orodes overcame his brother and arranged his murder.

Almost immediately Orodes was faced by a massive Roman invasion. The Roman leader Marcus Crassus was eager to win a military reputation to match that of his rivals in Rome, Caesar and Pompey. He used the murder of the Roman ally Mithradates III and the unfinished arrangements of Pompey as an excuse to act against the Parthians.

In the summer of 53 BC Crassus led an army of about 40,000 men into Mesopotamia. In response Orodes sent a force of some 10,000 horsemen under his general Surena. Surena was supported by a highly efficient transport system which brought food and arrows to his horse archers. So extensive was this support system that Surena could spare 200 wagons to carry his harem. The two armies met at Carrhae where the swirling horse archers decimated the ponderous Roman legions. Some 20,000 Romans were killed, including Crassus, and a further 10,000 were captured and sold as slaves.

When Orodes received the news from Carrhae he knew that his throne was safe from Rome. However, he was not so certain that he would not be removed by internal troubles. Orodes grew suspicious of the growing popularity of the successful Surena. The general showed no signs of having designs on the throne, but Orodes remained wary. A few months after Carrhae, in a disgraceful act of treachery and ingratitude, Orodes had Surena murdered.

ARISTOBULUS II (?–49 BC)

Usurped: Kingdom of Judaea
Social Origins: Royal Family

During the latter half of the 2nd century and the first half of the 1st century BC the Jews took advantage of the decline of the Seleucid and Ptolemaic dynasties in Syria and Egypt respectively to acquire increasing degrees of freedom. Eventually Judaea achieved independence for the first time in centuries under Hyrcanus I. The new dynasty combined the role of King and High Priest to produce a form of government peculiarly suited to the Jewish state.

By 70 BC, the Kingdom of Judaea had spread its borders to include Samaria and other nearby regions. When Hyrcanus II came to the throne he set in motion a train of events which would lead to the fall of the Kingdom of Judaea. Almost as soon as Hyrcanus II ascended the throne, his brother Aristobulus mounted a palace coup and overthrew him. Hyrcanus fled the palace and the country as fast as he could, knowing only too well the fate he would suffer if he fell into the hands of the newly crowned Aristobulus II.

Aristobulus II set about establishing his position in Jerusalem. He did this with energy and thoroughness, determined that he would not fall to such a coup as he had himself launched. Aristobulus II was, however, powerless against the forces his brother was gathering. Hyrcanus II made his way to the Roman army of Pompey, at that time campaigning in Armenia. In 63 BC Pompey marched his powerful army into Judaea, demanding that Hyrcanus II be reinstated as King and High Priest. Recognizing a lost cause when he saw one, Aristobulus II reluctantly acquiesced and left the kingdom to his brother. The price of Pompey's help was, however, high. Judaea became a client kingdom of Rome, losing its hard-won and short-lived freedom.

— 👑 —

PHRAATES IV (?–2 BC)

Usurped: Kingdom of Parthia
Social Origins: Royal Family

Phraates IV was born one of 32 sons of Orodes I, King of the Parthian Empire which extended from the frontier of the Roman Empire in Syria to the Himalayas. Mixing with the harem and court, Phraates IV passed his youth quietly. His elder brother Pacorus enjoyed the favour of Orodes I, was given governmental posts to gain experience and was generally accepted as the heir to the throne.

In 40 BC Pacorus led a huge Parthian army on an invasion of the Roman Empire, ostensibly to support a Roman rebel named Labienus. While the Roman armies and politicians were concerned with their own internal struggle for power, Pacorus seized Syria and surrounding areas for his father. However, Pacorus allowed himself to be caught at Gindarus by a superior Roman force in 38 BC and he was killed.

When the news of the prince's death reached Parthia, the succession suddenly became open. Orodes was expected to begin grooming another son to follow him, and chose Phraates. The young man, however, decided not to wait his turn on the throne. The unexpected death of Pacorus had opened up the prospect of absolute power to Phraates, and he did not want to risk losing his chance. In 37 BC, only a few weeks after he had been chosen as heir, Phraates IV murdered his father. He then led a band of soldiers through the royal apartments and ordered the murder of all 30 of his brothers.

By this brutal action, Phraates IV hoped to make his grip on the throne secure. He had certainly removed all immediate rivals for the crown, and in 36 BC strengthened his power by defeating a Roman invasion led by Mark Antony. These measures may have helped Phraates IV to the throne, but his abuse of power aroused much resentment. His rule was marked by a brutality and tyranny not common in the Parthian Empire, semi-barbaric though it was. Eventually an internal revolution wrested the throne from his grip.

In desperation Phraates IV fled to the lands of his Scythian subjects. It was among these nomadic horsemen that the Parthian dynasty had originated many years earlier. Phraates IV gained their support and used it to regain his throne. For several more years Phraates continued to rule the mighty Parthian Empire. When his death came it was in just such a coup as had gained him the throne in the first place. In 4 BC Phraates IV's wife slipped poison into his meal in order to secure the throne for her son, Phraates V.

HEROD THE GREAT (73–4 BC)

Usurped: Kingdom of Judaea 37 BC
Social Origins: Royal Family

Herod was born in 74 BC as a prince of the ruling dynasty of Judaea, a small Jewish client kingdom of Rome in the Near East. His rise to the kingship was brought about by the interference of the great powers in the affairs of Judaea. Herod used his undoubted abilities to turn events to his own ends.

In 59 BC Herod became Governor of Galilee and seems to have performed this task well. His life changed irrevocably in 40 BC when a huge Parthian army swept over the borders and overran Judaea. King Hyrcanus II of Judaea was captured and taken to Parthia as a prisoner.

Herod wasted no time in fleeing the country and hastened to Italy. Since 63 BC, Judaea had been a client kingdom of the Roman Empire, so it was natural that Herod should travel to Rome. Once in the city, Herod persuaded Mark Antony and the young Octavius that he was the man to recover Judaea from the Parthians and return it to the sphere of Rome. Octavius and Antony persuaded the Senate to make Herod King of Judaea, and then sent him back to the Middle East to claim his kingdom.

Acting in co-operation with the Roman armies resisting the Parthian invasion, Herod slowly gained ground. In 37 BC he captured Jerusalem and became king in fact as well as in name. Perhaps hoping to strengthen his hold on the throne, Herod immediately married the beautiful Marianne, a grand-daughter of Hyrcanus II.

The true king, Hyrcanus II, remained alive as a prisoner of the Parthians, who seem to have been hanging on to him in case he became a useful political pawn. The continued existence of this rival may have made Herod feel insecure. He embarked on a massive building programme, erecting fortresses, town walls and rebuilding the Temple in Jerusalem. When Herod learnt that his brother and sister had taken a dislike to his children, Herod had them murdered. Perhaps this was a sign of his continued insecurity. Few usurpers rest happily once they have secured the crown, and Herod seems to have been no exception.

In 31 BC, Octavius established himself as the master of the whole Roman Empire. Herod hurried to Rhodes to congratulate Octavius on his victory. He also secured Octavius's promise that he could remain as King of Judaea. The following year the Parthians released Hyrcanus II, who returned to Judaea. Quite what Hyrcanus's motives were for returning to his old kingdom is uncertain. He may have hoped to regain the throne, or conceivably might have been content with a pension. Herod took no chances. He ordered men to meet Hyrcanus on the road to Jerusalem and kill him. After this assassination, Herod may have felt more secure. He continued to reign without serious opposition until 4 BC.

Note: Herod's paranoid suspicions about potential usurpers were almost certainly responsible for his murder of small children in the small village of Bethlehem, an event recorded in the Bible.

Gaius JULIUS CAESAR (102–44 BC)

Usurped: Power in Rome 47 BC
Social Origins: Nobleman

Considered by many to be the greatest figure in ancient history, Julius Caesar clawed his way to supreme political power against enormous odds. Only his ruthless determination and prodigious talents ensured his success.

In the mid-1st century BC Rome was in crisis. The Republican form of government had been designed for a city state with a population of a few thousands. The citizens of Rome were divided into three classes, the noble Patricians, the moderately wealthy Equites or Knights and the common Plebeians. Each class had varying powers and responsibilities. For a time the system worked well but when Rome acquired an enormous and incredibly wealthy empire, the government began to crumble.

The few thousand citizens were in control of an empire of millions. The

Julius Caesar
A marble bust of Julius Caesar, dictator of Rome. Caesar is shown here in the
ceremonial robes befitting a member of a proud patrician family, rather than in the
more familiar armour, emphasizing the military successes through which he gained
power. A clear join can be seen around the neck of the bust. This is due to the fact
that the bodies of such statues were mass-produced in workshops while the heads were
completed to order by master craftsmen. (*Macdonald/Aldus*)

Plebeians had been impoverished by constant wars, while some of the Patricians and Equites had amassed vast fortunes. Huge amounts of money and antiquated governmental procedures ensured that Roman government became increasingly corrupt and degenerate.

Caesar was born into an impoverished, but highly respectable Patrician family. Family influence was used by Caesar to acquire a series of minor military and diplomatic posts. Through these Caesar became friends with the immensely rich Crassus. The young Caesar persuaded Crassus to advance him large sums of money in return for political favours. With the money Caesar provided lavish entertainments for the Plebeians, thus winning their support.

In 67 BC Caesar married Pompeia, cousin of the powerful and victorious general Pompey the Great. Through bribery and the influence of Pompey, Caesar gained increasingly important posts. In 59 BC he secured the position of Consul, the most important in the Republic. His march to power had begun. Pompey, Caesar and Crassus now formed an unconstitutional partnership, known as the Triumvirate, and used their influence to manipu- late the state to their own ends. All three gained more influence and money as a result.

In 58 BC Caesar became Governor of southern Gaul. He used the appointment to conquer the whole of modern France and launch raids on Britain and Germany. These brought him large amounts of loot, enormous glory and the loyalty of his sizeable army. In 53 BC Crassus died and Pompey was becoming increasingly jealous of Caesar's rise. Senators trying to break up the Triumvirate encouraged Pompey's distrust of Caesar. In 49 BC the Senate sent Caesar orders which, if had followed them, would have entailed his ruin and probable death.

Up to this point Caesar's ambitions seem to have been set on amassing vast wealth and personal power within the framework of the Republic. But now he changed his aims toward acquiring complete control of the Empire. In a series of lightning campaigns Caesar smashed the armies of Pompey and the Senate. Marching his troops into Rome Caesar demanded and received the post of Dictator. The position had been given to army commanders in times of crisis before, but only for a few months. Caesar forced the Senate to grant him the position for ten years. Later this was changed to a life appointment.

By this action in 45 BC Caesar had overthrown the power of the Republic and made himself supreme master of the greatest empire in the known world. However, Caesar's political judgement then deserted him. He demanded that he be allowed to use the title of King in the eastern provinces. Caesar was correct when he said that the new title would give him greater respect in those countries used to rule by kings. However, in Rome the title 'king' was hated. Only after terrible struggles had Rome ousted her tyrannical kings, and nobody wanted to see a new king installed. A conspiracy of leading noblemen was formed. On the Ides of March 44 BC, Caesar was murdered. His ambitions had risen one step too high.

— ♔ —

MARCUS ANTONIUS (MARK ANTONY) (c. 83–30 BC)

Kingmaker of the Middle East 34 BC
Social Origins: Roman General

Mark Antony spent a dissolute and drunken youth before rising to high command in the Roman army and becoming one of the most powerful men in the known world. He took power by force and imposed his decisions on several kingdoms. However, it is his relationship with Cleopatra VII of Egypt and his famous kingmaking ceremony at Alexandria in 34 BC for which he is best known.

After the death of the Dictator Julius Caesar (see above) the Roman Empire was split by civil war as Caesar's friends fought against his murderers. By 42 BC Caesar's party had emerged victorious. The three leaders, Lepidus, Octavian and Mark Antony, divided the Empire between them, Octavian took the western provinces, Lepidus acquired Africa and Mark Antony the East. It was a fateful decision for Antony.

In 41 BC he met and fell hopelessly in love with Queen Cleopatra of Egypt. Thereafter his actions and policies changed. Instead of behaving as an ambitious Roman general, Antony became obsessed with his role as a divine eastern monarch. He began calling himself 'The New Dionysus', taking the name of the eastern wine god. Under the spell of Cleopatra, Antony launched military campaigns and interfered in the politics of other nations, all for the benefit of Egypt.

By 34 BC Antony was married to Cleopatra and ruled Egypt with her, as well as having control over the whole eastern Mediterranean. He decided to hold a great ceremony in Alexandria to emphasize his power and impress his subjects. It was to be Antony's greatest victory, and his worst mistake.

A great platform was built in an immense square in Alexandria. On the platform were erected six gilded thrones. On the appointed day tens of thousands of Alexandrians poured into the square to watch the spectacle. Antony and Cleopatra appeared and sat on two of the thrones.

On to the platform came Ptolemy Caesarion, Julius Caesar's son by Cleopatra. He was crowned deputy Pharaoh and King of Kings, the ancient title of the Persian Emperors. Next came Antony's son by Cleopatra, Alexander Helios. He was enthroned as King of Armenia and Media. Third into the public eye was Cleopatra Selene, twin sister of Alexander Helios. She was given the crown of Lybia and much of North Africa. Finally the little toddler Ptolemy Philadelphus, recently born to Antony and Cleopatra, was made King of Syria and Macedonia.

In this single ceremony Antony was not only making kings, but launching a usurpation of great scope. He had been appointed to rule the Eastern Mediterranean territories of Rome and liaise with Egypt. He was now declaring that he was Pharaoh and lord of all his lands to do with as he wished. In the east such behaviour was accepted as the natural prerogative of a ruler and for a while Antony succeeded in his aims. He became the ruler of perhaps the wealthiest empire in existence.

However, in Rome Antony's kingmaking activities were seen as treachery and a gross insult. Octavian was able to rouse the people and Senate of Rome to his cause. He marched against Antony and crushed his forces at the battle of Actium in 31 BC. The following year, stripped of his possessions and abandoned by Cleopatra, Mark Antony stabbed himself to death. His power had lasted just four years.

TIRIDATES II (fl. 1st century BC)

Usurped: Parthian Empire 32 BC
Social Origins: Nobleman

Tiridates II led a rebellion against the tyrannical Phraates IV (see above) after the latter had been on the throne just five years. In that short time Phraates IV had shown himself to be a violent, suspicious and unpredictable king. Few people were safe in his court. His most successful general was murdered after having achieved a great victory because Phraates IV grew jealous of the man's popularity. Other, less important people also fell victim to the tyrant's whims.

Tiridates led the coup against his monarch in 32 BC and succeeded in driving the king from the country. However, Phraates soon returned with the support of wild Scythian tribesmen and forced his way back onto the throne. Resistance to his reign remained. Not long afterwards Tiridates headed another coup and once again grabbed power. This time, however, Phraates IV returned in dangerous mood. Tiridates wisely fled Parthia and travelled to Rome. Here he was welcomed by the Roman ruler Augustus Caesar and given a pension.

CLEOPATRA VII (69–30 BC)

Usurped: Crown of Egypt 47 BC
Social Origins: Royal Family

Cleopatra VII was brought up in the court of the Ptolemies of Egypt where duplicity, deceit and savage revenge were commonplace. It was no wonder that when she became an adult Cleopatra would throw herself into intrigues of tortuous complexity. The only surprise is that she remained alive long enough to do so.

In 51 BC Ptolemy XI Auletes died. He left the throne jointly to Cleopatra, his eldest child, and his eldest son Ptolemy XII Philopator who was just ten years old. The couple were duly married and guardians were set up to advise Philopator. These guardians at once came into conflict with Cleopatra, who was aged 18 and had her own ideas about government. In 48 BC Cleopatra narrowly avoided an assasination attempt and fled to Syria. Here she raised an army and invaded Egypt. Civil war was imminent.

At this moment Julius Caesar, the great Roman general, arrived in Egypt. He tried to patch up the quarrel between the royal couple and asked Cleopatra to visit him in Alexandria. Cleopatra was astute enough to trust Caesar, but not her fellow Egyptians. She knew that if Philopator's guardians caught her before she reached Caesar they would kill her. Cleopatra therefore secretly sailed to Alexandria harbour. Here she had herself tied up in a carpet which a trusted servant carried ashore pretending it was a present for Caesar. When the 'present' was untied Caesar found himself confronted by the beautiful young queen.

Cleopatra quickly used her charms to become Caesar's lover. She turned the great Roman from an impartial outsider into her own partisan. In 47 BC Philopator began a war against Cleopatra and Caesar. His troops were defeated in battle by Caesar's Romans and Philopator drowned in flight.

Cleopatra persuaded Caesar not to take Egypt for Rome but to install her as queen, reigning jointly with a second brother who became Ptolemy XIII. Caesar then returned to Rome to take part in his own struggle for power. By 44 BC Cleopatra had lost her use for Ptolemy XIII and had him murdered. Her son by Caesar, Ptolemy Caesarion became joint ruler in his place.

After the murder of Caesar, Cleopatra realized that she had to win the friendship of the new masters of the Roman Empire. In 41 BC she visited Mark Antony and again used her charms to make a Roman her lover. Antony became fiercely partisan to Cleopatra, using his Roman troops and Roman provinces for the benefit of Egypt. For a few years Cleopatra was at the height of her success. she had virtual control over the whole Eastern Mediterranean, far more power than any of her ancestors. However, Antony's behaviour infuriated Octavian and the Senate in Rome. A brief war followed in which Antony and Cleopatra were heavily defeated and Antony committed suicide.

In 31 BC Octavian entered Alexandria in triumph. Cleopatra must have hoped to salvage something from the wreck of her plans. But after meeting Octavian she realized that she could expect no mercy. In traditional Roman manner she would be dragged through the streets of Rome in chains and then killed. Rather than face this disgrace, Cleopatra decided to kill herself. Octavian, however, wanted to keep her alive. He placed guards on the doors of her apartments and forbade any weapons to enter her possession.

Cleopatra was, as usual, more cunning than her opponents. She had a poisonous snake smuggled to her in a basket of fruit. After bathing and dressing herself in her robes as Queen-Goddess of Egypt, Cleopatra made the snake bite her and lay down to die. Octavian was furious, but had enough respect for Cleopatra to bury her beside Antony, as she had requested.

— 👑 —

JUBA II (?–AD 20)

Usurped: Kingdom of Numidia 29 BC
Social Origins: Royal Family

In 46 BC the North African monarch Juba I sent a powerful army under the nominal rule of his infant son Juba II to aid the Pompeian side in the Roman civil war. At Thapsus the combined armies were smashed by Julius Caesar (see above). Knowing that he had only an humiliating death to look forward to, Juba I challenged his general Petreius to a duel. The two men ate a sumptuous banquet and then fought to the death. Juba II, now titulary King of Numidia, had been captured by Caesar at Thapsus and was taken to Rome.

For 17 years Juba lived in Rome under house arrest. He passed his time studying history and writing treatises on geography. Eventually Juba managed to persuade Augustus Caesar, who now held supreme power in Rome, that he was a trustworthy man. Augustus allowed Juba to marry Cleopatra Selene, a daughter of Antony and Cleopatra who was also being held captive in Rome. Perhaps the two hapless inmates had found some solace in love during their long imprisonments.

In 29 BC Juba II returned to North Africa and, with the aid of Roman troops, imposed his rule on the Numidians. Later he extended his kingdom westwards to the Straits of Gibraltar, being careful to check with Rome beforehand that such action was acceptable. Juba II took the title of King of Mauretania after these acquisitions. He died in AD 20.

— 👑 —

LIVIA DRUSILLA (58 BC [-] AD 29)

Usurped: Power in Rome
Social Origins: Noblewoman

Livia Drusilla is one of the most enigmatic figures in Roman history. She was the wife of Augustus and the mother of Tiberius, over both of whom she exercised a large degree of influence. Exactly how great this influence was and how cynically she used it has never been determined. If she was responsible for even half the deeds blamed on her, she was a ruthless woman indeed.

She was born in 58 BC a member of the Claudian family, the proudest and most respected noble family in Rome. She married a fellow nobleman and bore him two sons, Tiberius and Drusus. During the civil wars the Claudians were opposed by Julius Caesar and Octavian, later to be known as Augustus Caesar. At one point Octavian besieged Livia and her husband in Perusia.

In 39 BC Livia met Octavian and the two immediately fell in love. Risking both scandal and political difficulties, the two divorced their respective spouses and married each other. By 30 BC Octavian was master of the Roman World. In 23 BC he revised the constitution to give the appearance of Republican democracy, but to reserve real authority for himself under the title of Augustus. It is more than probable that the highly intelligent and well educated Livia had a hand in this legislation.

It is probable that tensions were building up within the Imperial family. The question of the succession lay open. Augustus had a daughter, Julia, by an earlier marriage, but he had no children by Livia. In 12 BC Julia's husband, by whom she had had two sons named Gaius and Lucius, died. Livia promptly persuaded Augustus to marry the young widow to Tiberius, her own son. To achieve this she had to overcome the objections of Tiberius who was very much in love with his own wife. Livia ignored her son's objections and the marriage went ahead.

The intrigue was a failure. Tiberius disliked Julia, who took solace in numerous affairs. The resentful Tiberius then left Rome for a quiet and voluntary exile in Rhodes. After a few years Tiberius wished to return to Rome, but Augustus refused. His grandsons, Gaius and Lucius were rising in importance and appeared to be learning the business of government well. Augustus did not want his stepson, and the boys' stepfather, to return to Rome and complicate the succession. Livia, on the other hand, wanted her son back and urged Augustus to relent.

At this critical point Gaius and Lucius died. It was widely believed that Livia ordered their murders. If she was responsible for their deaths, she covered her tracks well for there was little or no evidence to suggest that they did not die natural deaths. Tiberius returned to Rome soon afterwards and Livia persuaded Augustus to adopt him as his heir.

In AD 14 Augustus died and Tiberius assumed the purple toga of power. He shared power with his mother and, after his virtual retirement, she took full power for herself. In AD 19 Germanicus, grandson of Livia through Drusus, was murdered. Again rumours flew that Livia was responsible, though there is little direct evidence.

Whether or not Livia was responsible for the many murders and crimes which have been blamed on her is unclear. It is known, however, that she took enormous powers for herself to which she had no right. Her influence on Rome and the Imperial succession was great.

PRAETORIAN GUARD

Emperormakers of Rome AD 41
Social Origins: Imperial Bodyguard

In AD 37 the popular young man Caligula succeeded his great uncle Tiberius as Emperor of Rome. The new ruler soon revealed himself to be cruel and licentious to an extraordinary degree. He ordered executions on whims and forced his senators and noblemen to undergo the most humiliating ordeals. Nowhere was this behaviour resented more than in the army. Caligula's father had been a popular general, and the soldiers had hoped for favours from the new emperor. Instead they received nothing but abuse.

On one occasion Caligula humiliated his troops by ordering them to collect shells to celebrate their 'victory' over the ocean. Caligula, like other emperors, used the Praetorian Guard, the only soldiers stationed within Rome itself, as a personal bodyguard. He made the mistake of alienating this powerful body. First he ordered the death of their commander and then humiliated their officers.

One particularly popular officer, named Cassius Chaerea, was singled out by Caligula for insults and unpleasant duties. Chaerea was an elderly man with an heroic career behind him, and furthermore came from one of the leading aristocratic families in the city. He came to head the resentful discussions in the Praetorian barracks.

On 24 January AD 41 Chaerea found himself responsible for guarding the Emperor at a theatre. When the Emperor left his seat, Chaerea and some chosen guardsmen followed him into a corridor and stabbed him to death. Other Praetorians were sent off to kill Caligula's wife and daughter.

Caligula had appointed no heir so constitutional power returned to the Senate. In the chaotic hours after Caligula's death, those Senators present in Rome called a hurried meeting. They drew up hasty plans for a return to democratic, Republican government. Events were soon to overtake them.

After the assassination, the Praetorians searched the Imperial Palace looking for supporters of Caligula. In the palace was the dead emperor's uncle, Claudius, a man noted for his slobbering stupidity and amiably simple mind. Fearing for his life, Claudius hid behind a curtain. One of the passing soldiers noticed the man's shoes projecting from beneath the curtain, seized him and dragged him off to the guardroom.

The Praetorian officers recognized Claudius as a member of the Imperial family and swore allegiance to him as the new emperor. Other troops followed their lead and soon Claudius was being paraded through the streets. The crowd of citizens and soldiers carried Claudius to the Senate. Shrinking from the Praetorian swords and thinking they could control the simple Claudius, the Senate proclaimed him Emperor. The accession of Claudius set a precedent by allowing the army to dispose of ultimate power. It was a precedent which would be followed many times.

Claudius quickly rewarded the Praetorian with a cash payment. The Senate, however, found itself faced not by an amiable idiot, but by a rather shrewd politician. Claudius reigned for 13 years, during which time he conquered Britain and introduced many reforms.

— ♔ —

AGRIPPINA THE YOUNGER (c. AD 15–59)

Emperormaker of Rome AD 54

Social Origins: Noblewoman

Agrippina the Younger was born into a junior branch of the Imperial Family of Rome during the reign of Augustus. She saw no reason why her birth or female sex need bar her from power. The instrument she chose was her son Nero, whom she determined to instal on the throne somehow. Unfortunately, Agrippina fell victim to Caligula. She was exiled from Rome and had her properties confiscated. Nero was brought up in comparative poverty. The experience must have made Agrippina all the more determined.

In AD 48, when Agrippina was aged 33, the Emperor Claudius ordered the execution of his beautiful, but wanton wife Messalina after learning about her numerous infidelities and intrigues. Almost immediately Agrippina began plotting her way into power.

She made advances to her uncle and managed to arouse his passions more strongly than her rival Lolia, widow of Caligula. Agrippina married Claudius, despite the fact that marriage between uncle and niece was illegal, and persuaded him to marry his daughter Octavia to Nero. This action placed Nero closer to the throne than he had been before. The only remaining obstacle for Agrippina to overcome was Britannicus, Claudius's ten-year-old son. Knowing the Emperor's affection for the boy, Agrippina dared not murder him. Instead she gradually edged Britannicus out of public life, giving his role and responsibilities to Nero.

Finally, Agrippina persuaded the Emperor to adopt Nero officially. As Nero was older than Britannicus, this made him heir. Having gained everything she wanted from Claudius, Agrippina decided not to give him the chance to change his mind. In October 54 she prepared for her husband a dish of mushrooms, Claudius's favourite, and laced them heavily with poison. That night the Emperor died and Agrippina installed Nero as the new ruler.

For a time everything went as Agrippina had planned. Nero was Emperor, but she held the reins of power. Nero delivered a moving speech, written by a noted philospher, and did everything expected of an Emperor, except exercise power. A clash came when Nero took a beautiful ex-slave as a mistress, abandoning Octavia. Agrippina was horrified, fearing that Nero might lose power through popular indignation at the liaison. She quarrelled with her son and was banished.

Under the influence of his new mistress, Nero then became convinced that Agrippina was plotting against him. Though there was no evidence against his mother, Nero invited her to court and then sent her to sea in an unseaworthy boat. When Agrippina unexpectedly swam ashore, Nero sent two soldiers to kill her. It is an interesting sidelight on the limits of Imperial power that the first officer Nero ordered to carry out the murder refused out of hand. He obviously felt self-confident enough in his own position to be able to refuse what he regarded as an irregular order.

— ♕ —

Servius Sulpicius GALBA (3 BC [-] AD 69)

Usurped: Roman Empire AD 68
Social Origins: Nobleman

Galba's rise to power was a see-saw of fortune and disaster. He nearly won the crown only to lose it and then gain it again before falling victim to his own character. The train of events was set in motion by others, but it was Galba who saw them through to the bitter end.

The Emperor Nero had begun his reign well, choosing able administrators and ruling with an absence of cruelty unusual in his age. But as the years passed he became increasingly extravagant and profligate. Government posts went to those who flattered Nero the most and the provinces became uneasy under maladministration. By 68 Nero had become a very unpopular man. In that year a series of revolts broke out and the finances of the Empire plunged into chaos. The Senate boldly declared Nero a public enemy and the Praetorians abandoned him. In the depths of despair, Nero committed suicide. The Empire was without an Emperor. Since the establishment of the office of Emperor by Augustus almost a century earlier, power had been held by a member of the Imperial family, but with the death of Nero the family was extinct. The Imperial purple robe was open to anyone who could take it.

In Gaul a rebellion by Governor Vindex had been put down, but not before Vindex had persuaded Galba, a governor in Spain, to join him. Vindex had promised Galba the Imperial throne in return for a share of power. Servius Galba would have made an ideal front for Vindex. The elderly Galba was known as an efficient and careful governor, a complete contrast to the extravagant Nero. However, Vindex was beaten and Imperial troops moved on to face Galba. After being declared Emperor, it seemed Galba was to lose it all.

It was at this moment that Nero died. Encouraged by the lack of a rival, Galba hurried to Rome where he was welcomed by the Senate and immediately made Emperor. Throughout his life Galba had acquired a reputation for frugality. Once in power, this became miserliness. Furthermore his increasingly severe attacks of gout made Galba bad-tempered and irritable. He ordered executions and tortures irrationally and unpredictably. The Senate and Praetorians began to loathe the man they had previously welcomed. Galba had gambled and won, soon he would lose. Abandoned by both the Praetorians and the Senate, Galba was overthrown by Otho, one of his chief supporters.

Marcus Salvius OTHO (AD 32–69)

Usurped Roman Empire AD 69
Social Origins: Equites (Lesser Nobility)

It has been said that Marcus Salvius Otho was better at dying than at living. It is a statement with which it is difficult to argue. Otho first came to prominence in 58 when Nero became enamoured with his wife. Otho refused to countenance any adulterous liaison and said so publicly. Nero then thought of offering Otho a rich province far from Rome to get him out of the way. This was, of course, exactly what Otho had wanted. He took Lusitania in western Spain and left his wife in Rome.

In Spain, Otho carved a career for himself as an efficient administrator and amassed a sizeable fortune. He also came to know Galba, and took part in the rising which brought the old man to Rome. Once in Rome Otho noticed the resentment which Galba's meanness and unpredictable temper were arousing. He decided to make a bid for the Imperial title himself. In contrast to Galba, Otho made a point of ostentatiously tipping those who served him and paying high wages. Having acquired a desirable reputation, he then tried to become adopted by Galba on the grounds that the old man could not live long. When Galba refused, Otho decided to take more drastic action.

Organizing the troops from Spain and some of the Praetorians under his command, Otho seized power on 15 January 69. Galba shut himself up in the palace with a strong contingent of troops. There was little Otho could do to reach the Emperor, so he tricked him into leaving the building. Messages were sent to Galba stating that loyal troops had killed Otho. Galba believed them and opened the palace doors, whereupon he was murdered.

Almost immediately news reached Otho that Vitellius, commander of troops on the German frontier, was marching on Rome. Otho sent his troops north to block the Alpine passes, but they were heavily defeated. When a messenger arrived with the news, Otho did not believe him. Whereupon the messenger, who had only execution to look forward to under Vitellius, killed himself on the spot. Otho looked sadly at the body and declared 'I shall not subject brave and loyal men to danger.' He then held a small party for his family, said goodbye to his friends and committed suicide.

Aulus VITELLIUS (AD 15–69)

Usurped: Roman Empire AD 69
Social Origins: Nobleman

Aulus Vitellius was 55 years old when his soldiers acclaimed him Emperor. He had spent most of his life at the Imperial court, flattering and pampering successive Emperors to gain money and appointments. He had only recently taken up his command on the German frontier when he received the news that Nero was dead and Galba (see above) was Emperor.

Vitellius himself may well not have acted on the news, but his troops did. They remembered Vitellius's generosity and praises and considered that he would prove to be even more generous as Emperor. His officers immediately led the troops to Italy where they fought their way to Rome and installed Vitellius in power. Having gained the Imperial purple, Vitellius was determined to enjoy it. For five months Vitellius ruled as Emperor. He proved to be an incompetent ruler who was more concerned with satisfying his prodigious appetite by constant meals than with affairs of state. He was also exceptionally cruel, having men tortured before his eyes. He was known to murder heirs so that wealthy men would die intestate and he could seize their money.

When, in December, rebellious troops supporting the rebel general Vespasian arrived in Italy, many of Vitellius's men deserted. The Emperor disguised himself as the palace caretaker in the hopes of escaping. But he was recognized and dragged out of the palace. The wretched Emperor's enemies gathered together, tortured him savagely and then drowned him in the Tiber.

— ♛ —

Titus Flavius Sabinus VESPASIAN (AD 9–79)

Usurped: Roman Empire AD 69
Social Origins: Commoner

Titus Flavius Vespasian was the fourth usurper to seize power in Rome in the troubled year 69. Yet unlike the others he was no debauchee, innured to the court intrigues and decadence which had become increasingly common since the death of Augustus. He was the first Emperor to be born outside the Patrician circle. Perhaps his humble birth had something to do with his honesty.

He was born the son of a customs inspector, but joined the army and quickly earned his way to high command. He incurred Nero's displeasure by falling asleep when one of the Emperor's poems was being read aloud. However, Vespasian was too good a soldier to be punished. In 67 he was sent to command the army in the East. He was still there when the news of Nero's death arrived.

In July the legions of Egypt and Judaea proclaimed Vespasian as Emperor. He left the East in the care of his son Titus, later to become Emperor, and marched on Rome. However, even before he reached Italy the Danube legions had risen to his support and killed Vitellius. Vespasian found Rome open and waiting.

In his ten year reign Vespasian set about putting Rome in good order. He himself lived a modest and respectable life, and passed laws enforcing morality on the citizens of Rome. He recognized the terrible state into which public finances had fallen, and put them right. Some of his financial methods may have been less than honest, but he brought the Empire back into solvency. He quickly reformed the process of administration making ability, not bribery, the test for promotion. Above all, Vespasian was popular. He

D. VESPASIANVS AVGVSTVS.
LE GAIN SENT TOVSIOVRS BON DE QVELQVE PART Q'VIL VIENNE

Vespasian
The Roman Emperor Vespasian was a great soldier and was placed in power by the
army. His military character is emphasized by this 18th-century French engraving,
based on an ancient bust. It is, therefore, surprising that Vespasian called a halt to
continuous foreign conquest and closed the doors of the temple of Janus, thus
declaring that Rome was at peace. He even built a huge Temple of Peace in Rome
in his later years. (*Mansell Collection*)

71

was a blunt, no-nonsense soldier who loved to crack jokes and was always ready for a laugh.

Vespasian restored the self-esteem of Rome and reformed the Empire's finances and administration. He was exactly the type of tough, practical man who was needed. Even his last act could have been designed to instil pride into Rome. Feeling the end was near, Vespasian declared 'An emperor should die on his feet.' He struggled upright, swayed on his feet for a moment and then died. It was a noble end to a noble reign.

— 👑 —

Publius Helvius PERTINAX (?–AD 193)

Usurped: Roman Empire AD 193
Social Origins: Army Officer

By the year 192 the behaviour of the Roman Emperor Commodus, son of the popular Marcus Aurelius, had reached a ridiculous level. After a fairly promising start to his reign, the Emperor refused to do any work or take official duties seriously. Instead he fought in the gladiatorial arena, delighted in executing criminals and in visiting brothels. Leading politicians and generals quickly became discontented with the rule of Commodus and several plots against his life were made. At first all of these were discovered and the conspirators executed. However, it was not long before a successful plot was hatched.

Pertinax, an able and distinguished general who held office in Rome, hatched the plot and was joined by Marcia, Commodus's mistress, and Laetus, prefect of the Praetorian Guard, the Imperial bodyguard. On the last day of 192 Marcia fed poisoned mushrooms to the Emperor. Commodus fell ill, but then showed signs of recovering, whereupon Laetus called upon a wrestler to strangle him.

The next day Pertinax hurried to a special meeting of the Senate. There he carried out what was probably a shrewd and well-planned act. He declared that he had been put on the throne by soldiers, but that the Senate should be the body to choose the next Emperor. He then suggested that the senior Senator Glabrio should be chosen. It was a brilliant move. He had flattered the Senate by pretending that power lay with them. At the same time his carefully worded hint about the soldiers ensured that the Senate would choose him as Emperor. The Senate knew only too well the fate they might suffer if the soldiers learnt that Pertinax was not to be the man. In a single stroke, Pertinax had gained the support of both Senate and army.

Having gained the Imperial power, Pertinax set about restoring the glories of Marcus Aurelius. He solved the financial difficulties by selling off the fabulous treasures and extensive lands confiscated by Commodus. A stringent economy drive was instituted. Banquets were curtailed and public entertainments almost vanished. Pertinax was showing himself to be an able, if uninspiring, master for the Roman world. However, he made one mistake, a slip which was to cost him his life. He did not adequately reward those who had helped him to gain the throne. Less than three months after coming to power he was murdered by a band of Praetorians.

PRAETORIAN GUARD

Emperormakers of Rome AD 193
Social Origins: Imperial Bodyguard

After becoming Emperor of Rome by murdering Commodus, Pertinax (see above) paid the Praetorian Guards a reward for having helped him, but otherwise seemed hostile to them. At this time some 4,500 Praetorians were stationed in and around Rome. There were paid twice as much as ordinary legionaries and had gained immunity from prosecution for a number of crimes. Under Commodus, many abused these immunities to lead a criminal career. Pertinax abolished the abuses and severely restricted the Praetorians.

Laetus, Praetorian Prefect who had helped Pertinax to the throne, quickly tired of the continual insults and controls heaped on his men. On 28 March 193 a group of 300 Praetorians marched from their barracks to the Imperial palace. Instead of protecting their master, the Praetorians on duty looked the other way. Realizing his danger, Pertinax bravely tried to retrieve the situation by making a speech to the insurgents. He began pointing out the benefits of his rule, but the audience was in no mood to listen. A spear was thrown and slammed into Pertinax's chest. The Emperor toppled forwards and was killed by a rain of sword blows.

Meanwhile, Pertinax's father-in-law and Governor of Rome, Sulpicianus had heard the uproar and rushed to the Praetorian barracks to try to calm the situation. He had almost succeeded when the 300 guardsmen returned from the palace with the head of Pertinax. In what was probably an attempt to regain control of the situation and prevent anarchy, Sulpicianus immediately put himself forwards as the next Emperor. Laetus and most of the Praetorian officers may have been in favour of this move, for Sulpicianus had made a good governor of the city. They asked that Sulpicianus promise to pay the Praetorians a reward for making him Emperor, to which Sulpicianus agreed. At this point events suddenly slipped out of control.

A wealthy Senator named Marcus Didius Julianus, who had led a distinguished public career in the provinces, heard what was occurring and made his way to the Praetorian barracks. He immediately offered the guards a higher sum of money than Sulpicianus had done. Exactly what Julianus's motives were is hard to determine. He could scarcely have expected to receive the honour accorded to earlier emperors who had gained the throne by merit. Perhaps he hoped to make a fortune and then retire!

There then followed a disgraceful spectacle. The common guardsmen, scenting easy money, forced their officers to accept the higher offer. Sulpicius then raised his bid, as did Julianus. In effect the Roman Empire was up for auction with the greedy Praetorians acting as auctioneers. The Imperial dignity had fallen a long way from the pinnacle of Marcus Aurelius just 13 years earlier.

Eventually Julianus offered each guardsman 6,250 denarii, the equivalent of five year's pay. He won the day. The guardsmen carried him to the Senate and forced his appointment at swordpoint. The only concession the officers could wring was that Sulpicianus should not suffer for his opposition to Julianus. The Emperor who had bought his way into power proved a tragic and dismal failure. The Senate refused his instructions and the mob threw stones at him in the street. At the first sign of opposition, Julianus was abandoned to his fate.

Lucius Septimus SEVERUS (AD 146–211)

Usurped: Roman Empire AD 193
Social Origins: Provincial General

In 193 the Praetorian Guards in Rome auctioned the title of Emperor to the man who would pay them the most money. It was a disgraceful abuse of their power and when the news reached the provinces the regular army rose in rebellion. In Syria the legions proclaimed their general, Pescennius Niger, as Emperor, in Britain Clodius Albinus was invested with the Empire, while on the Danube frontier the commander Septimus Severus became the third Emperor to be announced by the troops on receiving the news. He immediately set out for Rome.

Severus was not a Roman, but a Carthaginian who had joined the army and risen to high command. He spoke Latin as a second language and never lost his strong African accent. Though not a native Roman, Severus was a good soldier and fine organizer. This reputation may account for the welcome he received in his march to Rome. Wherever he went Severus was greeted with open arms. When he reached Rome, Severus found that Julianus had already been murdered and he took power with ease.

However, Severus was not yet in control of the whole Empire. In 194, having first allied himself with Albinus, Severus led his legions to the east where he first defeated and then executed Niger. Three years later he moved against Albinus and crushed his armies at Lyons.

Severus soon showed his background by a complete lack of respect for Roman institutions. The Senate was ignored and lost much of its remaining powers. He installed many new Senators from the provinces, ensuring that native Romans lost their majority in the most important body of government. He quickly disbanded the dangerously ambitious Praetorian Guard, replacing them with a Praetorian loyal to himself. The whole balance of power within the Empire shifted from Rome to the provinces.

Caesar Marcus Opellius Severus MACRINUS (AD 164–218)

Usurped: Roman Empire AD 217
Social Origins: Lawyer

Opellius Macrinus seized power out of fear—fear for his life and fear for his relatives. If he had not acted it is more than likely that he would have been killed. This fear was brought about by the statement of an elderly Egyptian named Serapis.

One day in 217 Serapis suddenly announced that the gods had revealed to him that Macrinus, at that time the commander of the Imperial bodyguard, would become Emperor. Servants of Caracalla, the reigning Emperor, had Serapis put to death for his temerity, and sent a message to Caracalla. The Emperor was in Palestine at the time and Macrinus in Rome. By chance Macrinus came across the letter about Serapis before it reached the Emperor. He knew that as soon as the brutal Caracalla heard about the prophecy his execution would be ordered. As commander of the bodyguard, Macrinus had control over a large section of the army and the civil administration. He used these contacts to save himself.

Macrinus secretly involved Martiallus, a soldier of the bodyguard, in his plans and ordered him to kill Caracalla at the first opportunity. The Emperor was still in Palestine on a visit to his wealthiest provinces. While travelling one day, Caracalla called a halt and slipped into some bushes to relieve himself. Martiallus followed and stabbed the Emperor to death. A second member of the bodyguard, who seemed to be taking his job unusually seriously, then killed Martiallus.

Back in Rome, Macrinus immediately seized power. He assumed the ancient titles of the Emperors, to which he had no right either by birth or achievement. He created Caracalla a god, thus hiding his part in the murder from the public, and bullied the Senate into doing his bidding. Having now gained a throne which he had not wanted, Macrinus knew his only chance of staying alive was to keep it. He hoped to gain the respect and support of the army by gaining a great victory. He therefore organized a great invasion of Parthia, the age old enemy of Rome. The invasion was only a partial success. Macrinus gained little glory, and his troops little loot. The failure sealed his fate.

Julia MAESA (?–AD 222)

Emperormaker of Rome AD 218
Social Origins: Provincial Nobility

An accident of birth and circumstance created the conditions for Julia to launch her bid for power. She proved herself to be an unscrupulous schemer more than equal to the task.

When Julia Maesa was still a young woman, her sister, Julia Domna, married the man who later became Emperor Severus. While her sister reached dizzying political heights in Rome, Maesa remained in her home town of Emesa, in Syria. Here she had two daughters, one of whom, Soaemias, had a son named Varius. At the age of 14, Varius followed family tradition by becoming high priest of the local sun god Elagabalus, whose name he thus took as his own.

When Macrinus assassinated Caracalla and took the throne, Maesa found herself the head of the only living relatives of the much loved Severus. She used this circumstance to launch her bid for power. First she made sure that Elagabalus mixed freely with the Roman troops of the area. He was given plenty of money and allowed to spend it freely. Having ensured her young grandson had a reputation for generosity, likely to impress soldiers, she then announced that the boy was actually the illegitimate son of Caracalla. Soaemias supported this spurious claim, which brought Elagabalus closer to the throne.

The cunning old woman then linked Elagabalus's divine role as priest with his Imperial relatives' posthumous deification. She was careful, however, not to allow the publicity to reach a point where Macrinus might feel the boy was a threat. At least not until she was ready.

In 218 Maesa declared Elagabalus to be Emperor. Macrinus rushed to confront the forces of the boy in Asia. The battle which followed was something of a farce. The troops of Elagabalus fled the field, but Macrinus had already panicked and run, being killed by agents of Maesa as he tried to escape.

When he entered Rome as Emperor in 219 Elagabalus brought with him his oriental god and other eastern traditions. He married one of the Vestal virgins on the grounds of his own divinity. Maesa had achieved her aim and placed Elagabalus on the throne. She now set about organizing power into her own hands while Elagabalus indulged in his pleasures.

The palace was bathed in perfumes and sumptuous banquets were arranged where the guests literally waded through flowers to their tables. The delicate luxury and feminine touches were typical of Elagabalus. It may have been these which lost him the respect of the army, which was transferred to his young cousin, Alexander.

Elagablus grew jealous and tried to kill his cousin, however the Praetorian guards were too quick for him. They rescued Alexander and then killed Elagabalus in revenge. Alexander took the throne and proved himself to be an able ruler during his 18 years in power.

ARDASHIR (?–AD 241)

Usurped: Power in Persia AD 226
Social Origins: Commoner

As with many great rulers with humble origins, the exact details of Ardashir's early life are obscure. His brilliant triumphs of later years, by contrast, are well known and dazzling in their magnificence.

Ardashir was born as the illegitimate son of a soldier named Sassan and a clothworker. He was born and brought up in Parsa, roughly equivalent to the southern section of modern Persia and then a small province of the much larger Parthian Empire. Ardashir later claimed that Sassan was, in civilian life, a high priest and a descendant of the ancient royal house of Persia. It is impossible to ascertain the truth of these claims.

In 226, however, Ardashir proclaimed his supposed family ancestry and claimed the titles and powers of King of Parsa. His fellow countrymen seem to have been in the mood for rebellion, and eagerly followed him. Ardashir quickly established his control over Parsa and raised an army. Atrabanus V, the Parthian Emperor, marched against Ardashir, whom he considered an upstart who had usurped power in a small province. In three hard battles, however, Ardashir defeated the military might of the Parthians, and killed Atrabanus. Ardashir then led his jubilant Persians on to seize all the territories of the Parthian Empire.

With this stunning success behind him Ardashir assumed the title King of Kings, which had belonged to his supposed ancestors. He now announced his intention of uniting all the territories which had once belonged to the great Persian Empire of about 300 BC. Many of these lands now belonged to Rome. In the great clash which followed, Rome came off worst, but Ardashir was never able to take all the lands he wanted. He died in 241, leaving an enormous empire to his dynasty.

BOADICEA (?–AD 61)

Usurped: Kingdom of the Iceni AD 61
Social Origins: Royal Family

Boadicea, also known as Boudicca, usurped power for one reason; revenge. In her brief and dramatic reign, she exacted a bloody and violent retribution from her enemies.

Boadicea seems to have been born a princess in one of the half-dozen or so Celtic kingdoms of southern Britain. She married Prasutagus, King of the Iceni in Norfolk, about the time of the Roman invasion of 43. Prasutagus managed to win Roman friendship and was allowed to keep his kingdom as a tributary of Rome. The Iceni escaped Roman taxation fairly lightly as a consequence, but their neighbours suffered terribly. Most resented was a tax to pay for the public buildings in the Roman colony of Camulodunum, now Colchester.

When Prasutagus died in 61 he left some of his kingdom to Rome, and the rest to his two daughters. The Roman procurator of the time, however, was a ruthless man named Catus Decianus. Decianus ignored Prasutagus's wishes and the legal position. He sent Roman troops into Iceni territory and seized vast amounts of land and money, as if the Iceni were enemies not friends. When Boadicea protested she was tied to a stake and whipped. Her daughters were brutally raped.

Boadicea immediately took control of the kingdom. She raised an army of many thousand warriors and set out, determined on exacting a terrible revenge on the Romans. Neighbouring tribes joined the rising and soon Boadicea had over 100,000 warriors at her back. The infuriated force fell upon Camulodunum and butchered everybody in the colony. The IXth Legion set out to put down the rising. It was ambushed by Boadicea and virtually annihilated.

Boadicea next wreaked her wrath on London. Her ferocious men poured into the city, looted it and then burnt it to the ground. Some 70,000 citizens perished in the orgy of violence. Boadicea was taking an awful revenge for the injuries done to her and her daughters. The Roman governor Suetonius then appeared on the scene with the main Roman army in Britain and defeated the Iceni. He claimed that he killed 80,000 Britons and that Boadicea took poison on the battlefield. A short and extremely violent reign was over.

TANG (fl. c. 1760 BC)

Usurped: Chinese Empire circa 1760 BC
Social Origins: Nobleman

The details of Tang's usurpation remain obscure. It is not even certain that he ever existed. No Chinese documents remain from this early period, the history of events rests on later legends and traditions. However, the king lists have been found to be remarkably accurate when they can be checked against archaeological evidence.

In the 18th century BC China consisted of a series of towns and vast agricultural lands along the valley of the Yellow River. The Emperor seems to have held a position of authority over a number of local warlords. Tang was probably one of these warlords who used bronze weapons and chariots to enforce their authority on the peasants and border tribesmen.

According to tradition the rule of the Emperor Ji was so cruel that the celestial gods removed their approval from him and conferred it on Tang instead. With such divine aid, Tang simply took over the title and power of Emperor. Behind this tale may lie a military coup launched by disgruntled local nobles against an Emperor too eager to impose his authority. Tang established the Shang Dynasty which was to preside over the rapidly expanding Chinese Empire until about 1122 BC.

PING WANG (fl. c. 770 BC)

Usurped: Chinese Empire 771 BC
Social Origins: Imperial Family

Ping Wang was brought to the throne by a military rising against the Emperor You Wang, Ping's father. Exactly how central Ping was to the conspiracy is unclear, but he was the main benefactor of the upheavals. China was to prove the ultimate loser of the events of 771 BC.

You Wang was an autocratic Emperor who paid little attention to his advisors, and thus incurred the enmity of many powerful nobles. The events which caused his overthrow, however, were precipitated when he abandoned his Empress for a beautiful young mistress. Burning with indignaiton the Empress and her son Ping Wang organized an alliance between their relatives and barbarian tribes beyond the frontiers of the Empire. Together these forces burst into the Imperial capital of Hao. You Wang was killed and Ping Wang took his place.

The usurpation placed the new Emperor in the hands of those noblemen and tribal leaders who had put him on the throne. The Emperor was unable to regain his authority and China slowly slid towards anarchy. Noblemen increasingly seized power from the Emperor and China became a collection of warring states.

HUAN KUNG (?–642 BC)

Usurped: Power in China circa 680 BC
Social Origins: Nobleman

Huan Kung came to power by a combination of force and tact. For a time he was able to hold together the crumbling Chinese Empire, but his efforts were ultimately futile.

By the early 7th century BC China had almost collapsed as an Empire. The Emperor controlled little more than a few square miles of land around his capital at Lo Yang. The rest of the Empire was in the hands of numerous local nobleman who paid lip service to Imperial authority, but were virtually independent rulers. In 685 the ruler of Chi, a state in northeast China died, leaving two sons. The young princes then plunged into a murderous squabble for power. Eventually Huan emerged successful, after killing his brother.

Now Lord of Chi, Huan set about extending his power. In this aim he was ably advised by Kuan Chung whom he made his chief minister. Huan called a meeting of all the lords of China to discuss such matters as irrigation, defence and the rule of law. Using a combination of soft words and military bullying, Huan persuaded the other lords to do as he asked.

For the following forty years, Huan held these meetings at which he organized the affairs of the Empire. Throughout this time Huan always maintained the fiction that he was acting on behalf of the Emperor in Lo Yang. In fact he was doing nothing of the sort and treated the Emperor as if

he were just another provincial ruler. Real power lay in the hands of Huan
and Kuan Chung.

— 👑 —

CHAO KAO (fl. late 3rd century BC)

Emperor maker of China 210–208 BC
Social Origins: Courtier

Chao Kao was prompted to seize power behind the scenes in order to save
his life. His later attempt to establish himself in the full glare of open power
led to his downfall.

In his later years Hwang-ti, the first Emperor to really unify the whole of
China, relied on the advice of two courtiers, the minister Li Ssu and the
eunuch Chao Kao. When Hwang-ti died far from his capital, the two
courtiers knew that their lives might well be taken by Hwang-ti's eldest son
Fu Su, whom they had banished from court some years earlier. In a
desperate attempt to save their lives Chao and Li stopped news of the
Emperor's death from leaking out. They forged a document ordering the
death of Fu Su and then set out for the capital. They pretended that all was
well, with the Emperor's body travelling in the Imperial carriage as if still
alive. In order to hide the smell of the rotting corpse, Chao ordered a cart of
fish to travel beside the royal carriage.

When they reached the capital, the two conspirators found that Fu Su was
dead. They then announced the death of Hwang-ti and proclaimed Ershi
Huangdi, a younger brother of Fu Su, as Emperor. Chao Kao quickly
gathered power into his own hands. He had Li Ssu executed on trumped-up
charges and enforced his will on the Emperor. After just two years, Chao felt
strong enough to mount a bid for open power. He ordered the death of Ershi
Huangdi and declared himself Emperor. However, at his very first session at
court, Chao Kao found his orders ignored and some ministers even attacked
him. His attempt to take power directly was resented. Imperial authority
collapsed and China entered a period of anarchy as strong men bid for the
throne. The name Chao Kao is sometimes spelt Zhao Gao.

— 👑 —

WANG MANG (?–AD 23)

Usurped: Chinese Empire AD 9

Social Origins: Nobleman

Wang Mang came to power in the midst of terrible social problems, and was dragged down by those same problems. Towards the end of the 1st century BC the Han Dynasty was faced by troubles over land ownership, with peasants being ousted by nobles, severe financial shortage and dynastic weakness caused by a succession of boy-emperors.

After the death of Emperor Han Ai Di in 1 BC government fell into the hands of Wang Mang, regent for the under-age Emperor who had assumed the throne. Wang Mang belonged to the family of an earlier Empress and had risen to his high position by a mixture of family influence and personal ability.

After eight years of controlling the government from behind the scenes, Wang Mang seems to have decided that he could control things far better as Emperor than as Chief Minister. He forced the Emperor to go through an elaborate ceremony at which he read out a statement renouncing the throne. Wang Mang then took the title of Emperor. There was nobody powerful enough to stop him.

For some years Wang Mang tried valiantly to solve the problems of the Empire. He introduced widespread reforms, but these were largely resisted by the landowners and petty officials who stood to lose most. Defeat in a war against barbarian nomads to the north added to Wang Mang's problems. In 14 a small peasant rebellion broke out under the commmand of a secret society called the Red Eyebrows. Wang Mang failed to react in time and by 23 the rebellion had spread and become almost Empire-wide. Wang Mang was overthrown by the rebels and murdered. A junior branch of the former Imperial family was then installed on the throne.

TSAO PEI (fl. 3rd century AD)

Usurped: Chinese Empire AD 221

Social Origins: Nobleman

Tsao Pei owed his success to his father Tsao Tsao, who used the actions of others to further his quest for power. By the early 3rd century, China had expanded to reach from what is now Korea to Vietnam and westward to Burma. This extensive Empire, under the Han Dynasty, was increasingly wealthy and prosperous. However, the country was wracked by a series of rebellions, many consisting of peasant revolts.

Perhaps the most dangerous of these was the Yellow Turban rebellion. The Emperor asked Tsao Tsao, at this time one of the Imperial generals, to put down the movement. Tsao Tsao did so with frightening ruthlessness, killing half a million rebels. Soon afterwards one of Tsao Tsao's fellow generals was murdered by a powerful faction of court eunuchs. The soldiers immediately burst into the palace and butchered the eunuchs. This incident removed two of the major forces opposed to Tsao Tsao in one stroke. The general's influence over government then became paramount.

When Tsao Tsao died in 221 he left his power to his son Tsao Pei. The younger man does not seem to have had the patience to act through a puppet Han Emperor. He deposed the reigning sovereign and declared himself to be Emperor. However, he soon found that his direct power extended over barely a third of the Empire. By greedily trying to assume supreme power Tsao Pei found that he had lost much of his authority. His name is sometimes spelt Cao Pi.

— 👑 —

LIU PEI (AD 161–223)

Usurped: Power in China AD 221
Social Origins: Imperial Family

Liu Pei was born into a junior branch of the Han Imperial family which had fallen upon misfortune and been reduced to near poverty. Liu Pei, however, seems to have been an able and ambitious general. In the early years of the 3rd century he rose to positions of high command, placing him in a position to mount his bid for power.

In 221 the last legitimate Han Emperor was dethroned by the general Tsao Pei (see above), who took his place. Liu Pei would have nothing to do with the usurper. He announced that as the only available successor of Han blood, he was the true Emperor. Many malcontents flocked to Liu Pei's banner, but he was unable to make headway against the more powerful Tsao Pei. Instead Liu Pei set up a separate Empire, usually referred to as the Shu Han in southwestern China. Here he and his son ruled as if they were legitimate Emperors, until Shu was conquered by Tsao Pei's successor.

— 👑 —

SSU-MA YEN or WU TI (?–AD 289)
Usurped: Chinese Empire AD 265
Social Origins: Nobleman

Ssu-ma Yen came to power because of his undoubted abilites and almost
limitless ambition. He held on to power throughout his life, but eventually
sowed the seeds for the destruction of his line. During the partition of the
Chinese Empire caused by numerous military risings after the usurpation of
Tsao Pei (see above), Ssu-ma Yen was probably a junior officer who followed
Tsao Pei.

In the army of the resulting state of Wei in northern China, Ssu-ma Yen
became the chief army officer, leading the troops to many dramatic victories.
In 263 he achieved his greatest triumph when he overran the Shu Empire,
adding it to the territories of his master the Tsao Emperor. However, Ssu-ma
Yen soon grew discontented with the rule of the Emperor. Perhaps he felt he
had not been rewarded properly for his efforts, or he may have felt that the
affairs of state were not being run as well as they could.

In 265 Ssu-ma Yen turned his troops on his own monarch, ousting him in
a swift military coup. The successful general then declared himself Emperor
as the founder of Chin Dynasty. As Emperor Ssu-ma Yen is usually referred
to by one of his titles; that of Wu-ti. Wu-ti proved himself to be an energetic
monarch. He conquered the kindom of Wu, also established in 221, thus
reuniting the whole of China under his own rule. Wu-ti tried to cope with
the continuing social and agricultural problems of the Empire. In large part
he seems to have been successful.

However, Wu-ti performed one act which was to have disastrous consequences for China. For administrative purposes he divided the Empire into
15 districts and placed one of his sons in control of each. Presumably Wu-ti
wished to have men he could trust in such powerful positions. The plan
worked well during the Emperor's lifetime for his sons served him well and
loyally. But when in 289 Wu-ti died, his sons refused to acknowledge the
supreme authority of one of their own number. China fell into the grip of
civil war. Ssu-ma Yen's name is sometimes given as Sima Yan.

— 👑 —

LIU YUAN (?–318)

Usurped: Power in China 308
Social Origins: Barbarian King

Liu Yuan used the superb military forces of his own kingdom to exploit an opportunity given him by his enemies the Chinese. After a promising start Liu Yuan had to settle for partial success, and even this was lost by his successors.

It was regular Chinese policy to protect their weak northern border by playing off one band of barbarians against another. Barbarian kings loyal to Chinese interests were rewarded with gold, titles and Chinese brides. The habit of Chinese Emperors of keeping large harems, one had 10,000 wives, led to the existence of a vast number of eligible Imperial princesses to be married off to barbarian leaders. Such marriages impressed the barbarians, but scarcely bothered the Chinese.

One of the most powerful barbarian tribes was the Hsuing-nu. This nomadic tribe specialized in horse and cattle breeding. They were a tough people who could undergo tremendous hardships, and handed out equally fearful sufferings to their enemies. At some time in the 2nd or 3rd centuries, the Han Dynasty gave the king of the Hsuing-nu a royal bride. Perhaps this was in gratitude for his having raised tens of thousands of mounted warriors in Chinese service.

In the late 3rd century, the Hsuing-nu throne was occupied by Liu Yuan, a descendent of the Chinese princess, but a true nomad at heart. He carefully watched the squabblings of the Chin princes and in 304 felt his chance had come. He announced that he was the only legitimate successor to the Han, which may well have been the truth, and proclaimed himself Emperor of China.

Very few Chinese recognized Liu Yuan's title, being too busy with their disputes about the Chin succession. Nothing daunted, Liu Yuan called out the entire military force of the Hsuing-nu. This may have amounted to nearly 100,000 men, all expert horse archers and hardy fighters. These ferocious forces poured over the Great Wall and slammed into China. The feuding Chinese princes could put up no effective resistance. The barbarian Hsuing-nu looted and pillaged where they wished, capturing cities and towns with ease and adding them to the Empire of Liu Yuan.

Liu Yuan was succeeded by his son Liu Tsung who continued the conquest. Eventually the new Han Dynasty controlled the whole of northern China. The native Chinese rulers were squeezed into a small state along the Yangtse River.

— 👑 —

MAHAPADMA Nanda (fl. c. 360 BC)

Usurped: Kingdom of Magadha circa 363 BC
Social Orgins: Low Caste

By the 4th century BC, Magadha had become the most important and powerful of the many kingdoms in the Ganges Basin. However, its internal order was far from stable. The ancient dynasty of kings was overthrown in about 413 BC by a popular rising. It is said that this was brought on by disgust at the dynasty's orgy of internecine murder and feud. A family belonging to the Kshatriya, or warrior caste, was installed. It was this dynasty which was overthrown by Mahapadma.

Mahapadma may have been the son of a barber and a prostitute, or have been born to a virtuous, but low-caste woman. The records are unclear on this point. Equally imprecise is the path this humble man took to the throne. His achievements have been obscured by later legends and inventions. Once king, however, Mahapadma energetically enlarged his dominions and established his family's grip on power. However, throughout his life he seems to have been regarded as a coarse *nouveau riche* by the establishment figures of his realm.

PUSHYMITRA Sunga (fl. early 2nd century BC)

Usurped: Mauryan Empire circa 183 BC
Social Origins: Priest Caste

Under three great and energetic rulers the Maurya Dynasty built up a huge empire, which covered nearly the whole of India. Asoka was possibly the most powerful Maurya Emperor. When he died in 232 BC he had reformed government and religion and nearly unified the entire sub-continent. After the death of Asoka, however, the Maurya dynasty weakened as royal princes bickered about their share in government and provincial governors took powers properly belonging to the Mauryas.

By about 183 BC the prestige of the Mauryan kings had become so reduced that the Empire seemed ripe for take over. The man to whom this idea occurred was Pushymitra Sunga, a successful general belonging to the priest caste. Brahadratha, the Mauryan Emperor, used Pushymitra to lead his armies against various foes. It is possible that the successful general lost patience with the ineffectual rule of the Emperor.

Whatever his motives, Pushymitra organized a highly successful coup within the palace, killed Brahadratha and took over the mantle of Emperor. As might be expected of a man of his caste, he restored the power and influence of traditional religion at the expense of the new Buddhist faith which had recently gained ground.

Elsewhere, Pushymitra was less successful. The outlying provinces took advantage of the assassination of Brahadratha to declare their independence. Even in the Ganges Basin, heartland of Maurya power, Pushymitra was unable to enforce complete obedience. It seems that various states had degrees of allegiance to the central authority which they kept or flouted according to their strength. The slow disintegration of the Maurya Empire was accelerated.

KANISHKA (fl. c. late 1st century)

Usurped: Kushana Empire circa 78 (?)
Social Origins: Unknown

The Kushana Empire of northern India was founded in the mid-1st century AD by wild Turkic tribesmen named Yueh-chih. These barbarians poured down over the passes from the northwest and conquered large territories of the Indus valley and Hindu Kush. When Vima Kadphises, the second Kushana Emperor, died there followed a period of anarchy. Details of this time have long since been lost, but Kanishka emerged as the undoubted victor and established himself on the throne. It is not known if he was related to the old royal family in any way, or even whether he was a nobleman. Accurate dating is virtually impossible in this era of Indian history and Kanishka may have gained power any time between about 78 and 145.

We do know, however, that he was a Yueh-chih. Later Chinese records state that Kanishka asked for a Chinese Imperial bride (see Liu Yuan for Chinese marriage policy), but that a Chinese general managed to defeat him in battle and send him home to India still a bachelor.

Marcus Julius PHILIP (THE ARAB) (?–AD 249)

Usurped: Roman Empire AD 244
Social Origins: Army Officer

Marcus Julius Phillipus was an Arab who carved a path to power which brought him to the pinnacle of his career in time to preside over what may have been the greatest celebrations of the ancient world. Philip took service in the Roman army when still a young man. He has come down in history as an arrogant and ruthless personality who schemed and plotted his way to high command. By 244 Philip had risen to the position of Praetorian Prefect and was second in command to the Emperor Gordian III during the latter's campaigns against the Sassanians.

Soon after the campaign opened, supplies began to fail and the troops suffered privations in the distant Eastern provinces. Philip managed to persuade the legionaries that the fault lay with the young Emperor, though he was probably deliberately reducing supplies himself. When the troops were sufficiently uneasy, Philip led them in a mutiny and murdered Gordian III.

Philip bought peace with the Sassanians by giving them extensive territories. Then he hurried to the German frontier to repel a barbarian invasion. In 248 Philip travelled to Rome to preside over the magnificent celebrations of the city's thousandth anniversary. The gladiatorial games and wild animal fights were on a scale never seen before, and lavish displays of emotion became common in the city. Philip no doubt enjoyed these crude pleasures, but he was soon to be betrayed and killed, albeit reluctantly, by a trusted aide.

— ♔ —

Gaius Messius Quintus Trajanus DECIUS (AD 201–251)

Usurped: Roman Empire AD 249
Social Origins: Senator

Decius did not want to become Emperor, but the structure of Imperial command and the workings of chance brought about circumstances in which he had no choice but to don the Imperial purple. With poor communications and a bureaucracy continually insensitive to the problems of underlings, ordinary soldiers had few legitimate methods of voicing a grievance. When pay fell too far in arrears or conditions became unbearable, the legions would revolt. It was their only method of effective protest.

Often a revolt was put down fairly tolerantly, but some mutinies involved the claiming of the title Emperor for a local officer. Perhaps the troops hoped a local man in power would understand their problems better than the existing Emperor. Such a revolt broke out in Pannonia in 248 and a man named Pactianus was proclaimed Emperor.

When he received the news, the Emperor Philip, known as The Arab, sent an army under his trusted general Decius to deal with the situation. Decius arrived in Pannonia to find that the mutinous troops had killed Pactianus. Any hopes Decius entertained that this signalled a return to loyalty were quickly dashed. The troops declared that they now wanted Decius to be Emperor. When news of this reached Decius's camp his own men supported the rebels and hailed their general as Emperor.

Realizing the terrible danger in which such a move placed him, Decius at once protested. He declared that Philip was Emperor and that he was himself a loyal general. A group of mutinous officers then took Decius aside and informed him that if he did not lead the rebellion, they would kill him and find somebody who would. The threat brought about a change of heart. Decius took command of the army and led it to victory over Philip's forces. Philip the Arab was killed and Decius took his place. He acted as Emperor as he had done as general; efficiently and honestly. In 250 Decius marched north to fight the invading Goths. At first he was successful but in the summer of 251 he was killed along with most of his army.

Aemilius AEMILIANUS (c. AD 206–253)

Usurped: Roman Empire AD 253
Social Origins: Army officer

After the death of the Emperor Decius in battle against the barbarian Goths, his second in command, Vibius Trebonianus Gallus, was made Emperor in his place. Anxious to end a war which was proving very dangerous for the Romans, Gallus paid the Goths an enormous tribute in return for a promise to return across the frontier. He then hastened to Rome where he led a riotous life and rapidly became unpopular.

At this time Aemilius Aemilianus was Governor of Moesia on the Danube. When the Goths invaded his territory he defeated them and captured much loot, which he handed out to his men. The contrast between this heroic action and the peace bought by Gallus were clear. The frontier legions proclaimed Aemilianus to be Emperor and marched on Rome.

Gallus left his feasting tables to lead his men against the usurper. The armies met at Spoleta, but did not fight. Aemilianus sent messengers to Gallus's camp offering money to any deserters and announcing the great extent of his victories over the Goths. The ploy worked. Gallus's troops murdered their master and flocked to the banner of Aemilianus. The new Emperor marched into Rome to the ecstatic cheers of the crowd and the flattering plaudits of the Senate. He was not to have time to reveal if he would have made as fine an Emperor as he had a general, for he was murdered four months later by his own men who had received a better offer from another general.

— 👑 —

Publius Licinius VALERIAN (c. AD 190–266)

Usurped: Roman Empire AD 253
Social Origins: Senator

Valerian was an honourable man whose sense of duty drove him to take power as Emperor of Rome, and finally led to his downfall. The train of events which set Valerian on his unique career began when Gallus heard of the approach of the rebel Aemilianus (see above). The beleagured Emperor sent Valerian to Gaul to raise loyal troops against Aemilianus. It seems that Valerian was chosen because he was a senior senator with a reputation for honesty and honour.

True to his mission Valerian raised a mighty army, but by the time he reached Italy Gallus was already dead. Valerian decided to march against Aemilianus all the same, perhaps in the hope of avenging Gallus and thus preserving his own honour. In what was almost a replay of events of just four months earlier, the armies met at Spoleta. Valerian had the larger army and promised amnesty to the common soldiers who came over to his side. Aemilianus was murdered by his own men who hailed Valerian as Emperor.

Valerian proved himself to be an able soldier and Emperor. He administered the Imperial bureaucracy with a firm and fair hand. Realizing that to allow any general to gain too much glory and fame was to invite a rebellion, Valerian personally led his army on all major expeditions. In 257 he defeated the Goths, who had once again invaded Roman territory.

At the same time the Sassanians launched a major attack on the Eastern provinces. Their fast moving scouts even reached the Mediterranean. Valerian marched east to face them. He was approaching his greatest and his darkest hours. Valerian marched into Asia at the head of a mighty army. He fought tenaciously against the invaders, organized heroic defences of besieged cities and led his troops to some hard fought victories. The fighting rocked backwards and forwards as first one side, then the other gained the upper hand. Such an epic struggle between two great powers had not been seen for many centuries.

Then disaster struck. Plague spread through the Roman army, slashing its numbers in a matter of weeks. Valerian was defeated and captured. He spent the rest of his years as a household slave at the court of King Shapur of the Sassanians. It seems that the gleeful Sassanian monarch enjoyed parading Valerian in his Imperial robes before house guests. It was a sad downfall for a great ruler.

ZENOBIA (fl. late 3rd century AD)

Usurped: Kingdom of Palmyra AD 267
Social Origins: Noblewoman

Zenobia was the most beautiful and powerful ruler of the most beautiful and powerful city of the Near East in the 3rd century. Palmyra stood at a large oasis in the desert, commanding the trade routes between the Mediterranean and Asia. The city reaped the benefits of the huge qualitites of luxury goods, including silk, gold and spices which passed through. By 250 it had grown to great size and wealth, boasting finer civic buildings and amenities than many other cities. At the same time Palmyra had retained a certain amount of self-government though it lay within the Roman Empire.

The city, and surrounding lands, were governed in the 250s by the nobleman Odaenathus, who was married to the noted beauty Zenobia. Odaenathus aided Valerian in his epic struggle with the Sassanian Empire, and after the Roman defeat managed to hold the invaders at bay. In return Odaenathus was made governor of vast areas and given great power. In 267 he was murdered. Zenobia at once arrested the culprit and executed him, though it was strongly suspected that she had had a hand in the crime.

The powers of Odaenathus passed to his son, Wahballat, but Zenobia made herself regent and gathered all power into her hands. Zenobia soon realized the true extent of Roman weakness in the East and of her own strength. She raised an army of nearly 70,000 men and set about building up a mighty empire for Palmyra. She took advantage of internal unrest in Egypt to invade and capture that wealthy nation. She used the pretext of acting in

Zenobia

Zenobia was famed as the most beautiful and forceful woman of her time. She ruled the city of Palmyra and extended her authority over much of the Eastern Mediterranean. In this imaginative 19th-century picture she is shown taking a last look at her magnificent capital before she was dragged to Rome in chains and the city put to the torch. (*Herbert Schmalz*) the interests of Rome, but was careful to establish men loyal to her in Alexandria. She next took over large areas of Asia Minor.

At this time Zenobia became famous as a patron of the arts and philosophy. She entertained the greatest figures at her court and encouraged culture in all its forms, while her own beauty and athletic ability became legendary. But Zenobia's years of glory were soon to end.

By 272 the Roman Emperor Aurelian had settled the barbarian invasions which had weakened the West. He decided to curb the power of Zenobia. Aurelian marched to Antioch, where he defeated the formidable Palmyran army after a long and hard fought battle. Both Palmyra and Zenobia were captured. Palmyra was stripped of its wealth and razed to the ground, the majority of its population being put to the sword. Zenobia was taken to Rome where she was forced to walk in chains through the streets as part of Aurelian's triumph.

Unlike other defeated monarchs, Zenobia was not put to death on the Capitoline Hill. Instead Aurelian gave Zenobia a country villa at Tivoli where she lived in comfort for many years. If her great dreams of empire had crumbled, Zenobia at least avoided the terrible death of so many others who fell foul of Rome.

— ♔ —

Marcus Aurelius CLAUDIUS II (?–AD 270)

Usurped: Roman Empire AD 268
Social Origins: Obscure Provincial

In 268 the Roman Empire was being ruled by the energetic and quick-witted Gallienus, son of Valerian (see above). Gallienus was an active military commander who toured the frontiers, defeating foes and throwing back invasions. He acted equally decisively against rebels and so managed to stay in power for fifteen years, a remarkable achievement in Rome at this time.

When an army officer name Aureolus launched a rebellion in Milan, Gallienus moved with his usual speed. However, the Emperor did not realize that there were other traitors in his own army. As he waited before Milan, Gallienus was murdered by a group of his own officers.

The conspiracy was led by Marcus Aurelius Claudius, an Illyrian soldier who had risen to high command. Claudius quickly established his control of Imperial administration. However, the slow disintegration of the Empire continued. Within a year of his violent accession, Claudius was fighting off a Germanic invasion and the following summer faced the Goths. Though he failed to tackle the underlying reasons for Roman weakness, Claudius successfully held the barbarians at bay. He was engaged in further operations when, in 270, he died of disease.

— ♔ —

Marcus Mausaeus CARAUSIUS (?–AD 293)

Usurped: Power in Britain AD 287
Social Origins: Soldier

Carausius was a low-born officer who seems to have performed his duty as he saw it. Unfortunately his concept of defending the Empire did not accord with that of the Emperor, a fact which forced Carausius's hand.

In the 280s the Roman Empire was facing a crisis. Central authority had been weakened by constant upheavals and ineffective government. The mounting pressure of barbarian attacks had reached a climax. Provincial towns and cities were forced to defend themselves unaided. Massive walls were built around once peaceful towns and troops were raised locally.

When Diocletian became Emperor in 284 he attempted to resolve the situation. The northern German frontier was being continually broken by Saxon raids. The Saxons would come either by land or, more frequently, by sea, raid an area and sneak back home. Carausius was the man entrusted with holding the Saxons back. He had at his disposal a powerful fleet to patrol the Channel and large fortresses on both coasts. Carausius quickly proved himself to be an energetic commander who was able to keep the Saxon raids to a manageable level.

The methods Carausius employed, however, were rather unusual and led him into trouble. Starved of funds for his expensive fleet, Carausius refused to hand booty over to Imperial officials, but kept it for his command instead. Even worse, Carausius never attacked Saxon ships on their way to a raid, only on the return journey when they would be loaded with loot. At the same time, his dealings with Saxon kings were rather too friendly for the liking of his superiors. Carausius seems to have reached an unofficial working relationship with the Saxons, whereby neither pursued the other too closely.

When these facts came to the notice of the Imperial government it ordered the execution of Carausius. The hapless general took the only action he could, he announced a rebellion and assumed the title of Emperor. Unlike other men, however, Carausius knew his limitations. He had been born near the mouth of the Rhine and knew that his power was limited to Britain and Northern Gaul. He never attempted to march on Rome, but simply to maintain his position.

For some years this policy succeeded, but then an ambitious Roman named Constantius was made commander in Gaul. Constantius determined to bring Britain back under Imperial control. He launched a massive attack and captured all Carausius's fortresses on the south Channel coast. Soon after this defeat Carausius was murdered by one of his officers named Allectus.

Marcus Aurelius Valerius MAXENTIUS (?–312)

Usurped: Western Roman Empire 307
Social Origins: Imperial family

The ultimate cause of Maxentius's bid for power was his own jealous temperament and the complicated Imperial system, known as the Tetrarchy, which had been introduced by the Emperor Diocletian. Under the Tetrarchy there were two senior Emperors, called Augustus, and two junior Emperors, known as Caesar. It was expected that the Augusti would rule jointly, one in the east and one in the west, while the Caesars were in effect trainee Emperors. Diocletian chose as his fellow Augustus a distinguished soldier named Maximian.

Later Diocletian and Maximian abdicated in favour of their Caesars: Galerius in the east and Constantius in the West. They chose as Caesars Daia and Severus respectively. Maxentius, the son of Maximian resented the way in which he had been ignored. Under the pre-Tetrarchy system he could have expected to become Emperor after his father. The young man's anger grew even greater when Constantius died and Severus became Augustus with Constantine, Constantius's son as Caesar.

In 307 Severus announced that he was taking the prestige of capital city away from Rome. Henceforth Italy and Rome would be taxed on the same lines as the rest of the Empire. The citizens of Rome were furious. Not only were they going to be taxed but the Imperial dignity of their city was besmirched. When officials arrived to carry out the measures, the Romans refused to co-operate. The city guards would not disband and the citizens rose in protest.

Maxentius was nearby at the time and heard what was happening. Seeing his chance, he raced to Rome and had himself declared Emperor on the promise that he would reinstate the ancient honours of the city. Maxentius called his father out of retirement to help with administration. Then he laid a cunning trap for Severus and had him killed.

Galerius then intervened and tried to defuse the situation by announcing that Constantine was the new Augustus in the West while Maxentius was to be Caesar. Maxentius was furious, believing he had been slighted. When his father, Maximian, tried to take the purple robe of an Augustus from his shoulders, Maxentius had him arrested and thrown out of Rome.

Maxentius continued to rule in Rome and extended his power throughout much of the western Empire. But Constantine was not willing to tolerate a usurper Augustus. In 312 the armies of the two men met just outside Rome. Constantine was victorious and Maxentius was drowned as he tried to escape across the Tiber.

Magnus Clemens MAXIMUS (?–388)

Usurped: Western Roman Empire 383
Social Origins: Army Officer

Magnus Maximus came to power on the back of religious discontent and military rebellion, though he was clever enough not to allow these to dominate his policy. The Emperor Gratian was a staunch Christian who relentlessly persecuted paganism and stripped the temples of their wealth. This policy was resented, particularly in the more remote provinces where the people were still devoted to their traditional gods.

In Britain the pagan backlash combined with the growing discontent of local troops to produce an explosive situation. Maximus was the military commander in Britain and had recently won a victory against the Picts to the north. He may have been worried that his success would incur the jealousy of Gratian. Whatever the motives, Maximus declared himself Emperor in Britain, announcing his tolerance of paganism. He immediately took his army to Gaul and began the march south.

Gratian mustered an army and set out to meet Maximus. The troops of Gratian were clearly as discontented with his rule as were the men in Britain for they deserted in droves. Gratian was captured and executed with scarcely a struggle. Maximus at once set up an Imperial court in Gaul. He had himself baptized as a Catholic, perhaps to win over those Christians disturbed by the pagan origins of the usurpation.

Meanwhile in Italy Valentinian II, a younger brother of Gratian, had assumed the Imperial purple. Gratian did not cross the Alps to deal with his rival immediately. Instead he spent four years consolidating his hold on Gaul and Spain. Only then did he march over the mountains, chase Valentinian II from his capital of Milan and become undisputed master of the Western Empire. However, it soon proved that Maximus had over-reached himself for the Eastern Emperor, Theodosius, intervened and had Maximus killed.

THEODOSIUS I THE GREAT (346–395)

Kingmaker of Western Roman Empire 383–395
Social Origins: Army Officer

By the later part of the 4th century the Roman Empire had been divided into two halves, East and West, for administrative reasons. Each half had its own Emperor and the two were expected to co-operate. However, all too often the colleagues became rivals. Theodosius was no exception. Before becoming Emperor of the eastern half of the Roman Empire in 379 Theodosus I had led a successful career in the army, fighting in Britain and central Europe. The reign of Theodosius marks with startling clarity the continued strength of the Eastern Empire and the sad decline of the West.

In 383 the Western Emperor Gratian was murdered and succeeded by the general Magnus Maximus (see above), though Gratian's brother Valentinian II managed to hold on to power in Italy. In 387 Maximus drove Valentinian II from his capital, Milan. The young refugee fled to the east and arrived at the court of Theodosius. The astute Eastern Emperor at once saw the opportunities which the situation offered. If he could install an Emperor at Milan who was loyal to him, the rewards could be great.

Theodosius at once mustered his army and marched westwards. Maximus knew very well what was afoot and led his troops into Pannonia, part of modern Yugoslavia, to block Theodosius's advance. In two sharp battles the western troops were overrun and Maximus was killed.

Theodosius returned Valentinian II to the Imperial purple in Milan and carefully gathered his rewards. The most important government posts were distributed to eastern men, upon whose loyalty Theodosius could rely. One of these men, Flavius Arbogastes was made the senior general in the west. It was this man who, one day in 392, found the body of Valentinian II hanging in the Imperial bedroom. Arbogastes appointed a man named Eugenius as Emperor and sent messages to Theodosius informing him of what had happened.

Theodosius did not believe the tale of suicide, and suspected that Arbogastes had murdered Valentinian. Once again Theodosius marched westward. In 394 he smashed the western army and killed Eugenius. Arbogastes preferred suicide. Theodosius did not risk installing a second puppet emperor in the west, instead he re-united the Empire under his own rule. The unification did not last long. In less than a year, Theodosius had died leaving the empire to his two sons. This time there was to be no further unification. The two halves of the Empire followed very different courses.

Flavius STILICHO (c. 360–408)

Usurped: Power in the Western Roman Empire 395–408

Social Origins: Barbarian

Stilicho was born a Vandal at a time when that barbarian tribe was causing trouble for the Roman Empire along the Danube. Early in his life Stilicho took service with the Eastern Emperors, possibly as a mercenary leader. He rapidly rose to a position of great influence under Theodosius I.

When Theodosius died he bequeathed the Western Empire to his infant son Honorius. Stilicho was part of the military organization intended to uphold the authority of Honorius until the boy was old enough to rule for himself. However, Stilicho quickly gathered power into his own hands. He became the true ruler of the Western Empire, though Honorius was kept as the legitimate Emperor.

In the 390s the barbarian Goths pushed south towards Greece. The Eastern Emperor drove the Goths away into Pannonia, in modern Yugoslavia, where the barbarians disrupted contact between the two halves of the crumbling Empire. It was a rupture which was never repaired. In 401 Stilicho drove bands of invading Goths out of Italy and moved on to defeat his own tribesmen, the Vandals, near the Danube.

Stilicho then caused the Senate to pay Alaric, the King of the Goths (see below), a large amount of gold and to make him a Senator. Stilicho hoped thus to buy off this dangerous leader. However, some in Rome saw the action as an attempt by Stilicho to arm the barbarians. They whispered that Stilicho had never forgotten his own barbarian birth. In 408 the intriguers gained the support of the young Honorius by playing on his fear of these rough outsiders. Honorius ordered the murder of Stilicho.

ALARIC (376–410)

Kingmaker of Western Roman Empire 410

Social Origins: Barbarian King

Born into a noble family of the barbarian Goths, Alaric spent some years in the Roman army, which may account for his understanding of the mentality of his enemies. In about 396, however, Alaric returned to the Visigoths to become their king. He first led his tribesmen through Greece, but from 402 onwards hovered around the northern frontiers of Italy. Only the actions of the Roman General Stilicho (see above) kept Alaric at bay.

When, in 408, Alaric received the news of Stilicho's murder he at once raised the warriors of the Visigoths and marched into Italy. By the end of 409 Alaric was outside the gates of Rome. He tried negotiating with the Emperor Honorius, but eventually lost patience. Alaric cunningly took the side of the Senate in a dispute with Honorius and raised a new Emperor to the Imperial purple. It is possible that Alaric wished to play the role of Stilicho.

However, early in 410 the new puppet Emperor Attalus betrayed Alaric. The furious barbarian unleashed his warriors, fought his way into Rome and sacked the city. The actual sacking was rather restrained for a barbarian attack, for Alaric did not wish to destroy the city, merely to make his point. Nevertheless, the shock of the event reverberated through the known world. Neither Roman nor Barbarian had thought that Rome could be defeated, despite her many weaknesses. The Empire had existed for so long that men knew no other form of government. Alaric had shown that Rome was finished. Authority collapsed and the world plunged into anarchy. A few months after the sacking, Alaric died.

— ♔ —

ATTILA (?–453)
Usurped: Kingdom of the Huns 444
Social Origins: Nobleman

Attila's usurpation was swift and bloody. It was the start of a career which was to be even more violent and terrible than the murder which brought him to power. At this time the Huns were an Asiatic warrior nation. They fought on horseback, being expert archers and swordsmen. The Huns moved quickly on their wiry horses, outmanoeuvering any army sent against them and were savage in the extreme. By the 430s the Hun tribes were concentrated on the Hungarian plains and were loosely ruled by a nobleman named Rua.

In 434 Rua died, leaving the leadership of the Huns to his nephews Attila and Bleda. In a swift campaign in 441 the Huns butchered the army of the Eastern Roman Empire and exacted a massive tribute of 6,000 pounds weight of gold. Four years later, Attila tired of sharing power. He had always been the dominant brother and now seems simply to have become irritated by the need to refer decisions to Bleda.

In 445 Attila murdered his brother. Thereafter Attila introduced an autocratic style of government previously unknown to the Huns. He found an old sword, which he declared to be the sword of the God of War. Any disagreement with Attila now became heresy as well as treason and was brutally rewarded. Attila dispensed judgement and planned the government without reference to any advisers. His word became law.

In 447 Attila smashed the Eastern Empire, devastated vast areas and exacted another huge tribute. In 451 Attila led his warriors into the Western Empire and carried out the frightful carnage and destruction for which the Huns were becoming notorious, and which earned him the sobriquet of 'The Scourge of God'. He was, however, driven back and the following year he was kept out of Italy by plague.

In 453 Attila married a beautiful young German girl named Ildico. The wedding was a grand affair with thousands of warriors drinking themselves insensible and indulging in barbaric sports. Attila retired to bed with his young bride, but during the night died by choking on blood from a nosebleed. The following morning the unfortunate girl had to explain to the hundreds of bloodthirsty warriors that their beloved leader was dead. One cannot help having sympathy for the poor bride.

HENGIST (?–488)

Usurped: Power in Kent 455
Social Origins: Barbarian

Hengist and his brother Horsa were vigorous warleaders of the north Germanic tribe, the Jutes. They took advantage of the weakness of others to become independent rulers on their own account.

By the 440s Britain had been cut off from Roman help and was faced by attacks from the Picts beyond Hadrian's wall. The British leader, Vortigern, employed Hengist and Horsa as mercenary captains with a force of about 200 Jutes. It appears that the two brothers had been forced to leave home after becoming involved in a murderous brawl during a feast. Once in Britain, Hengist and Horsa showed themselves to be able and efficient warriors. Vortigern asked them to recruit more fighters from the Jutes.

The brothers eagerly accepted and brought a massive force to Britain. At first they served Vortigern, but Hengist and Horsa quickly recognized the wealth and weakness of the Britons which contrasted with their own poverty, but great military prowess. The Jutes were given land in Kent in return for their services, but this was not enough for the brothers. In 445 they led their men against Vortigern and soundly defeated him, though Horsa was killed in battle.

Hengist
A medieval representation of the death of Hengist in battle with King Arthur. Later traditions mingled legends of the two men, leaders of the Saxons and Britons respectively. In fact little is known of the death of Hengist, save that tradition held it to have occurred in the year 488. While a battle between the two great leaders may have taken place, it is unlikely, for Arthur, if such a man existed, probably came to power around the year 500. The later incorporation of Hengist into legend is a clue to his greatness. (*Michael Holford*)

Vortigern lost his position as leader of post-Roman Britain while Hengist managed to impose his authority on the whole of Kent. For the next thirty years Hengist engaged in almost constant warfare with the Britons, but they never managed to throw the Germanic invaders out of Kent. He died in 488.

— 👑 —

RICIMER (?–472)

Kingmaker of Western Roman Empire 456
Social Origins: Army Officer

Ricimer came from a barbarian Suevian family which was related to the Gothic royal clan but which had become assimilated into Roman society and granted Patrician, or noble, status. After a childhood in Rome, Ricimer joined the army and served with distinction. While his fellow generals, Aetius and Avitus, were struggling against Attila and the Huns, Ricimer was making a name for himself fighting the Vandals in North Africa and in the Mediterranean.

In 455 Avitus became Emperor. Ricimer may have suspected that his old rival would order his execution, or he may have acted simply out of ambition. Whatever the motives, Ricimer led his troops against Avitus. The armies met at Placentia, modern Piacenza, and Ricimer won a devastating victory. Avitus was imprisoned and died a suspiciously swift death. In 457 Ricimer raised Julius Valerius Majorian to power as Emperor.

Majorian ruled wisely and reformed the tax system. However, Majorian showed favour to a general named Aegidius to whom he entrusted the reconquest of Gaul from the barbarians. Ricimer resented the move. He murdered Aegidius and forced Majorian to abdicate at swordpoint. Majorian, like Avitus before him, then died within a matter of days.

Ricimer decided to take no chances with the Imperial dignity in future. Though he did not take the purple himself, Ricimer made sure that the new Emperor was entirely under his domination. He placed on the throne a nonentity named Libius Severus, who was followed in 467 by Anthemius. Ricimer remained the true power in Italy, a fact emphasized when in 472 he placed yet another puppet, Olybrius, in the Imperial palace. On 18 August 472 Ricimer died.

— 👑 —

ZENO (426–491)

Usurped: Byzantine Empire 474 and 476
Social Origins: Army Officer

Coming from a provincial family from Isauri, an area of southern Asia Minor, Zeno climbed to supreme power in the emerging Byzantine Empire. Throughout his troubled career he was able to rely on help from his friends in Isauri.

Early in his life Zeno joined the army of the Eastern Roman Empire, now changing in character and becoming the Byzantine Empire. He was appointed to the influential position of chief bodyguard to the Emperor Leo I. At court he met, and later married, Leo's daughter Ariadne. In 474 Leo I died whereupon Zeno managed to engineer the accession of his own son as Leo II. No doubt Zeno hoped to achieve great power as the Emperor's father. These hopes were dashed when Leo II died after only a few months.

Zeno had himself proclaimed Emperor, but he lacked support at court. Verina, the widow of Leo I, secured the elevation of her brother Basiliscus to the Imperial throne and Zeno fled for his life. He travelled to Isauri where he found safety from Imperial pursuit. For two years Zeno worked at gaining support for his pretensions to the purple. In 476 Zeno emerged from Isauri and marched on Constantinople. Basiliscus and Verina were ousted and Zeno reassumed supreme power. Though quiet his reign of 16 years was undistinguished. Perhaps the most notable event was the humiliating act of buying off the barbarian Ostrogoths.

ORESTES (?–476)

Kingmaker of Western Roman Empire 475
Social Origins: Army Office

Orestes first rose to fame as one of the officers loyal to the terrible Attila the Hun who ravaged much of Europe early in the 5th century. After the death of Attila, the Hun power collapsed and Orestes was left without employment. With an eye for a good opportunity, Orestes transferred his allegiance to his old enemy, the crumbling Western Roman Empire.

By the time Orestes arrived at the Imperial court at Ravenna, in northern Italy, the Emperor had ceased to wield any real power. The Western Empire was restricted to the Italian peninsula, and even there powerful generals dominated the Emperors. Orestes soon determined to take advantage of this situation for his own ends.

In a series of clever, if brutal, court intrigues Orestes managed to remove most of his rivals. In 475 the ex-Hun leader confronted the Emperor Julius Nepos at the head of his troops. Faced by a military mutiny on such a scale, Julius had no choice but to abdicate. In his place Orestes invested his own son with the Imperium of Rome. By a strange twist of fate the young man who thus became the last Emperor of Rome was named Romulus, the name of the founder of the great city.

The new Romulus was invested with the title of Augustus, but the contemptuous populace soon changed this to the diminutive Augustulus for the boy was so obviously a puppet of his father. Orestes quickly gathered the reins of Imperial government, or at least what remained of them, into his own hands. He was not to enjoy power for long. The following year he was murdered during a military mutiny led by the mercenary Odoacer (see below).

ODOACER (435-493)

Usurped: Western Roman Empire 476
Social Origins: Barbarian mercenary

By the late 5th century the military might of the Western Roman Empire had almost completely vanished. Successive waves of invaders and corrupt actions by wealthy Romans had destroyed the armed forces. The weak Emperors of the time relied upon large numbers of barbarian, or semi-civilized mercenaries. Odoacer was one such man.

The man who was destined to usurp power in Italy came from the Danubian tribe of the Heruli. Odoacer was employed by Rome to hire a large force of his fellow tribesmen and lead them against the enemies of the Empire. Soon after arriving in Italy, however, Odoacer realized the true weakness of the Imperial system. He quickly decided to wring as much as possible from the Emperor for himself and his men.

In the summer of 476 Odoacer and his mercenaries demanded one third of Italy as farmland on which to settle. When Orestes (see above), the strong man of Imperial politics, refused, Odoacer murdered him. Odoacer next led his barbarian mercenaries to the Imperial capital of Ravenna. Here he forced the emperor Romulus Augustulus to abdicate. Odoacer did not bother trying to set up a puppet Emperor. Instead he collected the Imperial insignia and sent them to the Eastern Emperor, Zeno.

Zeno wisely accepted the fictional reunification of the Empire under his control and appointed Odoacer to Patrician, or noble, rank. In effect Odoacer had set himself up as an independent King of Italy while pretending to act on behalf of the Eastern Emperor. The usurpation marked the end of the Roman Empire in the West. Odoacer is sometimes referred to as Odovakar or Ottokar.

CERDIC (fl. c. 500)

Usurped: Power in Southern England circa 495
Social Origins: Obscure

The details of Cerdic's violent assumption of power are as obscure as the origins and character of the man himself. For an usurpation of such historic importance, the event is frustratingly poorly recorded.

In the closing years of the 5th century, Britain was a troubled land. The native Romano-Britons were struggling to maintain their civilization in the face of repeated Anglo-Saxon attacks. The rebellion of the mercenary Hengist (see above) in the 440s had set a precedent for future usurpers by grabbing power from weak British leaders. It seems that Cerdic decided to follow the lead.

According to chronicles written some generations later, Cerdic and a band of Saxons landed in Hampshire in 495 and violently wrested the area from the Britons. However, it is known that Cerdic is a British, not Saxon, name and that many Germanic mercenaries were already established in Hampshire. It is possible that Cerdic was a local man who used mercenaries to overthrow legitimate authority in the region. The Kingdom of Wessex, which Cerdic established, later united the whole of England and provided the ancestors of Britain's present Royal Family. It is a pity we do not know more about this man.

— ♕ —

AMALSWINTHA (?–535)

Usurped: Kingdom of the Ostrogoths 526
Social Origins: Royal Family

Having been brought up in a court of luxury and opulence, Amalswintha, whose name is often spelt Amalasuntha, tried desperately to hang on to her privileged position. In the attempt, she tragically lost everything.

The Ostrogoths were a barbarian people who had lived for many years on the fringes of the Roman Empire. They had acquired a great regard for Roman civilization and had absorbed many aspects of it. Under Theodoric the Great (reigned 473–526) the Ostrogoths moved into Italy and established a wealthy and prosperous kingdom. It was here that Amalswintha, eldest daughter of Theodoric, was born and brought up.

When Theodoric died in 526, he left no sons and was succeeded by Amalswintha's ten year old son Athalaric. Amalswintha immediately made herself regent for her son and began ruling in his name. In order to keep the boy from interfering in government, Amalswintha allowed him to indulge in every pleasure he desired. By the age of eighteen, drink and debauchery had ruined the young king's constitution. A minor illness carried him away.

His inconvenient death left Amalswintha with no official right to continue in power. She acted swiftly to overcome this problem. In the years before her son's death Amalswintha had made herself unpopular with the rough Ostrogoths by favouring Romans and providing a Roman education for her children. In an attempt to defuse this situation she ignored the claims of her remaining children and chose a cousin, Theodahad, as the next king. Her condition for raising this traditional Ostrogoth to the throne was that he share the throne with herself.

For a while this arrangement seemed to be working to Amalswintha's satisfaction. With Theodahad apparently content with a subordinate position, Amalswintha was able to continue ruling Italy as before. But Theodahad resented Amalswintha's pro-Roman leanings as much as anyone and while outwardly submissive, he was secretly canvassing support amongst Ostrogoth nobles.

In 535 Theodahad struck. He raised the Ostrogoths against Amalswintha. The Roman majority in Italy could do nothing to save her. She was imprisoned on an island in Lake Bolsena and later murdered. By desperately attempting to hold on to power and her beloved Roman culture and luxuries, Amalswintha had brought about her own death.

GELIMER (fl. early 6th century)

Usurped: Kingdom of the Vandals 530
Social Origins: Royal Family

By the early 6th century the Germanic tribe of the Vandals had fought their way through Gaul, Spain and North Africa. They had looted the Western Empire from end to end and were now firmly established in North Afica as a nation of marauding bandits and pirates on a grand scale. In 455 they had pillaged Rome itself. It was to the top of this violent society that Gelimer clawed his way.

Under King Hilderic the Vandals saw a diminution of their power. Their Moorish vassals rebelled and became independent while the Vandal control of the Mediterranean sea routes was being seriously threatened by the

Byzantines. Gelimer was a cousin of Hilderic and in the later 520s seems to have been an active freebooter in the best Vandal tradition.

In 530 Gelimer felt strong enough to launch a bid for power. No doubt he felt that his more vigorous leadership would restore the savage Vandals to their former pre-eminence. Gelimer surprised Hilderic and captured him. A short while later Hilderic was put to death.

With unfettered power over his people, Gelimer could now act as he wished. Unfortunately for Gelimer, the Byzantines chose this moment to launch a major attempt to regain the lands lost to the Vandals more than a century earlier. The Byzantine general Belisarius landed in Africa in 533 and crushed the Vandal army in two swift victories. Gelimer took to horseback and fled, but early in 534 he was captured. The once proud King of the Vandals was dragged to Constantinople and paraded through the streets to the jeers of the populace.

FREDEGOND (?–597)

Kingmaker of Neustria 584–597
Social Origins: Serving Girl

In the late 6th century the old Roman province of Gaul had come under the sway of the Franks, a vigorous Germanic people from east of the Rhine. While the bulk of the population remained Gallo-Romans the ruling classes were Franks. Under their control the nation slowly fell into barbarism as old institutions collapsed. However, a certain level of prosperity and civilization survived.

The Royal Frank dynasty, known to history as the Merovingians, ruled over this semi-civilized state in great splendour. The Merovingian kings followed Frank custom by dividing their property amongst their sons. This inevitably led to a number of independent kingdoms within the Frank empire. The northwestern sub-kingdom, centred around Amiens, was known as Neustria. It was here that Fredegond rose to power through her wit, charm and frightening determination.

King Chilperic I of Neustria came across the young Fredegond when she was a humble serving maid. The charms and beauties of the girl attracted him enormously and from what we know of her later career it is unlikely that Fredegond did much to put him off. Within a few months, Chilperic had become so besotted by Fredegond that he murdered his wife, Galswintha, so as to be free to marry her.

Having gained her place beside Chilperic, Fredegond set about establishing herself. She first awaited the birth of a son, providing an heir to Chilperic through herself. Then, using her undoubted charms on Chilperic, she managed to evade blame for the deaths of Galswintha's children. It is fairly certain that Fredegond engineered this series of murders and accidents so as to clear the way for her own son to assume the throne.

By 584 all rival heirs had been eliminated. In that year King Chilperic was murdered, almost certainly on the orders of Fredegond whose use for the doting and elderly king had ended. Her son assumed the throne as Clothaire II, although he was scarcely old enough to walk. Fredegond, of course, seized power as regent and made sure that her growing son was carefully kept away from government.

For a full thirteen years, the ex-serving girl remained as the unchallenged supreme ruler of Neustria. Her crimes led her into bitter feuds with other Frankish sub-kingdoms, but she emerged triumphant from all these struggles. When Fredegond died in 597 Clothaire II became king in fact as well as in name. A few years later he managed to unite all the Franks under his rule.

BRUNHILD (?–613)

Usurped: Kingdom of Austrasia 576
Social Origins: Spanish Princess

The violent welter of bloodshed and feuding into which Brunhild threw herself seems almost incredible to modern readers. The sheer scale of the slaughter carried out for seemingly trivial reasons appears sadistic and mindless to an absurd degree. However, the role of a Dark Age ruler was very different from that of both later and earlier monarchs. There were no sophisticated governmental departments to enforce state decisions, and no civil service to administer regulations.

In such times a ruler relied upon prestige to enforce his will. If a sovereign were respected his subjects would obey him. But if the king was seen to be weak endless rebellions and assassination attempts would ensue. Only by fiercely preserving respect and honour could a monarch of this era hope to survive. It was this terrible and single-minded insistence on honour which lay behind the violent career of Brunhild and others like her.

Brunhild was born a princess of the Visgothic kingdom of Spain. She and her sister, Galswintha, were married to two Frankish princes, Sigibert and Chilperic respectively. When the Frank king died, Sigibert and Brunhild became rulers of Austrasia, the lands around the lower Rhine, while Chilperic and Galswintha became rulers of the Kingdom of Neustria to their west.

A few years later Chilperic murdered Galswintha in order to marry his lover, Fredegond (see above). This affront to the honour of Brunhild was intolerable for the proud queen. She pretended to be satisfied with the payment of wergild, a type of compensation, but secretly persuaded her husband to prepare for war. In 573 Sigibert unleashed his warriors and stormed through Neustria, raiding and pillaging as he wished. Caught unawares, Chilperic fought back as best he could, managing to lead a devastating raid into Austrasia.

In 575 Chilperic arranged the assassination of Sigibert and managed to capture Brunhild. The widowed queen now had a double reason for revenge. While a captive, she enticed Chilperic's son to fall in love with her and married him. Fredegond was furious at being thus outmanoeuvred and ordered the death of the young couple. Brunhild escaped but her lover was butchered.

Now with a sister and two husbands to avenge, Brunhild raced back to Austrasia. There she wasted no time in wresting power from the squabbling nobles who were arguing over the inheritance of Sigibert. Though she had no legitimate claim to power, Brunhild kept a tight control of affairs by the sheer force of her personality and the swiftness of action to which she could dedicate herself. Austrasia was mobilized for war to inflict revenge upon Fredegond. The Franks then plunged into one of history's most frightful civil wars as the supporters of the two queens slaughtered each other by the thousand and devastated each others' lands.

In 597 Fredegond died and Brunhild's fury abated somewhat. However, Clothaire, son and successor of Fredegond, could not forget the terrible wars. In 613 he tricked the now elderly Brunhild into captivity. He tied the old woman's ankles and wrists to wild horses and drove the horses to a gallop before the ropes snapped taught. Brunhild was torn to pieces. In this savage way the violent career of perhaps the most dominating woman in French history came to an end.

Note: Brunhild figured as an almost supernatural and legendary character in much Germanic heroic literature, with many stories told about her strength and cruelty.

RAEDWALD (?–625)
Kingmaker of Northumbria 617
Social Origins: King of East Anglia

By the late 6th century Britain was divided into Anglo-Saxon kingdoms and British states. The ethnic frontiers had not yet reached the present boundaries between English, Welsh and Scot, but the overall pattern was clear. The English were divided into several kingdoms of which two of the most powerful were Northumbria, stretching from the Humber to the Forth, and East Anglia.

In the year 588 Aelle, King of Northumbria died. For some reason his son, Edwin, could not establish himself on the throne and fled to Wales. The Kingdom passed instead to a nobleman named Aethelric. Five years later Aethelric died to be replaced by his son Aethelferth. About the same time Raedwald became King of East Anglia.

At this time East Anglia was possibly the wealthiest of the English kingdoms. By 616 Raedwald had exacted a vague oath of subservience from all the kingdoms south of the Humber. It was natural that the exile Edwin should find his way to the court of Raedwald at Rendlesham. When Aethelferth heard of Edwin's arrival he sent a messenger to Raedwald demanding Edwin's death or surrender.

It was a difficult moment for Raedwald. It would certainly be advantageous to win the friendship of Aethelferth by the murder. Yet as a guest Edwin was supposedly safe from attack. Raedwald sat up late into the night discussing the problem with his wife. In the end honour won the day and Raedwald refused Aethelferth's request.

War between East Anglia and Northumbria inevitably followed and Raedwald was the first to act. He led a large army northwards, taking with him Edwin who he declared to be the true King of Northumbria. Raedwald fought Aethleferth on the banks of the Idle and won a devastating victory. The Northumbrian king was killed and Edwin installed in his place. Edwin was only too happy to acknowledge Raedwald as overlord in return for his kingdom. For some years Raedwald basked in the glory of being Bretwalda or overlord, the most powerful man in Britain. He died peacefully in 625.

— ♔ —

HERACLIUS (575–642)

Usurped: Byzantine Empire 620
Social Origins: Army Officer

In the early 7th century the Byzantine Empire, which had once stretched the length of the Mediterranean suffered severe defeats as the Persian Sassanian Empire conquered large territories in Palestine and Asia Minor. The cruel and despotic Emperor Phocas was unable to stop the decline.

Heraclius, a native of Cappodocia, was at this time the highly successful governor of North Africa. In 620 he left his province for Constantinople. It seems that Heraclius had become frustrated by the incompetent leadership of Phocas and believed that he could do much better himself. It soon became clear that many others shared this opinion. When Heraclius reached Constantinople the population poured into the streets to cheer the strikingly attractive young man with his long blonde hair and steel-grey eyes. Phocas was overthrown and Heraclius took the throne.

In a series of lightning campaigns, Heraclius defeated the Sassanians. He then reorganized the army and established militarised frontier zones to protect the boundaries of his new Empire. Heraclius had been right when he had thought he could do better than the tyrannical Phocas. Heraclius died in 642 in the midst of the first advance of Islam in the Middle East.

— ♔ —

CADWALLA (?–689)

Usurped: Kingdom of Wessex 685
Social Origins: Royal Family

Cadwalla was described by a contemporary as 'a daring young man, exiled from his own country.' It is an apt description of a character who for three years carved a bloody path across English history, only to leave as suddenly as he had come.

Before 685 Cadwalla seems to have been a young member of a junior branch of the royal family of Wessex, one of several small kingdoms in England. He may have earned a living as a warrior in other English kingdoms. In that year, however, Cadwalla recruited a band of followers and launched his bid for power. He began by attacking insecure frontier lands on the border of Wessex and Sussex. Having achieved success there, Cadwalla turned west and enforced his control on the whole of Wessex. There is little doubt that he did this by naked military force.

At some time during his wars, Cadwalla was seriously wounded. By the summer of 688 it became clear that the new king would not survive for long. Though a Christian, Cadwalla had never been baptized. He therefore abdicated the throne, handing it to a kinsman named Ine, and travelled to Rome. There on Easter Saturday 689 he was baptized by Pope St Sergius and given the Christian name of Peter. Ten days later Cadwalla Peter died.

— ♔ —

GAO YANG (?–550)

Usurped: Power in Northern China 534
Social Origins: Chinese Military Officer

By the 530s the barbarian nomads who had overrun northern China two centuries earlier had settled down to a more sedentary existence. However, the barbarian tactics of lightning cavalry actions remained common on the grassy plains of northern China. The Wei Dynasty of the area is known to have adopted Chinese customs and religion to a large extent, becoming estranged from their barbarian supporters.

Gao Yang was a Chinese who took service in the Wei army and learnt the mounted tactics of barbarian horse warfare so thoroughly that he became assimilated into Wei society. In 534 Gao Yang galloped up to the Imperial entourage at the head of a band of followers. Under threat of instant death the Emperor was forced to surrender to Gao Yang and take up residence at the latter's stronghold. Here Gao Yang dictated measures to the Emperor and became effectual ruler of the Eastern Wei Empire. After Gao Yang's death in 550 his son dismissed the Emperor and made himself ruler as the first representative of the Northern Chi Dynasty.

YANG CHIEN (?–614)

Usurped: Chinese Empire 581
Social Origins: Army Officer

Yang Chien was a tough soldier hardened by long years on campaign and intolerant of what he considered useless civilian luxury. It may have been this which prompted his bid for power in the Northern Chinese Empire in 581.

Yang Chien was a highly successful general who had been instrumental in the Chou conquest of the Chi, which reunited the whole of northern China. It was just four years after this conquest that Yang Chien took power and massacred the entire Chou royal family. The new ruler took the Imperial name of Wen-ti, by which name he is more often known, and thus started the Sui Dynasty.

Wen-ti immediately introduced laws banning shows of luxury and opulence. Civilians were subject to a strict census and were made to pay their taxes on time and in full. Henceforth the wealth of his nation was to be directed towards warfare, for Wen-ti was determined on a great war of conquest. The struggle began in 587 when Sui troops overran the Yangtse River basin. Two years later Wen-ti reached the southern coast of China and could announce the first unification of China for 400 years. The name of this Emperor is sometimes spelt Yang Jian, and his title Wen Di.

LI YUAN (?–626)

Usurped: Chinese Empire 618
Social Origins: Nobleman

The rise to power of the nobleman Li Yuan might have shown the way for other ambitious aristocrats, but vigorous action by the new dynasty which he established virtually eliminated the chances of such a coup being repeated.

When the Emperor Yang-ti was murdered Li Yuan, Duke of Tang, was the governor of the huge province of Taiyuan. His main task at that time was the recruiting and training of an army of 200,000 men to replace losses recently sustained by the Emperor. When he received news of the murder of the Emperor, Li Yuan decided to use his new army to gain power for himself. A swift campaign eliminated all rivals and within a year Li Yuan had been proclaimed Emperor as Kao-tsu, first of the great Tang Dynasty.

Under the early Tangs, the power of the nobility was stripped away. No longer were government appointments made to men solely because of their birth or regional power. The massive civil service for which China has become famous was first organized at this time. Under strong Confucian influence entrance examinations were introduced for the civil service and a strong emphasis on service laid down. Henceforth, the administration was run by professionals with allegiance to the throne and a strong sense of duty. The years of anarchy in China were coming to an end. Li Yuan is often referred to as Gao Zu.

CHANDRA GUPTA II (?–c. 415)

Usurped: Gupta Empire circa 375
Social Origins: Imperial Family

The circumstances surrounding Chandra Gupta II's assumption of power in the strong Gupta Empire of northern India are not properly known. The first detailed account was not written until nearly two centuries after the event. According to this account Chandra Gupta was a younger brother of the Emperor Rama Gupta. He is said to have been in love with his brother's wife, the Empress Dhruvadevi.

After a particularly disgraceful defeat at the hands of the King of Shaka, Rama Gupta was forced to hand over a number of hostages, including Dhruvadevi. Chandra Gupta was horrified at the idea. He immediately rescued Dhruvadevi from her fate and then killed his brother. He then took his brother's place as Emperor and married Dhruvadevi.

— ♔ —

SKANDA GUPTA (?–c. 467)

Usurped: Gupta Empire circa 454
Social Origins: Imperial Family

Skanda Gupta came to power in response to an emergency. He appeared to be the only man able to stave off disaster and for this reason he was able to become Emperor. The mid 5th century saw northern India in turmoil. For some decades the Gupta Empire had held sway over a vast area of land from the Indus to the Ganges Delta. Within this land peace and prosperity flourished on a scale rarely seen before. However trouble soon intruded on this idyllic scene.

Some time in the 440s a devastating attack was launched across the northwest frontier by barbarians whom the Guptas called Hunas. Fighting on horseback and capable of great cruelty, the Hunas are almost certainly a branch of the Huns who ravaged Europe at about the same time.

The elderly Emperor, Kumara Gupta, reacted vigorously to the attack. Though unable to take the field himself, Kumara sent his son Skanda Gupta into the Indus Valley at the head of a great army. Skanda was a son of an inferior wife and therefore was not heir to the throne. He was, however, a royal prince and had shown marked military ability. In a long and bloody series of running fights, Skanda managed to halt the advance of the Hunas. He was unable to throw the invaders back to the mountains, but at least he kept them away from the Gupta heartlands.

In the midst of this war Kumara died. The Hunas were still a potent threat. To the courtiers and nobles it seemed that only the energetic Skanda could hold off the barbarians. They readily agreed that Skanda should be the next Emperor, the claims of more senior children being conveniently forgotten. For the rest of his life Skanda fought ceaselessly to preserve his kingdom. He was successful, but after his death the Gupta Empire collapsed.

ARUNASVA (fl. mid-7th century)

Usurped: Kingdom of Harsha circa 647

Social Origins: Obscure

Arunasva took advantage of circumstances to launch his bid for power, but he made one mistake. It was a mistake which was to cost him dear. After the collapse of the Gupta Empire in northern India, the area fell into the hands of numerous petty kings. In the early 7th century one of these, Harsha Vardhana, managed to weld the numerous kingdoms together into a loose alliance. Though he rarely displaced rulers, Harsha made them his subjects and enforced his will over a wide area of the Ganges and Indus plains.

In 647 Harsha died without an heir. A courtier named Arunasva immediately seized the throne. He knew that the tributary kings would take any opportunity to break their oaths of allegiance. It was essential that Arunasva show that he was as strong and powerful as Harsha had been. It was this which probably led Arunasva to take the action which brought about his downfall.

Soon after Arunasva had taken power, Wang Hsuan arrived as the ambassador of the Chinese Emperor Tai Tsung. Perhaps hoping to show that he was able to stand against the power of a monarch as mighty as the Chinese Emperor, Arunasva attacked Wang Hsuan. The Chinese ambassador managed to escape the attempted murder and fled northwards to Nepal. Here he raised an army on his authority as a representative of the Chinese Emperor and marched against Arunasva. The forces of the tributary kings joined Wang Hsuan, who easily overthrew Arunasva. The usurper was dragged back to China and paraded in front of Tai Tsung. The Indian monarch had learnt that he could not interfere with a Chinese ambassador with impunity.

CHARLES MARTEL (c. 690–741)

Usurped: Power in Kingdom of Franks
Social Origins: Nobleman

Charles Martel has been described as the last barbarian and first mediaeval king. In many ways his violent and meteoric career had features of both.

Charles was born some time around 690 as the son of Pepin, Mayor of the Palace to the ineffectual Merovingian kings. As the son of the most powerful Frankish noble, Charles was brought up in a violent but privileged situation. Constant warfare combined with wealth made up Charles's childhood. In 714 Pepin died and the post of Mayor of the Palace did not come to Charles for it was not, in theory at least, hereditary.

Charles at once set about recovering his father's position. He first took service in the army of the Frankish kingdom of Austrasia in a civil war against the Frankish territory of Neustria. In 716 Charles won a great victory and thus established himself as Mayor of the Palace of Austrasia. A few years later Charles used his newly acquired power to secure his appointment as Mayor in Neustria as well.

Charles stripped the kings of more power than any earlier Mayor of the Palace. Soon after acquiring his appointment in Neustria, Charles scarcely bothered to consult the king at all. He acted as if he held all power in his own hands. To all intents and purposes, he did.

Charles encouraged missionaries amongst his people, but otherwise had an ambivalent attitude to the Church. He confiscated vast monastic lands and parcelled them out to warriors in return for military service. This gave him a heavily armoured, highly trained, mobile striking force. It was the start of the feudal system and of Charles's greatness.

Charles used his warriors to extend the Frankish kingdom eastwards into Bavaria and other German lands. In 732, however, the greatest threat to his power emerged from the south. The Moslems had already overrun Spain and were now probing into France. A massive army under Abd-ar-Rahman crossed the Pyrenees and marched as far as Tours. Charles hurried south and the two armies met at Poitiers. Charles's troops smashed the Moslem army and sent it running back to Spain. France was safe from conquest by Islam and Charles had earned his nickname of Martel, or Hammer. He died in 741, still at the height of his power.

AN LUSHAN (c. 700–757)

Usurped: Chinese Empire 756
Social Origins: Barbarian Nobleman

Born into a tribe of barbaric nomads, An Lushan achieved the dizzy heights of Imperial power before illness and treachery pulled him down. It was common for the Chinese to exploit tribal rivalries by employing barbarian mercenaries to help protect the Empire against other barbarians. It seems that An Lushan entered Chinese service during the 730s as a warrior paid to fight against his own kind.

An Lushan soon proved himself to be a born general and astute diplomat. He concluded treaties with various tribes, recruiting thousands of warriors to his own banner and using them to maintain the frontier. By 752 An Lushan had a professional bodyguard of 8,000 horsemen and a trained army of 100,000 warriors to call upon. He had gained the trust and favour of the Imperial government and of the Emperor Xuan Zong himself. It is probable that An Lushan would have remained happy with this arrangement.

However, in 752 the Chief Minister died and was replaced by Yang Kuo Chung, a man hostile to An Lushan and his barbarian frontier guards. Chung circulated rumours and slander about An Lushan while the warlord was on the distant frontiers and unable to contradict the stories. In 755 An Lushan was summoned to court, ostensibly to attend a wedding. The cunning barbarian suspected that he was being recalled to stand trial for imagined crimes. He had no doubt that Chung would pack the court.

An Lushan travelled to the capital of Lo Yang, but he travelled at the head of his 100,000 strong army. Xuan Zong fled and An Lushan was able to proclaim himself Emperor under a name which translates as 'Heroically Martial'. A fresh Imperial army was sent against An Lushan, but was smashed and routed.

Soon after this success, An Lushan lost everything. Failing eyesight, extreme obesity and a painful skin condition, made the new Emperor irritable. He began ordering executions for trivial offences and whipped his advisers if he did not care for what they said. After just a year as Emperor, An Lushan was murdered by his son, An Chung-hsu. The younger man, however, was not the equal of his father. After a struggle lasting six years the Tang Dynasty was back in control of China.

PEPIN THE SHORT (?–768)

Usurped: Kingdom of the Franks 751
Social Origins: Nobleman

The usurpation of Pepin the Short was not a cataclysmic change of power. It was more a recognition of fact than an alteration. However his assumption of the kingship involved some difficult problems and became a matter for international politics.

The activities of Charles Martel and Pepin of Heristal had stripped all true power from the Frankish Kings of the Merovingian Dynasty who ruled large areas of modern France and Germany. Soon after Pepin succeeded his father as Mayor of the Palace, he decided to rid himself of the fiction of a Merovingian king, at this time Childeric III. However, the Merovingians were descended from the ancient heroes of the Franks and had much popular support. Also Childeric III was a king anointed with Holy Oil. To dethrone him, Pepin would risk earning the enmity of both Church and people. It was a risk he could not take.

In order to circumvent the religious objection, Pepin sent messengers to Pope Zacharias. Pepin asked for approval to dethrone Childeric and take his place. The Frankish ruler was willing to offer the Papacy military aid in Italy in return for the dispensation. Eager to gain Frankish aid against troublesome Lombards, Zacharias agreed. He cited the instance of Samuel proclaiming David as King of Israel while King Saul still ruled. The precedent had no connection either with Frankish customs or the political situation, but neither Zacharias nor Pepin were too concerned. They had a precedent on which to act.

In 751 Pepin called a council of the Frankish nobles at Soissons and announced the Papal decision. The nobles, following Frank custom, then acclaimed Pepin as their king with the title Pepin III. Childeric III was quietly eased from the throne and sent into retirement. In 754 Pepin fulfilled his promise to the Pope and defeated the Lombards in Italy. He died in 768 leaving his kingdom to two sons, Carloman and the mighty Charlemagne.

— ♛ —

CHRISTOPHER (?–770)
Kingmaker of the Papacy 768–770
Social Origins: Priest

By 768 the Pope had become not only the spiritual authority of Western Christendom, but also the ruler of extensive territories in central Italy and the heir to the immense prestige of the Roman Emperors. Christopher, a senior official in Rome, struggled to maintain some semblance of order in the chaotic situation of 768.

Pope Paul I (757–767) had used his position to impose a tough, autocratic rule on Rome and surrounding lands. When he died in July 767 a group of Roman nobles, led by Toto, staged a sham election which raised Toto's brother Constantine, to the throne of St Peter. Though Constantine's election was clearly irregular, the actual method of electing a new pope was very different from that practised today, when only cardinals may vote. In the 8th century the nobility of Rome and the ordinary populace had a voice in the elections, as well as the clergy of Rome.

At this time Christopher was the Chief Notary of the Vatican. He objected to the enthronement of Constantine, insisting that the election should be carried out properly according to the established rules of the time . When the new Pope and the nobles ignored him, Christopher began plotting.

He wrote to King Desiderius of the Lombards of northern Italy asking for military help and began organizing support amongst the mob and soldiery of Rome. In July 768 a group of Lombard troops entered Rome and Christopher struck. The Roman troops mutinied against Constantine and killed Toto. The Lombards, meanwhile, rushed to a nearby monastery and dragged a monk named Philip to the Lateran Palace. Here Philip was installed as Pope, though he strongly objected to the whole charade. It seems that Desiderius wanted a Pope whom he would be able to control.

Christopher, however, was too sharp to be caught. He announced that so long as Philip remained in the Lateran Palace, he would not enter Rome. A band of clerics then dragged Philip from his throne and took him back to the monastery. Christopher then organized a regular election at which Stephen III was chosen. It was at this time that the laity were excluded from papal elections for the first time and the choice placed in the hands of the cardinals. For two years, Christopher virtually ruled Rome through Stephen. However in 770 the Pope tired of such control. He handed Christopher over to the vengeful Desiderius in return for territory.

— ♛ —

CYNEHEARD (?-786)

Usurped: Kingdom of Wessex 786
Social Origins: Royal Family

In the late 8th century the Kingdom of Wessex occupied most of southwest England and was ruled by Cynewulf, who had been placed on the throne by a council of nobles. Though perfectly legal the enthronement of Cynewulf had bypassed Cyneheard, a brother of the previous king Sigebryht. Cyneheard smarted under the insult and caused some trouble for Cynewulf. The youthful Cyneheard launchad an audacious bid for power which was initially successful, but in its very success laid the foundations for its failure.

One night in 786 Cyneheard learnt that the king was dining with his mistress at a remote house. Cyneheard gathered a group of 84 men and hurried to the scene. Bursting in to the house, Cyneheard's men killed Cynewulf before the king's bodyguard could intervene. Cyneheard then offered the bodyguard great wealth if they would support him and back up a false story about the killing. The bodyguard, to their great honour, refused and attacked Cyneheard. They were, however, heavily outnumbered and were cut down.

Cyneheard then proclaimed himself king and was hailed as such by his supporters. However, the kinsmen of the warriors killed in the coup refused to accept Cyneheard's authority and plotted revenge. Eventually, the aggrieved kinsmen were able to reach Cyneheard and kill him, as he had killed Cynewulf. After this bloody debacle a remote cousin named Brihtric became King of Wessex.

— 👑 —

OFFA (?-796)

Usurped: Kingdom of Mercia 757
Social Origins: Royal Family

At the time of Offa's usurpation Mercia occupied most of the English midlands and was the most powerful kingdom in England. The details of the coup are poorly known. In later years Offa became an extremely powerful monarch and it is possible that contemporary writers were wary of recording anything which might anger him. It is, however, possible to reconstruct the outline of events.

For 41 years from 716, Mercia was ruled by King Athelbald, an extremely powerful monarch who exercised power over other English kings. Athelbald seems to have been inordinately fond of seducing nuns and becoming riotously drunk. He is also known to have engaged in murderous brawls on more than one occasion. In 757 Athelbald was murdered, perhaps by a subject who had a feud with this violent king.

Almost immediatly a nobleman named Beornraed seized power. Beornraed seems to have had no connection with the Royal Family and faced great troubles in enforcing his rule. The opposition was led by Offa, a cousin of Athelbald's. Resistance soon became open warfare and Offa drove Beornraed into exile and took the throne for himself. Offa re-established Mercian dominance in England and erected the great dyke along the Welsh Marches for which he is chiefly remembered.

— ♔ —

IRENE (752–803)

Usurped: Byzantine Empire 797
Social Origins: Noblewoman

Few women in history are as controversial as Irene. Some contemporaries reviled her in language which makes the reader wonder if he is learning about a woman or a devil. Other writers of her time praise Irene as next to a saint. These highly divergent views can be detected among the politicians and noblemen of her time. She was both loved and hated. Even today, historians are not quite sure what to make of this remarkable woman.

Irene first enters history when she married Leo who succeeded his father as Byzantine Emperor in 775. At this time the Empire was a powerful state extending deep into both Europe and the Middle East. However it was beset by invasions by the Arabs in the south and by bitter internal religious disputes. Irene soon revealed herself to be a beautiful and intensely emotional woman who was charged with a great religious fervour. Her great culture and tempestuous temper soon became famous.

In 780 Leo IV died, leaving his young son, Constantine VI, in the charge of the dowager Empress. Irene quickly enforced her control on the nobles and the army. She insisted that as regent for the young Emperor she was to be obeyed as if she were the Emperor herself. She acted decisively in government, cutting taxes, encouraging trade and becoming a great patron of the arts. She had definite views on religion, further exacerbating the already charged religious disputes. In particular she was a great lover of icons, the holy images of Eastern churches, and restored the worship of icons. To enforce these changes she punished the iconoclasts, who wished to remove the images from churches, among both the higher and lower ranks of the clergy.

Throughout these years, Irene completely controlled young Constantine. If he dared to disagree with her, Irene would beat him till he wept. On a more positive note, she arranged a sound dynastic marriage for the boy and supervised his education. When the boy-Emperor came of age, Irene excluded him from the real decisions of government. In 790, however, a military mutiny, caused largely by religious problems, coincided with a bid by Constantine to establish his personal rule. Irene was swept from power, but remained at court. She plotted and intrigued endlessly, constantly attempting to portray the young Emperor in a bad light. Constantine needed little help in this for he was a weak and indecisive ruler. In 797 Irene collected her supporters, deposed the young man and had him blinded.

She then took the title of the Emperor for herself and ruled alone. At this time Charlemagne, the new Holy Roman Emperor in Rome, considered marrying the tempestuous Irene to effect a reunification of Eastern and Western Roman Empires. Irene seems to have considered the idea favourably. Perhaps she thought that she could control a man she looked upon as an uncultured savage who could not even sign his name. She probably thought that through the marriage she would greatly extend her own empire. The Byzantine courtiers, however, hated the idea of bowing to a barbarian. In October 802, while Irene was ill in bed they overthrew her and sent her off to enforced retirement on the island of Lesbos.

NICEPHORUS I (?–811)

Usurped: Byzantine Empire 802

Social Origins: Nobleman

Nicephorus came to power because of the hatred directed against the former ruler, but he came to a peculiarly grisly end which may well be unique among Emperors.

The Empress Irene (see above) ruled in Constantinople from 780 until 802. During those years she achieved much, but at the expense of alienating sections of the state. Many clergy resented her interference in church affairs and her decision to tax church lands as if they were in secular hands. The army, meanwhile, was stripped of much influence at court and had to endure harsh spending cuts.

Nicephorus was the chief official at the Imperial treasury during this time. It is possible that he used his position to intimate to the Church and army that he did not agree with Irene's policies. Clearly he had an eager audience, for in the autumn of 802 he was able to organize a palace coup with army backing. Irene was imprisoned on the island of Lesbos, where she soon died.

Nicephorus ruled the Empire for 9 years with mixed fortunes. Then in 811 the notorious Khan Krum led his Bulgar warriors on a raid into Byzantine territory in Europe. Nicephorus gathered an army and marched to face the Bulgars. He threw the Bulgars back in a running battle, but at the Pass of Pliska the invaders turned and annihilated the Byzantines in a tough three-day battle. Nicephorus was killed in the fighting. Khan Krum took the Emperor's skull and had his craftsmen make it into a goblet from which he liked to drink his wine at his great barbaric feasts.

— 👑 —

LEO V (?–820)

Usurped: Byzantine Empire 813
Social Origins: Army Officer

The tremendous foreign pressures under which the Byzantine Empire suffered in the late 8th and early 9th centuries demanded a strong Emperor. In part this explains the rapid turn-over of Emperors in these years for as soon as a ruler proved inadequate he was replaced. Leo was just the type of tough soldier whom the Byzantines felt they needed and so his usurpation was popular. However, as soon as the foreign threats temporarily departed, the citizens began to resent his tough rule and like many of his predecessors, he died a violent death.

At his death in battle in 811, Emperor Nicephorus I left a son named Stauracius. However, this young man died of wounds sustained in battle with the Bulgars six months later. Next to mount the throne was Michael I, an intelligent and studious man. Though an able ruler, Michael was not a military man. The desperate situation with both Bulgars and Arabs attacking Byzantine lands in the north and south respectively was too much for him.

At this time Leo was the extremely able military commander of Anatolia. Realizing that the Empire both needed and wanted a soldier at the helm, he marched on Constantinople and used his troops to dethrone Michael. There was no animosity involved, and Michael seems to have accepted the usurpation with good grace. He was allowed to retire to a monastery where he spent the remaining 32 years of his life.

Leo V at once set about his military task. He smashed Bulgar power at a great battle in Thrace and erected massive fortifications to keep them out of the Empire. Khan Krum died soon afterwards, and Leo at once concluded a peace treaty with his son Khan Omurtag. These formidable achievements and some spectacular military demonstrations induced the Arabs to sign a treaty that ensured 20 years of peace.

Having achieved his task, Leo returned to Constantinople to enjoy the fruits of Imperial power. Unfortunately, he became enmeshed in the religious quarrel over the status of icons, or religious images, in worship. Leo took the part of those who disliked the worship of icons. In 820 he was murdered by those who wanted freedom to worship the icons.

BEORNWULF (?–825)

Usurped: Kingdom of Mercia 823
Social Origins: Nobleman

It is frustrating that we do not know more about Beornwulf and his usurpation for it was a momentous event in English history. Throughout their history the Midlands kingdom of Mercia had been ruled by members of the royal house of the Iclingas. This family had raised Mercia from an unimportant state to the position of the most powerful kingdom in Britain. The line came to a sudden end with Beornwulf.

In 821 Ceolwulf was crowned King of Mercia. As such he exercised control over Kent and Essex, and had considerable influence in East Anglia and Wessex. He opened his reign with an attack on the Welsh kingdom of Powys which brought that state under Mercian control. At this time Beornwulf was a rather unimportant elderman whose name appears well down the list of noblemen called upon to witness the royal signature on state documents.

In 823 a contemporary chronicle laconically records 'Ceolwulf is deprived of his kingdom.' That is all we know of the act of usurpation, but we know much more about its consequences. As a non-royal king Beornwulf had none of the immense prestige of the Iclingas. His subjects did not respect him as they had respected the old royal house. In the 9th century, a ruler without respect was in deep trouble.

First to act was King Egbert of Wessex. He lead an army into Mercia in 825 and crushed Beornwulf's army at Ellendun. Perhaps the Mercians had not been too keen on fighting for the usurper. Kent and Essex immediately threw off Mercian control to pass under the influence of Wessex. The East Anglians rose next and defeated the Mercian army, killing Beornwulf. Mercia's position as a great power was gone forever.

— ♔ —

ANASTASIUS Bibliothecarius (c. 805–c. 879)

Usurped: Papal Throne 855
Social Origins: Clerical Family

Anastasius was born around the year 810 to an Italian family which had already produced at least one bishop. He entered the church and soon became noted for his great learning. In 847 he was made a cardinal, but soon fell from the favour of Pope Leo IV because of his views and ambitions. Anastasius fled across the Alps to the court of the Frank Emperor Louis II. The disagreements with Leo IV continued unabated and in 850 Anastasius was excommunicated, a sentence he refused to accept.

When Anastasius heard the news of Leo's death in 855, he acted quickly. He persuaded Louis to back his claim to the papacy and lend him some troops. Anastasius then hurried towards Rome. Louis's support could be vital, but was not decisive for at this time the right to elect a new Pope was restricted to the people and clergy of Rome. On the way south Anastasius met messengers travelling to tell Louis that a new Pope had been elected in the person of Benedict III. Anastasius stopped the envoys and induced them to support his claim instead.

Anastasius hurriedly convened a meeting of clerics at the town of Orte which, quite illegally, elected him Pope. Armed with both an election and military muscle, Anastasius pushed on to Rome which he entered in September 855. Though the Romans clearly wanted Benedict as Pope, Anastasius overrode their objections. He maintained the Papacy was far too important a post to be decided by Romans alone for it affected the whole of Europe. No doubt, he was right but he had conveniently forgotten his irregular election.

For a while Anastasius managed to keep control of the situation with the aid of the Frank troops. However, the populace of Rome grew increasingly restive. Eventually, after only three years, open rebellion broke out, Anastasius was dragged from the Papal throne and Benedict installed in his place. Anastasius was allowed to retire to a monastery. Later in life he was reconciled with the Pope and returned to Rome as Chief Librarian. He became one of the leading Christian writers of his time during the last twenty years of his life.

RURIK (?–879)

Usurped: Power in Russia 862
Social Origins: Foreign Warrior

The career of Rurik was one of violence and ambition on a grand scale. Unfortunately, the times in which he lived were so unsettled that his story was not written down for posterity until many years after his death. As a result it is uncertain how much of the story of Rurik is true, and how much is fiction.

Rurik and his brothers, Sineus and Truvor, were born in Sweden some time around 830 when the great Viking raids were at their height. Rurik would have seen successful raiders returning from England and France while merchants came back from the East laden with silks and spices. No doubt he heard tales of the confused state of affairs in eastern Europe, where numerous petty Slavonic tribal kingdoms were in a state of continual warfare. Rurik and his brothers decided that this was a place for which adventurous young men should make. They gathered together a band of like-minded warriors, perhaps two hundred in all, and set out.

Rowing up the trade rivers from the Gulf of Riga in their longships, the brothers offered their swords to the first ruler who would pay their price. The local rulers were only too keen to hire such a formidable band of aggressive young men and readily came up with the cash. For a while Rurik and his men made a tough but well-paid living by acting as hired fighters for various tribes and rulers.

After a few years, however, Rurik took an important step. Rather than merely serve others, he decided to serve himself. It is unclear whether the tribesmen of Ladoga asked Rurik to take control or whether he seized control at sword point, though the latter seems more likely. Having gained power Rurik continued his warlike career. After the deaths of his brothers, Rurik seized Novgorod and moved his power base to that thriving city. From Novgorod Rurik built up a kingdom which stretched from the Dvina to the Volga and from Lagoda to Peipus. The native Slavs referred to Rurik and his men as the Rus. It was from Rurik's kingdom that Russia was to grow, and his descendants were to rule Russian lands for the next seven hundred years.

Rurik
A 19th-century depiction of Rurik which emphasizes the remarkably violent character of this young adventurer who carved out a kingdom for himself in a foreign country. Rurik's violent assumption of power marked the beginnings of the state which was to become Russia. (*Mansell Collection*)

BASIL I (c. 812–886)

Usurped: Byzantine Empire 867
Social Origins: Provincial Nobility

Born in about 812 into a noble but impoverished Macedonian family, Basil travelled to Constantinople in search of his fortune. He succeeded beyond his wildest dreams.

Exactly when Basil arrived in the Imperial capital is unclear, but he quickly secured a post in the Imperial stables. He proved to be an intelligent and trustworthy employee. Basil won rapid promotion and used his position and contacts to become extremely wealthy. The promising man soon came to the notice of the Emperor Michael III, who was known to contemporaries by the unpromising name of Michael the Drunkard. Perhaps Basil became a drinking companion of the Emperor, introducing him to new bars and vintages. Basil soon became a trusted confidante of the Emperor, but was secretly planning his own future.

In 866 Michael made his favourite co-Emperor. It was at this time that the two men fell out dramatically. It is not clear whether Basil deliberately provoked the quarrel or whether genuine feelings were involved, but the point at issue was who should be Patriarch of Constantinople. Michael favoured Ignatius, who preferred to negotiate with the Popes. Basil supported Photius who wanted to repudiate Papal superiority and lead the Eastern church on its own path.

The quarrel soon became extremely serious. Basil solved it by murdering both Michael and his powerful uncle Caesar Bardas. Seizing sole control of the Empire for himself, at the expense of Michael's family, Basil instituted a firm rule. Over the next 19 years, he revised the laws of the Empire, overhauled its financial system and strengthened the church. He died in 886, leaving a secure and prosperous throne to his son Leo VI.

AELLE (?–867)

Usurped: Kingdom of Northumbria 865 or 866
Social Origins: Nobleman

Aelle chose an entirely inappropriate moment to launch his usurpation. To Aelle's catastrophic sense of timing can be traced the collapse of the Kingdom of Northumbria.

In the summer of 865 an enormous force of Vikings landed in southern England. Unlike earlier Vikings, this army was not content to raid and retreat. Under the command of Ivar the Boneless, they had come to stay. In 866 the Vikings moved to East Anglia and forced the local population to pay large amounts of money and hand over food and horses. It was in this year that Aelle chose to launch his bid for power.

The Kingdom of Northumbria at this time stretched from the Humber to well into Scotland and from the North Sea to the Irish Sea. It was a rich and prosperous kingdom, but far from happy. The king, Osbriht, seems to have been extremely unpopular, though we do not know the reason for this. The discontented nobles were led by Aelle, who seems not to have been related to the royal family at all. Late in 865 or early in 866 Aelle rebelled against Osbriht and drove him from the throne. Osbriht fled and attempted to recruit an army with which to regain his power, while Aelle was establishing his control on the kingdom.

Hearing of these events, Ivar the Boneless decided to take advantage of a divided enemy. In the spring of 867 Ivar and his men marched north from East Anglia, crossed the Humber and stormed into the city of York. Aelle was absent from his capital at the time, trying to run Osbriht to ground. When he heard the news of the Viking attack, Aelle sent peace messengers to Osbriht. An ·agreement was patched up between the two men and their combined forces marched on York.

The Northumbrians launched a joint attack on the Vikings who were manning the city defences. Savage street fighting resulted, and both Aelle and Osbriht were killed. Left leaderless the Northumbrians submitted to the Vikings and accepted a puppet king named Egbert.

ARNULF (c. 850–899)

Usurped: Holy Roman Empire 887
Social Origins: Bavarian Royal Family

Arnulf was born in about 850 as an illegitimate son of Carloman, King of Bavaria. He grew up in an era when the once powerful Frank Empire was crumbling under repeated hammer blows. Already divided between Eastern and Western branches of the Imperial Family, the Empire suffered repeated attacks from Vikings in the north and Arabs in the south. Sensing the weakness of central authority local counts and kings attempted to appropriate powers to themselves. In this declining Empire Arnulf learnt his trade of soldier and ruler.

In 876 Charles the Bald, ruler of the Eastern Franks, created Arnulf Margrave, or governor, of the eastern border lands of Carinthia. Eight years later it suddenly seemed as if the Carolingian Empire was set for a revival when Charles the Fat, the new eastern king inherited the western kingdom as well. The Empire was reunited and Charles travelled to Rome to be crowned Emperor by the Pope.

However, Charles the Fat soon showed himself to be a lethargic and incompetent ruler. Rather than continue military action against the Vikings, Charles paid them to go away. This action, of course, merely ensured that the raiders returned the next year for another payment.

By the spring of 887, the nobles had had enough of Charles the Fat. Arnulf took leadership of the rebels and led their armies against Charles. As slow to act as ever, Charles did not rouse himself in time to take action. The nobles easily overcame him, forced his abdication and locked him up. As leader of the rebels, Arnulf coerced his fellow nobles to elect him as Emperor, although he had no connection with the Imperial family.

Though later crowned Emperor by the Pope, Arnulf was never able to enforce his rule throughout the Empire. His lack of Imperial ancestry and dubious accession persuaded several nobles that they owed him no allegiance. Guy, Duke of Spoletta, was a particularly truculent subject who rarely obeyed Imperial commands. It was during a punitive raid against Spoletta in 899 that Arnulf fell ill and died.

— ♛ —

ROLLO (c. 860–932)

Usurped: Duchy of Normandy 911
Social Origins: Norwegian Nobleman

Rollo was born in about 860 into an aggressively ambitious Viking family. His father, Rognvald, seems to have been an active Viking raider in the heyday of the Scandinavian plundering expeditions. Rollo, or Hrolfr as his name is given in his native tongue, was brought up in the tradition of raid and plunder which dominated the Viking nobility at this time.

In 876 Rollo sailed on his first raid, plundering the banks of the Lower Seine. In the following years Rollo led an active life as a leader of expeditions which penetrated deep into France and carried off huge amounts of booty. At this time the Frank Empire was wracked by internal disputes. The legitimate Carolingian dynasty faced rebellious nobles and even outright usurpation. There can be little doubt that these disputes allowed the Vikings to raid the Empire's lands in what are now France and Germany without facing serious resistance.

In the early 900s Rollo became involved in trouble at home, possibly one of the interminable blood feuds of the Vikings. He fled and settled permanently near the mouth of the Seine, continuing his career of plunder from his new base. Gradually, Rollo extended his power over a wide area. In 911 Charles the Simple, King of the West Franks, whose territories were roughly contiguous with modern France, decided to come to terms with Rollo.

Charles the Simple offered to recognize Rollo's illegal assumption of power on the Seine. The Viking would acquire legitimate authority and other benefits. In return Rollo had to become a Christian and promise to block the Seine to other Vikings. Rollo eagerly accepted the offer, being christened Robert, and began to enjoy his new position as Duke of Normandy. We do not know how successful Rollo was at keeping other Vikings from raiding up the Seine, but it is clear that he held on to power long enough to pass it on to his son William in 927.

BOLESLAV (c. 910–c. 940)

Usurped: Kingdom of Bohemia 929
Social Origins: Ducal Family

Boleslav coolly plotted a cruel usurpation and, though he was successful, the sheer frightfulness of his actions caused him to lose much of his power.

In the early 10th century Bohemia was a semi-independent kingdom within the Holy Roman Empire under its ruler Uratislas. In 925 Uratislas died, leaving his realm to his eldest son Wenceslas, the 'good king' of Christmas carol fame. Boleslav, the younger son, received nothing. This lack of inheritance annoyed Boleslav, and his temper was made worse by religious problems. Wenceslas was a devout Christian, as were many of his people. He built churches, encouraged learning and supervised the spreading of the gospel within his kingdom. Boleslav was a stout pagan who resented the introduction of what he considered an effete and foreign religion.

At some time Wenceslas had sworn a vow of chastity and had shown no signs of marriage. In the autumn of 929 a son was born to Boleslav. This seemed to guarantee that the throne would pass into Boleslav's, and pagan, hands. However, there was no guarantee that Wenceslas would not break his vow and produce an heir. Boleslav invited Wenceslas to celebrate the birth of the infant Boleslav. Wenceslas attended the party, but at midnight absented himself for his customary midnight prayers.

Boleslav knew his brother's habits and was waiting in the chapel with a band of six trusted henchmen. As the king knelt in prayer he was stabbed repeatedly, and finished off with a spear thrust from his brother. The dying

words of Wenceslas were 'why? why?.' When the Emperor Otto heard what
had happened, he was furious. Wenceslas had been one of his favourite and
most trusted subject rulers. Otto led a large army into Bohemia. Boleslav was
defeated and imprisoned. He was later released, but his power was much
curtailed. To his undying irritation, Boleslav had to tolerate Imperial
missionaries spreading the Gospel through his lands.

ROBERT I (c. 865–923)

Usurped: Kingdom of the Franks 921

Social Origins: Nobleman

Robert was born in the 860s as a younger son of the Marquis of Neustria.
The Marquisate of Neustria was one of the richest properties in the Frank
Empire. Indeed, the Marquis controlled more land and wealth than came
under the direct control of the Emperors. In 888 Odo, Robert's elder brother,
was elected King of the Western Franks, whose territory covered most of
modern France. He created Robert Duke of the Franks and entrusted vast
estates to him.

In 898 Odo died and Charles the Simple, who already ruled much of
France, claimed the throne. Charles was a member of the legitimate Royal
Family, being descended from the mighty Emperor Charlemagne. Robert
bowed to Charles's superior claims and accepted him as king. However,
Charles proved unable either to halt the Viking raids or to persuade his
powerful nobles to act together instead of fighting private wars.

In 922, Robert seems to have lost patience with the ineffectual monarch.
As one of the most powerful of all the Frank nobles, and the brother of a
previous king, Robert was in a commanding position. He canvassed opinion
amongst his fellow nobles and found that they too had tired of Charles the
Simple. Robert gathered his troops and forcibly removed Charles from the
throne.

As king Robert had far more resources at his disposal than had Charles.
He was in a better position to enforce his rule, and made valiant attempts to
do so. In 923 Charles tried to stage a return. He raised an army and gained
a surprise victory over Robert in which the latter was killed. Charles proved
himself still unable to impose order and died in 929. Robert's descendants
later returned to the throne as the highly successful Capetian dynasty (see
Hugh Capet below).

Taira MASAKADO (?–940)

Usurped: *Japanese Emperor 935*
Social Origins: Samurai

Masakado belonged to the aristocratic Taira samurai clan. Such clans of warriors formed the elite of Japanese society at this time, and for several centuries afterwards. Each clan had a core based upon a family, while the other members had been adopted into the family and boosted the fighting strength of the clan.

In 935 Masakado asked to be given the immensely important government post of *Kebiishi* or Police Commissioner. The Emperor refused, whereupon Masakado immediately began a rebellion by killing his own uncle, an important official, and raising an army. Ineffectual attempts by the Emperor to resist the armed might of Masakado were brushed aside. In 936 Masakado announced that he was the new Emperor and took the name of Heishin.

For four years Masakado was able to exercise power, but the Emperor had never been captured or properly defeated. In 940 Hidesato, of the Fujiwara clan, caught Masakado at a disadvantage. After a running battle lasting 13 days, Masakado was killed. His brief rule was over.

— ♔ —

ERIC BLOODAXE (c. 925–954)

Usurped: *Kingdom of York 947 and 952*
Social Origins: Norwegian Royal Family

Eric Bloodaxe is unusual among usurpers in that he managed to stage a successful coup not once, but twice, in the same place and in almost exactly similar circumstances. The key to this double success lay in the situation at York and in Eric's ancestry and undoubted abilities.

Since 866 York had been the centre of the large and powerful Viking kingdom of Northumbria, and there were large numbers of Scandinavians mixed in with the native English population. Though Christianised by the mid-10th century, the Northumbrians were a fiercely proud people. In 937 Athelstan, King of Wessex, conquered Northumbria. He installed a puppet king of his own and took the title 'King of the English'. The Northumbrians resented their loss of independence even if it was to an enlightened and strong king.

It was into these circumstances that Eric strode in the summer of 947. Eric was the son of King Harald Fairhair of Norway. As he grew up, Eric proved himself to be a magnificent warrior and born leader of men, earning his sobriquet of 'Bloodaxe'. Unfortunately his passionate and fiery temper involved him in much trouble. When he argued with, and killed, a younger brother, Eric had to flee from Norway. Perhaps looking for recruits, Eric made for the Viking lands of York.

When he arrived, Eric was probably rather surprised to find that he was being welcomed as a liberator. The Northumbrians knew of Eric's prestige as a fighter and wanted to make use of it. The leading nobles persuaded him to take the kingship and proclaim Northumbrian independence. The footloose Eric was only too happy to oblige, even if he had to become a nominal Christian to do so.

In the spring of 948 Eadred, the successor of Athelstan, led a punitive raid to the north. In the only major battle of the campaign, Eric caught a section of Eadred's army fording a river and annihilated it. However, the Wessex army was too powerful and the Northumbrians were forced to submit. Eric fled, perhaps to the Viking settlements in Ireland.

Four years later the rule of the Wessex puppet had irritated the Northumbrians beyond endurance. Eric heard of the situation and hurried back to York. This time Eric himself was the main driving force. Storming into the Royal Halls at the head of a tough band of Viking warriors, Eric seized power. Realizing the haphazard nature of his claim, Eric enforced his position with brutal force. He ruled with all the trappings of a Viking king. His band of warriors brooked no insult and exacted bloody revenge on any who spoke against Eric.

The merciless rule was too much for the Northumbrians, even though Eric proved himself more than capable of maintaining the independence of York. In 954 a rising of noblemen drove Eric from his throne. As he fled York once again, he was murdered by a nobleman named Maccus at Steinmor.

— 👑 —

AELFTHRYTH (?–c. 1000)

Kingmaker of England 978
Social Origins: Noblewoman

In 964 Aelfthryth married King Edgar of England as his second wife. By his first wife, Athelflaed the 'White Duck', the king already had a son named Edward. Two years after the marriage Aelfthryth bore a son named Ethelred, and the scene was set for a dynastic dispute.

In 975 Edgar died unexpectedly and the nobles acclaimed the elder brother, Edward as king. The young man had a foul temper, which sent the courtiers into hiding whenever it burst forth, and he was apt to act rashly. In addition to these faults Edward attempted to curtail the rise to wealth and influence of the monasteries. This action inevitably incurred the wrath of the Church.

Powerful factions were working to frustrate Edward's policies. It seems that Aelfthryth planned to take advantage of this discontent for her own purposes. She identified herself and her son with the clerical cause, hoping to gain the Church's support.

On 18 March 978 Edward rode to his stepmother's house at Corfe to pay a visit to his half-brother. As he entered the courtyard, Aelfthryth's retainers came forward with a cup of wine. When Edward reached forwards to take it, the men seized his arms to restrain him, and stabbed him. The young king spurred his horse forwards in an attempt to escape, but he tumbled to the ground and Aefthryth's men killed him.

Aelfthryth immediately proclaimed her son Ethelred as king and ordered Edward to be buried without even a short service. No doubt Aefthryth hoped that the opponents of Edward would rally to her support. If so, she was badly mistaken. The English were used to open feuding and violence, but not the treacherous murder of a guest. Also, though Edward had been rather unpopular, he had had his good points.

Ethelred was accepted as king, but he never enjoyed the unconditional loyalty of his subjects. They recalled the underhand way in which he had come to the throne. Perhaps because of this lack of support, Ethelred earned his nickname of the Unready. When Danish invasions increased some years later, Ethelred found himself without a loyal army and was forced to flee abroad. Aefthryth herself had to surrender much of her influence over the boy to Archbishop Dunstan and eventually withdrew from court to live in a convent.

— ♔ —

OLAF TRYGGVASSON (963–1000)

Usurped: Kingdom of Norway 995
Social Origins: Royal Family

Olaf was the son of a Norwegian ruler named Tryggve. This gave him great prestige, though it is difficult to be precise about the extent of Tryggve's power in the land of fjords. When Tryggve was murdered, Olaf was still a young man. He promptly set sail from Norway to lead a spectacularly successful career as a Viking.

Not only was Olaf a magnificent fighter, and leader of men, but he also excelled in the barbaric sports so admired by his subjects. One of his favourite tricks was to run from end to end of his ship by jumping from oar to oar while they were in use. To add excitement to the sport, Olaf would ask his men to attach sharp swords to some of the oars, so that he would have to leap over them to the next oar.

While raiding in England during the early 990s Olaf acquired enormous wealth, great fame and the Christian religion. In 995 Olaf decided that it was time to return home and claim his lands. He landed in Trondelag with a large fleet of followers. Then Jarl Haakon, the most powerful nobleman in Norway, moved against him. In the ensuing battle Haakon was killed. Olaf took the title of king and gained undisputed power over Norway.

Such a situation did not please Swein Forkbeard of Denmark who had exercised considerable influence over the Norwegian nobility before Olaf's return. In 1000 Swein ambushed Olaf at Svoldr when the latter was returning from a raid and was accompanied by only 11 ships. The Norwegians fought valiantly, but towards evening the Danes closed in for the kill. Olaf's magnificent ship, known as the 'Long Serpent' and the largest vessel of its day, was boarded. As the Danes gathered around him, Olaf knew that there was only one way to avoid the disgrace of capture. He leapt overboard to be dragged down by the weight of his armour.

ADELAIDE (931–999)

Usurped: Power in the Holy Roman Empire
Social Origins: Noblewoman

Adelaide was clearly a very dominant character and took a hand in politics wherever she lived. However, it is still far from clear to what extent she was motivated by personal ambition and how much by expediency.

She was born in 931 as the daughter of Rudolph of Burgundy. At the time of her birth the Frank Empire, covering most of modern France and Germany and parts of Italy, was in a perilously weak condition. The actual power throughout the land was held by local magnates, such as her father, while the Imperial family had divided the Empire into two, or sometimes three, portions. The legitimate Carolingian dynasty could not hold on to power and before long the nobles were electing Emperors from amongst their own ranks. It was against this background that Adelaide lived.

While still in her teens she was married to Lothair II, King of Italy, a scion of the Imperial house. In 951 Lothair died and the Italian nobles at once rose

Adelaide
A romanticized engraving of Adelaide, Queen of Italy and Germany. This remarkable dominant woman not only controlled politics but also had a wide influence over Churchmen. She was a very devout lady who lavished valuable gifts on the Church and endowed many religious establishments. She was later made a saint by the Church. (*Mary Evans*)

in rebellion against the idea of monarchy. The beleaguered Adelaide tried to keep control of the situation, but it was beyond her. She therefore appealed for help to Otto I, the recently-widowed King of Germany.

Otto came south with an enormous army, crushed the rebels and married Adelaide. Taking the title of King of Lombardy, an area of northern Italy, Otto returned north to deal with a rising of his own nobles. Soon after the marriage Otto's eldest son, Duke Liudolf of Swabia, rebelled on the grounds that Adelaide wished to oust him from the succession. We do not know the truth of these accusations, but Liudolf was killed in the fighting.

For the next twenty two years, Otto ruled Germany and Italy with a firm hand. In 962 the Pope crowned him Holy Roman Emperor after he had smashed an invasion of eastern Germany by the barbarian Magyars. When Otto died in 973 he was succeeded by his and Adelaide's son Otto II, who ruled with the advice of Adelaide and his Byzantine wife, Theophano. When Otto II died in 983 he left an infant son, also named Otto. Again Adelaide stepped to the fore, taking a leading role in politics until Otto III came of age. She died in 999.

JOHN TZIMISCES (925–976)

Usurped: Byzantine Empire 970
Social Origins: Army Officer

In making his successful bid for the Imperial crown, John Tzimisces probably felt that he had achieved the ultimate goal of Byzantine soldiers. In fact he was almost certainly being manipulated by a mind more subtle and cunning than his own.

Under the Emperor Constantine VII Byzantium enjoyed a period of unequalled cultural brilliance. However, the frontiers were constantly threatened by Muslims and barbarians. In 959 Constantine died and was succeeded by Romanus II, who may have murdered him. Romanus did not survive long, dying in 964. The Empire was left to Romanus II's wife, Theophano.

This accomplished and cultured woman knew full well that the 960s were not the time for a woman to rule the Byzantine Empire. The tough military men on whom the Empire relied disliked civilian control and were unlikely to tolerate rule by a woman. She therefore took one of the most accomplished generals, a man named Nicephorus Phocas, as her lover. Nicephorus became joint ruler with Theophano, who immediately sent him off to control the armies. He soon conquered Syria and Mesopotamia.

These successes may have encouraged Nicephorus to believe he was more powerful than he was and to start taking decisions on his own initiative. Theophano looked around for a general likely to be more pliable to her will. Her eye alighted upon John Tzimisces, a nephew of Nicephorus. She encouraged both the ambition and lusts of John to such an extent that he murdered his uncle in 970 and took his place in the Empress's bed.

As before, Theophano made certain the new Emperor was kept busy with the army. John fought the Russians, driving them out of the Balkans, and retook the Euphrates from the Muslims. John died in 976.

VLADIMIR I (956–1015)

Usurped: Grand Duchy of Kiev 972
Social Origins: Ducal Family

Vladimir's usurpation was little more than a squabble between brothers over an inheritance, but it had a profound effect on the balance of power in Eastern Europe. An effect which has persisted to this day.

By the late 10th century Russia was firmly in the hands of the Viking adventurers who had accompanied Rurik (see above) and his brothers about a century earlier. However, the Scandinavian culture of these men was slowly, but firmly, being swamped by that of the Slavonic peoples of Russia. In 972 Vladimir's father died to be replaced on the throne of the Grand Duchy of Kiev by Yaropolk. Vladimir resented the accession of his elder brother. Almost immediately he killed the new Grand Duke and stormed into Kiev at the head of his warrior band. The civil authorities surrendered to him without a struggle. Vladimir had acquired the Grand Duchy.

As ruler of Kiev, Vladimir realigned Russian allegiances away from Scandinavia in favour of Byzantium. In 988 he married Anna, sister to the Emperor Basil II, accepted Orthodox Christianity and agreed a treaty with the Empire. It is partly from these events that the Russians derived the long-cherished belief that they represented the 'Third Rome'. Vladimir went on to conquer large territories in Eastern Europe and found the future greatness of Russia.

HUGH CAPET (?–996)

Usurped: Power in France 996
Social Origins: Nobleman

Hugh Capet achieved a quite remarkable break with tradition, though at the time few people, least of all himself, could have foreseen the consequences of his action. By the late 10th century the Kingdom of France had sunk to a low ebb. The position of king carried with it very few lands, and less power. Many nobles in France were more powerful than the king himself, and only obeyed royal edicts when it suited them to do so. When a king died, the nobles gathered to elect the successor. Usually they chose the man they felt would give them least trouble. In 987 Louis V died and the nobles gathered to choose the next king. They elected Hugh Capet, son of Hugh Duke of Burgundy.

In itself the election of Hugh was not remarkable, and the aristocracy no doubt congratulated themselves on having continued the tradition of weak kings. They were to be proved wrong. Hugh Capet was an extremely cunning and astute man. He also had the type of constitution which would not have disgraced an ox.

Unlike the earlier kings, Hugh had a substantial amount of territory under his direct control. This was roughly the County of Paris, stretching from that city to Orleans. From these lands Hugh was able to draw enough money and military might to maintain the royal dignity. Before he died in 996, Hugh took an important step. He nominated his son Robert as the next king and had him crowned. The nobles were persuaded to swear allegiance to the young heir. When Hugh died in 996, the nobles accepted this arrangement and made Robert the next king.

Robert copied his father and installed his son as king before he died himself. The first five monarchs of the Capetian line followed the same policy, until the nobles had forgone their right of election in favour of the right of legitimacy. At the same time, the Capetians were extremely long-lived men, the average reign lasted 27 years. Hugh Capet's action had made France into an hereditary monarchy, stripping the nobles of their power over the throne.

Ibu Abi Amir Mohammed, ALMANZOR (939–1002)

Usurped: Caliphate of Andalusia 996
Social Origins: Lawyer

Almanzor, or Al-mansur as he is more properly called, was the last great ruler of Muslim Spain. After his death in 1002, the nation of Andalusia collapsed into a collection of petty states which warred continuously with each other and the Christian kingdoms to the north.

Almanzor was born in 939 into a distinguished Arab family which had migrated to Spain in the wake of the Islamic conquest of the peninsula. Until the age of 28, Almanzor practised as a lawyer in Cordoba. In 967 he became a legal adviser at the court of the Caliph Hakam II. At court he came to the notice of the favourite, Subh, and the military commander, Ghalib. Through their influence, Almansur became chief minister in 978.

After the death of Hakam, the three powerful men, Almansur, Ghalib and Subh, formed a government between them. In theory the three men were acting for the new Caliph, an infant. In reality, they were working for their own interests. In 981 Almanzor fell out with Ghalib. In a swift campaign he achieved a rather surprising victory over the old general, smashing his armies. Almanzor hurried back to Cordoba where he purged the supporters of Ghalib and enforced his will on Subh.

From that point on Almanzor was the real power in Andalusia. In 996 he quietly shuffled the Caliph out of the way and took regal power for himself. For the remainder of his reign, Almanzor concentrated on curbing the power of local governors and extending his rule into North Africa. Possibly the most lasting monument to his reign, however, is the magnificent Mosque of Cordoba which he extended and completed. The vast size of the pillared main hall is stunning, while the graceful line of the innumerable pillars is a pleasure to behold.

BRIAN BORU (926–1014)

Usurped: High Kingship of Ireland 1002
Social Origins: Local King

Brian Boru was born a younger son of King Kennedy of Thomond, one of numerous petty kings in 10th century Ireland. Some Irish kings, with the title

King of Peaks, ruled little more than a single village. These petty kings owed allegiance to various Kings of Kings who in turn were subject to the Kings of Fifths. The Fifths of Ireland, of which there were only four, divided the whole island between them. The O'Neills of the Ulster Fifth were the designated High Kings of All Ireland.

This political system was both set and in a state of flux. The overlordship of the High King was more theoretical than actual while allegiances among lesser kings were constantly shifting. Only the four Fifths showed any semblance of permanence.

In his twenties Brian Boru became chieftain of the Dal Cais, a tribe living near the mouth of the Shannon. In 952 the Dal Cais under Brian Boru captured and brutally sacked the city of Limerick. This success made Brian a famous warrior and attracted men to his standard. He spent the next decades conquering surrounding kings and extending his power until he could claim the kingship of the Fifth of Munster.

In the year 1000 Brian raised the forces of Munster and invaded the Fifth of Leinster. He was totally successful. He now cast his eyes on the High Kingship, which was hereditary within the O'Neill dynasty. The High King Maelsechnaill mac Domnaill appealed for help to his O'Neill relatives, but they refused, as did the kings of Meath. In the year 1002 Brian marched on Tara, ejected Maelsechnaill and had himself proclaimed High King. He had replaced not only the High King, but the entire dynasty. Fourteen years later Brian Boru was killed fighting the Vikings of Dublin who had rebelled. His name is more properly spelt Brian Boruma.

MELUS (?–c. 1018)

Usurped: Power in Bari 1009
Social Origins: Obscure

The origins of Melus are not clearly known. His concern for his native city of Bari may indicate that he was one of the wealthy landowners or merchants who were to be found in Italy at this time.

In the early 11th century much of southern Italy owed allegiance to the Byzantine Empire, and Bari was no exception. However, the Greek rule was unpopular and unrest was common. In 1009 Melus led a full scale revolt in which he seized power in Bari and took the title of Duke of Apulia. For some time Melus held power successfully, but by 1015 he was little better than a fugitive on the run from Byzantine forces.

In that year he travelled to pray at a shrine on Monte Gargano. There he had a meeting which was to change not only his life, but that of southern Italy as a whole. In the shrine he came across a party of some 40 tough warriors. They were Norman knights on their way home from Jerusalem who had stopped off in Italy. Melus asked them to join him, but the men refused for they were anxious to be on their way. They did, however, promise to pass the offer on to their friends when they got home.

Melus may not have held much hope of a result from this meeting, but in fact the Normans did a good publicity job. Soon hundreds of Norman knights were flooding into southern Italy looking for work as mercenaries. They were, on the whole, younger sons who could not hope to inherit lands at home. Melus employed the first arrivals to help him regain power in Bari, which he achieved with great speed. Later arrivals, however, were more interested in furthering their own ends than in remaining loyal to their employers.

WU ZE TIAN (623–705)

Usurped: Chinese Empire 698
Social Origins: Imperial Concubine

Originally rising to prominence as a favourite concubine of the Emperor Tai-tsung, Wu later married his son and successor Tai Zong. Wu has come down to us by repute as a highly cultured lady of great presence; she was also ruthless in the extreme and indifferent to inflicting cruelty on a grand scale.

Soon after his accession in 650, Tai Zong showed himself to be a weak man who was frequently unable to attend to government business due to ill health. Wu deputised for him and slowly gathered power into her own hands. By the time Tai died in 683, Wu was the undisputed mistress of China. She elevated her son Chung-tsung to the Imperial throne as a front for her own rule. Wu soon tired of Chung and replaced him with a second son Jui-tsung.

In 690 Wu decided that her power was secure enough for her to do away with the fiction of her position. She dethroned her son and announced her accession as the Emperor Sheng Shen. She was the first woman ever to rule China, and there was neither the vocabulary nor the institutions for a reigning Empress. As Emperor, Wu encouraged the growth of the civil service at the expense of the nobles. She gave important government tasks to those who performed best at the examinations for the bureaucracy. Wu seems to have maintained her rule with the aid of spies and assassination squads. In 705 a palace coup ousted Wu and returned Chung-tsung to power. She is sometimes referred to as Wu Chao.

HUANG CHAO (?–c. 884)

Usurped: Chinese Empire 880
Social Origins: Merchant

The later Chinese Emperors of the Tang dynasty (618–906) were weak rulers who allowed power to slip into the hands of the bureaucrats, and in particular the palace eunuchs. Local governors took powers upon themselves and corruption became rife. The delicate system of land management broke down, bringing starvation in its wake, and officials imposed harsh taxation, most of which found its way into their own pockets. This inevitably created great discontent, and the most discontented of all was Huang Chao.

Huang Chao was a merchant but with the economic decline there were few trading opportunities. In the early 870s he sat the prestigious entrance examinations for the civil service. He failed. Stirring up the discontented peasants of Hopei, Huang Chao began a great rebellion. The Tang government, led by a simple-minded Emperor and a clique of eunuchs was unable to command the loyalty of its own troops.

In 879 Chao captured the city of Canton and sacked it with great cruelty. He then moved into the Yangtze Valley, conquering vast territories. In 880 Chao led his peasant army into the Imperial capital of Loyang. The Tang government fled before him and Chao marched in unopposed. He then massacred all the senior civil servants who had been foolish enough to remain. Perhaps he blamed them for his examination failure.

Chao proclaimed himself Emperor and set about organizing his government. Two years later a massive barbarian invasion from the north struck China. The invaders, led by a man with the colourful name of 'One Eyed Dragon' smashed Chao's army and he died in the consequent flight.

— ♔ —

KUANG-YIN (927–976)

Usurped: Chinese Empire 690
Social Origins: Army Office

In 904 the last of the Tang Emperors was murdered together with his entire family by an official named Chu Wen. Wen tried to establish control but failed. Southern China split up into ten kingdoms, while the north passed into the hands of military dictators and suffered frequent attacks by Khitan barbarians from the north . The last of these dictators styled himself the Emperor of the Chou Dynasty.

In 960 Chao Kuang-yin, leader of the Chou Imperial Guard, was leading an army against the Khitan. While in his tent enjoying a drinking session with his officers, Chao was surprised by a band of soldiers who rushed in and dressed him in Imperial robes. Hearing what had happened, the remainder of the army saluted Chao as Emperor. Chao immediately abandoned the campaign and rushed home. With the aid of the Guard, Chao overthrew the Emperor and proclaimed himself as the Emperor Tai-tsu.

Chao proved himself to be both astute and practical. Breaking with tradition he did not murder the previous Imperial family and officials, preferring to use their experience and advice for himself. He realized that the main threat came from the army. He therefore invited all his senior officers to a banquet and asked them to resign their commands. In return he offered them enough money 'to live at ease, drinking night and day, in the knowledge that you have provided for your heirs'. The generals agreed and resigned *en masse*. The army was then brought under direct Imperial control and no future general allowed to gain too much power. By 979 the Sung Dynasty, which Chao had founded, had reunited the whole of China. This emperor's name is sometimes given as Zhao Kuangyin and his title as Sung Tai Tsu.

— 👑 —

MAHMUD of Ghazni (971–1030)

Usurped: Principality of Ghazni 997
Social Origins: Princely Family

Mahmud of Ghazni is a name with lives in India as the epitome of evil and destruction. In his native Afghanistan, however, he was regarded as a fine and cultured monarch. The difference in outlook is largely one of perspective.

Mahmud's father was Sabuktagin, a petty ruler from Ghazni who extended his rule to include most of Afghanistan and the Hindu Kush. In 997 Sabuktagin died and left the throne to his younger son Ismail, whom he considered far more fitted to rule than any of his other sons. The 26–year-old Mahmud, however, took a very different view. He felt that he was a more worthy successor to his father than his younger brother. He therefore promptly imprisoned his brother, seized power and set about proving that he was, indeed, an able ruler.

He moved into Turkestan, taking control of the highly lucrative caravan routes between China and Europe. Next, in the year 1000, Mahmud launched his first attack on India. Using a highly mobile force of mounted mountain-fighters, Mahmud swept down into the Indus Valley, defeated King Jayapala of Shahiya and plundered several towns. It may have been on this exploratory raid that Mahmud realized that the Hindus stored their wealth in their temples. As a good Muslim, it was Mahmud's duty to destroy such idolatrous buildings, and it was more than convenient that this religious duty coincided with his insatiable greed for gold.

In 1004 Mahmud attacked the city of Multan on the Indus and in what became almost annual raids, he later plundered the Punjab, Mathura and Thanesar. Mahmud was clever enough to attack in the autumn when the farmland was close to harvest. His fast moving armies could therefore find enough food in India and were unburdened by transport. In 1025 he achieved his greatest success when he captured the holy city of Somnat. Some 50,000 inhabitants were slaughtered in the fighting and he carried off an immense amount of booty. It was almost his last raid, for he died in 1030.

ZOE (?–1050)

Kingmaker of Byzantine Empire 1034–1050
Social Origins: Imperial Family

Zoe was the most dominant woman of her time and remains one of the most fascinating characters of Byzantine history. She was born into a family of Emperors and by skilful scheming managed to maintain an important position throughout her life.

She was born to Constantine VIII, who may have been disappointed not to have produced a male heir. In fact Zoe proved herself more capable than any son was likely to have been. Constantine married her to a certain Romanus, who duly succeeded to power as joint Emperor with his wife when Constantine died in 1028.

It is clear that Zoe did not share her father's views of Romanus III. The marriage was not a happy one, and Zoe took a lover in the shape of Michael Paphlagonian. In 1034 the Empress poisoned her husband and raised her lover to joint Imperial power as Michael IV. The Imperial pair ruled well for several years, with Michael successfully countering the Bulgar threat in the Balkans and Zoe administering the Empire from Constantinople.

In 1041 Michael died. Zoe immediately raised a youthful nephew of Michael, also named Michael, to joint power. Young Michael V did not appreciate what he saw as the meddlesome activities of Zoe. He had her arrested and banished to a convent on Prinkipo Island. For once Zoe had been outmanoeuvred and there seemed little prospect that she would return to power.

However, Zoe had made many friends when in power. After barely a year of rule by Michael V, the people of Constantinople rose in rebellion. Court officials took the hint, and sent for Zoe to restore order. Michael V was strangled. Back in Constantinople, Zoe had her sister Theodora enthroned as joint Empress. She then married an aging, but still handsome adventurer named Constantine. For the next eight years the Imperial trio reigned peacefully. After Zoe's death Constantine IX continued his rule.

— ♔ —

GODWIN (?–1053)
Kingmaker of England 1040–1053
Social Origins: Obscure

The exact origins of Godwin are unknown, though he seems to have been of Danish extraction. Whatever his birth, Godwin dominated England for several decades and was instrumental in the election of two kings. It is likely that he fought alongside Canute when that Danish monarch was invading England in 1014. He was early recognized as a man of ability and power, and in 1020 Canute created Godwin Earl of Wessex. This was the largest and wealthiest earldom in England and carried with it immense prestige and great power.

When Canute suddenly died in 1035, Godwin supported the claims of the legitimate son Hardecanute over those of the bastard Harold. However, he was outvoted at the Witan and Harold became first regent and later king.

In 1036 Alfred, the eldest son of Ethelred the Unready, the King of England defeated by Canute, visited England to see his mother Emma, now the widow of both Ethelred and Canute. The arrival of a prince of English royal blood would clearly have upset the already difficult succession problem. As soon as the young man landed, Godwin arrested him. Godwin then handed the boy over to gaolers who took their job too seriously and tortured Alfred to such an extent that he later died. Whether or not Godwin ordered this action is unclear.

In 1040 Harold died and Hardecanute came to England to be welcomed by Godwin, who smoothed his way to the throne. Soon afterwards Hardecanute invited Alfred's brother Edward to come to England as a prospective heir pending the birth of a son to the king himself. It must have been an uncomfortable time for Godwin and no doubt he wished for the quick appearance of an heir. He was to be disappointed.

On 8 June 1042 Hardecanute attended the riotous wedding feast of a friend Tovi the Proud. When the feast was in full swing, the king leapt to his feet with his drinking horn in his hand. Perhaps he intended to drink a toast. Instead he staggered, fell to the ground and died. Godwin immediately led the nobles in acclaiming Edward as king.

Godwin managed to exert tremendous influence over Edward. He married the king, who was not interested in women, to his daughter Edith. Perhaps more important, Godwin secured Earldoms for his five sons; Tostig, Sweyn, Gurth, Leofwine and Harold. The king came to resent this overmighty subject family. He attempted to counter-balance them by using knights and churchmen from Normandy, where he had been brought up in exile. In fact the vast majority of Englishmen resented the high-handed Normans and supported Godwin in his opposition to them.

In 1051 Edward felt strong enough to exile the Godwin clan. But Earl Godwin organized his support and returned in 1052 with such massive backing that Edward was forced to restore him. The following year Godwin died leaving his power and prestige to his son Harold, later to become King of England.

MACBETH (?–1057)

Usurped: Kingdom of Scotland 1040
Social Origins: Royal Family

Macbeth is one of the few early kings of Scotland familiar to the general public. In the main, of course, this is due to the tragedy written by Shakespeare about his life and death. The play is a fairly accurate account of the reign, though it is highly dramatized and some events are glossed over for the sake of a good story.

Macbeth first enters history in the 1030s as a grandnephew of King Kenneth and therefore a cousin of the reigning King Duncan. Duncan made his cousin commander-in-chief of the army and largely left military affairs in his hands. In 1040 Macbeth suddenly turned on Duncan and killed him. Perhaps the tough Scottish nobles had lost respect for a king who left the fighting to someone else. It is highly unlikely that the murder took place, as Shakespeare suggests, while Duncan was a guest at Macbeth's house. Perhaps the king was killed when Macbeth's troops burst into court.

Macbeth ruled for a total of seventeen years. It seems that he made a reasonably good king. However, Duncan's son Malcolm had escaped Macbeth and was in England trying to gain support. He was to remain a dangerously unsettling influence throughout Macbeth's reign and eventually brought about his death (see Siward below).

— ♛ —

WILLIAM d'HAUTVILLE (?–1045)

Usurped: Countship of Apulia 1043

Social Origins: Foreign Adventurer

William d'Hautville is probably the greatest self-made man of any period in history. He was born the son of a Norman knight so obscure that not much more is known about him than his name. Through his own efforts and abilities, William managed to raise himself to the position of sovereign lord over a vast and wealthy territory. It was a remarkable career.

William's rise to greatness began in 1032 when he received a message from a fellow Norman named Rainulf. The previous year Rainulf had been rewarded with the town of Aversa and a rich heiress by the Duke of Naples for his services as a mercenary. Rainulf had written to Normandy asking for more knights to come south to act as mercenaries. William and his brother Drogo needed no further prompting. They mounted their warhorses, donned their armour and spurred southward.

Taking service with the Count of Capua, the d'Hautville brothers gained both wealth and influence. They sent messages home asking their brothers to join them. Soon no fewer than ten d'Hautville brothers were in southern Italy; William, Drogo, Roger, Mauger, Tancred, Robert, Geoffry, Serlo, Humphrey and a second William. In 1038 the brothers hired themselves to a Byzantine force invading Sicily. The invasion failed and William realized the weakness of the Byzantine forces, who then ruled much of southern Italy.

In 1041 William and his brothers joined the army of various Lombard lords, including Gaimar of Salerno, who were rebelling against the Byzantines. The rebellion was staggeringly successful. At the battle of Monte Maggiore 2,000 Normans, including some 700 heavily-armoured knights, faced a numerically superior Byzantine army. The Normans launched an overwhelming charge in triangular formations. They rode through the leading Byzantine forces, throwing them back on the reserve units in confusion. The Byzantines fled and the Normans chased them so effectively that Byzantine power in Italy ceased to exist.

The Lombards were delighted, but their joy soon turned to impotent anger. William calmly announced that since the Normans had won the battle, they deserved the spoils. There was nothing the Lombards could do against the superior Norman might. William then carved up southern Italy between his Norman supporters, apportioning land as he saw fit. Though William and his Normans owed nominal allegiance to Gaimar, they ignored any requests he made and were virtually independent. In 1043 William threw off all pretence of subservience when he announced that he was taking the title of Count of Apulia. On William's death in 1045, his brother Drogo inherited the Countship.

— ♛ —

SIWARD (?–1055)

Kingmaker of Scotland 1054
Social Origins: English Nobleman

In 1040 Siward, Earl of Northumbria, must have been surprised to find his teenage nephew, Malcolm Canmore at his gate asking for protection. Malcolm was the son of King Duncan of Scotland and was at that moment fleeing from the usurper Macbeth (see above) who had recently murdered Duncan. Siward admitted the young man, giving him both protection and a home.

For fourteen years Malcolm lived with Siward, during which time he grew into an able and attractive young man. Finally Siward decided it was time that his nephew was returned to his inheritance. We do not know what messages, if any, passed between Siward and Macbeth, but clearly no agreement was reached.

In 1054 Siward raised the military forces of his Earldom. He gathered a mighty army and a fleet and set out northwards with Malcolm in his train. At some unidentified site, Siward met the Scottish army in a great battle. The Scots were utterly defeated, and many noblemen killed. Macbeth fled northwards. However, the English also suffered heavy casualties and Siward's son Osbern was killed. The victory established Malcolm Canmore as the ruler of the borderlands of Cumbria and Lothian.

The following spring Siward died. His place as Earl was taken by Tostig, son of the powerful Earl of Wessex, Godwin (see above). Malcolm at once made friends with Tostig and in 1047 was able to defeat and kill Macbeth at the Battle of Dunsinane.

— ♛ —

ISAAC COMNENUS (?–1061)

Usurped: Byzantine Empire 1057
Social Origins: Provincial Aristocracy

The Comnenus family came originally from southern Italy, but by the opening of the second millenium were firmly established as landed nobility in Asia Minor. The family was destined to provide Byzantine Emperors for much of the 11th and 12th centuries. The base of their power was laid by Isaac and his father Manuel Eroticus.

Manuel served as a highly successful general under Basil II, gaining great distinction. His son, Isaac, likewise entered the army and led a brilliant military career. In 1056 the popular Empress Theodora was succeeded by Michael VI, her designated heir. The Emperor was not popular, however, and the ambitious Isaac decided that his time had come.

He began organizing a conspiracy, and recruited many generals to his cause. Perhaps they had become exasperated by the degenerate state of Imperial finances which had a serious influence on their own military effectiveness. Assured of military support, Isaac travelled to Constantinople where he stirred up the people and overthrew Michael.

Isaac held power for two years, during which time he reorganized Imperial administration and set the finances in order. In 1059 Isaac retired to a monastery where he spent the remaining two years of his life.

Peter Cadalus HONORIUS II (1009–1072)

Usurped: Papal Throne 1061
Social Origins: Bishop

By the mid-11th century the whole Roman Church was in the throes of a massive reform movement. The eager young idealists wished the Church to take a great spiritual lead, staffed by men of the highest moral tone. They were opposed by secular rulers who felt their power was threatened and by older clerics who had a more pragmatic approach to moral leadership of a wayward flock. The great reforming Pope, Leo IX (Pope 1049–1054) was succeeded by other, equally fervent Popes. The reformation was gaining ground fast. It was against this background that Peter Cadalus made his bid for the papacy.

In April 1061 the reforming Pope Nicholas II died. There was an immediate anti-reforming backlash. The nobility of Rome, whose powers were being stripped away by the new ideas, immediately sent messengers to the Emperor Henry IV, hailing him as Patrician of the Romans. The holder of this ancient office had, before the reforms, been empowered to nominate a Pope. The nobles urged Henry to declare a reactionary as Pope. A group of Italian bishops arrived at about the same time with a similar request.

Henry, at this time, was only 11 years old and power lay with his mother Agnes. A member of the royal family, Peter Cadalus, who was Bishop of Parma, heard what was going on and made his way to the Imperial court. Here he gained the backing of Agnes and on 28 October 1061 was elected Pope by Henry IV and a collection of bishops. He took the name of Honorius II.

With a strong force of German troops, Honorius made the difficult winter crossing of the Alps and marched on Rome. He arrived in April to find that the reforming clergy had already gathered in Rome and elected Alexander II as Pope. Honorius wasted little time in ejecting Alexander and taking over the pontifical throne.

By the autumn of 1062 the claims and counterclaims of the rival Popes had reached such a stage that the Imperial court decided to sort out the matter. Agnes had by this time died and the new regent was in favour of the church reform movement. The court accordingly found in favour of Alexander.

Honorius was far from discouraged. He fortified himself and his troops in the Castel Sant'Angelo and refused to leave Rome. Only after a grand international synod of bishops had repudiated him and acknowledged Alexander did Honorius abandon his attempts to hold the papal throne. He retired to northern Italy and died in 1072.

— 👑 —

ALEXIUS I Comnenus (1048–1118)

Usurped: Byzantine Empire 1081
Social Origins: Imperial Family

In 1071 the army of the Byzantine Empire was smashed by the Turks and much territory in Asia Minor lost. Other defeats followed in Italy. The Emperor Nicephorus III was clearly unable to cope with the situation. Alexius Comnenus, a senior general and a relative of the earlier Emperor Isaac Comnenus, decided that the time had come for a firm hand on government. Naturally he thought that he could provide it.

In 1081 Alexius led his troops in rebellion and ousted Nicephorus, who retired to a monastery. Alexius began his reign badly. At the Battle of Durazzo, in modern Albania, his forces were overwhelmed by an invading force of Italian Normans. However, later successes against the Pecheneg barbarians and the Normans restored his prestige.

Alexius's great contribution to history came in 1095. In that year he decided to tackle the Turkish problem on the Empire's eastern frontier. He sent a message to Pope Urban II asking for military aid from the West to throw back the rising tide of Islam. There can be little doubt that Alexius had intended that the Pope should recruit some mercenaries and send them to the East. Instead the Pope sent messengers throughout Europe preaching a holy war against the Muslims. The result was a massive army numbering over 100,000 men which set out on what became known as the First Crusade.

In 1096 Alexius had to call on all his reserves of tact and diplomacy to ensure the passage of such a huge force through his territories. In the event the Crusade brought him mixed fortune. The Crusaders defeated the Turks, but refused to hand over their conquests to the Empire, but at least the Islamic pressure was relieved for a number of years.

Rodrigo Diaz y Vivar, EL CID (c. 1040–1099)

Usurped: Power in Valencia 1094
Social Origins: Nobleman

Known to history by his title of El Cid, which means 'the leader' or 'the lord', Rodrigo Diaz y Vivar is one of the most famous and dominating figures of Spanish history. He is also one of the least understood. El Cid is often represented as a valiant Christian knight struggling against the Moslems. The truth is far more complicated and romantic.

El Cid was the leading noble and military commander of Castille in 1072 when Alfonso VI became king. After some early difficulties, the nobles accepted Alfonso, but the king never forgot these early suspicions. For nine years El Cid led the forces of Castille in a series of brilliant campaigns, defeating the Moslems at every turn. El Cid was a military commander of genius, able to use and inspire his troops with great skill. His name became the terror of the enemy and the mere knowledge that he commanded an opposing force was enough to dishearten the Moslems.

In 1081, however, Alfonso argued with El Cid and banished him. El Cid then sold his sword to the Moslem ruler in Saragossa, but was careful to avoid fighting against his home kingdom. By 1094 El Cid had built up a private army of nearly 10,000 men. These warriors followed him because of his fame, skill and extraordinary luck.

Cid ruydiaz.

El Cid
The heroic qualities of the Spanish knight Rodrigo Diaz are depicted in this early engraving. It was the unbroken string of military successes which gave this man his sobriquets of El Cid, meaning Lord, and El Campeador, meaning Champion. By combining military glory with political acumen, this landless adventurer made himself master of one of the greatest cities of Medieval Spain.

In 1094 El Cid captured the city of Valencia for his master. As soon as he was installed, however, El Cid renounced his allegiance and declared for Alfonso. In reality, El Cid had set himself up as an independent Prince. Alfonso was too distant and El Cid too strong for the announcement of allegiance to have any real meaning. For five years the Moslem rulers of southern Spain threw their forces against El Cid, but every attack came to grief. It was during these years that El Cid won his reputation as a champion of Christianity. In 1099 he died and Valencia was at once recaptured by the Moors.

TANCRED (c. 1050–1112)
Usurped: Power in Antioch 1111
Social Origins: Italo-Norman nobleman

When the First Crusade left Europe for the East in 1096, Tancred was one of the most enthusiastic members of the movement. He served under his uncle Bohemond of Tarentum. Along with other Crusaders, Tancred promised to enter the service of the Byzantine Emperor Alexius I (see above), and to hand over all conquests to the Empire, as the price for transport to Asia Minor.

He took part in the successful siege of Antioch in 1098 and fought valiantly at the storming of Jerusalem. After achieving this staggering success the Crusaders settled down to rule their lands. Forgetting the promises to the Emperor, they divided the lands amongst themselves. Bohemond was given the great city of Antioch and surrounding lands. After a serious defeat by the Moslems, Bohemond accepted Byzantine overlordship. All this time Tancred had taken a leading role in the civil government and military operations of the city. On occasion he acted as deputy when Bohemond was absent.

In 1111 Bohemond died. The claims of his son were ignored by Tancred who immediately seized the reins of power. Taking the title of Prince of Antioch, Tancred threw off the power of the Byzantines. He now acted as the completely independent monarch he had become. He died after only a year in power, but his fame lived on in the songs of minstrels and troubadours.

HENRY I (1068–1135)
Usurped: Kingdom of England 1100
Social Origins: Royal Family

The usurpation carried out by Henry I of England was one of the smoothest and most efficient in history. So well executed was the power bid that even today we cannot be certain exactly how it was carried out, nor the extent of Henry's role.

Henry was the best educated, strongest and most able of the sons of William the Conqueror, but it was his misfortune to be the youngest. When William died the eldest son, Robert, received Normandy, while the second son, William was made king of England. Henry, though well provided for, received no share of power. He had to await the death of one of his brothers. It seems that in the year 1100, Henry decided to take action. Robert was away on the First Crusade, while William Rufus stayed in England. If Henry stood any chance at all of gaining power, he would have to act before Robert returned.

On 2 August 1100, William led a hunting party, which included Henry, into the New Forest. Towards evening an arrow slammed into the king's chest and killed him outright. The party later announced that an arrow shot by a man named Tirel had glanced off a stag and hit the king. The story was patently false. Not only did Tirel deny the story, but a glancing arrow was unlikely to have enough force to cause instant death.

Henry at once made for the Royal Treasury at nearby Winchester. Three days later Henry was crowned king. He issued a long and complicated charter in which he promised to put right the evil's of William's reign, imprisoned the powerful and unpopular Prince Bishop of Durham who was one of the three most powerful men in England other than the King, and married a member of the old Royal House of England. The usurpation was complete.

The rapid coronation and other equally decisive actions seem to indicate that Henry had his bid for power well planned. If Robert had been in Normandy, instead of in distant Palestine, he might have intervened and taken the throne himself. It is clear that Henry acted swiftly to stop Robert claiming a crown which should have been his. The question remains; how was Henry ready to act with such speed unless he knew when William was going to die? The truth behind the arrow which struck down William Rufus on that summer evening will probably never be known, but it came at a very fortuitous moment for Henry.

Maurice, GREGORY VIII (c. 1070–c. 1140)

Usurped: Papal Throne 1118
Social Origins: Commoner

Maurice, who was later to become the anti-Pope Gregory VIII seems to have been a very difficult man. There can be no doubt about his learning and intelligence, but he was constantly involved in arguments with other churchmen. It may have been this which predisposed him to launch his bid for power.

After a distinguished early career, and a pilgrimage to the Holy Land, Maurice became Archbishop of Braga, in Spain. He immediately fell out with the Bishop of Toledo as to the extent of the latter's diocese. No sooner was this matter settled by Pope Paschal II than Maurice argued with the clergy of Santiago, precipitating another complicated controversy. In 1116 Maurice visited Rome, hoping to gain a favourable decision.

Instead Paschal sent Maurice on a delicate diplomatic mission to the Emperor Henry V. It was a disastrous decision. Still smarting from the wrongs he believed had been done to him, Maurice at once took the Emperor's part in a dispute with Paschal. In 1117 Maurice crowned Henry against Paschal's wishes. Maurice was excommunicated, which he saw as yet another unprovoked insult.

The year 1118 saw Henry V in Rome to meet the new Pope Gelasius II. The new Pope, however, refused to meet him and fled the city. Henry was furious and announced that Gelasius had been deposed. Maurice was on hand and put himself forward to replace Gelasius. He was duly enthroned and took the title and powers of the Pope, though Gelasius was still alive.

The following year Gelasius died and his clergy elected Calistus II to take his place. Calistus II came to an agreement with Henry, leaving Gregory without support. He managed to hold on for a while, but in 1121 he was captured by Calistus and imprisoned for life.

WILLIAM THE MISERABLE (?–1128)

Usurped: County of Flanders 1128
Social Origins: Nobleman

William was given the name of 'the Miserable' during his own lifetime, and it was a name he earned. His life was one of constant ill-fortune which would have made anyone miserable. He did not even enjoy his final triumph, for at the moment of victory he died in agony.

William was the son of Robert, Duke of Normandy, and grandson of William the Conqueror. No doubt he looked forward to inheriting this wealthy Duchy. However, in 1106 Robert was defeated by his ambitious brother Henry, King of England, and imprisoned. Robert himself probably did not resent the event too much. He was given a fine mansion and allowed as much food, wine and women as he wanted, and indeed did not make any attempt to escape.

William, however, became a footloose nobleman wandering through Europe. He tried several times to regain his Duchy, but the attempts never came to anything. After twenty years without a home, William became betrothed to the daughter of the Count of Anjou. The lady's inheritance would have made him a wealthy nobleman. However his watchful Uncle Henry stepped in and halted the marriage.

Then, in 1128, Count Charles of Flanders died without an heir. William was a distant relative and hurriedly persuaded King Louis V of France to back his claim. Louis gave William the core of an army and William set out for Flanders. However, the nobles of Flanders had already chosen Thierry of Alsace as the new Count. On 21 June 1128 William's army met that of Thierry at Thielt. By cunningly posting a sizeable reserve in hiding, William was able to launch a surprise attack at a crucial moment and he won the day.

William took over government in Flanders with the aid of his French troops. He then received the welcome news that the nobles of Normandy, who resented Henry's plan to install his daughter Matilda as heiress, wanted him as their Duke. Fortune seemed to be smiling on William the Miserable at last. However in a skirmish with supporters of Henry, William was injured. The wound turned septic and he died five days later.

STEPHEN (c. 1097–1154)

Usurped: Kingdom of England 1135
Social Origins: Royal Family

Stephen launched a swift and decisive coup which swept all before it and installed him on the throne, though he was not the heir and had an elder brother still living. Once in power, however, Stephen showed himself incapable of keeping it.

Henry I, King of England, choked to death on a lamprey on 1 December 1135. Before his death he had named his daughter Matilda as heir and made all the nobles, including Stephen, swear to follow her. Unfortunately, Matilda's spiteful temper and haughty pride had alienated the nobles. The unpopular actions of her husband, Geoffrey Plantagenet, did little to help her. Stephen must have known of this dislike, he was, after all, one of the most powerful nobles in England. He realized that his royal blood, distant though it was, gave him a good claim to the throne. He carefully laid his plans.

When Henry died, Stephen was on the continent. He at once rode to the coast and took ship for England. The first port he tried was Dover, but the civic authorities realized what he was up to and refused to admit him into the town. The same thing happened at Canterbury, but Stephen was undeterred and spurred on to London. Here he was both known and liked. The Londoners opened their gates and cheered Stephen. He promised to be a good king, and promptly executed some robbers to prove his point.

Barely pausing, Stephen and his entourage galloped down to Winchester where the Royal Treasure was kept. Here he met his brother, Henry, and together they persuaded the officials to open the treasury. On 22 December Stephen had himself crowned by the Archbishop of Canterbury. The excuse given for ignoring the true heir, Matilda, was that she had married the unpopular Geoffrey without the consent of the council of nobles. This consent had not been needed for the marriage, but Stephen managed to get the Church to sanction this spurious reason by giving the clergy enormous legal freedoms and benefits.

By Christmas, Stephen was firmly installed as king. Matilda, however, refused to accept the usurpation without a struggle. With the aid of Robert Earl of Gloucester she began a civil war which was to drag on for years. Stephen never quite lost his throne, but neither did he entirely suppress Matilda. He died in 1154 and the throne passed to Matilda's son Henry II.

LOTHAIR II (c. 1060–1137)

Usurped: Holy Roman Empire 1125
Social Origins: Lesser Nobility

By the 12th century the Holy Roman Empire had evolved a complex system of succession, based upon the old system of election. Before his death, the Emperor was expected to nominate a successor. When the Emperor died the chief nobles would meet, the Archbishop of Mainz would formally put forward the claim of the designated heir and the nobles would then acclaim him. Lothair wrecked the system and seized power, but in the process began a struggle which was to endure for centuries.

Henry V nominated as his successor Frederick Hohenstaufen, Duke of Swabia. However both Henry and Frederick had fallen out with Archbishop Adalbert of Mainz. Lothair, Duke of Saxony decided to take advantage of this. Born into a minor noble family, Lothair had gained his duchy through a marriage arranged by Henry V. Any thoughts of gratitude to Henry which may have occurred to Lothair were soon suppressed.

When Henry died and the nobles met, Lothair persuaded Adalbert to nominate him, instead of Frederick. Lothair had no connection whatsoever with the Imperial Family, but merely claimed that the nobles were entitled to choose the Emperor they wished, and that he was the best man for the task. Adalbert, recognizing a useful tool when he saw one, duly nominated Lothair. The dukes were somewhat suprised, as they had expected Frederick to be named. In a rather stormy meeting the nobles were induced to elect Lothair as Emperor.

Though beaten, Frederick was not finished. He consistently resisted Lothair's policies. The Emperor, meanwhile, gave in to the demands of the Church and nobles in order to gain support. For decades afterwards the Hohenstaufens and the Welfs, as Lothair's family was known, were bitter enemies. The rivalry spilled over into Italy and rumbled on for centuries. The novel form of Lothair's election set a precedent. Thereafter the nobles elected the man they wanted. This inevitably led to a succession of weak Emperors, and the gradual break up of the Empire.

Taira KIYOMORI (?–1181)

Usurped: Power in Japan circa 1156
Social Origins: Samurai

The rise to power of Taira Kiyomori was a long process of intrigue and violence. It is difficult to pinpoint a date at which his power became unassailable. But if such a moment must be chosen, it would be the celebrated Hogen Incident of 1156.

Kiyomori belonged to the powerful Taira clan of samurai. Early in life he entered court politics. The usual infighting at court which was accepted behaviour in Japan at this time, was made more ruthless by Kiyomori's ready recourse to the support of samurai warriors. In 1156 one of the court intrigues between factions of the Imperial family came to blows. Kiyomori took the side of the Emperor and set out to attack his rivals at the palace of Shirakawaden.

The ensuing battle was one of the earliest full scale encounters between samurai. Kiyomori and his chief protagonist Tametomo, of the powerful Minamoto clan, went through all the niceties of samurai honour. Challenges were read, duels fought and ritual arrows exchanged. When the fighting began in earnest, however, Kiyomori won a devastating victory. He had made himself indispensable to the Emperor and at the same time had crushed rival samurai clans.

Soon Kiyomori was made chief minister and other government posts distributed to the Taira. In 1164 Taira power was threatened by turbulent monks, who wished to gain court influence. The monks marched through the streets of the capital, carrying sacred objects with them to show their holy power. It could have been a difficult time for Kiyomori, for the influence of the monks was great and their moral ascendency taken for granted. As the monks approached the Imperial palace, Kiyomori stepped out to meet them. He did not even attempt to parley with them. Instead he picked up his bow and sent an arrow slamming into the shrine of holy objects. The monks wisely took the hint, bowed before the power of violence over that of morals and withdrew.

Kiyomori strengthened his position by a series of marriages. In 1180 he was gratified to see his grandson assume the throne. As chief minister for an infant, Kiyomori had undisputed power. He enjoyed it for a full year before his death.

SALADIN (1138–1193)

Usurped: Sultanate of Egypt 1169
Social Origins: Military Family

Saladin, or Salah al Din as his name is more correctly spelt, is best known for his implacable opposition to the Christian Crusaders. In particular, the long struggle between himself and Richard the Lionheart of England is known for its excitement and romance. Yet Saladin came to power through at least two acts of treachery and violence.

Born the son of a successful general, Saladin also followed a military career. In 1154 he was made Governor of Damascus by the great leader Nur ed Din. Fifteen years later Saladin travelled to Egypt ostensibly on a good-will visit to Sultan Shawar, but in reality to seize his throne for Nur ed Din. Soon after arriving, Saladin invited Shawar to accompany him on a pilgrimage to a nearby shrine. The Sultan accepted at once. If he had any suspicions of Saladin's motives they were dispelled by the fact that pilgrimages were a holy duty and pilgrims were sacred. To interfere with a pilgrim would have been sacrilege of the worst kind. Shawar felt safe, but he did not know Saladin.

As the two men rode side by side, Saladin leapt on Shawar and bore him from the saddle. Saladin pinned the Sultan to the ground and ordered him to be beheaded. With the Sultan dead, Saladin moved quickly. He ruthlessly crushed all opposition to the new regime. Within six months he could report to Nur ed Din that the vast resources of Egypt were at his command.

Saladin
A European view of Saladin dressed in the sumptuous robes he wore as Sultan of Egypt, a throne he gained through murder. Later in his career, Saladin became famous as the opponent of the Christian Crusaders in the Holy Land and for his great battles against the English warrior-king Richard the Lionheart. (*Mary Evans*)

Saladin became governor of Egypt for Nur ed Din and fought valiantly against the Crusaders. He was winning a great reputation for himself and building a power base among the army.

In 1175 Nur ed Din died leaving the throne to his young son. When Saladin heard the news, he gathered a highly mobile force from his Egyptian army and raced to Damascus. Once there, Saladin ensured the disappearance of the true heir, and used his troops to persuade the people to accept him as Sultan. With the resources of Egypt and Syria at his command, Saladin turned on the Crusading states. He very nearly succeeded in gaining complete victory. But the arrival of the Third Crusade and King Richard halted his triumphal progress. His final years were taken up with almost constant warfare.

RICHARD De Clare, STRONGBOW (?–1176)

Usurped: Power in Leinster 1171

Social Origins: Anglo-Norman Nobleman

Strongbow came to Ireland as the result of a deadly feud which had begun many years earlier. His interference did not halt the hostility he found, but merely gave it a new direction.

In 1151 King Dermot McMurchad of Leinster carried off the beautiful Derbforgail, wife of a minor king. A short time later Roderick O'Connor, High King of Ireland, ordered Dermot to return the woman. When Dermot refused a bloody feud became inevitable. Eventually the struggle resolved itself into a battle for the position of High King. After 15 years of warfare Roderick O'Connor was clearly getting the better of the struggle. Dermot came to England to ask for military aid. He found it in the shape of Richard de Clare, Earl of Pembroke, known to friends and enemies alike as Strongbow.

In the summer of 1170 Strongbow arrived in Ireland with an army of 1,200 men, including a large contingent of heavily-armoured knights. Within a matter of days he had captured Waterford for Dermot. Strongbow then raced on to Dublin, where his men forced their way into the city and rampaged through the streets until the authorities surrendered.

At about this time Dermot married his daughter Aife to Strongbow. With the bride, Strongbow received the promise that he would inherit the Kingdom of Leinster under the High Kingship of Dermot. Strongbow must have been greatly pleased, but he was being tricked by Dermot. Under Irish custom thrones could not be inherited through the female line, nor could a king bequeath his title outside his kinship group. Dermot's promise had no validity in law. The kingdom should have passed to one of his numerous male relatives.

Early in 1171, Dermot unexpectedly died. Strongbow, not unnaturally, claimed his inheritance of Leinster, but was faced with the opposition of the royal kinship and Irish law. Strongbow found an effective counter-argument: the lances of his Anglo-Norman knights. The Leinstermen could not face this show of force and Strongbow was hailed as King.

Soon afterwards King Henry II of England summoned Strongbow. He was becoming worried about the growing power of his subject. Strongbow hastened to the English court to reaffirm his loyalty and lay all his conquests at the disposal of King Henry. Henry paid a short visit to Ireland and then left Strongbow to enjoy his new-found power.

— ♔ —

ANDRONICUS Comnenus (c. 1110–1185)

Usurped: Byzantine Empire 1183
Social Origins: Imperial Family

Long before he became Emperor, Andronicus had an unpleasant reputation as a self-interested, untrustworthy adventurer of the most ruthless kind. His career more than justifies his reputation.

Born in about 1110, Andronicus was a grandson of Emperor Alexius Comnenus I but he belonged to a cadet branch of the Imperial family and had little prospect of reaching the throne. He entered the army and fought in frequent wars against the Muslim enemies of the Empire. Here he won many battles and acquired an enormous amount of loot. In 1153 Andronicus began plotting against the Emperor Manuel, but the conspiracy was discovered and Andronicus was thrown into gaol.

Twelve years later warfare flared between the Empire and the Hungarians. Andronicus managed to escape from prison at this point and raced northwards to the court of Yaroslav, Prince of Kiev. Using every argument he could think of, Andronicus persuaded Yaroslav to attack the Hungarians from the north while the Byzantines were advancing from the south. The plan resulted in defeat for the Hungarians. Manuel was so grateful that he appointed Andronicus as Governor of Cilicia. Three years later, however, Andronicus ran off with Theodora, Manuel's niece. Once again Andronicus was in disgrace.

In 1180 Manuel died and Alexius Comnenus II, a young boy, came to the throne. Andronicus moved back to court and quickly won influence with the young Emperor and the chief nobles. In 1183 Andronicus ordered the murder of Alexius II and seized the throne for himself. He turned on the nobles who had helped him and stripped them of much of their power. When they objected, he brutally crushed all opposition to his rule.

In the late summer of 1185 Andronicus left Constantinople for a few days. While he was absent the nobility stirred up the mob and a riot broke out. Andronicus raced back to restore order. Entering the Hippodrome to address the populace, he was set upon by rioters and, quite literally, torn to pieces.

Minamoto YORITOMO (?–1195)
Usurped: Power in Japan 1185
Social Origins: Samurai

Yoritomo, chief of the Minamoto clan, was the head of one of the most powerful samurai families in Japan. He was not, however, a great fighter himself. He preferred to leave that dangerous occupation to other Minamoto. It is likely he would never have achieved supreme power if it had not been for the rash action of one of his clan.

In 1180 the courtier Minamoto Yorimasa raised a rebellion against the infant Emperor Antoku, who was dominated by the Taira clan. The palace rising was a fiasco and Yorimasa and his Minamoto supporters were soon fleeing before the Taira army. Yorimasa himself committed hara-kiri. This extremely painful form of suicide involved slitting open the abdomen with two sword cuts. It was considered the only method by which a defeated samurai could preserve his honour.

Yorimasa was dead, but the Taira leader, Kiyomori was determined to destroy all the rebels. This inevitably involved Yoritomo, who was honour bound to protect his fellow clan members. In the first clash Yoritomo took personal control of the Minamoto army, but was heavily defeated. Thereafter he gave military command to his extremely capable younger brother Yoshitsune. Yorimoto devoted himself to weaving political alliances against the Taira and administering the Minamoto war machine. The talents of Yoritomo were well recognized by his enemy Kiyomori. As the latter lay on his deathbed he called his followers and announced his dying wish. 'Lay the head of Yoritomo on my tomb' he said.

But Kiyomori's successors were not as able as he and by 1185 the Taira had been totally defeated. Yorimoto was the undisputed power in Japan. He confiscated Taira estates, distributing them to his loyal Minamoto. Over the

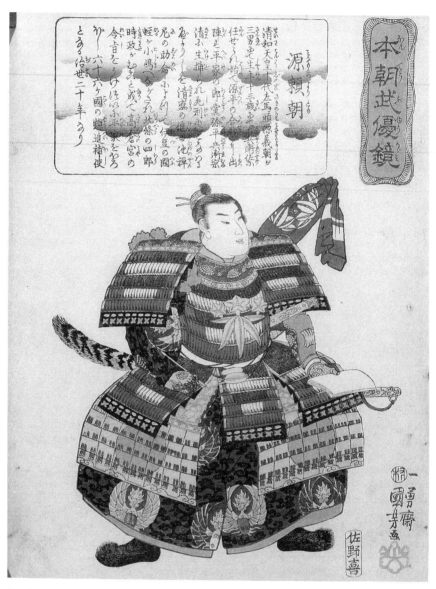

Yoritomo Minamoto

Yoritomo Minamoto is depicted here in the lacquered armour of the samurai warrior class to which he belonged. Although Yoritomo often emphasized the military nature of his regime, he was actually a rather poor general who left the business of fighting to other members of his clan. He himself preferred to concentrate on diplomacy and politics, the real basis of his success. (*Macdonald/Aldus*) following years, Yoritomo completely reshaped Japanese government institutions.

He was given the title of Shogun by the helpless Emperor. The title was a form of temporary military dictatorship which had previously been granted to able generals for limited periods of time. It literally translated as 'barbarian-quelling generalissimo'. Yoritomo's shogunate, additionally, had no time limit. In fact the title and powers were to pass to his successors for nearly seven centuries before the Emperors regained power. As Shogun, Yoritomo had a military representative working alongside the civilian governor of each province. With this formidable network of military strongmen, Yoritomo imposed his reforms and maintained his power undisturbed.

— 👑 —

ISAAC II Angelus (?–1204)

Usurped: Byzantine Empire 1185
Social Origins: Nobleman

Isaac Angelus considered himself a wronged man, and launched his bid for the Imperial throne to right his grievances. The path he took led only to greater sufferings and hardships.

The Angelus family was a minor branch of the Imperial Comnenus clan, but the connection was so distant that they behaved and were treated as were other nobles. When the Emperor Andronicus (see above) instituted his supression of the power of the nobility, the Angeli suffered more than most. Isaac felt that he had been dealt a personal blow by his remote kinsman. Together with other disgruntled nobles he roused a mob which killed Andronicus in September 1185.

Isaac then persuaded the noblemen to install him as Emperor in place of the murdered monarch. During his reign, Isaac energetically fought against the enemies of the Empire. When he was campaigning with the army in 1195, Isaac heard that his brother Alexius had ousted the Imperial advisers and installed himself as Emperor. Isaac hurried home, but he was seized by partisans of his brother, blinded and locked up in prison.

Isaac's son, also named Alexius, fled to the court of the Holy Roman Emperor Philip. Philip sent the young prince south to join the German contingent mustering for the Fourth Crusade. In the younger Alexius the Venetians and Germans saw a useful tool. On the pretext of reinstating the imprisoned Isaac, the Crusader leaders attacked Constantinople. In 1204, after a long and bloody siege the city fell.

The aging Isaac was taken from prison and installed as a puppet Emperor.

It was hardly surprising that the Byzantines refused to acknowledge an Emperor elevated by such a barbaric foreign invasion and Alexius the Elder set up a rival Imperial government at Trebizond. Isaac died in 1204 and was succeeded by the younger Alexius who was entirely dominated by the Doge of Venice. The Byzantine Empire seemed poised on the edge of chaos and total collapse.

CATHAL Crobderg (?–1224)
Usurped: High Kingship of Ireland 1191
Social Origins: Royal Family

The fact that Cathal was able to launch his usurpation shows that the exploits of the adventurer Strongbow (see above) and his fellow Anglo-Normans did not have as great an effect on Ireland as might be supposed. The Strongbow and his companions fitted into the prevailing Irish political situation, rather than overthrowing it. Only when later English involvement grew in scale did the activities of Strongbow appear so significant.

The many great and petty kingdoms of Ireland had a complex network of relationships which culminated in the title of High King of Ireland. At this time this position was not strictly confined to a single dynasty, nor did it carry supreme political power. The title was simply a recognition that a king had more power and influence than any of the other 150 or so kings.

In 1166 the position of High King was secured by Roderick O'Connor. Nine years later Roderick accepted Henry II of England as overlord in return for a restraining hand on Anglo-Norman adventurers in Ireland. In fact Roderick took little notice of his overlord. He continued to exercise his power in Ireland and to indulge in the feuds for which Irish royalty were famous.

In 1191 Cathal, half-brother to Roderick, led a family faction against the High King and overthrew him. Cathal assumed the troubled title of High King while Roderick retired to a monastery. It would be interesting to know which brother was the happier after the usurpation.

ALEXIUS DUCAS (?–1205)

Usurped: Byzantine Empire 1204
Social Origins: Nobleman

Alexius Ducas came to power at a moment of great crisis for the Byzantine Empire. He proved unable to cope with the emergency and paid the ultimate price for failure.

In the autumn of 1204 the victorious army of the Fourth Crusade was camped outside the gates of Constantinople while their puppet Emperor Alexius IV carried out their wishes. (See Isaac Angelus above). As Chief Steward of the Empire, Alexius IV chose Alexius Ducas. This fiercely proud aristocrat came from one of the grandest families in Constantinople and greatly resented the demands imposed on the Empire by the Crusaders. He considered the westerners little better than barbarians.

In his capacity of Chief Steward, Ducas consistently tried to thwart the Crusaders' demands. Alexius IV admired the westerners and owed them a great debt for placing him on the throne. However, he was no match for Ducas in the ancient Byzantine skill of palace intrigue. By the late autumn, Ducas had rallied the proud Byzantines to his cause of resistance. He felt strong enough to take the throne from Alexius IV, puppet of the hated foreigners.

One day Ducas arrived at court unbidden and at the head of a sizeable band of soldiers. He brushed aside the protests of court officials and burst into the Emperor's apartments. Minutes later Alexius IV lay dead at Ducas's feet, strangled by a bowstring. Ducas immediately proclaimed himself to be Emperor Alexius V.

The new Emperor shut and barricaded the gates of the city, set about strengthening the defences and fired an arrow into the camp of the Crusaders. Through the winter a series of skirmishes took place before the walls, but no serious fighting occurred. On 9 April 1205 the Crusaders launched a massive and meticulously planned assault. Ducas took personal command of the defences, and after a long and bloody struggle the Crusaders were thrown back. Ducas was jubilant, his takeover had been vindicated.

But the Crusaders were not finished. They remained outside the walls. When they launched a second attack, a small group managed to break through a blocked gateway and enter the city. Ducas heard the news, panicked and fled. The great city was given over to slaughter and loot by the Crusaders. The magnificent library, with volumes dating back to before Christ, was burned. When the pillage was over, Count Henry of Flanders was proclaimed the new Emperor. Ducas went on the run, but by losing

Constantinople he had lost his support. He was quickly caught by his enemies, dragged back to the Imperial City and executed.

OTTOKAR I (?–1230)

Usurped: Kingdom of Bohemia 1196
Social Origins: Royal Family

In the late 12th century Bohemia was a relatively sparsely populated kingdom. It lay around the Upper Elbe and formed the easternmost frontier of the Holy Roman Empire where the lands of Western Christendom met those of the wild Magyars and Slavs.

Earlier rulers of Bohemia had secured for themselves the title of king, establishing virtual independence within the loose framework of the Empire. In the 1190s Ladislaus III was proving himself to be a remarkably undistinguished monarch A group of disaffected noblemen gathered around the king's younger and more dynamic brother, Ottokar. In 1196 Ottokar led a power seizure which ousted Ladislaus and placed himself firmly on the throne.

Almost immediately a dispute broke out over the Imperial title between Philip of Swabia and Otto of Saxony. Ottokar cunningly avoided declaring his outright support for either candidate. Instead he dangled the bait of Bohemian support before both candidates and so increased his wealth and power. By the time of his death in 1230, Ottokar had added the large province of Moravia to his kingdom.

OTTO IV (c. 1182–1218)

Usurped: Holy Roman Empire 1198
Social Origins: Nobleman

The usurpation of Otto IV was a long and confused affair. Few contemporaries understood the issues at stake, and even fewer modern historians have been able to sort out the claims and counterclaims put out by Otto and his rival Philip of Swabia. The tangled process was put in motion when the Emperor Henry VI died in 1197.

The Emperor left an heir in the shape of a one year old son named Frederick, but it was unthinkable that such a helpless infant should be Emperor. The boy was sent to Sicily as a ward of the Pope and the crown passed to Henry's younger brother Philip of Swabia. However the Hohenstaufen family had many enemies within the Empire. Otto of Saxony, of the Welf faction, decided that Henry's death marked the time to unite opposition under his own banner.

Otto immediately had himself crowned as Emperor by the Archbishop of Cologne. Unfortunately, Philip had the Imperial crown and regalia, so Otto had to make do with fakes. Nonetheless it was an impressive ceremony and was held at the Imperial Cathedral of Aachen. Philip, though he had the real crown had been crowned at a provincial cathedral, so that neither man had carried out the correct ritual. Otto then issued a torrent of claim and propaganda invoking ancient law and custom in his favour. Philip struck back with an equally formidable weight of argument. Both men appealed to Pope Innocent III to vindicate their claims, but the Pope prevaricated. He dare not risk endorsing a loser.

Germany plunged into civil war as the noble supporters of the rival Emperors fought out their differences. Early in 1208 Otto's forces were at their last gasp. The Imperial pretender fled Germany in defeat. Just one year later Philip was murdered. When he heard the news, Otto raced back to Germany. He hurriedly married Philip's daughter and set about uniting the two factions. By 1213 he had almost succeeded in producing a strong and united Empire. However, the application of pressure by the Pope and massive bribes by the French managed to de-stablize the situation. Otto was defeated by a French army at Bouvine in 1215. Rebellions broke out in Germany. He died in 1218, master of little more than his own Duchy of Saxony.

MANFRED (1231–1266)

Usurped: Kingdom of Naples 1254
Social Origins: Imperial Family

The Holy Roman Emperor Frederick II was brought up in Sicily as a ward of the Pope. Later Popes felt this gave them the right to interfere in the affairs of Sicily and Naples, which were united by a shared culture and government. In recent centuries the area had been controlled by Byzantium, the Moors and the Normans. Strong influences of each culture survived, along with sizeable minorities amongst the native population. The whole area was a cultural melting pot.

When he had gained the title and powers of Emperor, Frederick gave the territory of Taranto to his bastard son, Manfred. As governor of Taranto, Manfred was subject to the military ruler of Naples who in turn served the Empire. Frederick died in 1250, the Imperial title passing to his legitimate son Conrad IV. Conrad died soon after leaving an infant as heir.

Pope Innocent IV considered that this gave him a great opportunity to take over Southern Italy for the papacy. The Imperial governor was chased from Naples and local rulers, including Manfred, swore a vague allegiance to the Pope. When, in 1254, Innocent tried to enforce these claims, Manfred took up his sword. He stormed into the great treasury of Lucera and made off with everything he found there. With this money, Manfred recruited an army of Moslem mercenaries. He vigorously attacked the Papal troops, smashing them at Foggia. Innocent was suffering from an illness when he heard the news. The shock killed him.

The new Pope Alexander IV excommunicated Manfred. In reply Manfred invaded papal territory. In desperation Alexander turned to the belligerent French nobleman Charles of Anjou. He offered Charles the title of King of Naples if he would protect Rome. Charles led a great army south in 1265. At Benevento, early the next year, Manfred met the invaders in battle. His army was crushed and he himself killed. Naples and Sicily passed to the French. It was to prove a troublesome conquest.

— 👑 —

KUBLAI KHAN (1216–1294)

Usurped: Mongol Empire 1260

Social Origins: Imperial Family

By the late 1250s the mighty Mongol Empire was in crisis. The Great Khan Mangu managed to keep the internal pressures under control, but on his death factional violence broke out. Kublai emerged victorious from the confusion and bloodshed.

At this time the Mongol Empire stretched from Korea, through northern China, across the Central Asian steppes to the Black Sea. It had been conquered by nomadic horsemen from Mongolia under their leader Genghis Khan some 40 years earlier. There now appeared two distinct attitudes among the Mongols. Many Mongols wished to take advantage of the conquests by settling down to live as pampered lords amid luxury and opulence. The traditionalists wanted to remain nomads, milking the conquered lands of wealth and living in barbaric splendour. They looked on the faction which wished to settle as effete and soft.

Genghis Khan
A near-contemporary Chinese depiction of their great enemy Genghis Khan. Having usurped the leadership, of the Mongol tribes, Genghis Khan led them on a ruthless path of conquest and ´victory. His campaigns involved genocide and terrorism as a matter of course and probably claimed more than 35 million lives. (*Macdonald/Aldus*)

Mangu died when on campaign in western China against the remnants of the Sung Empire. Kublai, a supporter of the 'settler' faction was with him at the time. A third brother, Ariq, was at home in Mongolia living his favoured lifestyle as a nomad. The fourth brother, Hulagu, was waging a bloody war in distant Persia.

Ariq called a meeting at which he was proclaimed Great Khan. He soon made it clear his support lay with the traditionalist faction. Kublai, too, had himself proclaimed Great Khan and led his army to Mongolia. For four years the superb Mongolian warriors slaughtered each other by the thousand on the open steppes. Massive armies wheeled and manoeuvred at high speed. Eventually Ariq was killed and Kublai assumed the undisputed mantle of Great Khan.

By 1279 Kublai had completed the conquest of China. He took the title of Emperor of China. He turned his back on the steppes and settled down to lead the life of a Chinese Emperor. His court became as ostentatiously luxurious as any before it. For a while Kublai and his successors continued to rule as Mongol Emperors of China. But gradually the nobles and Emperors forgot their origins. They lost the natural hardness and tenacity of steppe peoples and became lacking in energy and determination. Eventually the Chinese drove the Mongols out. Ariq had been right after all. Kublai's name is sometimes given as Qubilai.

— 👑 —

BAIBERS Al Bundukdari (?–1277)

Usurped: Sultanate of Egypt 1260

Social Origins: Mameluke (Slave-soldier)

Baibers was born in the Caucasus Mountains to Christian parents. As a baby, however, he was sold to Moslem slave traders and taken to Egypt. There Baibers joined the ranks of the Mamelukes. These slave-soldiers were brought up as fundamentalist Moslems, trained to fight for Islam and to crush all resistance. They formed a powerful section of the army of Egypt, which was subject to Syria at this time.

Baibers grew up to be a tall, broad and immensely strong man. This physical prowess combined with military skill to bring Baibers high command. He installed fellow Mamelukes, whom he could trust, as senior officers. In 1260, after achieving a brilliant victory over Crusaders under Louis IX of France, Baibers received unpleasant news. The Sultan, Turanshah, was holding a feast for his leading emirs, or noblemen, in a tent beside the Nile. The Sultan had become jealous of Baibers's success and was demoting the Mamelukes in favour of emirs.

Baibers knew that he could not long survive such a change of heart by the Sultan. He gathered a band of Mamelukes and raced to the tent. With drawn sword, Baibers burst into the feast. Turanshah saw Baibers' angry face and fled. He hid in a tower, but Baibers set fire to the building. When the Sultan ran from the flames, Baibers gave chase. A mameluke spear struck Turanshah who dived into the Nile. Mamelukes leapt into the river and dragged Turanshah ashore, where Baibers hacked him to death.

Baibers replaced Turanshah as ruler of Egypt. Soon after this violent coup, Baibers found himself opposed by his overlord Sultan Kutuz of Syria. Baibers solved this problem by literally stabbing Kutuz in the back and taking over his territory. For the remaining 15 years of his life, Baibers maintained an iron grip on his lands. He waged ceaseless war on the Crusaders and succeeded in crushing the power of the Christians.

PETER III, King of Aragon (?–1285)

Usurped: Power in Sicily 1282
Social Origins: Spanish King

Peter of Aragon was already a crowned king when circumstances gave him the chance to seize power in Sicily and expand his kingdom. His opportunity was largely due to the activities of Charles of Anjou. In 1266 Charles had conquered Naples and Sicily at the request of the Pope (see Manfred above). He installed an administration of Frenchmen and papal officials. These men disregarded the customs and wishes of the people and relied on a strong military presence to enforce their rule. Local laws were brushed aside and tough new taxes imposed. Charles was aiming at building up a Mediterranean Empire and he needed every coin he could wring from his lands. The people suffered the impositions with growing impatience.

On the evening of 30 March 1282 a French soldier insulted a Sicilian woman at Vespers outside Palermo cathedral. The woman's husband whipped out a knife and avenged the insult in traditional fashion. The sight of a dead Frenchman released the pent-up anger of the crowd. Within seconds every Frenchmen at the service was dead. The murderous mob raced through Palermo killing any Frenchmen they met. The rising spread throughout Sicily and very few Frenchmen escaped the slaughter.

When news of the massacre reached Peter he saw his chance. Years earlier he had married the daughter of Manfred, one time King of Naples and

Sicily. Using this as the basis for a claim to the throne, Peter led a fleet to Sicily and had himself proclaimed King of Sicily. Charles of Anjou also launched an invasion and years of fighting resulted. Eventually, in 1302, Frederick, a younger son of Peter was recognized as King of Sicily. The Sicilian Vespers, as the massacre was known, had gained independence for the island.

VISHNUVARDHANA (fl.early 12th century)

Usurped: Power in the Western Ghats circa 1130
Social Origins: Tribal Chief

At the opening of the 12th century India's Western Ghats were in theory subject to the Chola kingdom, but in reality were the home of numerous mountain tribes which owed little in the way of real obedience to their distant overlords. They followed their chieftains on raids to plunder the lowlands.

Vishnuvardhana was born into one such tribe, the Hoysalas. By the time he came to lead the Hoysalas, the people of the lowlands were paying the mountain tribes to desist from attacking. Vishnuvardhana turned this ad hoc arrangement into the basis for a powerful kingdom. He led his fierce mountain tribesmen down into the lowlands. The bribes to desist from attack were converted into regular taxation. The Hoysalas then repudiated the overlordship of the Chola. Around the city of Dorasamudra, Vishnuvardhana built up a sizeable kingdom which resisted all attempts by the Chola to re-establish their dominance. The usurper's grandson Ballala was able to inherit a fine, strong kingdom which lasted for three centuries. Not a bad achievement for a bandit chief.

GOPALA (fl. mid-8th century)

Usurped: Kingdom of Bengal circa 740
Social Origins: Obscure

Virtually nothing is known of the usurpation of Gopala, and only slightly more about his reign. However, his seizure of power had a profound effect on Indian politics for several generations.

After the breakup of the powerful Empire of Harsa (see Arunasva above) many areas of northern India gained independence from the Imperial authorities. One of these was Bengal, south of the middle reaches of the Ganges. Sometime about 740 the ruler of Bengal died without an heir. A period of chaos ensued from which Gopala eventually emerged as the power in the land. His descendents later built Bengal into a major state.

Only a folk tale gives us a clue to the course of Gopala's takeover. According to this story the nobles of Bengal met to elect a new king. They did so, but that very night a demoness appeared and battered the new king to death with a club. Next day the nobles elected a second king, but he was killed in the same way. A third king was elected and followed the others to the grave. Eventually Gopala was elected. As he lay fearfully awaiting the arrival of the demoness, the goddess Chandi appeared and gave him a magical weapon. With this sacred tool, Gopala killed the demoness and so established himself in power. We shall probably never know what bloody series of murders and coups lies behind this folk tale.

— 👑 —

DIDDA (fl. mid-10th century)

Usurped: Kingdom of Kashmir circa 940
Social Origins: Royal Family

As a general rule the kingdoms of northern India did not accept rule by women. Monarchs were kings, not queens. Didda was an outstanding, if unusually brutal, exception to the rule.

A few years before Didda's takeover Kashmir had been dominated by bands of mercenaries called the Tantrins. These ruthless soldiers were only defeated by the kings with the aid of the landed nobility, who then demanded huge privileges and powers as payment for their service. At that moment the king died, leaving a number of sons, all of them infants. Didda at once took power as regent. She struggled to limit the powers of the nobles, with a small degree of success. However, the nominal king was fast approaching manhood and threatened to overthrow all Didda's arrangements.

Didda solved this problem by murdering him and transferring the kingship to a younger boy, while retaining the regency for herself. When this boy likewise grew older, Didda did not even attempt to discover his political leanings. She murdered him out of hand and transferred the title, but not the power, of King of Kashmir to a third prince. It was as well for the younger members of the royal family that Didda died soon afterwards.

— 👑 —

HULAGU (?–1265)

Usurped: Power in Persia 1260
Social Origins: Mongol Prince

The incident which set Hulagu on his path of conquest and usurpation must rank as one of the worst political decisions of history. In 1250 the Grand Master of the Assassins who controlled a small area of northwest Persia, sent a band of his followers to murder Mangu, Great Khan of the Mongols. The attempt failed and Mangu decided on revenge. In 1251 Mangu's brother, Hulagu left Mongolia at the head of a massive army. His instructions were simple. He was to destroy the Assassins, impose Mongol domination over the Caliph of Baghdad and return to Mongolia.

In 1256 Hulagu arrived in Persia. He quickly reduced Alamut, capital of the Assassins, and captured the Grand Master. The prisoner was sent off to Mongolia. Mangu refused even to see the Grand Master, who was savagely killed. Hulagu, meanwhile, captured all the lands and strongholds of the Assassins, putting to death every member of the sect he could find.

In 1258 Hulagu moved on to the second part of his task. The Caliph of Baghdad, spiritual leader of the entire Moslem faith, refused to accept Mongol overlordship. Hulagu led his forces in an assault on the city. Baghdad fell after a brief struggle and about 200,000 of its population were butchered. The Caliph was killed by being wrapped in a carpet and trampled by horses. The Mongol prince then raced on to capture Damascus and all of Syria.

Hulagu now set about establishing an administration to take care of his vast conquests. In 1260, before Hulagu returned to Mongolia, the Great Khan Mangu died. Hulagu's two brother's Kublai and Ariq began squabbling over their inheritance. Hulagu immediately moved his troops to the northern frontier of Persia. Here he was in a position to interfere in the fatricidal dispute or to stop the fighting spilling into his conquests.

In the event, Hulagu did not intervene. He kept on the sidelines. When Kublai killed Ariq, Hulagu sent a message to his brother and ruler that he intended staying in Persia and administering the lands he had conquered. In effect Hulagu was repudiating his allegiance to the Mongol Empire and usurping the Great Khan's powers in the area. After the long civil war, Kublai was in no position to enforce his rule. Hulagu gained power almost by default.

— ♔ —

CHARLES I (1226–1285)

Usurped: Kingdom of Naples 1261
Social Origins: French Royal Family

Charles was a younger brother of King Saint Louis IX of France. He was created Duke of Anjou by his brother and later gained the Countship of Provence through marriage. He seemed set to follow a life typical of the higher French nobility, but events were to thrust him forwards to kingship and great power.

Charles was an ambitious man, usually quick to grasp an opportunity to increase his wealth and power. When, in 1265, Pope Urban IV asked him to bring a French contingent to Italy to help put down the rebellious Manfred of Naples (see above), Charles leapt at the opportunity. He eagerly promised to reinstate church authority in the South of Italy and to pay the Papacy 10,000 ounces of gold each year, in return for Papal troops and recognition of his rule as King of Naples.

As the Angevin army advanced southwards, Charles sent messages ahead to the nobles of southern Italy. These promised to recognize their positions if they rose against Manfred. Many did so and Charles came to power in Naples as much by leading an internal rebellion as by heading an invasion force. For many years Charles ruled southern Italy with a firm hand. He tried to impose justice and order on his new subjects. They, however, found such tight control, especially by a Frenchman, irksome. In 1282 the Sicilians rose against Charles's rule and ousted him. The dreams Charles had been building of acquiring an Empire including southern Italy, Byzantium and the Crusader states were dashed. He died in 1285, his ambitions shattered.

MICHAEL VIII Palaeologus (1234–1282)

Usurped: Byzantine Empire 1261
Social Origins: Nobleman

After the Crusaders took Constantinople in 1205 (see Andronicus I above), the Byzantine Empire was divided in two. The area around the Imperial city was ruled by the Westerners, or Latins as they were known. The native Byzantine dynasty held that portion of the Empire which existed in Asia Minor and held court at the ancient city of Nicea. With the passing of the years, the Latin Empire declined. The treasures of Constantinople had been looted in its capture and the populace were unwilling to co-operate with the foreign regime.

It was at this time that Michael Palaeologus came to the fore. He came from a distinguished noble family which remained staunchly loyal to the Nicean Emperors. As a young man, Michael joined the army and led a successful military and civic career. This culminated in 1260 when he was made co-Emperor with the legitimate sovereign John Lascaris. There seems little doubt that Michael was the dominant personality of the two. He was merely using John as a legitimate front for his regime.

In 1261 Michael led the triumphant Nicean troops through the gates of Constantinople after a crushing defeat of Latin forces. For the first time in half a century, the Byzantine Empire was united under a Byzantine monarch. Michael now saw that John was no longer of any use to him in uniting the Byzantines against the Latins. The legitimate Emperor was seized on Michael's instructions, blinded and thrown into prison.

Michael remained sole Emperor for 21 years. During his rule, he attempted to reconstitute the Empire. Though partially successful, he was never able to recover the lands lost to the Bulgarians and the Seljuks during the division of Imperial power. He did, however, cunningly frustrate all attempts by the Latins to restore their control over the Empire. By making conciliatory noises towards the Papacy, Michael hoped to heal the split in Christendom and so allow a united effort against the Moslems. Religious intolerance among his own people frustrated these attempts. Nevertheless, he left a strong and united nation on his death in 1282.

ALBERT I (c. 1250–1308)

Usurped: Holy Roman Empire 1298
Social Origins: Imperial Family

Albert was the able son of an able monarch. When the peculiarities of German kingship deprived him of his father's throne, he began plotting his return.

In 1254 Conrad IV, the sole surviving male representative of the Hohenstaufen Imperial family marched into Italy to recover Naples from Charles of Anjou. He was defeated and executed. After his death several men claimed the Imperial title, but none were properly elected or able to impose even nominal power in Germany. In 1274, however, Rudolf of Hapsburg was nominated at a proper election and officially crowned at Aachen. In the 18 years of his rule, Rudolf proved himself to be a very competent monarch who regained much of the power and prestige of the office of Emperor.

The noble electors, however, felt that Rudolf had been too strong a monarch. On his death in 1291, they ignored his eldest son Albert in favour of an obscure nobleman named Adolf of Nassau. They hoped that a weak monarch would allow them to enlarge their estates and indulge in their private wars. They were right, but they had reckoned without Albert.

Although Albert acknowledged Adolf and retired to his ancestral estates on the Rhine, he had no intention of foregoing his Imperial legacy. Albert carefully built up his power and influence in the southwestern area of the Empire. In 1298 he struck. Raising an army of loyal followers, Albert marched against Adolf and heavily defeated him at Gollheim. Soon afterwards Adolf died, enabling Albert to call an election meeting on his own terms. The nobles accordingly elected him Emperor. Pope Boniface VIII, however, witheld his approval of the violent usurpation until 1303.

As Emperor, Albert ruthlessly increased the power of the Hapsburgs. He seized lands on the Rhine for himself and installed two of his sons as rulers of Bohemia and Moravia. But he was unable to control the internal feuding of the German nobles. On 1 May 1308 he was murdered by his nephew, John of Swabia. The elector nobles ignored the claims of Albert's sons and nominated Henry of Luxembourg as Emperor. It was to be 130 years before the Hapsburgs returned to Imperial power.

— 👑 —

MATTEO VISCONTI (1250–1322)

Usurped: Power in Milan 1295
Social Origins: Clerical Family

The Visconti were one of the great landed families of Milan and claimed descent from the 9th century Lombard Kings of northern Italy. At the time of Matteo's rise to power, Milan was a wealthy city of about 150,000 people which was the centre of a territory encompassing 50 other towns and numerous villages. The resurgence of urban life was in full swing. Milan was a centre for trade, finance and the arts. The glories of Roman town life were returning.

Milan, like most other Italian cities of the time, was a Republic. Political power was balanced between the nobles and the wealthy merchant classes. This semi-democratic style of government was coming under increasing pressures as the cities grew and greater wealth led to increasing opportunities for bribery and corruption. In Milan the pressures were relieved when much power came into the hands of the Archbishop. In 1255 Ottone Visconti became Archbishop, an office he held for 40 years.

In his lengthy term of power, Ottone relied heavily on his relatives to perform many of the offices of state. The Visconti became accustomed to exercising authority, though the Milanese did not forget their Republican state. In 1295 the elderly Ottone died and the Archibishopric passed away from the Viscontis. However the powerful family did not wish to lose control of Milanese affairs. The most determined of them was Matteo, grandnephew of the late archbishop.

By intrigue and the application of force where needed, Matteo managed to separate the ecclesiastical duties of the archbishop from his civic responsibilities. Matteo ensured that the temporal powers came into his own hands, though he was careful not to take any titles which might offend the Milanese sense of republicanism. It was 15 years before the Papacy accepted this usurpation of ecclesiastical power and recognized Matteo as Vicar of Lombardy. This confirmed Matteo in his behind-the-scenes power. Before his death in 1322, Matteo quarrelled with Rome again, but was able to pass on his power intact to his son Galeazzo.

— 👑 —

MALATESTA DI VEROCCHIO (?–1310)

Usurped: Supreme power in Rimini 1295
Social Origins: Wealthy Family

Malatesta di Verrochio rose to power as part of a movement sweeping Italy in the late 13th century. Like many other men of his time, he tried to take advantage of circumstances to ease himself into power. When the people he was replacing objected, the scene was set for usurpation.

In the early 13th century, the North Italian town of Rimini was a typical example of its type. The city was growing increasingly wealthy as trade and commerce improved. The city state had successfully thrown off the yoke of control by the Holy Roman Empire and was beginning to find its political feet. Like most Italian cities, Rimini looked to ancient Rome for a model for a method of government. A council was instituted with consuls serving as senior officers. However, the system had its problems and pressures.

Rivalry between wealthy families within the city led to bitter feuding which spilled over into the city government. To sort out these problems, many cities appointed a Podesta. Such a man held office for 6 months and had almost unlimited power. He was, however, subject to a strict investigation on leaving office and could be prosecuted for any irregularities.

In 1237, Rimini called upon a man named Giovanni Malatesta to act as Podesta. The choice was natural. The Malatesta were a wealthy family, but had only recently moved to the city. They had influence but were free of the old rivalries. Giovanni performed his task well. As the years passed members of the Malatesta family were frequently called upon to undertake the office of Podesta.

After about 50 years, however, the Malatesta were becoming very powerful within Rimini. The influential positions within the Podesta were becoming associated with this family only. Others grew jealous and plotted the downfall of the Malatesta. In fact these others set in motion the train of events which would lead to their own subjugation.

In 1288 the wealthy families of Rimini, notably the Parcitadi, engineered the exile of the whole Malatesta family on a trumped-up charge. It seemed that the family was outwitted. The council of Rimini celebrated, but Malatesta di Verocchio, the head of the family, was a determined man. After a short time away from Rimini, he returned.

Using the friends and influence he had won as Podesta, Malatesta di Verrochio had himself reinstated. The judicious use of violence and the threat of violence was allied with his political string-pulling to install him in an entirely new position. No longer Podesta, Malatesta di Verrochio took supreme power. His rivals were crushed into submission and the position of the Malatesta became unassailable. The new system, where one family held supreme power, was not new in Italy and was known as Signoria. Many cities in Italy were becoming dominated by Signoria at this time. Sometimes the Signoria came to power peacefully, as did the della Scala family at Verona, others employed the type of usurpation experienced at Rimini in 1295.

— 👑 —

ROBERT BRUCE (1274–1329)

Usurped: Kingdom of Scotland 1306
Social Origins: Nobleman

Robert Bruce was an opportunist who was forced into making his dramatic bid for power because of a rash and scandalous act which he committed. The reasons for this act remain unknown.

In 1390 Bruce's grandfather, also named Robert Bruce, had been one of the contestants for the disputed crown of Scotland. Edward I of England was asked to arbitrate and chose John Baliol as king. Edward insisted upon many benefits from Baliol for having favoured him. At first Baliol agreed, but in

1296 invaded England. Edward reacted swiftly, defeated the Scottish army and proclaimed himself King of Scotland.

This arrangement did not suit the bulk of the Scottish population. New taxes and laws were imposed by Edward. Many nobles gathered together to fight against Edward's English officials. The struggle dragged on for some years. Robert Bruce seems to have fought on whichever side suited him best at the time, but in 1306 he committed an act which forced him to declare himself.

As a possible heir to the throne, Bruce was under pressure to join the resistance. First, however, he had to come to some arrangement with John Comyn, another nobleman also with a claim to the throne. It was agreed that Comyn would support Bruce in return for land and money. In 1306 the two men met in a church in Dumfries to arrange the final details. Perhaps the men did not trust each other, and decided that the sanctuary of the church would restrain the other. The followers of both men waited outside. Suddenly they heard the two men shouting. Then a terrible scream rang out and Robert Bruce came running out. He had stabbed Comyn to death.

When news of this sacrilegious act spread, people were furious. The Pope excommunicated Bruce as soon as he learnt what had happened. Edward I gathered an army to crush the killer. Realizing that Edward was now his implacable enemy, Bruce joined the resistance party and had himself crowned king. Edward I died in 1307 to be replaced by his son Edward II who was not really interested in ruling Scotland. For the next 7 years Bruce fought the English and gradually pushed them south. His career culminated in 1314 at the Battle of Bannockburn when he utterly routed the English army.

EDWARD BRUCE (?–1318)

Usurped: High Kingship of Ireland 1316
Social Origins: Scottish Royal Family

After gaining control of Scotland, Robert Bruce wanted to strengthen his power. He therefore supported his brother Edward when the latter made his bid for power in Ireland. Robert even wrote a letter to the Irish chieftains reminding them of their common ancestry and language and urging them to support Edward.

Edward Bruce landed in northern Ireland in 1315 with a small army of Scots. He persuaded the O'Neils of Ulster to join him against the Anglo-Irish lords. Edward hoped that by appearing to be helping the Irish to fight the English he would be able to take power. He was quickly proved right in this assumption. In 1316 Edward had himself crowned High King of Ireland, though he had no real claim to the title and was not even an Irish king. The English were soon restricted to a few isolated strongholds.

However, Edward soon found that the Irish were not an easy people to govern. Local kings claimed privileges with which Edward was unfamiliar. The Irish also insisted on pursuing old feuds which threatened to upset Edward's control. The Irish, to their dismay, soon found that Edward was actually serious in his intention to impose the authority of his High Kingship in much the same way that Robert Bruce ruled Scotland. Unfortunately for Edward, the Irish High Kings had never wielded such power. The Irish resented the domineering attitude of Edward and they melted away from him.

In 1318 Edward met an English army at Carrickfergus. His reduced army was defeated and he himself killed. Edward had been too eager to impose his concept of kingship on a people who had ideas of their own.

ROGER MORTIMER (?–1330)

Usurped: Power in England 1327
Social Origins: Nobleman

Roger Mortimer came to power because of a woman, and lost it because of a boy who was scarcely old enough to shave. In an era of pride and violence, Mortimer was one of the proudest and most violent of all.

Mortimer grew to manhood during the reign of the strong and warlike Edward I. In 1307 Edward I died and was replaced on the throne by his effeminate son Edward II. A tough warrior baron such as Mortimer can have had little sympathy for the new king and his homosexual favourites. In 1321 the powerful Marcher Lords, whose lands bordered with the turbulent Welsh, saw that Edward II was trying to take their lands in order to give them to the favourite Despenser. Mortimer was one such lord and he took an active part in the rebellion which followed. For a while the Marchers, under the Duke of Lancaster, were successful, but they were ultimately defeated. Mortimer ended up imprisoned in the Tower of London.

Three years later Mortimer escaped and fled to France. There he met Isabella, Queen to Edward II. This proud woman had finally had enough of her husband's male favourites and the humiliations which they heaped upon her. Mortimer and the estranged Queen were instantly attracted and soon became lovers. In 1326 news reached them that England was thoroughly disgusted by Edward. Mortimer and Isabel landed near London, raised the standard of revolt and soon had Edward and Despenser in their power.

Despenser was executed. Edward was forced to abdicate and later murdered in a particularly unpleasant fashion.

Mortimer and Isabel proclaimed Edward's 15-year-old son king as Edward III. However the boy was kept well away from power. Nobody had any illusions about who was the real power in the land. Mortimer ruled, if he did not reign. Edward III was kept alive only because he served as a useful front for the regime. This situation lasted for three years.

Then, on 19 October 1330, the teenager Edward smuggled a group of his young friends into Nottingham Castle where he was staying with his mother and her lover. The small band of youths strode up to Mortimer's room, which was next to that of the Queen. When the guards refused to admit them, Edward drew a concealed weapon and fought his way into the room. Mortimer, who had never expected the boy to behave in such a determined manner, was utterly unprepared and could to nothing to save himself. Mortimer was hurried through a show trial in London and then hanged at Tyburn. He was not even accorded the dignity of a beheading.

LUIGI GONZAGA (?–c. 1340)

Usurped: Power in Mantua 1328
Social Origins: Possibly a Nobleman

The city state of Mantua followed the normal political trends of northern Italy during the 12th and 13th centuries progressing from being subject to the Holy Roman Empire to being an independant republic. The powers elsewhere vested in a semi-dictatorial Podesta were at Mantua given to the leader of the militia, the Capitano del Popolo. This office was monopolized after 1270 by the family of the Bonaccolsi. In 1308 Guido Bonaccolsi was named as hereditary Signore of Mantua. It seemed that the city had made a peaceful transition to government by Signoria, or lordship. Luigi Gonzaga was to change all that.

It is difficult to be certain as to Gonzaga's origins, but he seems to have been wealthy and well-connected. Perhaps he was one of the merchant-nobles so common in northern Italy at this time. Wherever he came from Luigi swiftly ousted the Bonaccolsi from power. He took over the position and rights of Signore of Mantua. In time the Gonzagas took the title of Marquis of Mantua and remained in sole control of the city state until 1708 when the line died out.

Ashikaga TAKAUJI (?–1352)

Usurped: Power in Japan 1335
Social Origins: Samurai

Head of the Ashikaga samurai clan, Takauji was in turn both Emperor-maker and later usurper. It is ironic that his amazing rise to power was begun by another man whose sole aim was to curb the influence of such men as Takauji.

That man was the Emperor Go-Daigo who launched a revolt in 1331. He wished to overthrow the Hojo Shogun and re-establish the Emperor as the actual power in the land. Such a situation had not existed for centuries. Despite early reversals, Go-Daigo soon found himself at the head of a great rising against the Hojo who were generally considered to be abusing their powers. Takauji was an enthusiastic supporter of the Go-Daigo rebellion. It was he who finally captured the Imperial capital of Kyoto from the Hojo in 1334.

No doubt Takauji hoped that he would gain wealth and influence for himself and his clan by his invaluable services. He was mistaken. Go-Daigo gathered all power into his own hands and appointed his son as Shogun. The new arrangement did not please Takauji nor many other samurai clan leaders. In 1335, Takauji raised his Ashikaga samurai against the Emperor. Go-Daigo fled to a mountain retreat in the south.

In Kyoto, Takauji was astute enough to realize that he should be seen to be acting constitutionally in his usurpation. He therefore found a pliant prince of the Imperial family and hailed him as Emperor. The new Emperor immediately relinquished all his powers to Takauji as Shogun. Despite Go-Daigo's efforts, nothing had changed except the Emperor and the Shogun. The Ashikaga samurai were to remain in power until 1573.

JOHN VI Cantacuzene (1292–1383)

Usurped: Byzantine Empire 1341
Social Origins: Nobleman

The Emperor Andronicus III was an easy-going man who loved luxury and enjoyed feasting and merrymaking, but he was also an astute judge of character. He chose John Cantacuzene to take over for him the more mundane duties of an Emperor. While Andronicus remained alive, Cantacuzene was loyal, but things were to change when Andronicus died.

The Emperor's death came in 1341 when his son, John Palaeologus, was no more than a boy. At the time Cantacuzene was on campaign in Thrace. He realized that courtiers jealous of his power and influence would lose little time in turning the boy against him. Cantacuzene knew that he might well find himself on trial for his life. To forestall the plotters, Cantacuzene had his troops hail him as Emperor John V. He sent messengers to Constantinople to inform the court that there were now joint Byzantine Emperors. The messengers, backed up by armed support, soon made it clear that Cantacuzene was the more senior of the two.

John Palaeologus was pushed into the background. Although Cantacuzene did not enter Constantinople until 1347, he kept a tight control on affairs of state. His rule proved to be unpopular, especially his policy of employing Turks, long standing enemies of the Empire, as mercenaries. Perhaps hoping to avoid the bloody death usually meted out to unpopular usurpers, Cantacuzene suddenly abdicated in favour of John Palaeologus. He retired to a monastery where he lived for a further 28 years.

— ♔ —

COLA di RIENZI (c. 1313–1354)

Usurped: Power in Rome 1347
Social Origins: Innkeeper's Son

Cola is an oddity in the Europe of the 14th century, a time of warring nobles and feuding kings. He was a charismatic man of humble origins who became the champion of commoners against the nobility. For a few brief months, he very nearly achieved his dreams.

Born about 1313, Cola received an education and earned a living as a notary. When his brother was murdered by a nobleman, Cola received no justice from the Roman courts. He took up the role of political orator, proving himself to be a magnificent speaker and fearsome opponent in debate. In 1343 he journeyed north to Avignon to try to persuade Pope Clement VI to return the Papal court to Rome. Innocent refused, but gave this strange character an official position and sent him back to Rome.

There Cola became increasingly infuriated by the rule of the nobles. On 20 May 1347 Cola called a meeting on the Capitol Hill. The very site was designed to remind the Romans of their ancient republican traditions. Cola made what was possibly the greatest speech of his life. It was certainly one of the most dramatic in history. The crowd which had gathered was turned into an organized citizenry, determined to assert their rights and privileges. The nobles sensed the situation and fled. Cola was appointed to the ancient position of tribune and given full powers.

Cola proved a just ruler, removing many iniquities of law and reforming the administration of the city. However, his sudden rise in power seems to have gone to his head. He sent messengers ordering the Holy Roman Emperor to appear before him, and renounced the authority of an absent Pope. In December the nobles and their troops returned to Rome. Cola's behaviour had alienated many people and the nobles sent him into exile. In 1354 he travelled to Rome as Papal messenger for Innocent VI. The visit was rash and ill considered. He was murdered.

— ♕ —

JOHN of GAUNT (1340–1399)
Kingmaker of Spain 1367
Social Origins: English Royal Family

John of Gaunt was a noted English military leader who became embroiled in Spanish politics almost by accident, but pursued them with determination for a number of years. His actions were indirectly to have great influence over the Iberian peninsula for many years.

In 1366 John of Gaunt, was campaigning in France with his brother Edward the Black Prince during an early stage of the Hundred Years War. During a lull in the fighting, the English were surprised to find themselves approached by King Pedro the Cruel of Castile. Pedro had been driven from the throne by his illegitimate half-brother Don Enrico Trastamara, aided by a sizeable French army under Bertrand du Guesclin. Pedro appealed to the English for help.

The two royal princes were only too happy to match lances once again with an old enemy and led their army south. On 3 April 1367, 24,000 English and Castillian troops faced 60,000 French and Spanish men. John of Gaunt and his brother won a resounding victory and replaced Pedro on his throne, whereupon John of Gaunt married Pedro's daughter Constance. When, in 1369, Don Enrico returned and murdered Pedro, John claimed the Castillian throne on behalf of his wife. He was, however, not in any position to do anything about the claim as he was virtually ruling England on behalf of his nephew Richard II at the time.

In 1385, however, John was free of commitments in France and England. He sailed to Spain to claim his crown. He found a willing ally in King John of Portugal whose throne was being claimed by King John of Castile due to some rather complicated dynastic reasons. On 14 August John of Gaunt and John of Portugal crushed the army of John of Castile. However a heavy defeat the following year robbed John of Gaunt of any hope of finally wearing the crown of Castile.

John of Gaunt remained in the south for three more years before returning to England. He resigned his regal claims in favour of a daughter whom he then married to the heir to Castile, thus joining the families of Pedro and Enrico and ensuring a strong and united Kingdom of Castile. A second daughter of John of Gaunt married John of Portugal. A son of this marriage was to be Henry the Navigator, the man so influential in opening up the trade routes to India and China in the following century.

— ♔ —

TAMERLANE the MAGNIFICENT (c. 1336–1405)

Usurped: Power in Transoxiania 1369

Social Origins: Tribal Chieftain

Tamerlane, or Timur i Leng as his name is more correctly spelled, had a difficult early career, but at the age of about 33 he managed to establish himself as ruler of Transoxiana, the fertile land north of the Hindu Kush. Far from satisfied, Tamerlane set out to build up a massive· empire. He very nearly succeeded.

Born in about 1336, Tamerlane became tribal chief of the Berlas at an early age. By cunningly playing off rival tribes, Tamerlane managed to become one of the most powerful men in Transoxiana. In 1360 Tughlak, Khan of the Jagatai Mongols invaded Transoxiana. Tamerlane quickly surrendered and then sat back to watch Tughlak crush his rival chiefs. Tamerlane gained the governorship of Kesh in the new regime. At Kesh Tamerlane collected all those discontented with the Mongol rule and made friendly contacts elsewhere throughout the land. In 1365 Tamerlane and his brother-in-law Hosain began a rebellion which drove out the invaders. Tamerlane then murdered Hosain and proclaimed himself sole Emir of Transoxiana.

Over the following 10 years, Tamerlane waged war on the Jagatai and finally succeeded in bringing them under his own rule. In 1376 Tamerlane took the title of Khan. With an ever-growing army of ferocious horsemen, he was set to begin his career of conquest.

The rich land of Khorassan, south of the Aral Sea was captured first. In 1381 he stormed into Afghanistan, captured Herat and buried thousands of men alive to dissuade the Afghans from rebellion. The year 1383 found

Tamerlane on the shores of the Caspian and four years later he had conquered all of Persia. When the town of Ispahan had the temerity to rise against his rule, Tamerlane charged down and crushed the rebellion. He put the population to the sword and constructed a mound of 70,000 skulls to remind passers-by of the punishment for resistance. In 1393 he captured Damascus and Armenia.

Trouble with the Mongols of the Golden Horde took Tamerlane north. In a devastating campaign he smashed the Golden Horde and harried the lands between the Volga and the Don as far north as Moscow, leaving towns and cities no more than smoking ruins filled with bodies. Tamerlane invaded India in 1398, looting Delhi and most of the cities of the Ganges and Indus basins. Next to fall was Syria. It seemed that nothing could stop Tamerlane's fearsome warriors and his military genius. In 1404 he set off with an enormous army to begin the conquest of China. He died before his army had covered 300 miles. The empire he had built collapsed after his death. Only the remnants of his magnificent capital of Samarkand remain.

— 👑 —

ENRICO II da Trastamara (?–1379)

Usurped: Kingdom of Castile 1369
Social Origins: Royal Family

Enrico da Trastamara, or Henry II as he is sometimes known, was an illegitimate son of Alphonso XI, King of Castile, then one of several Christian and Moslem states in Spain. When Alphonso died the legitimate heir, Pedro, ordered the death of all his bastard siblings, but Enrico managed to escape, and fled north to France. For a time Enrico could only live as a fugitive prince, but in 1366 he heard news from Spain. Pedro's queen, the sister of the Queen of France, had died in strange circumstances which indicated she had been killed on the orders of her husband. Enrico's moment had come.

Taking advantage of a temporary lull in the Hundred Years' War being fought between England and France, Enrico recruited a massive army of mercenaries. Perhaps as important, the renowned French leader Bertrand du Guesclin agreed to join as military commander. Enrico and his 30,000 freelancers marched into Spain and drove Pedro from the throne. The expensive army was then disbanded, a terrible mistake by Enrico. In the spring of 1367 a large English army led by the Black Prince, heir to the English throne, and the famous leader Sir John Chandos marched into Spain to help Pedro. On 3 April Enrico's Castillian troops were overwhelmed at Najera and he fled to the Kingdom of Aragon.

Pedro soon made himself even more unpopular than before by raising harsh taxes and using Moslem mercenaries to quell opposition. In 1369 Enrico judged the time right to return to Castile. He raised an army from the discontents of Castile and sent for du Guesclin. With du Guesclin's help, Enrico outmanoeuvred Pedro's army at Montiel and captured him. The royal half-brothers met in a tent and at once lost their tempers. Pedro called Enrico a whore's son and in the undignified scuffle which followed, Pedro was fatally wounded. Enrico was at last secure on his throne. He ruled for a further ten years, and was the ancestor of most future kings of the whole of Spain including the present monarch Juan Carlos.

— ♕ —

HUNG WU (c. 1328–1396)
Usurped: Chinese Empire 1367
Social Origins: Peasant

By the mid-14th century the Mongol rulers of China had almost lost control of their Empire. Decades of decadence and mismanagement had taken their toll. The administration of the Emperor Togan Temur was staggering from one crisis to the next. China was ripe for takeover. When the bid for power came, it emerged from an unexpected source, a monk-turned-bandit named Chu Yuan Chang.

Chu was born in about 1328 to a poor peasant family. In 1345 Chu's family was wiped out by plague and he became a destitute beggar. He found a brief home as a Buddhist monk, but in 1353 became a bandit by joining the Red Turban movement. This secret society aimed at social reform in favour of the peasants. Chu soon saw the flaw in this ideal and developed a policy of his own. He declared himself committed to achieving social reform by overthrowing the Mongols. His social reform was designed to appeal to landlords as much as to peasants while the educated classes would appreciate the ousting of the uncultured Mongols.

With his radical new ideas, Chu attracted a large following and by the early 1360s had most of the lower Yangtse Basin under his control. In 1367 he defeated his final rival as the anti-Mongolian leader at the Battle of Boyang. He immediately sent an army of over 200,000 men north to capture Peking. Togan Temur did not wait for the inevitable defeat, but fled north to Mongolia.

Chu at once proclaimed himself the first Emperor of a new dynasty. He took the name Hung Wu, by which he is usually known, and named his dynasty the Ming, which means 'bright light'. Hung Wu set about reorganizing the Empire. He established the provincial system which survives to this day and redistributed land to ease the economic problems of the peasantry. He reintroduced the policy of appointing bureaucrats by examination and merit. However, the independent authority of senior ministers was abolished and all power was concentrated in the hands of Hung Wu.

In later years, Hung Wu seems to have become obsessed by the thought that he might fall victim to a palace plot. Perhaps his humble origins were scorned by the haughty and highly educated bureaucrats, causing the Emperor to feel that he was resented by those meant to serve him. In 1380 a high-ranking bureaucrat named Hu Weiyong was discovered attempting to thwart an Imperial order. Hung Wu ordered his immediate execution, along with his entire family. Not content, Hung Wu extended the suspicion of guilt to the officials who had served Weiyong and their families. In all 30,000 people were put to death. Through such brutal measures, Hung Wu managed to keep his throne and push through his reforms. Hung Wu died in 1396.

BAYAZID I (1347–1403)

Usurped: Sultanate of the Turks 1389
Social Origins: Royal Family

Only a few decades before the time of Bayazid, the Ottoman Turks had been a savage pagan tribe from the steppes of Eastern Europe. But by the mid-14th century they had become converted to Islam and were a relatively settled, if still warlike nation.

The ruler of the Turks after 1359, Murad I, led the Turks out of their homeland in northern Anatolia on an invasion of Europe. In 1382 the Turks had reached Sofia and Murad now ruled his growing state from Adrianople. In 1389 Murad defeated a combined Balkan force at Kossovo, but died almost at once. Though he may well have died of wounds sustained in the fighting, there were strong rumours that he had been assassinated, or at least that his end had been hastened, by agents of his son Bayazid.

Whatever the truth of this allegation, Bayazid immediately seized power. He announced that henceforth he would take the title of Sultan of the Ottoman Turks, the first to use the title which was to survive until the early 20th century. In 1394 Bayazid attacked the Byzantine Empire, bringing down upon himself a massive Christian alliance from the West. In 1396 he crushed this expedition. Six years later, however, Bayazid was himself defeated by the savage Asian ruler Tamerlane (see above). The Sultan of the

Ottoman Turks was imprisoned in an iron cage where he spent the rest of his life, much to the amusement of Tamerlane.

— 👑 —

HENRY IV (1367–1413)

Usurped: Kingdom of England 1399
Social Origins: Royal Family

Henry IV was one of the most reluctant usurpers ever to lay hands on a crown. Until the age of 31 Henry seemed quite content to lead the life of a typical nobleman, but then he was forced into rebellion by the king to whom he had always been loyal. Almost to the last moment, Henry tried to avoid taking the throne.

Henry, known as Bolingbroke, was born in 1367 as the son of the powerful John of Gaunt, Duke of Lancaster (see above). He grew up as cousin to King Richard II and moved in circles of wealth and privilege. As an influential nobleman, he became involved in politics and opposed Richard on some occasions. It was this that was to turn the king against him.

In 1397, Richard ceased to reign with the advice of Parliament and his nobles. He insisted that his every whim should be law and spent money lavishly on luxury and waste. A few nobles dared to oppose him. They were murdered or executed for their pains. Henry, wisely, kept quiet. But he became involved in a quarrel with the Earl of Nottingham. Richard seized on this to repay Henry for his previous opposition.

Richard demanded that the two noblemen settle their dispute by trial by combat. When the two men armed themselves for the fight, Richard declared that to preserve the peace both men had to be exiled. Henry obeyed and left for France. But Richard was not yet content. In 1399 John of Gaunt died. Richard promptly seized the money and lands belonging to the Duchy of Lancaster, which should have gone to Henry. Aghast at this loss, Henry found himself left a penniless exile. He decided to take action.

On 4 July Henry landed in Yorkshire. He came, he said, to persuade Richard to give him back his lands. Whether this was the real reason or not, we do not know. But Henry was quickly joined by noblemen and knights who were thoroughly disgusted by Richard's autocratic rule. Henry's journey to London rapidly became a triumphal procession. By the time Richard realized the danger it was too late. Nobody would follow him.

Henry met Richard at Flint and treated him with all the respect due to a king. On 30 September Richard abdicated. Henry presented himself to Parliament, which hailed him as king through his descent from King Henry

Henry IV
The tomb effigy of Henry IV in Canterbury Cathedral. Henry IV took a troubled
throne and faced several rebellions and risings in his early years in power. The
strength and stability which he brought to royal power in his later years is
demonstrated by the splendour he lavished on his tomb, and by its survival.
(*Michael Holford*)

— ♛ —

III. Richard was locked up at Pontefract Castle where he died the following February.

Henry had succeeded in a usurpation he had not wanted and now had to rule a kingdom he had gained against his will. For 14 years, Henry struggled against rebellion at home and trouble from the Scots. Eventually he succeeded in asserting his power and when he died in 1413, Henry left a strong and prosperous throne to his son, the warlike Henry V.

— 👑 —

JOHN THE FEARLESS (1371–1419)

Usurped: Power in France 1407
Social Origins: Nobleman

John the Fearless, Duke of Burgundy, inherited an awkward political situation from his father. The Dukes of Burgundy held lands in both the Kingdom of France and the Holy Roman Empire, and thus had divided loyalties. Though descended from the royal house of France, the Burgundians were pursuing an increasingly separate policy.

As a young man John took part in various campaigns against the Turks in Eastern Europe. He fought with such bravery that he earnt for himself the sobriquet of The Fearless. In 1404 he inherited the titles and lands of Duke of Burgundy. As such he became immediately embroiled in the internal struggle in France. King Charles VI was mad and power was being contested by the Dukes of Orleans and Burgundy, both descended from the royal family.

At first John was politically outmanoeuvred by Duke Louis of Orleans and seemed to be losing the struggle. In 1407, however, John solved this problem by having Louis murdered and seizing the powers which should have been held by the mad king. For six years John was the master of France. Then in 1413 he made the mistake of stirring up a riot in Paris. The lesser nobility turned to the Armagnac, or Orleanist, party who were now united with Queen Isabella and the Dauphin Charles, heir to the throne. Civil war broke out in earnest.

In 1419 John was invited to attend a peace meeting with the Orleanists on a bridge at Montereau. John and his advisers left their armed escort on the river bank, as did the Armagnac party. The two groups met at the centre of the bridge and exchanged pleasantries. Suddenly the Armagnacs drew concealed weapons and stabbed John the Fearless to death. Nothing was solved by this treacherous murder. The long struggle between Burgundian and Armagnac became even more bitter and dragged on for many more years.

Robert CLEMENT VII (1342–1394)

Usurped: Papal Crown 1378

Social Origins: German Nobleman

In 1378 Pope Gregory XI, who had spent most of his pontificate in France, died. The people of Rome were determined to have an Italian as Pope and that the Papal seat should stay in Rome. While the cardinals cast their votes, the mob burst in to the chapel and demanded the election of an Italian. Faced with the threat of violence, the cardinals hastily made Bartolomeo Prignano Pope as Urban VI.

Urban seems to have become obsessed by his own importance. He threatened those who opposed him and flew into violent, frightening rages. The cardinals were horrified by what they had done. The majority fled to Agnani. There they declared the election of Urban void and elected Robert of Geneva as Clement VII.

Clement came from a distinguished family and was related by blood or marriage to many of the crowned heads of Europe. Almost the whole papal civil service joined Clement in Naples and the Kings of France, Naples and Scotland acknowledged him as Pope. Despite this promising start Clement failed to gain control of the Papacy. His election was as irregular, if not more so, than that of Urban VI. England and Germany refused to acknowledge him. More disturbingly he was unable to enter Rome. Tough mercenaries hired by Urban beat off all attempts by Neapolitan and French troops to instal Clement.

In 1389 Urban died. Clement stood ready to enter Rome once he was accepted as the one Pope. But the Roman cardinals elected Boniface IX as Pope, ignoring Clement. Thereafter the influence of Clement went into a decline. He died in 1394, whereupon the French cardinals elected Benedict XIII in opposition to Boniface. The schism dragged on for years.

JOAN of ARC (1412–1432)

Kingmaker of France 1429
Social Origins: Peasant

Joan was a remarkable woman. In an age when warfare was an exclusively male occupation, she raised and led an army to victory over a seemingly invincible foe. From her humble origins she rose to mix with the highest in the land and established the king upon a throne he thought lost. Only her burning religious convictions drove this young girl on.

In 1428, at the age of 16, Joan believed she had a vision from God which commanded her to save France and place the Dauphin, the title borne by the heir to the French crown, on the throne. At this time France was suffering from terrible defeats from England and the Dauphin Charles was discredited by rumours of his illegitimacy. At first Joan was ignored, but her honest conviction won over those who met her. She was introduced to the Dauphin in early 1429 and won his support. After being examined by a theological board, Joan was sent to join the army.

Joan's faith and her startling bravery made her a natural leader. The common soldiers adored her and gained fresh confidence from this slight girl. She led an army to Orleans, then being besieged by the English. Leading the attack herself, Joan captured the English siege works, although she was badly wounded.

Further victories followed. The holy, or demonic, reputation of Joan inspired her own troops and demoralised the English. On 14 July 1429 she captured Reims, the traditional coronation city. Two days later the Dauphin was crowned as Charles VII of France. Believing her mission fulfilled, Joan wanted to go home, but the new king showed signs of retreating before the English. Joan stayed to lead the French armies.

In May 1430 Joan was captured in a minor skirmish by Burgundian allies of England. The Burgundians handed her over to the English who sent her to an ecclesiastical court for trial. The fact that Joan worked miracles was not doubted, but was it God or the Devil which inspired her? The fact that she claimed to appeal to God, bypassing the Church angered the clericals trying her. For nearly a year Joan was kept in prison. The English Duke of Bedford tried repeatedly to make her confess that her vision was not from God so that her life would be spared. Joan refused and so, on 30 May 1431, she was burned at the stake. Throughout the year of her imprisonement Charles VII, the king she had made and had crowned, made no attempt to rescue her. It was the most shameful act of his reign.

— ♔ —

FRANCESCO Alessandro SFORZA (1401–1466)

Usurped: Duchy of Milan 1450
Social Origins: Mercenary Captain

During the mid-15th century, Italy was dominated by the rivalries of the city states and by the mercenaries they employed. As a leading mercenary, Francesco Sforza was in an ideal position to take advantage of this anarchy. He lost little time in doing so.

Francesco was the son of a peasant-turned-mercenary named Muzio Attendolo. When Muzio took to a life as a condottiere, or mercenary captain, he took the name of Sforza, which means 'The Force'. Young Francesco was brought up in the mercenary camp and was trained from birth for the task of leading men into battle.

In 1426, at the age of 25, Francesco took over his father's mercenary band and entered the service of the Milanese Visconti family. When this contract came to an end he was employed by the Florentines, the bitter enemies of Milan. By the late 1430s Francesco had shown himself to be the finest and most dynamic condottiere in Italy. His services were in great demand, and he had little qualms about changing sides when his contract of employment ran out.

He served both the Visconti and the Florentines three times during the 1430s and 1440s. There seems to have been little hard feeling about this changing of sides. Condottieri were expected to remain loyal only as long as the contract lasted. Sforza remained true to this principle, but extorted huge sums and vast estates as his price for renewing a contract. He married the daughter of Filippo Visconti, Duke of Milan, during this period of warfare.

In 1447 Filippo died and Francesco immediately claimed the Duchy through his wife. The claim was disputed, not only by many Milanese uncertain of Francesco's loyalties, but also by Alfonso of Naples who wanted the city for himself. Francesco plunged himself into intrigue and political moves of a truly Machiavellian style, combined with outright violence by his mercenaries. Eventually, in 1450 Francesco emerged as the master of Milan and took the title of Duke, which he held until his death 16 years later. The Sforzas remained Dukes of Milan until 1535 when the family died out.

— ♔ —

Vlad DRACULA (c. 1430–1476)

Usurped: Principality of Wallachia 1447 and 1456
Social Origins: Princely Family

Dracula gained power through violence, and maintained his position by the use of naked force and fear. This savage behaviour may have been at least partly caused by his upbringing.

Dracula was the son of Dracul, Prince of Wallachia. As a Christian monarch on the frontiers of the great Islamic Ottoman Empire in what is now part of Romania, Dracul was in a delicate position. He handed Dracula and a second son, Radu, over to the Turks as hostages while trying to keep the friendship of the Hungarian king. As hostages the boys were treated well at first, but later subjected to the most horrific treatment. Radu, if not Dracula himself, was submitted to homosexual rape by the Sultan.

In 1447, Dracul was dethroned and killed by his Hungarian overlords. The Turks released Dracula, hoping he would try to claim his father's lands and destabilize the Christian war effort. Taking advantage of the fact that the Hungarian army was busy with the Turks, Dracula rode hard for Wallachia with a picked force of loyal men. He forced the people to accept him as Prince at swordpoint. A few months later the Hungarians returned and drove Dracula from his new found power.

In 1455 Constantinople fell to the Turks, and Wallachia collapsed. Dracula hurried to the Hungarian court to offer his sword to the general Hunyadi. The offer was accepted and Dracula was made commander of a local army. In 1456, on the pretence of attacking the Turks, Dracula led his small army into Wallachia and once again seized power with the aid of military might. He then invited the entire nobility of Wallachia, whom he blamed for the death of his father, to a feast pretending to have forgiven them. Suddenly Dracula's bodyguard entered and began killing the noblemen. None escaped.

Dracula maintained his savagely-won position by executing his subjects on the least suspicion of disloyalty and paying tribute to both the Ottomans and the Hungarians. In 1462 the relationship with the Turks broke down and Dracula was faced by a major invasion. The Turks were only halted by a violent night attack, after which Dracula mounted 20,000 Turkish bodies on tall stakes. Sultan Mehmet II retreated, but did not give up the struggle.

The Sultan released Radu, who hurried to Wallachia with promises of peace from the Turks. The new nobility happily agreed and abandoned the tyrannical Dracula. The unseated Prince of Wallachia fled to King Matthias of Hungary who placed him under house arrest, but otherwise treated the fugitive well. In 1476 war broke out between Hungary and the Turks. Matthias gave Dracula an army to invade Wallachia and stir up trouble. At

Dracula
A 16th-century woodcut of Dracula, based on a contemporary portrait. This unflattering picture was cut by a German, a people against whom Dracula carried out frightful atrocities as part of his brutally repressive home policy. It is, therefore unlikely to be a sympathetic portrayal but it captures the hard eyes and long nose in other depictions of this violent man. (*Mary Evans*)

first Dracula was successful. Once again he was made Prince of Wallachia on the lance points of foreign troops. But the Wallachians did not want a repeat of Dracula's former savage reign. As Christmas approached they murdered him and sent his head to the Turkish Sultan.

Amadeus of Savoy, FELIX V (1383–1451)

Usurped: Papal Crown 1439
Social Origins: Duke of Savoy

Felix V is one of the few men in history to gain, and abdicate, two entirely different crowns. Born Amadeus, son of Duke Amadeus VII of Savoy, the future Felix succeeded to his north Italian Duchy in 1416. He was, however, a deeply religious man who found himself both unsuited to and unhappy with his role as temporal ruler. In 1434 he retired to a hermitage where he gained a reputation for learning and holiness. His retirement was not to last long.

In 1431 Eugene IV was elected Pope and at once tried to dismiss the Council of Basle, which was meeting to discuss church reforms. It was clear that Eugene's motives were less than honourable, for he had a strong personal interest in resisting the reforms which would have removed bribery and patronage. He failed, but the struggle between reforming council and self-interested Pope continued.

In 1439 the struggle reached a climax. The cardinals and bishops at the Council decided to replace Eugene. They sent a message to Amadeus. As a layman he would be free of clerical factionalism, but his holiness would guarantee recognition. Amadeus accepted, took the name of Felix V and hurried to Basle. Acting through the Council, Felix endeavoured to gain recognition of his papacy. Several states accepted him, or at least ignored Eugene, but Felix was never able to occupy Rome.

In 1447 Eugene died and was replaced in Rome by the more amenable Nicholas V. With the cause of the schism removed, Felix found himself without support and without a purpose. He abdicated in 1449, being granted a large pension by Nicholas, and died two years later. Felix was the last of the antipopes. Henceforth dissatisfaction with the Church in Rome would take the form of Reformation, which tore Christendom apart and established the modern pattern of Christianity.

Georg Boczkos von PODIEBRAD (1420–1471)

Kingmaker of Bohemia 1453
Social Origins: Czech Nobleman

In 1437 the native royal dynasty of Bohemia came to an end and the throne passed to King Albert of Hungary. Though initially accepted in Bohemia, the new king soon proved to be immensely unpopular. Large sections of the Bohemian nobility and peasantry had been won over by the religious teachings of John Hus, who had been executed in 1415, which embodied many features of the later Reformation. Albert, by contrast, was a strict Catholic who had nothing but contempt for the Taborites, as the followers of Hus were known.

Bohemian resentment grew at the rule of a foreign Catholic. Rebellion began to spread through the land and a Polish nobleman named Casimir was suggested as a more favourable king. Podiebrad was active in this movement, being a veteran of the religious Hussite Wars which had wracked the area some years earlier.

In 1439 Albert died. There was a move to place Casimir on the throne, but Podibrad now disagreed. He pointed out that Albert's heir, Ladislas V, was not old enough to walk, let alone rule. If the Bohemians accepted the legitimate heir, they could rule themselves. But if they overthrew the legitimate monarch, they might find themselves invaded. At a stormy meeting of the nobility, Podiebrad managed to win the majority to his way of thinking. He then had himself nominated as Regent in Bohemia for the young king. This move skilfully excluded Hungarian officials from claiming to rule for the king and seemed to ensure the Bohemians at least 20 years of self-rule.

In 1457 this cosy arrangement was destroyed when Ladislas died. Again the nobles met in a series of tumultuous meetings. However, the majority had been satisfied with Podiebrad's regency. He had little trouble having himself made king, taking the throne from the true heir, Matthias Corvinus, an adult Catholic.

The accession of Podiebrad enraged the few Catholic nobles in Bohemia, who had looked forward to the coming of age of Ladislas. They allied themselves with King Matthais Corvinus. The climax to the struggle came in 1466, when Podiebrad was completely victorious. He ruled until his death in 1471.

— ♛ —

LUDOVICO il MORO (1451–1508)

Usurped: Duchy of Milan 1476
Social Origins: Ducal Family

The turbulent country of Renaissance Italy was no place for a weak monarch. This was a fact recognized by Ludovico, and turned to his own advantage with great skill and cunning. He created a court which established new standards of opulence and achievement.

As a younger son of the mercenary-captain-turned-Duke Francesco Sforza (see above) Ludovico had plenty of opportunity to study his father's methods of government. When in 1466 Ludovico's elder brother Galeazzo became Duke, Ludovico showed himself to be an able and loyal helper. But ten years later Galeazzo died, leaving as heir his seven year old son named Gian. The treacherous and tortuous intrigues of intercity politics and internal rivalries were quite beyond such a young boy. Ludovico was nominated as regent.

Ludovico made an alliance with the powerful Kingdom of Naples and Gian was married to a daughter of the Neapolitan royal house to cement the alliance. Ludovico, meanwhile, married the beautiful and highly cultured Beatrice d'Este, daughter of the Duke of Ferrara. As Gian reached maturity, the Neapolitans and others applied pressure on Ludovico to resign. By this time, however, Ludovico had gained a liking for power and had little wish to relinquish his position. He refused to hand over power to the teenage Gian. Pressure built up and Ludovico became desperate.

Suddenly, in 1494 King Charles VIII of France invaded Italy to enforce a remote claim to the throne of Naples. Seeing a chance to escape his allies, Ludovico joined forces with Charles. The combined French-Milanese army swept southwards and Charles was crowned in Naples. Ludovico felt strong enough to abandon all pretence of ruling as Regent and proclaimed himself Duke of Milan. At this extremely convenient moment Gian dropped dead. It seems almost certain, reading contemporary accounts, that he was poisoned on the orders of Ludovico.

For the remaining 6 years of his rule, Ludovico governed Milan both wisely and well. His court became a shining example of Renaissance culture. Leonardo da Vinci was employed for a total of 16 years, completing the famous Last Supper mural and many other works of art. In 1500 Ludovico fell out with the new French King Louis XII. He was captured and kept a prisoner until his death in 1508.

— ♔ —

GIOVANNI BENTIVOGLI (1443–1508)

Usurped: Power in Bologna 1462
Social Origins: Gentry

The private papers of the Bentivoglia were destroyed when the magnificent Palazzo di Bentivoglia was burnt in 1507. It is therefore more difficult for the historian to piece together the story of their climb to power than that of other great families of the Italian Renaissance, such as the Medici or the Sforza.

During the early 15th century the Bentivoglia family rose to be one of the wealthiest and most influential in the great university city of Bologna in northern Italy. In 1446, however, the head of the household, Annibale, was murdered by a rival faction. He left a three year old son, Giovanni. Leadership of the family was taken over by Sante, an illegitimate but very able man. In 1462 Sante died, leaving the 19-year-old Giovanni as head of the most powerful family in the city.

Giovanni at once set about seizing power. Over the following few years he gathered all control into his own hands. However, Giovanni never took any title which indicated his position. He remained, in law, a private citizen like many others. However his enormous wealth and readiness to resort to violence or bribery as occasion demanded assured his position. He controlled the lucrative grain supplies of the city and distributed all government appointments.

During the 44 years Giovanni remained in power Bologna improved both financially and culturally. The city became increasingly concerned with trade and commerce. The narrow, muddy streets of the mediaeval city were swept away to be replaced by the broad, arcaded streets which remain to this day. Magnificent public buildings were constructed. The Bolognese cuisine came to be highly regarded, producing both a special form of pasta and the Bolognese sauce to adorn it.

Through all this time, Bologna had remained a Papal fief. The city had long since slipped from Papal control, though the titular authority remained with the Pope. In 1506 Pope Julius launched a surprise attack on Bologna to enforce his rule and drove Giovanni from the city. Giovanni died in exile two years later.

— ♛ —

MANFRED LANCIA (fl. mid-13th century)

Usurped: Power in Milan 1252

Social Origins: German Soldier

In 1252 the Holy Roman Emperor Conrad IV marched over the Alps into Italy to assert his control over his Italian inheritance. He was opposed both by Pope Innocent IV, and by the many communities which had won some form of independence from Imperial control. One such was the city of Milan.

Conrad sent his trusted commander Manfred Lancia with a thousand cavalrymen to impose Imperial authority on Milan. Manfred stormed into the city, overwhelming the citizens with his superior military force. However, Manfred had no more intention of paying heed to Imperial orders than had the Milanese. Using money looted from Milanese merchants to buy the loyalty of his cavalry, Manfred set himself up as sole dictator of Milan. Manfred's success proved to be ephemeral. He was soon overthrown and power was restored to the citizen republic.

— ♔ —

YUNG-LO (?–1424)

Usurped: Chinese Empire 1403

Social Origins: Imperial Family

Yung-lo, or Yong-le, took the throne of his nephew, believing that he had killed the young man. Not until much later was it learnt that the true Emperor still lived. After overthrowing the Mongol Dynasty, the peasant leader Hung Wu (see above) took power as Emperor and reorganized the Chinese Empire. He introduced many reforms and set his relatives, whom he could trust implicitly, in important positions.

When Hung Wu died in 1399 his young grandson Hui-ti ascended the throne. Almost at once the Empire began to fall apart. The Emperor's relatives felt less loyalty to the boy Emperor than they had to the tough warrior who had installed them in authority. Fighting broke out between factions of the family, in defiance of Imperial orders.

The conflict came to a height in 1403 when Yung-lo, a brother of Hung Wu, launched a determined attack on the capital city of Nanking. Yung-lo's troops smashed through the city walls, set fire to the city and began a general massacre. All those who had remained loyal to the Emperor were put to death. It was assumed that Hui-ti had been killed in the fighting, but forty years later he was found living as a monk in a remote area of the Empire. By this time Yung-lo was dead and Hui-ti was allowed to live the rest of his life in comfortable retirement.

Yung-lo, meanwhile, established his rule with an iron fist. After murdering the supporters of Hui-ti, Yung-lo moved on to his many relatives who held regional commands and ordered their executions. He concentrated even more power into the hands of the Emperor, stripping his officials of authority. Great voyages of discovery and trade were sponsored in the Pacific and Indian Oceans. Yung-lo also moved the capital north to Peking, where he ordered the construction of a mighty city. Thousands of peasants laboured on the building of Peking, raising the glittering palaces and the Forbidden City which remain to this day. Yung-lo died at the height of his powers in 1424.

QUTBUD din AIBAK (?–1215)
Usurped: Sultanate of Delhi 1206
Social Origins: Army Officer

In the early 11th century Afghans and Turks poured across the Hindu Kush to conquer much of northern India and convert large numbers to Islam. The state they set up became known as the Sultanate of Delhi. For many years the Sultanate remained part of the Afghan state, itself subject to the Abbasid Empire, based in the Arab heartlands. That situation was to change in 1206 when Qutbad din Aibak took Delhi out of the mainstream of Islamic organization.

The Afghan ruler Muhammed Ghuri had built up his power in Delhi and surrounding lands, but had not ignored his homeland. When Ghuri died in 1206, the general Qutbud din Aibak, who had once been a slave, was in Delhi. He at once proclaimed himself independent as the Sultan of Delhi, separating the Indian lands from those of Afghanistan. The Sultanate of Delhi was thus cut off from the homeland of Islam. Although it kept the faith pure, the Delhi rulers were culturally assimilated by Indian civilization. The Delhi Sultanate became a purely Indian state.

ALA UD DIN (?–1316)
Usurped: Sultanate of Delhi 1296
Social Origins: Royal Family

Under his uncle, Sultan Khalji, Ala Ud Din proved himself to be an able and ambitious general. He fought many successful campaigns against the enemies of the Sultanate of Delhi, which ruled most of northern India. In 1296 he was sent south to Devagiri where he defeated the state of Yadava and acquired a vast amount of booty. Returning to Delhi, Ala Ud Din bribed the nobles with his loot. Gaining their support and backing, he immediately murdered his uncle and proclaimed himself Sultan.

Once established, Ala Ud Din reorganized the taxation system of the Sultanate and concentrated more power into his own hands. These reforms greatly increased the power and authority of the Sultan. He was able to launch military expeditions against other Indian states, reviving the dreams of earlier Delhi Sultans to extend their empire over the entire subcontinent. In 1311 he reached Madurai, at the southern tip of India, but was unable to capture the city. Called back to Delhi by troubles amongst his nobles, Ala Ud Din was involved with internal disputes for the remaining ten years of his reign.

Zahir-ud-Din Mahomet BABARS (1483–1530)
Usurped: Delhi Sultanate 1525
Social Origins: Mongol Nobleman

Born Zahir-ud-Din Mahomet, Babars took the name by which he is better known to emphasize his fighting qualities. Babars means 'The Tiger' and it was this bellicose reputation which led to Babars being invited to attempt to take power in Delhi. The reputation was well deserved.

In 1495 Babars became Khan of Ferghana, south of the Aral Sea. He was very conscious that he was the descendant of two great Mongol conquerors, Genghis Khan and Tamerlane the Magnificent, and at once set about following their lead. He captured the wealthy city of Samarkand and soon afterwards established himself in Kabul. Defeated on his northern frontier, Babars was looking for conquests in the upper Indus Valley when messengers arrived from Delhi.

By the early 16th century, the Delhi Sultanate had fallen from its previous grandeur under such rulers as Ala Ud Din (see above). The Sultanate had come under the control of an Afghan dynasty which installed fellow Afghans in positions of power and granted them wide ranging privileges and powers. The Sultans relied upon the traditional tribal rivalries of the nobles to maintain power. The Sultan Ibrahim, however, felt strong enough to enforce his power more directly. He began stripping provincial nobles of their authority and wealth. The nobles wanted to be rid of Ibrahim, but knew they were not strong enough. They therefore turned to Babars.

In 1525 Babars led a strong force down from Afghanistan to join with the army of the nobles and marched on Delhi. Ibrahim marched out to meet him with a much larger army. The two forces met at Panipat, and Babars won a devastating victory. Marching on to Delhi, Babars proclaimed himself Sultan. The local dynasts soon found that they had only exchanged a harsh master for one even harsher. Using his foreign troops, Babars imposed his authority throughout the lands of the Sultanate and reconquered areas which had been lost. In time his descendents, the great Mughal or Mogul Dynasty would bring all of India beneath their sway.

— 👑 —

EDWARD IV (1442–1483)
Usurped: Kingdom of England 1461
Social Origins: Royal Family

One of the most romantic figures in English history, Edward of York was intelligent, witty and handsome, but above all he was successful. In the turbulent years which followed Henry VI's lapse into madness, Edward showed himself to be the only man able to master the situation. One of his few weaknesses was a liking for women. It was a fault which nearly destroyed him.

In 1453, at the age of 29 King Henry VI went mad. For years his government had been dominated by two factions, one led by Cardinal Beaufort and the Duke of Somerset, the other headed by Richard, Duke of York and the fabulously wealthy Neville family (see Earl of Warwick below). As soon as the king became ill the squabble between the two factions grew more heated. Beaufort gained the confidence of Queen Margaret, Henry's wife, and so won power. His administration proved to be both corrupt and inept. The Yorkists resisted the government, and fighting broke out which soon turned into a civil war.

In 1460 the Duke of York was killed at the Battle of Wakefield. Leadership of the Yorkist cause fell on the 18-year-old Edward, son of the Duke. Allied with his 32-year-old friend Richard Neville, Earl of Warwick, Edward set out to avenge his father.

Edward actually had a better claim to the throne than King Henry, who was the grandson of the usurper Henry IV (see above), while Edward was descended from a more senior branch of the royal family. While the Henrys ruled well, the Yorks had not pushed their claim. Now that civil war had broken out, Edward declared himself the true king and set about taking Henry's crown.

Within three months of Wakefield, Edward had raised a fresh Yorkist army and marched on the Lancastrians, as the Beaufort party was now known. At Towton, in Yorkshire, the armies met in the middle of a snowstorm. Edward won a devastating victory, causing Henry and Margaret to flee to Scotland. Edward had won his crown.

Three years later Edward married Elizabeth Woodville, the widow of a Lancastrian knight and a low-born woman. The nobles had wanted the king to make a political marriage and were furious. Edward's constant philanderings increased their anger, for the nobles believed this showed that Edward did not love Queen Elizabeth. Other policies of Edward caused unrest and in 1469 the nobles rose against him. Edward fled to the continent.

In March 1471 he returned with a tiny army. In a dramatic and well conducted campaign he defeated his enemies and killed Henry's son, Prince Edward. A few weeks later King Henry himself died, almost certainly murdered on the orders of Edward, who now felt himself secure on the throne. None dared face the brilliant, handsome young king again, and Edward ruled in comparative peace until his death in 1483.

Richard Neville, Earl of WARWICK (1428–1471)

Kingmaker of England 1461–1471
Social Origins: Nobleman

Richard Neville, Earl of Warwick, was one of the richest men in England, owning vast estates and holding positions of power. He did not hesitate to use these advantages to advance himself and his family during the chaos of the Wars of the Roses. He did not scruple to change sides when it suited him, helping raise two men to the throne, but he met his match in one of his protégés.

When, in 1453, King Henry VI went mad Warwick joined the Duke of York, throwing the enormous weight of the Neville resources into the struggle. By 1459 York had reached a position where he could claim the

Warwick
An engraving of Richard Neville, Earl of Warwick, based on a portrait. Warwick was the richest man in England and could raise large armies from among his retainers. He used them first to install Edward IV and then to remove him in favour of Henry VI. Before the Battle of Barnet in 1471, Warwick showed his retainers he would not desert them, as rumour had indicated, by publicly killing his horse and taking his place in the battleline on foot. He was killed in the subsequent rout. (*Mary Evans*)

crown, but the following year he was killed in battle. Warwick then placed the military might of his retainers at the disposal of York's son Edward, Earl of March. With Warwick's men, Edward defeated his enemies in the opposing Lancastrian faction, imprisoned King Henry VI and made himself king in 1461.

Warwick, considerably older and more experienced than Edward, took over the reins of government. He presided over the internal reform of institutions and over foreign policy. After four years, however, Edward decided to take control for himself. While Warwick was in France negotiating an alliance, Edward went behind his back to seal a pact with the Duke of Burgundy. Warwick was furious and stormed back to England. Edward then blocked the marriage between Warwick's daughter and his own brother, Duke of Clarence, on the grounds that this would dangerously increase the influence of both Clarence and the Nevilles. Warwick retired from court and began plotting his return to power.

In 1469 the marriage with Clarence went ahead and Warwick raised an army from his own men and the defeated Lancastrians. Edward was caught without an army and had to surrender. He agreed to rule under the direction of Warwick, but secretly raised fresh forces and obliged Warwick to flee to France. There Warwick met Margaret, Queen of Henry VI, and managed to organize a formal Lancastrian-Neville alliance. In 1470 Warwick landed in England and raised a massive army. Now it was Edward's turn to run. Warwick marched to London, released Henry VI and restored him to the throne. The newly re-instated king, of course, had little real power. That lay with Warwick.

In March 1471 Edward returned with a small army, Warwick hurried to fight him, the armies meeting at Barnet on 14 April. The battle took place in a thick fog. Though Warwick was a brave man, he could not cope with the complexities of controlling an army in fog. Hacking at the enemy with sword and axe, Warwick's men became disorientated in the mist. Confusion reigned and Warwick was defeated. Though Edward had given orders that Warwick was to be taken alive, the Earl was killed in the rout. Warwick's career as kingmaker was over.

— 👑 —

RICHARD III (1452–1485)

Usurped: Kingdom of England 1483
Social Origins: Royal Family

For generations Richard III of England has been castigated as the epitome of the unscrupulous usurper and wicked uncle. That he was a violent man is beyond doubt, and he could be capable of great cruelty. However, it is possible, if not probable, that he honestly believed he was acting for the best and that personal ambition played only a small role in his seizure of power.

Richard's brother, King Edward IV died on 9 April 1483, leaving two young sons. Richard, then Duke of Gloucester, immediately proclaimed the elder boy King Edward V and set off to take on his duties as Protector and Regent. He was staggered to learn that the Woodvilles, the young King's maternal relatives, were raising a rebellion to seize the regency for themselves. Richard put the rising down, but the coronation had to be postponed. While arrangements for a fresh ceremony were being made, almost unbelievable news rocked the nation.

The Bishop of Bath and Wells came forward to state that the young King Edward V was a bastard. Before Edward IV had married his queen, Elizabeth Woodville, he had formally betrothed himself to a woman named Eleanor Butler. The engagement had never been formally broken so, according to the law of the time, the Woodville marriage was null and void.

Richard was placed in a difficult position. The Woodvilles began secretly to raise troops to enforce the position of Edward V while the long-defeated Lancastrian faction began to raise its head again. On 13 June Richard attended a meeting of the Royal Council. He suddenly interrupted the debate to point out Lord Hastings as the leader of the Woodville conspiracy. Richard had Hastings hacked to death on the spot. Other Woodville plotters were arrested and similarly despatched.

Through all this young Edward V remained in the royal apartments of the Tower of London. After the collapse of the Woodville plot, Edward was joined by his younger brother Richard. Richard of Gloucester knew that a boy king was a weak king. Now that Edward V's right to reign was in doubt he was even weaker. The horrors of the civil war known as the Wars of the Roses (see Warwick and Edward IV above) were still fresh in the memory. The nation did not want a fresh outbreak of civil war and needed a strong king. Richard put himself forwards, and allowed Parliament to choose between him and Edward V.

Parliament did not hesitate. They chose to believe the Bishop of Bath and Wells, though his statement was unsubstantiated, and declared Edward and his brother illegitimate. Richard, Duke of Gloucester was made King Richard III. It was at this point that Richard's darkest crime is said to have been committed. His young nephews suddenly vanished. According to histories written some time later, Richard had the boys murdered. But the evidence for this is thin, based on rumour, hearsay and statements by Richard's enemies. Other rumours stated that the boys had been given a pension and sent into secret exile in Hungary or that they had died a natural death. We do not really know what happened to the boys, but certainly Richard got them out of the way somehow.

Richard was now secure on the throne, but his reign was to be neither long nor happy for his enemies were plotting together and raising fresh armies. In 1485 Richard died on the field of battle.

— ♛ —

Abu Abdullah, BOABDIL (?–c. 1495)

Usurped: Kingdom of Granada 1482
Social Origins: Royal Family

The small but densely populated and immensely prosperous Kingdom of Granada was, by the dawn of the 15th century, the only Moslem state remaining in Spain. It had managed to survive centuries of Christian attack because of its high population, nearly a quarter more than that of Castile, and the North African allies who could be relied upon to help throw back a Christian attack. Unfortunately Granada had a tradition of political intrigue and treachery beside which even the Borgia pale into insignificance. It was into this wealthy, but strife-torn and beseiged kingdom that Boabdil was born sometime in the mid-15th century.

Boabdil, or Abu Abdullah, was the son of King Abul-Hassan and, as soon as he was old enough to do so, plunged into the vicious intrigues at court. His chief supporters were the members of the powerful Abencerrages family, which had accompanied the original Moslem invaders of Spain in the 8th century. Boabdil's mother was cast aside by Abul-Hassan in favour of a slave girl and her family moved into the camp of Boabdil. After years of rivalry, between Boabdil with the Abencerrages and the supporters of Abul-Hassan and his new wife, Boabdil was forced to flee. Abul-Hassan invited the seven leading Abencerragas into a hall at the Alhambra, or royal palace, and had them all slaughtered. The beautiful room where this terrible deed took place is still known as the Hall of the Abencerrages. Turning against the cruelty of Abul-Hassan the people of Granada clamoured for the return of Boabdil, but the king refused.

In 1482, Boabdil entered the Alhambra of Granada at the head of a band of Abencerrages. Abul-Hassan fled allowing Boabdil to assume the throne as Mohammed XI. Abul-Hassan, however, was able to retain a grip on some of his kingdom and remained a constant threat to Boabdil. Sensing this disunity Ferdinand and Isabella, joint monarchs of Castile, attacked. For ten years a long three-cornered struggle continued between Castile, Boabdil and Abul-Hassan. In 1486 Abul-Hassan died, but his place was taken by his younger brother Mohammed XII. Even extreme danger could not unite the two Moslem factions. When Malaga was on the point of surrendering to the Christians, Mohammed XII sent an army of 40,000 men to its relief. The column was ambushed and destroyed by no other than Boabdil. Malaga fell.

In 1492 Boabdil found himself besieged in his capital city of Granada. Realizing that the forces of his kingdom, dissipated in long civil war, were unequal to the struggle, Boabdil surrendered. As part of the peace treaty he made the Christian monarchs guarantee the same freedom of worship to the Moslems, as he had given his Christian subjects. In the event the promise was not honoured. In 1499 the Granada Moslems were forced to convert to Christianity or to leave Spain.

Girolamo SAVANAROLA (1452–1498)

Usurped: Power in Florence 1494
Social Origins: Monk

The rule of Savanarola in Florence is an aberration of the Italian Renaissance. At a time when princes ruled in splendour, dominating courts of unequalled magnificence and patronizing artists of the calibre of Michelangelo and Leonardo da Vinci, Savanarola imposed a puritannical rule, burning paintings and musical instruments. His rise to power is as curious as his use of power.

Born in 1452 to a well-to-do family in Ferrara, Savanarola received a good education and began training for a medical career. When just 21 Savanarola fell completely in love with a daughter of the local noble house. His suit was thrown aside with little attempt at tact. Savanarola bitterly renounced the world and entered a Dominican monastery at Bologna where he brooded on his injury.

Over the following 16 years, Savanarola won a reputation as a great orator and strict moralist. In 1490 he transferred to the Monastery of San Marco in Florence. Enormous crowds came to listen to his sermons, which were masterpieces of oratory, calling on every possible use of imagery, poetry and rhetoric. Savanarola's constant theme was the wickedness of luxury and the need to establish a Christian commonwealth. In 1492 Lorenzo the Magnificent, ruler of Florence died, leaving the city to his son Piero.

Piero Medici proved unequal to the task. His conduct of affairs was indecisive and muddled. In 1494 Piero was driven from the city and the people turned to Savanarola to establish the longed-for Christian state. Savanarola joyfully took power, making himself dictator with far more control than the Medici had ever exercised. He burnt such luxurious signs of decadence as paintings, lace, fine clothes and musical instruments. For three years he ruled triumphant, but in 1497 his fall from power began.

Savanarola refused to attend the Pope in Rome and frequently disobeyed Papal instructions. In 1497 he was excommunicated and much of the religious impact of his speeches was lost. The following year the supporters of the Medici gained office and ordered Savanarola to stop public speaking. Savanarola refused, for this was the true basis of his influence. An ordeal by fire between Savanarola and a Franciscan was then ordered, but the event ended in a shambles and the mob turned on Savanarola. He was hurried off

to a swift trial, found guilty of heresey and hanged. The Medici returned to
rule Florence.

— ♔ —

OLIVEROTTO Euffreducci (?–1502)

Usurped: Power in Fermo 1501
Social Origins: Citizen

Orphaned when an infant, Oliverotto was brought up by his uncle Giovanni
Fogliani, a leading citizen of the Italian city of Fermo. When he was old
enough, Oliverotto was sent off to act as a mercenary under the famous
condotierre, or mercenary captain, Paulo Vitelli. In 1501, after some years of
fighting, Oliverotto decided the time had come to return home. He did not
return alone, nor without plans.

Oliverotto asked his uncle Giovanni to organize a great banquet for all the
leading citizens so that he could show them all that he had learnt and gained
during his years away. The unsuspecting Giovanni happily complied, glad
that his nephew was returning home. When he entered the city, Oliverotto
rode at the head of a magnificent entourage of over 100 servants and guards.
A few days later the welcoming feast was held.

The leading citizens of Fermo entered Giovanni's house, to be welcomed
by entertainments and foods more luxurious than Fermo had seen for many
years. Oliverotto had paid for the feast, and the influential guests were duly
impressed. Perhaps they considered asking the rich young soldier to serve in
some civic capacity. We do not know, for Oliverotto suddenly gave a signal
and in rushed his soldiers, swords in hand. All the guests, including Giovanni
were butchered.

Leaping on his horse Oliverotto raced to the town hall with a band of his
men. He stormed in and demanded that the officials now obey him as Prince,
rather than the elected council, most of whose members were now dead.
Those officials who refused were killed. Over the next few weeks Oliverotto
swept away the entire municipal government of Fermo, replacing it with
institutions of his own invention. Anyone who objected, or who Oliverotto
thought might resist, was killed out of hand. Within a short time the brutal
dictatorship of Oliverotto was securely imposed on Fermo. If he had not been
killed aiding his old employer Vitelli in a matter of international politics just
a year later, Oliverotto may have set up an hereditary Principality. As it was
Fermo fell back gratefully into the hands of the citizens.

— ♔ —

CESARE BORGIA (1476–1507)

Usurped: Power in the Romagna 1503
Social Origins: Clerical Family

A typical son of the Italian Renaissance, Cesare Borgia was highly educated, artistic and extremely intelligent. He was also unscrupulous, ruthless and intensely ambitious. In him the conflicting urges of the Renaissance became one.

Cesare was just 17 when his father, Rodrigo Borgia, became Pope as Alexander VI in 1492. Leaving his studies at Pisa University, Cesare hurried to Rome. Within a fortnight he had been created Archbishop of Valencia and a few months later he was made a cardinal. However, Cesare found that the life of a high-ranking cleric was not for him. He was too fond of hunting, war and chasing women to be happy in even the corrupt Papacy of his father. Cesare coveted the office of commander of the Papal army, but this was held by his elder brother, Duke John of Gandia. At the time it was rumoured that the brothers were also rivals in an incestuous love for their sister Lucrezia.

In June 1496 Duke John was brutally murdered and his body dumped in the Tiber. It is highly likely, though not proven, that Cesare was responsible. Nonetheless he succeeded to his brother's position as military commander of the Papal forces. Alexander was determined that the Papacy should regain its temporal authority in the Romagna, a fertile region of central Italy. As military commander, Cesare was destined to play a crucial role in this.

In October 1498 Cesare visited the court of the French king. He arrived at the head of a magnificent retinue, clothed in silk. After negotiating a treaty between France and the Pope, Cesare married Charlotte of Navarre. Having stayed with his wife for only a few days, he took the promised French troops and marched south.

The Romagna was a patchwork of republics and duchies which owed nominal allegiance to the Pope but were in reality independent, Cesare was determined to bring them under Borgia control, using the pretence of Papal authority. In 1480 he used French and Papal troops to capture Imoa, Camerina and Forli. Dealing with the treacherous Princess Catherine of Forli, Cesare nearly lost his life, but managed to outwit the woman and imprison her. The following year he took Faenze, Pesaro and Rimini. When Capua was taken, Cesare allowed his soldiers to plunder and loot the city. He took 40 of the prettiest girls to Rome to satify the lusts of himself and his father. The grateful Alexander grouped the captured towns into a single Duchy of Romagna and gave them to his son.

In January 1503 Cesare won his greatest success, by a combination of treachery and cruelty, and established himself as undisputed ruler of the Romagna. The noblemen of the area were uneasy at Cesare's success and tried constantly to evade his instructions and orders. They were led by Vitellozzo Oliverotto (see above), Gravina Orsini and Pagolo. Cesare noted their suspicions and launched a successful deception. He told them that he was happy to leave them their power if they supported him in foreign wars. He also promised that they need not meet him unless they wished to do so.

For weeks, Cesare smiled at the four nobles, heaping them with gifts and paying careful deference to their local jurisdiction. In December 1502 Cesare captured the town of Sinigaglia with troops drafted from the lands of the four nobles. He invited them to attend the victory celebrations and they, now trusting Cesare, did so. As soon as they arrived, Cesare had the men seized and strangled.

Having secured his power, Cesare ruled firmly and without mercy. Any person who opposed him or his father was killed. At least one archbishop and a duke fell to Borgia daggers or poisons. Lesser men were killed in their hundreds. Despite this Cesare's rule was generally beneficient. He imposed order on a chaotic land and allowed trade and industry to flourish. His success, however, was to be short-lived.

In August 1503 both Cesare and Alexander suddenly fell ill after a meal. It was rumoured that they had accidentally eaten a poisoned dish intended for a guest. Alexander died, but Cesare survived. While Cesare lay ill, his enemies were busy. A new Pope, Julius II, was elected who was opposed to the Borgia and many of Cesare's men were dislodged from their positions. Cesare was thrown into prison and only released when he gave up his title of Duke of the Romagna. He later said 'I had thought of everything to do in case my father died, the only thing I did not think of was that I should be ill at that moment myself.'

Cesare fled to the court of his father-in-law, King John of Navarre. There he was treated well and given a command in the army. King John hoped to take advantage of the undoubted military gifts of Cesare. For a while Cesare flourished in his new home. But on 12 March 1507 he was killed in a skirmish with Spanish troops. He was just 32 years old.

SELIM I (c. 1465–1521)

Usurped: Sultanate of Turkey 1512
Social Origins: Royal Family

Known to contemporaries as Selim the Grim, this Sultan expanded the realm of the Turks to include vast new territories. He also extended the position of the Sultan to make himself virtually unassailable. All this was built on the back of a usurpation of terrible brutality.

The Turks were at this period still culturally a nomadic, Asian people. They had conquered large areas of the Balkans and Asia Minor, but still had little conception of settled civilization or diplomacy. The Sultan Bayazid II, Selim's father, pursued an active foreign policy based upon attacking any neighbouring state whenever he got the chance.

In 1512 Selim, by now well into his forties turned on Bayazid. Perhaps he felt that the old man was passed his prime, or Selim may simply have been hungry for the power so long denied him. The younger, more dynamic Selim gained the support of the army officers so powerful in early Turkish society. Bayazid was forced to abdicate in favour of Selim. At a banquet soon afterwards Selim slipped poison into his father's meal. As soon as the old man had breathed his last, Selim ordered the execution of all his brothers and nephews. None, no matter how young, escaped the carnage. Viziers and other officials whom Selim could not trust were next to die. Within a short time Selim had a secure grip on the nation.

As Sultan, Selim led his armies to a series of brilliant victories. He captured Mesopotamia, Armenia and Egypt, adding them to the growing Turkish Empire centred on Constantinople. He defeated the last of the Abbasids, now a decadent dynasty, and took from them the title of Caliph. This endowed him with the spiritual leadership of the entire Moslem world, while his armies gave him temporal pre-eminence. He was able to pass this potent combination of religious and military power on to his son, Suleiman the Magnificent when he died in 1521.

Hernando CORTES (1485–1547)

Kingmaker of Mexico 1519
Social Origins: Spanish Nobleman

Cortes was an ambitious adventurer who left Spain in 1503, at the age of 19, to seek his fortune in the newly discovered Caribbean Islands. Through a remarkable series of circumstances and his own amazing abilities, Cortes became master of a mighty empire, and dispensed kingdoms as he wished. It was his tragedy to fall foul of an unfeeling bureaucracy.

In 1518 Velasquez, Governor of Cuba, gave Cortes command of an expedition to set up a new colony, to be named Vera Cruz, on the Mexican coast. Cortes had 500 men, a few horses and some guns. He soon fell out with Velasquez, renounced the Governor's authority and hurriedly sent a ship to Spain to reaffirm his loyalty to the crown.

At Vera Cruz Cortes was astounded to receive ambassadors claiming to

Cortes

Hernando Cortes was born of a wealthy noble family and travelled to America at an early age. After overthrowing the Aztec Empire, Cortes was made a Marquis in his own right and was granted a coat of arms. This manuscript illustration dates from the years of his greatness and may have been drawn from life. His body now rests in Mexico City, the Christian city which he founded on the ruins of the pagan Aztec capital.

come from a mighty Emperor. The strangers carried gifts of gold and silver worth a fortune and promised more if Cortes agreed not to visit Montezuma, Emperor of the Aztecs. Cortes took perhaps the only decision a brave and ambitious man in his position could take. He mustered his little army and set off to visit the Emperor. Several subject tribes of the Aztecs joined Cortes's force, as did many individual Indians. A chieftain named Ixtlilxochitl was particularly useful, giving supplies to the Spaniards.

After a short skirmish, Cortes entered the fabulously wealthy and enormous city of Tenochtitlan, now Mexico City. Montezuma surrendered to Cortes, whom he took to be a god, and the Spaniard became master of the vast wealth of the Aztec Empire. At first Cortes ruled through the Aztec officials, but a rising which nearly succeeded in ousting Cortes led to terrible bloodshed and the destruction of Tenochtitlan. Cortes then imposed a harsh rule on Mexico, but rewarded the Indians who had helped him. Ixtlilxochitl, for instance, was made King of Texcuca.

Created a Marquis and Governor of Mexico by King Charles of Spain, Cortes ruled Mexico for 10 years. However, the royal officials sent to help Cortes disapproved of his policies and programmes. They managed to engineer Cortes's removal from office. Cortes travelled to Spain to clear his name, but Charles preferred to trust his officials. Cortes, the man who had gained Mexico and set up kings, died in poverty in 1547.

— ♕ —

ATAHUALPA (c. 1495–1533) .

Usurped: Inca Empire
Social Origins: Royal Family

In 1525 Huayna Capac, the Inca, or God-Emperor of the Quechua, died. He left the control of his mighty mountain empire to his son Huascar, but the young man was not destined to have a happy or trouble-free reign.

The vast Inca Empire stretched along western South America from modern Quito to Valparaiso, spreading from the coastal lowlands to the highest peaks of the Andes. Millions of people lived within the highly complex society of the Empire. Farmlands were operated on a communal system, while craftsmen lived in great cities, often built of stone and decorated with gold and silver. This great empire had arisen almost in isolation, with only infrequent contact with other settled lands to the north. The entire structure was built around the holy Emperor, the Inca.

Huascar took over the reins of power, but he was not a particularly able man. Far more popular was an illegitimate son of Huayna Capac called

Atahualpa
A European engraving showing the Inca Atahualpa bound in chains as the prisoner of the Spanish Conquistador Francisco Pizarro. Atahualpa was held to ransom by Pizarro who extorted a vast quantity of gold and silver before being executed on a trumped-up charge. The engraving was completed a few years later and may be based on eye-witness accounts. (*Mary Evans*)

Atahualpa. This intelligent and brave young man had been given the governorship of Quito by his father. His good rule contrasted with the poor administration of his brother the Inca.

In 1532 Atahualpa repudiated his brother's overlordship and declared himself independent. Huascar sent an army against Quito and the Inca Empire plunged into a bloody civil war. After three years of fighting Atahualpa had won and Huascar was imprisoned. Atahualpa was the Inca, but not for long.

At this moment of triumph, Atahualpa received disturbing news. Strangers with white skins, weapons which flashed fire and killed at a distance, and ferocious monsters which they could ride had landed in the territory of the Inca. Accompanied by several hundred nobles and attendants, Atahualpa went to visit the advancing white men. The Spaniards were led by Hernando Pizarro, a cruel and ruthless man.

When Atahualpa arrived he was faced by a demand to surrender his Empire to King Charles of Spain, of whom Atahualpa had never heard. He refused. The Spaniards attacked the unarmed Indians, killing hundreds of them. Atahualpa was captured and thrown into a prison cell. In an effort to gain his freedom, Atahualpa offered to fill the room with gold. Pizarro accepted the deal. Messengers were sent out from the Inca to gather the gold of the Empire and within a few weeks the room was filled, but Pizarro did not release Atahualpa. Instead he executed him by strangulation. The government collapsed without its Inca and the whole Empire fell into the hands of Spain.

COSIMO de MEDICI (1519–1574)

Usurped: Duchy of Florence 1537
Social Origins: Ducal Family

Cosimo de Medici belonged to a junior branch of the great Medici family, the Dukes of Florence. Though far from poor, his family was only distantly connected to the main Medici family. At birth he seemed destined to lead the quiet life of a country gentleman. Nothing could have been further from the truth.

In January 1537, when Cosimo was just 17 years old, Duke Alessandro de Medici was murdered in a private feud. With Alessandro the senior branch of the Medici died out. The great men of Florence gathered to discuss what should be done about the government of their city and its surrounding lands. The institutions of republican government had been stripped of all power by the Medici, but they remained in existence. It was decided to revive the republic and return power to the Council. Then Cosimo arrived.

As soon as he had heard of the death of Alessandro, Cosimo had decided to become master of Florence. He had no troops on whom to rely, nor was he well-known in the city. He decided to use guile to gain his end. He came to Florence with just two friends, presented himself to the Council and claimed the title of Duke. The Council were undecided. Cosimo had a claim to the Duchy, but the Council had wanted a Republic.

Cosimo, however, gave the impression of being an easily-led youth. He pretended to be interested only in hunting and luxury. When one of the chief ministers, Francesco Guicciardini, suggested Cosimo might like to marry his pretty daughter, Cosimo pretended to be delighted. Guicciardini and three others, Filippo Strozzi, Valori and Acciajuoli, believed Cosimo to be a flighty youth who could easily be kept satisfied with entertainments and women. They saw in Cosimo a way to keep power to themselves without the risks of seeking power through elections and assemblies. They hailed Cosimo as Duke, and the rest of the Council followed their lead.

Once installed as Duke, however, Cosimo revealed his true colours. He hired a band of tough, ruthless bodyguards and set about imposing his will on Florence. He dismissed his advisers and appointed men he could trust, or bribe, to positions of authority. Strozzi and Valori were banished, along with many other men of influence.

In the late summer of 1537 these exiles raised an army of mercenaries and French troops lent by King Henry II. This formidable force was met at Montemurlo by mercenaries hired by Cosimo. The troops of Cosimo outmanoeuvred the insurgents, totally defeated them and captured all the leaders, except Piero Strozzi, son of Filippo. Cosimo had the captives led back to Florence where they were executed in a series of judicial murders such as even Florence had never seen before.

In 1539 Cosimo married Elenora of Naples, thus assuring himself of a rich and powerful ally. He imposed a tough, ruthless rule on Florence which allowed for no opposition. However, his policies were generally wise and productive. Florence increased in size, swallowing Siena in 1555, and became even wealthier as merchants and craftsmen flourished. Cosimo was particularly careful to encourage new industries, especially that of tapestry weaving. He was a great patron of the arts and sponsored many excavations of ancient Etruscan and Roman sites.

In 1569 he was granted the title Grand Duke of Tuscany by the Pope. By the time of his death in 1574 Cosimo had turned Florence into the dominant city of Tuscany, the most powerful state in Italy. If his accession and rule had not been so tinged with violence and cruelty, Cosimo might be counted as one of the greatest rulers of Italian history.

— ♛ —

John Dudley, Earl of NORTHUMBERLAND (1502–1553)

Kingmaker of England 1553
Social Origins: Lawyer

John Dudley was the son of Edmund Dudley, a clever lawyer who helped King Henry VII to fiddle huge amounts of money from the nation. John was to outdo even his father in audacity and illegal dealings.

When Henry VIII died in 1547 he left a young son, Edward VI, under the control of a Council of Regency led by the Duke of Somerset, the new King's uncle. Dudley was a member of the Council. Within a few months he had put Somerset in a bad light and persuaded the Council to make himself Protector of the Realm. He then took the title Duke of Northumberland to match the dignity of his new role.

As Protector, Dudley reformed the coinage, pocketing a huge amount of money in the process, and instituted other measures. By late 1552, Dudley had made himself unpopular enough for men to look to Somerset. Dudley feared for his position and ordered the arrest of Somerset. The Duke was found guilty of a trumped-up charge of treason and beheaded in January 1553. Dudley's power had become unassailable. Only the king could remove him from office, but King Edward VI was still only a boy.

Late in the spring of 1553, Edward fell ill. Dudley was worried, for his position rested on the survival of the young king. The next heir to the throne was Princess Mary, Edward's elder and strong-willed sister. Dudley knew that Mary would rule for herself and dismiss him from office. Therefore, Dudley began to plot.

On 21 May 1553 he married his son, Lord Guildford Dudley, to the king's cousin Lady Jane Grey. Lady Jane was just 17 at this time. She was beautiful, well educated and highly respected. Dudley hoped to use her to secure his own position. Using religion as a pretext, Dudley persuaded Edward to make the Protestant Lady Jane his heir, rather than the Catholic Princess Mary. Edward, a staunch Protestant, was only too happy to agree. The king then died on July 6 1553.

At once Dudley proclaimed Lady Jane as Queen of England, with his son as royal consort. He ordered the immediate arrest of Mary, but she escaped and fled to Norfolk. The people saw through Dudley's scheme, recognizing it as an attempt to prolong his Protectorship, and preferred to have a monarch of blood royal. Many nobles and ordinary folk flocked to Norfolk to support Mary. Dudley knew he had to act fast.

He gathered a small army and left London to confront Mary. As soon as he was out of sight, the Londoners slammed shut the gates of the city and declared for Mary. Dudley's army melted away from him once it became clear that the country was for Mary. He was captured by the Earl of

Arundel, a supporter of Mary. Mary quickly ordered the execution of Dudley and his son, together with the beautiful, but dangerous Lady Jane Grey.

CALVAGH O'DONNELL (?-1566)

Usurped: Lordship of Tyrconnel 1556
Social Origins: Nobleman

By the mid-16th century the English were making serious attempts to enforce the rule of the King of England, nominal High King of Ireland, on an unruly populace. The O'Donnell's of Donegal, for many years one of the most powerful families in Ireland, were in the forefront of the struggle.

In 1538 Manus O'Donnell formed an alliance with the O'Neills and the O'Briens, traditional enemies of his clan, against the English. For some years the alliance successfully opposed the English, a prominant role being taken by Manus's son Calvagh O'Donnell. The English King Henry VIII managed to disrupt the alliance by offering to recognize Manus as Earl of Tyrconnel and place him in charge of surrounding lands, including those of the O'Neills. Manus defected to the English cause.

The new Earl of Tyrconnel soon found himself in trouble at home. His son, Calvagh felt that he was not being properly rewarded for his services. He overthrew his father and took the title of Earl of Tyrconnel, though this was not recognized by the English until 1557. Four years later Calvagh was captured by the O'Neills and thrown into prison. He died in 1566.

— 👑 —

CATHERINE de MEDICI (1519–1589)

Usurped: Power in France 1559
Social Origins: Italian Noblewoman

Catherine de Medici was a true product of the Italian Renaissance. She was highly educated, a great connoisseur of the arts, and an insatiably ambitious schemer who balked at no amount of intrigue or treachery in the pursuit of power. When she came to France in 1533 as the 14-year-old bride of the Dauphin Henri she brought the Italian Renaissance with her. It was to prove a mixed blessing for her new country.

As wife to the Dauphin, or heir to the throne, Catherine led a dazzling existence. She was able to influence the social life of the court, and so of the nation. Her Italian chefs greatly improved French cuisine, and her appreciation of the arts had a profound effect on the attitudes of the French nobility. In 1547 her husband became King Henri (or Henry) II and her influence increased accordingly, but it was still restricted to society.

In 1559 Henry II died, leaving the throne to his 15-year-old son, Francis II. Power was placed in the hands of a Regency Council in which Catherine and the Duke of Guise were paramount. Catherine gained a taste for power which she would never lose. In her attempts to maintain her grip on power, she plunged France deep into civil war.

At this time France was in the throes of the Reformation. A minority of her people, popularly known as the Huguenots, had embraced Protestantism while the majority remained Catholic. Catherine hoped to heal the breaches between the two factions, but Guise, a staunch Catholic, opposed any compromise with the Huguenots.

In 1560 Francis II died to be replaced by his 10-year-old brother Charles IX. Catherine found herself struggling with the Guise faction to maintain her grip on power. She tried to play the Guise off against the Huguenots so that the two factions would weaken each other. As part of this policy she condoned the terrible St Bartholomew's Day Massacre in 1572. In a few days, the Guise party treacherously murdered some 50,000 Huguenots, including many Protestant noblemen. Rather than weaken the factions, this merely increased religious violence.

In 1574 Charles died and his brother Henry III ascended the throne. Aged 23 Henry happily handed power to his mother in return for luxuries and dissolute behaviour. Catherine continued to rule, but the increasing violence robbed her of real power. Civil war between the Catholic Guise faction and the Huguenots split France. Catherine's attempts to seize power had only brought ruin to the kingdom.

— ♛ —

ABBAS the GREAT (c. 1557–c. 1628)

Usurped: Persia 1586
Social Origins: Royal Family

By the 16th century the unity of Islam was a thing of the past. Only the great Empire of the Ottoman Turks, stretching from the Danube to the Arabian Gulf, presented a semblance of cohesion to the Christian world. Though as Caliph, the Ottoman Sultan held nominal power over all Moslems he could not enforce it. One of the many splinter states of Islam was Persia, now Iran. It was here that Abbas rose to greatness.

Abbas was born in about 1557 as the son of Shah Mahommed, a weak ruler who failed to maintain the unity of his nation. As a younger son, Abbas could hope for little from his father's nation. He travelled north to Nishapur in Khorassan where he had himself made Shah. However, in 1586 Abbas's elder brother was murdered and Abbas became heir to Persia.

Realizing that his chance had come, Abbas hurried back to Persia. Entering the capital, Abbas found his father beset by rebellious nobles and warring factions. The court hailed Abbas as Shah, whereupon Mahommed vanished from sight. His exact fate is unknown, but it seems probable that Abbas ordered his execution.

In a series of lightning moves, Abbas crushed dissension within Persia. He then led his nobles on a series of foreign wars, capturing enormous booty and great tracts of land. By the time of his death in 1628, Abbas had captured Baghdad, Hormuz and Herat. Within Persia, Abbas constructed a great road system and built many fine palaces. He was a great patron of the arts and of learning. However, he never forgot his troublesome early years and never completely trusted his subjects. When he suspected the tributary Khan of Mazendaran of plotting to throw off Persian rule, Abbas invited the Khan and his family to a feast and poisoned them all.

— 👑 —

IVAN the TERRIBLE (1530–1584)
Usurped: Power in Russia
Social Origins: Royal Family

When Ivan IV became Prince of Muscovy in 1533 he was only 3 years old. The nation, too, was in its infancy. Power was divided between the nobles, or boyars, who wielded power over their petty domains and only obeyed the Prince when they wanted to do so. In his reign of over 50 years, Ivan overthrew the power structure of Muscovy, and established Russia. But in so doing he won the name of Ivan the Terrible. It was a name he richly deserved.

Until the age of 13, Ivan took no part in affairs of state. The boyars pursued their own policies and struggles unhindered. At Christmas 1543, however, Ivan stepped in. He announced that from that moment on his power was to be absolute. The rights and privileges of the boyars were to be at an end. Ivan was usurping the powers which rightly belonged to his nobles and his councils. To make his point, Ivan ordered Andri, a leading boyar, to be bound and thrown to a pack of starving dogs.

Ivan the Terrible
A contemporary woodcut of Tsar Ivan the Terrible in the heavy, ceremonial robes of the Russian court. The title of Tsar, taken by Ivan, was a derivative of the Roman title Caesar and emphasized Moscow's claim to be the Third Rome, after the fall of Constantinople to the Turks in 1453. The Roman-style pillar in the engraving further enforces the image, though the Moscow of the times was little more than a large collection of wooden huts with unpaved streets.

Four years later Ivan was crowned. But he was not invested with the title of Prince of Muscovy, which was his by birth. He insisted that he should be crowned Tsar. This title was the Russian version of Caesar, the title of the rulers of the recently destroyed Byzantine Empire. He saw himself as the successor to the Byzantine Emperors. He was the champion of Orthodox Christianity and the ruler of a great empire stretching from the Baltic to the Black Sea. He was crowned Tsar of All the Russias in 1547.

To keep the power he had usurped from the councils and boyars of Muscovy Ivan embarked on a reign of terror designed to crush all resistance. When the chief citizens of the great city of Novgorod were suspected of corresponding with the King of Poland, Ivan marched on the city. He invited the citizens to a feast, and only then revealed the purpose for his visit. Courts were set up to determine guilt, but none were found innocent. Some 60,000 people were killed, many by being drowned in the River Volga. The city was burnt and left a smoking ruin.

Ivan seemed to delight in inflicting suffering. When nobles or others were suspected of plotting against Ivan, the Tsar himself took great delight in watching the tortures or executions. He carried out many of them himself. By such brutal methods, Ivan maintained his power over a turbulent people. Under this iron rule, Russia became a unified state, expanded greatly to the south and east and made itself a powerful nation. But Russia had to pay a high price for its greatness.

TOYOTOMI HIDEYOSHI (1536–1598)

Usurped: Power in Japan 1582

Social Origins: Samurai

Toyotomi Hideyoshi originated from the very lowest ranks of the samurai, but through his own cunning and the chance of fate came to wield supreme power. It was a power which seems to have turned his mind.

Born in 1536, Hideyoshi at an early age threw himself energetically into the main business of the samurai, fighting. By 1582, Hideyoshi had made himself one of the trusted generals of the warlord Nobunaga, the effective ruler of Japan. In that year Hideyoshi was campaigning in western Japan in an attempt to bring the area under the control of Nobunaga. One night Nobunaga was attacked by the rebellious general Akechi Mitsuhide and murdered.

Hideyoshi at once hurried back to Kyoto to avenge his master's death. Within a fortnight he had defeated Mitsuhide and reimposed order. At a great meeting of the samurai, Hideyoshi proposed that Nobunaga's grandson be made the next warlord. The samurai agreed. Since the grandson was not yet a year old, Hideyoshi took the powers of regent. He at once began ruling on his own account.

With no power superior to his own, Hideyoshi completely reorganized the samurai and their strategies. He created the most effective armies ever seen in Japan. He used them to impose his will on all of Japan, even the recalcitrant rebel areas which had escaped the authority of Nobunaga. In 1592 he threw his mighty army at Korea, overrunning much of the country. His rapid rise to supreme power may have brought on a form of megalomania for Hideyoshi then planned the conquest of China and other lands. A second army was sent to Korea in 1597 to prepare the way for the projected campaigns. Hideyoshi's death in the following year brought an end to the project. The armies returned to Japan to take part in the power squabble which rapidly developed.

JAN ZAMOYSKI (1541–1605)

Kingmaker of Poland 1587–1605
Social Origins: Lesser Nobility

Poland in the late 16th century was culturally highly advanced, but politically it was weak, ineffective and in serious decline. The king was elected by the nobles, who always made certain they chose a man unable to control the kingdom. That Jan Zamoyski was able to keep a firm grip on such a turbulent country is a mark of his greatness.

Zamoyski was born in 1541 as a son of the lesser nobility and showed an early aptitude for education. When still in his teens he left Poland for the University of Paris, moving on later to Padua and other seats of learning. He became famous as a scholar throughout the academic circles of Europe. At the age of 25 he returned to Poland and played a major role in redrafting the constitution of the kingdom on the death of King Sigismund II. The Polish constitution at this time provided for a very weak central government and allowed the nobles almost unlimited powers.

Under the new king, Stephen Bathory, Zamoyski became Chancellor. When King Stephen died in 1586 Poland plunged into confusion. Different factions of the nobility put forward their own candidates for the throne, demanding privileges and freedoms for themselves. When the Diet, or parliament of nobles, met in 1587 to elect the new king, Zamoyski showed his great skill at negotiation and intrigue. He managed to persuade a majority of nobles to back Sigismund of Sweden who thus became King Sigismund III of Poland. The nobles who opposed Zamoyski began raising troops to support their own candidate, Maximilian of Austria. Zamoyski took command of the royal army and resoundingly defeated his enemies at Byczyna in 1588.

Having shown himself to be not only a scholar, but also a politician and a soldier, Zamoyski was supreme. Together with Sigismund he set about trying to impose central authority on the turbulent nobles. Unfortunately Zamoyski soon fell out with King Sigismund, who felt that he should be allowed to rule his own kingdom. The nobles ranged themselves behind the two men and the nation again fell into turmoil. Only with difficulty did Zamoyski manage to reimpose his control, while at the same time defeating the Tartars. After 1600 Zamoyski and King Sigismund co-operated peacefully. Zamoyski died in 1605 after which Sigismund ruled for a further 27 years.

— ♕ —

MICHAEL the BRAVE (1558–1601)

Usurped: Province of Wallachia 1593
Social Origins: Nobleman

The late 16th century was a dangerous time for Christians in Eastern Europe. The Ottoman Empire was at this time an aggressive and powerful state with little regard for the Christian nations. In 1571 the Turks launched a massive slave raid into the lands north of Wallachia and carried 100,000 Christians back to the markets of Constantinople. It was a time when men were willing to surrender freedoms and liberties to a leader strong enough to protect them. No doubt it was this which helped Michael the Brave to power.

Born in Wallachia in 1558 Michael was a strong, but rather lawless nobleman who offended the reigning voivode (or ruler) Alexander and was banished. In 1593 Michael returned to Wallachia with a band of supporters and expelled Alexander. He took the powers and titles of voivode for his own and at once turned on the Turks. In a series of brilliant campaigns, Michael defeated the Turks and in 1595 drove them south of the Danube. Almost the entire Romanian people rose to the support of Michael and formed themselves into a new national state.

Jan Zamoyski of Poland (see above), however, did not welcome the rise of a strong state on the southern frontiers of his own. He first tried to foment trouble for Michael by backing a rebel named Andreas Bathory. Michael put down the rising, but on 19 August 1601 was murdered. It may be possible to see the hand of Zamoyski in the crime.

— ♕ —

BORIS GODUNOV (c. 1550–1605)

Usurped: Tsardom of Russia 1598
Social Origins: Nobleman

Boris Godunov first enters history at the court of Tsar Ivan the Terrible some time before 1570. He was at this time a young man, and apparently able to make friends easily. His sister, Irene, married Feodore, the eldest son of Ivan the Terrible and Boris became an increasingly important figure at court. He had started along his path to power.

In 1584 Ivan died and Feodore came to the throne. He was, however, a weak monarch and real power devolved on Boris. Now aged about 35 Boris showed himself to be an energetic ruler. He annexed large areas of western Siberia, encouraged trade with Western Europe and even attempted to found towns, though these remained little more than large villages in his lifetime. Boris's regency seemed threatened when, in 1598, Feodore died.

Boris Godunov, however, was equal to the occasion. He gathered together the nobles, or boyars, of Russia and bullied and bribed them into declaring him the new Tsar of all the Russias. The succession of power from Boris the Regent to Boris the Tsar should have been smooth. But the illegality of the move made the new Tsar insecure.

Within a few months a pretender had arisen claiming to be a son of Ivan the Terrible who had died some years earlier. No sooner had Boris put down this rising than Poland began to cause trouble. The beleagured Tsar died on 13 April 1605 having gained little but worry and insecurity from his assumption of power. Boris was succeeded by his son Theodore, but the latter was murdered three months later.

CHARLES IX (1550–1611)

Usurped: Kingdom of Sweden 1599
Social Origins: Royal Family

Charles IX came to power at a troubled time, when religious and personal differences threatened to tear Sweden apart. But he managed to re-establish authority and paved the way for Sweden to become the most powerful nation in northern Europe.

Charles was a child of 10 when his father King Gustavus Vasa died in 1560 and his eldest brother Eric became king. Eric was a bold man of action who conquered Estonia, but had an unfortunate taste for cruelty. Anyone who opposed him was murdered, often by the king himself. In 1567 he massacred the noble Stores and the following year led an unsuccessful invasion of Denmark. These two rash actions persuaded Eric's younger brothers, Charles and John, that he was no longer fit to rule.

At a meal held on 24 February 1568 the brothers arranged for poison to be slipped into Eric's meal. The king was immediately taken ill and died. Putting about the story that Eric had been mad, John took the throne with Charles's enthusiastic support. John was a Catholic and married the daughter of the Catholic King of Poland. His attempts to bring Sweden back within the fold of Roman Catholicism angered his fiercely Lutheran subjects. The failure of campaigns against Denmark did nothing to improve John's popularity. Charles, on the other hand, was immensely popular both as a man and for his staunch Lutheran religion.

In 1587 John's son, Sigismund, became King of Poland (see Jan Zamoyski, above). The two kings, father and son, co-operated in foreign policy and maintained an amicable relationship. The stage was being set for Charles's rise to power. In 1591 King John died, leaving the throne of Sweden to Sigismund, already King of Poland. Sigismund was at this time too busy in Poland to take up daily control of affairs. These he left in the hands of his uncle Charles. Sigismund was, however, crowned King of Sweden at an impressive ceremony in Uppsala in 1592.

For a time the arrangement worked well. The Swedes were happy with the regency of Charles and were content to keep Sigismund at a distance. In Poland, Sigismund revealed himself to be a staunch Catholic and a difficult man to work with. The Swedish nobles were dubious about accepting Sigismund's personal rule. In 1598 Sigismund announced he wanted to take control of Swedish affairs from Charles. He gathered together a Polish army and a group of Polish officials to implement his rule, which would include a strict enforcement of Catholicism.

The Swedes refused to obey their king. Charles sensed the way the wind was blowing, declared his undying support for Lutheranism, and raised his standard as the upholder of Swedish rights. The nobles and common folk flocked to Charles. In 1598 Sigismund's Polish army was smashed and thrown out of Sweden. Charles continued to rule in Sigismund's name but in reality was the sole power in Sweden. In 1600 the Riksdag, or Parliament, deposed Sigismund and Sweden became, in effect, a republic.

Clearly Charles was uncertain of his ground. He already had power and did not want to risk that by assuming titles which might anger others. Not until 1604 did Charles take the crown as Charles IX, and he was not crowned for a further three years. Charles died in 1611, having reorganized the army and given his nation a unity and purpose it had not known before. Within a few years his son Gustavus Adolphus would earn the title Lion of the North.

Gabriel BETHLEN (1580-1629)

Usurped: Principality of Transylvania 1613 and Kingdom of Hungary 1620

Social Origins: Nobleman

The history of Transylvania in the early 17th century is tangled and confused. The small principality maintained a shaky independence sandwiched between the Holy Roman and Ottoman Empires. Gabriel Bethlen was one of the strongest and most astute men to hold power in Transylvania in these troubled years.

Born to a Hungarian nobleman, Bethlen took service with his compatriot Sigismund Bathory who had become Prince of Transylvania in 1576. In 1595 Sigismund defeated a Turkish army at Giurgevo, and four years later retired to a monastery. Bethlen and the rest of Transylvania transferred their allegiance first to Stephen Bockskay and then to Gabriel Bathory, a cousin of Sigismund.

Gabriel was a poor successor to his cousin. He achieved notoriety in 1610 by attempting to cover up the atrocious crimes of his kinswoman Elizabeth Bathory who kidnapped and murdered hundreds of young women so that she could bathe in their blood in the belief that this would help maintain her beauty. By such action Gabriel Bathory lost the confidence and support of his nobles. For a nation like Transylvania this was disastrous.

By 1613 Bethlen had been acting in the heart of Transylvanian politics for several years. He decided on firm and direct action. He called together the nobles and warleaders and denounced the inadequacies of Gabriel Bathory. He sent messengers to the Ottomans asking for their support in opposing Gabriel Bathory, which was readily given. As Bethlen's support grew, that of Bathory diminished. Then Bathory was murdered, probably on the orders of Bethlen. Gabriel Bethlen immediately claimed the title of Prince. There was nobody strong enough to oppose him and he swept to power.

On 23 May 1618 a group of infuriated Protestant Bohemian nobleman threw three Catholic Austrian civil servants out of a window in Hradshin Castle. When news of the event spread, Bohemia rose in revolt against Austria. The Bohemians invited the staunchly Protestant Frederick, Prince of the Palatinate, to be their king and so sparked off the Thirty Years War.

Bethlen, ever an opportunist, assured himself of Turkish neutrality and then marched into Hungary. There he exploited anti-Austrian feelings and encouraged a series of rebellions. He took the title of King of Hungary, which properly belonged to the King of Austria. In November 1620 the Austrians smashed the army of Frederick and turned their forces on Hungary. Bethlen fled his new subjects and returned to Transylvania. He maintained a desultory war with the Austrians until his death in 1629.

— ♔ —

TOKUGAWA IEYASU (1542–1616)

Usurped: Power in Japan 1600

Social Origins: Samurai

Japan in the mid-16th century was dominated by warfare between rival samurai clans. It was as an unwilling actor in one of these dramas that Ieyasu first enters history. In 1546, at the age of four, Ieyasu was sent as a hostage to seal a bond between the samurai clans of the Tokugawa and the Imagawa. On the way he was kidnapped by the Oda clan who held him for four years. In 1550 Ieyasu was handed over to the Imagawa in an exchange of prisoners.

At the age of 17 Ieyasu succeeded to the leadership of the Tokugawa, now a considerably impoverished clan, and bound himself by oaths of loyalty to the Imagawa. Two years later the Imagawa were smashed and Ieyasu switched his clan to an allegiance with Oda Nobunaga. Nobunaga's power was extended and consolidated by his successor Toyotomi Hideyoshi, whom Ieyasu continued to serve.

In 1598 Hideyoshi died, leaving a 5-year-old son as his heir. Ieyasu was appointed a member of the five-man council of regents. Soon Ieyasu became the dominant regent and began to exercise power. His actions, however, angered the powerful samurai leader Ishida Mitsunari and other samurai clans.

In 1600 a plot by Mitsunari was sprung. A small revolt was organized in northern Honshu and Ieyasu marched out to deal with the rebellion. At once Mitsunari acted. While Ieyasu was away the capital Kyoto was seized and a large army recruited to defend it. Ieyasu, however, was more cunning than his enemies had thought. Sensing a trap, Ieyasu had not marched north, but made for his own lands to raise an army. He was, therefore, able to return to Kyoto much sooner than expected.

On 21 October the two armies met in the Sekigahara Valley, just north of Kyoto. The armies were larger than any seen before in Japan, numbering many tens of thousands on either side. So many warriors were present that there was no room for manoeuvre. The battle took the form of a struggling mass of men hacking at each other with the favoured samurai weapons of sword and polearm. Ieyasu's Tokugwara samurai proved tougher fighters and swept their enemies from the valley.

Firmly in control, Ieyasu set about reorganizing Japan. He moved the

Tokugawa Ieyasu
Ieyasu is shown here in the voluminous robes he wore at court, but he retains his
sword, which was the mark of samurai status. Ieyasu commanded his first army at
the age of 17 and used his formidable military skills to gain high command under the
warlord Hideyoshi and to seize power after his death. (*Mary Evans*)

capital to Edo, now Tokyo, and took the title of Shogun in 1603. He placed
the samurai firmly above all other social classes in Japan. A samurai was
legally entitled to kill instantly any member of a lower social class who did
not display the proper respect. The samurai were themselves divided into
those who were loyal and those whose loyalty was dubious. Rewards and
offices were distributed accordingly and the whole governement system overhauled. Through all this, Ieyasu left the Emperor, or Mikado, untouched. He
had no real power and Ieyasu was content to leave the office intact. The
system organized by Ieyasu and his immediate successors remained the basis
for Japanese society down to the end of the 19th century.

Arouj BARBAROSSA (?–1518)

Usurped: Bey of Algiers 1516
Social Origins: Pirate

Arouj Barbarossa was one of the more romantic swashbucklers to take his place among the North African corsairs. Born the son of a Greek Christian potter in Mitylene, Arouj and his brother Khizr left home at an early age to take to the sea. Here the brothers became Muslims and became captains of ships. They at once turned pirate. Arouj, a strikingly tall man, became known as Barbarossa because of his fiery red beard.

It was the custom of the time for the ports of North Africa to offer shelter to corsairs, providing them with stores and a market for their captured goods. In return the corsairs paid the Beys or governors of the ports a proportion of the loot and promised to support them in times of war. Arouj came to a suitable arrangement with the Bey of Tunis some time before 1509. Soon he was the leader of a formidable fleet of pirates and was able to blockade the Mediterranean coast of Spain, snapping up any ships which dared put to sea.

In 1516 Salim, Bey of Algiers, became aware that the King of Spain was sending a fleet to attack his city. Salim realised that he could not hope to resist with the forces at his disposal. He sent a message to Arouj Barbarossa asking for help. Arouj marched on Algiers at once, at the head of 5,000 men, while the Bey of Tunis led the fleet along the coast. Arouj, however, was intent upon taking advantage of the situation, not on helping Salim.

When Arouj and his army arrived, Salim ordered the gates of Algiers to be thrown open. Arouj marched in to be greeted by loud cheers, and by the grateful Salim. With the formidable force of tough pirates at his back, Arouj marched up to the welcoming committee. Taking the Bey Salim in his arms, Arouj suddenly shifted his grip and strangled the unfortunate Bey. With Salim dead, Arouj took over the reins of government, imposing a regime so harsh that he soon became unpopular.

In 1518 the threatened Spanish invasion came about. Arouj had lost the support of the people of Algiers by his tyrannical actions. In the ensuing battle he was abandoned by his subjects and killed.

— 👑 —

Armand Jean du Plessis de RICHELIEU (1585–1642)

Usurped: Power in France 1624–1642

Social Origins: Lesser Nobility

Richelieu was born into an impoverished Poitevin noble family. His father held the traditional right to appoint the Bishop of Lucon, and he chose 19-year-old Armand Jean in 1606. Many other men might have been happy with the quiet, but secure provincial life the bishopric brought, but not Armand Jean. He was unscrupulous, merciless and ambitious to an almost incredible degree. The young Bishop of Lucon was determined to make his mark on the world.

In 1614 he travelled to Paris as the local representative to the States General, an elected advisory Parliament. In the capital, Richelieu embarked on a determined policy of flattery and ingratiation which brought him to the notice of Queen Marie de Medici, the mother of the young King Louis XIII and virtual ruler of France. Through her Richelieu obtained the post of Secretary to the King.

Marie de Medici fell from power in 1617 and Richelieu was removed from office. He then began informing on his old allies and flattering the new administration. This new campaign of ingratiation failed to achieve its purpose. In 1621, however, Marie de Medici returned to court. The following year Richelieu became a Cardinal and in 1624 was appointed to the King's Council.

Within a few months, Richelieu had built up a network of spies and agents which he used cold-bloodedly and without any apparent emotion. Those who opposed his will were quietly murdered, or disappeared into state prisons. His control of government became absolute. In 1626 the Duc d'Orleans, the king's brother, tried to oust Richelieu. The Cardinal discovered the plot and had its chief supporters killed. Other conspiracies met a similar fate, partly because King Louis XIII believed Richelieu to be indispensable to the government and gave him Royal support.

During his many years in power, Richelieu pursued a consistent policy of centralization which brought France to the forefront of European power politics. Richelieu believed in the system of absolute monarchy. He ruthlessly crushed any who attempted to resist royal commands, though these were often the commands of Richelieu rather than Louis.

In 1626 all fortified houses and castles were demolished, save those under royal control. Three years later the political power of the Huguenots, French Protestants, was broken. The authority of the nobility was stripped away, to be replaced by financial and legal privileges which made the nobility rich and allowed them a life of luxury, but excluded them from power.

By the time of his death in 1642 Richelieu had successfully centralized

French government, removing any threat by the nobles to the power of the throne. This enabled France to build up an impressive army and become a first-rate power. The success had been achieved at the cost of crippling taxation and a slow strangulation of local government and initiative.

OLIVER CROMWELL (1599–1658)

Usurped: Power in England
Social Origins: Farmer

Cromwell was born a simple farmer in Huntingdonshire but died as the Lord Protector of England, one of the most powerful men in Europe. Yet he was not ambitious. If he had been, Cromwell would have taken power long before he did. The motives behind this strange rise may have been best revealed when Cromwell remarked that he only took power because he could no longer bear to watch others make so many mistakes.

It was not until the age of 41 that Cromwell became known outside his home county. In 1640 he was elected to represent Cambridge at Parliament. He soon attracted attention as a powerful speaker and a fervent Puritan. Cromwell became convinced of the justice of Parliament's rights to advise the king Charles I and to represent the people. When the English Civil War broke out in the summer of 1642 between the King and Parliament Cromwell raised a troop of cavalry in Cambridge.

At the Battle of Edgehill, Cromwell became convinced that only disciplined soldiers, secure in the faith of God, could overcome the Royalist cavaliers. He therefore set about reorganizing his men and training them to perfection. The victories he won brought him high command and more troops to be drilled and trained. By 1645 Cromwell was the leader of the New Model Army and the greatest general in England.

Though a man of great influence, Cromwell still acted as merely the military commander of the forces of Parliament. He obeyed their instructions, though he often argued his case on the floor of the House. Late in 1648 the House purged itself of Royalist supporters and began the trial of King Charles on charges of treason. The King was found guilty and executed, a move which Cromwell supported.

For the next four years Cromwell remained chief of the Parliamentary military forces. He put down numerous Royalist risings in Scotland and Ireland with a decisiveness which was effective but brutal. However, the Rump Parliament, as the remaining Members of Parliament were known, were not keeping their promises. They refused to carry out reforms and ignored the wishes of the people.

In spring 1653 Parliament began drafting legislation which would remove the need for further elections. The members were intent upon making themselves an oligarchy. This was too much for Cromwell and he decided to take action. On 20 April Cromwell marched into Parliament at the head of an armed guard of musketeers. He drove the members from Westminster at gunpoint and took the title of Lord Protector.

In 1654 Cromwell called a new Parliament, but instead of passing badly-needed laws, the body fell to bickering about how much power they should have. Cromwell dissolved the Parliament. A new body in 1656 proved little better and it was dissolved in 1658. Thereafter Cromwell gave up all pretence of ruling by Parliamentary authority and established a military government. He continued to rule until his death on 3 September 1658. The titles and powers of Lord Protector passed to his son Richard Cromwell.

Mahomed AURUNGZEBE (1618–1707)

Usurped: Mogul Empire 1658
Social Origins: Royal Family

At the time of Aurungzebe's birth, the Mogul Empire was at the height of its power. The Emperor in Delhi presided over the rich plains of northern India and held power over the many smaller states of the Deccan. The Imperial court was an artistic centre of great splendour, attended by the finest poets and craftsmen of India. It was Aurungzebe's father, Jahan, who built the famous Taj Mahal as a memorial to a beloved wife.

Originally named Mahomed, Aurungzebe grew up in these splendid surroundings. He was a strict Muslim, though he tolerated Hindu religion in his realm. In 1655 Jahan made Aurungzebe governor of territories in the Deccan. By this time Jahan seems to have lost interest in wielding power. He devoted his days to the pleasures of the harem and his gardens. Real power was held by ministers and nobles. In the Deccan Aurungzebe began to lose patience with his father's lax rule. He may have felt that his life was threatened by the sycophants at court.

In 1658 Aurungzebe took action. He led a small force of loyal soldiers down from the Deccan hills and rode north to Delhi. Arriving at the Imperial palace, Aurungzebe ordered his soldiers to seize his father and lock him up. The prince then turned on his brothers, had them all imprisoned and then executed. Nephews and cousins followed the royal princes to prison and death. The following year Aurungzebe had himself crowned Emperor as Al-Amgir, a name which means 'world conqueror'. The aging Jahan was transferred to the royal apartments at the Agra Fort, from where he could see the Taj Mahal and live a life of luxury.

Aurungzebe ruled the Mugul Empire for 49 years during which time the Empire reached new heights of wealth and artistic splendour, but began the slow decline which would end in its conquest by the British.

— 👑 —

George Monck, Duke of ALBEMARLE (1608–1670)

Kingmaker of England 1660

Social Origins: Soldier

George Monck was one of the first of a new breed of men, the professional soldier. For centuries military command had been the preserve of nobles trained from birth to lead men, but the complexities of 17th century warfare called for specialists. George Monck was one such man and proved his worth as a soldier in France and the Netherlands before returning to England to serve King Charles I in the Civil War. In 1644 he was captured by Parliamentarian troops but released two years later to serve under Oliver Cromwell (see above).

Monck was first Governor of Ulster and later made a General-at-Sea in command of the English fleet against the Dutch. After these successes he was appointed Commander-in-Chief of the troops in Scotland. Oliver Cromwell died in 1658 to be replaced by his son Richard, who soon revealed that he was not equal to the task of governing England. At this point Monck was approached by supporters of the king in exile, Charles II. Though Monck was quite happy to switch his allegiance once again, he did not want to risk his life. Cleverly encouraging the Royalists without committing himself, Monck awaited events.

In 1659 Richard Cromwell was ousted by a council of generals who proceeded to rule England with an iron hand. The people became restive and unhappy. Still Monck waited. In the autumn Royalist demonstrations were suppressed with such brutality that the generals lost what little support they had left. Monck sensed the mood of the nation and decided to act.

Still caution ruled Monck's actions. He gathered together the 7,000 men under his command and made a vague speech about restoring the freedoms of the kingdom. Then he started marching south. Nobody was quite sure what Monck intended to do, possibly even Monck himself was not certain.

By not committing himself to any particular cause, Monck had left open a path of retreat.

The people of England, however, had made their minds up. They had heard of the handsome, dashing young Charles II leading an adventurous life in Europe. Some remembered Charles from the days before Cromwell's rule. Contrasting Charles with the generals, the people were keen for a restoration of the monarchy. Yet they were uncertain of Monck's intentions.

Yorkshire was the first county to rise. When Monck marched his troops into the county he found himself surrounded by vast crowds shouting support for Charles and urging Monck to overthrow the generals. By the time Monck and his men reached the Humber few doubted that he was backing Charles. The armies of the generals melted away as the men deserted. Monck marched unopposed into London on 3 February 1660.

In London, Monck ordered the recall of a Parliament to include the Royalists previously banned. On 15 March a workman shouted 'God Bless King Charles the Second' in a city street. It is possible that Monck arranged the event to test city opinion. He need not have worried. The cry was taken up and ran through the city, Exchange and Parliament. Next day Monck sent an official message to Charles asking him to return.

On 28 April Parliament voted for a return of King Charles II. The city spent the night celebrating with parties and dances. A warship was sent to fetch Charles from the continent, who arrived in London on 29 May. Monck welcomed King Charles amid scenes of great rejoicing. Charles, for his part, created Monck Duke of Albemarle, gave him high military command and heaped him with honours and rewards. Monck died on 3 January 1670 and is buried in Westminster Abbey.

JOHN IV (?–1670)

Usurped: Power in Portugal 1640
Social Origins: Nobleman

For 60 years after the death of the childless Cardinal-King Henry in 1581 Portugal was ruled by Spain. When taking over the nation, Philip II of Spain had promised to respect Portuguese laws and institutions. However, time caused Philip II and his son Philip III to forget these promises. By the reign of Philip IV Portugal was being treated as merely an appendage of Spain. Her laws and traditions were ignored by insensitive officials working for the regent, the Count of Olivares.

By 1639 the Portuguese people and nobles had become tired of paying for

Spain's wars and Spain's policies. Duke John of Braganza noted the discontent. He was descended from the now extinct royal family, albeit through an illegitimate son of the 15th century. John of Braganza raised the standard of revolt and by skilful use of his meagre resources managed to throw out the Spanish garrisons. Spain was at this time preoccupied with the Thirty Years War and unable to divert her full military might to Portugal.

In 1641 John summoned the Cortes, or Portuguese Parliament, and had himself acclaimed as King John IV of Portugal. Spain retaliated immediately and warfare dragged on until 1668 when a series of Portuguese victories enabled John to force Spain to recognize Portuguese independence. John strengthened his alliance with other countries in Europe, in particular by the marriage of his daughter Catherine to Charles II of England in 1662.

— ♔ —

JOHN SOBIESKI (1624–1696)

Usurped: Kingdom of Poland 1674
Social Origins: Soldier

John Sobieski has attained the status of a hero by virtue of his great achievements at the siege of Vienna, but his early life was a web of intrigue, treachery and murder such as few villains have been able to match.

He was born the son of the Castellan or Governor of Cracow and from an early age was determined to follow his father in the profession of soldier. In 1624 John was appointed Captain of the Guard and took part in various campaigns against the Tartars, Cossacks and Swedes. In 1665 he was made Grand Marshal of Poland, with command of all troops in wartime. Already he seems to have had his eyes on the throne, and would stop at nothing to gain it.

In a new war with the Turks, John Sobieski played the traitor, holding his armies back until his king was defeated. King Vladislav IV was forced to make a humiliating peace and cede large territories to the Ottoman Empire. John then turned on the Turks and defeated them. His military glory began to outshine that of Vladislav, just as he had planned it should.

In 1674 the king called a meeting of the Diet, or council of nobles, but died on the day it was due to open. Sobieski was rather conveniently on hand with a large body of soldiers. He marched into the Diet with a troop of armed men at his back and forced the nobles to elect him as king. He at once set out at the head of his troops and inflicted a sharp defeat on an invading Ottoman army.

Sobieski's greatest feat came in 1683. In that year a huge army of 300,000

244

John Sobieski
The Polish king John Sobieski is shown here at his greatest moment, leading a combined German/Polish army to crush the Turkish host which had been laying siege to Vienna. The battle ensured the survival of Austria, and secured the liberation of Hungary. However, Sobieski gained little from his victory and Poland soon entered a long period of decline. (*Macdonald/Aldus*)

Turks marched on Austria and laid siege to Vienna. John Sobieski marched out of Cracow at the head of his small household army. He announced his intention of attacking the Turks and rescuing Vienna. On the banks of the Danube John was met by an army of the Holy Roman Empire, which agreed to follow his orders. By the time he reached Vienna, Sobieski had 70,000 men under his command. He launched an immediate attack and virtually annihilated the Turkish army.

Sobieski's final years were an anti-climax to the glory he won in Austria at Vienna. The nobles of Poland began squabbling amongst each other, and John was unable to control the intrigues. The Turks invaded again and snatched the Ukraine from Poland. A broken and disappointed man, Sobieski died on 17 June 1696.

— ♛ —

SOPHIA Alexycevna (1657–1704)

Usurped: Power in Russia 1682
Social Origins: Royal Family

Russia, in the third quarter of the 17th century, was a nation in turmoil. The Orthodox Church was split by reform movements and countless anarchic splinter churches arose. The boyars, or nobles, flouted the authority of the Tsar and peasants rose in rebellion.

On 27 April 1682 Tsar Feodore III, the ineffective son of Tsar Alexis, died leaving no children, but two younger brothers. Of these one, Ivan, was a half-wit, and the other, Peter, was a child. The boyars passed over Ivan in favour of Peter and set about organizing a regency. It was at this moment that Sophia Alexycevna struck.

Sophia was a daughter of Tsar Alexis by his first marriage. She and a powerful faction of boyars resented the reforms initiated by Alexis under the influence of his second wife and continued by Feodore. Sophia had the fanatical devotion of the elite guard corps, the Royal Musketeers, who were also opposed to reforms. As soon as the boyars had declared for Peter, she organized a rising of the Musketeers. The men stormed into the royal palace and forced the boyars to install Ivan as joint Tsar and elect Sophia as sole regent.

Firmly in power, Sophia ruled Russia with the aid of her lover Vasili Galitzin. She allowed Peter and Ivan to perform the ceremonial duties of Tsar, but always made certain that she was close enough to intervene. In 1689 Sophia made her final bid for total power. Galitzin returned from a campaign against the Turks to be welcomed by triumphal arches and the acclamations of a grateful regent. Sophia tried to use the occasion to install the 'conquering hero' as Tsar with herself as Tsarina and so dethrone the two young Tsars. Peter, however, learnt that Galitzin had actually been defeated, and the news spread quickly. The boyars turned against Sophia, while Peter persuaded some troops to follow him. Sophia was besieged in a convent and made to agree to retire from public life altogether.

WILLIAM III (1650–1702)

Usurped: Kingdom of England 1688
Social Origins: Dutch Nobleman

William was first and foremost Stadtholder of the Netherlands. His usurpation of the English and Scottish thrones, though it brought immense benefits to those countries, was probably seen by William as merely a part of his policy in the Netherlands.

William acceded to the position of Stadtholder, or leader of the Dutch Republic, in 1672 when Louis XIV of France launched an invasion of the Low Countries. William was promptly beaten in the field, but managed to halt the French by skilful use of his fleet. The effects of a second defeat two years later and a third in 1677 were likewise averted by prompt action on other fronts.

William began organizing a great alliance of European powers against the growing might of France. Austria and Spain quickly joined William. The marriage between William and Princess Mary, daughter of the future King James II of England, held out hopes that Britain would join the alliance. By 1687 Sweden and various German states had joined the anti-French alliance but England still refused to be drawn into the war. It is against this background that William's actions should be judged.

In 1687 James II was becoming increasingly unpopular in England. He put down the rising of the Duke of Monmouth with terrible savagery and vindictiveness and went on to attempt the re-establishment of Catholicism in England. Laws prohibiting Catholic worship were repealed and government jobs given only to Catholics. In a country as staunchly Protestant as England was at the time, such a policy could only lead to trouble.

William, across the Channel, was well aware of events in England. He made a point of publicising his, and his wife Mary's, strong Protestant leanings. He also pointed out that Mary was the next heir to the English throne and that he, too, was descended from the English Royal Family.

Many people in England expected William and Mary to become King and Queen when James died.

In 1688 James arrested seven bishops on a highly controversial religious charge, but they were acquitted at their trial. Days later a son was born to James. This stripped William and Mary of their hopes of inheriting the throne. James was determined to bring his son up as a Catholic so that he could continue the Catholicisation of England. The lords, Church and people were appalled by this prospect. William sensed his chance.

Messages came to William asking him to come to England and assume the throne. A message from the House of Lords specifically promised William all the help he wanted, if only he would come to England. William was delighted. If he became King of England all the wealth and power of England could be thrown into the war against France. It might conceivably be enough to tip the balance. However, William did not want to base his bid for power on English support which might not materialize. He gathered together a large army and sailed for Torbay.

Landing at Brixham on 5 November 1688, William began his march on London. Everywhere he went the people cheered him and shouted their support. The royal officials melted away from James II. When the king tried to raise an army virtually nobody turned up to support him. James knew that he was beaten and fled.

Before Parliament would allow William into London they made him agree to what became known as the Bill of Rights. This agreement stated that William and Mary would rule jointly, that they would allow free speech within Parliament, would summon Parliament regularly, would raise no taxes without Parliament's consent and that no Roman Catholic would ever again sit on the English throne.

William agreed to all the conditions put to him, and so became King of England. He gained the resources he needed for the war with France, and so could be said to have achieved his ends. At the same time the Bill of Rights laid the foundation in law for the democratic monarchy which gradually became the form of government of Britain.

DANILO PETROVITCH (1677–1735)
Usurped: Power in Montenegro 1697
Social Origins: Priest

At the Battle of Kossovo in 1389 the Ottoman Turks smashed the Serbian Kingdom and overran large areas of the Balkans. Only the mountain people of Montenegro managed to hold on to some form of independence, and even they had to pay tribute to the new rulers.

By the late 17th century, Montenegro was a small state which was subject to the Turks and had to face regular attacks by Turkish armies. Authority was wielded by the Bishop of Montenegro, a position which was elective by the clergy of the country. The survival of Montenegro might be ascribed to the combination of rugged mountain landscapes and the combined religious/military leadership of a succession of able Bishops.

In 1696 Danilo Petrovitch from the village of Nyegosh, became Bishop of Montenegro. He at once set about changing the constitution of his new realm. Within a year Danilo had overhauled the functions and institutions of the government. Most importantly he took the election of Bishop out of the hands of the electors. Instead he decreed that he would be empowered to elect his own successor. The change was nothing short of revolutionary for Montenegro. Before his death in 1735, Danilo nominated his nephew Sava as the next Vladika, or Prince-Bishop. The dynasty continued, passing from uncle to nephew, for bishops were required to be celibate, until Montenegro was swallowed up by Yugoslavia after the First World War.

NADIR KULI (1688–1747)

Usurped: Shah of Iran 1732

Social Origins: Foreign Soldier

Nadir Kuli was a brilliant soldier and the last of the great rulers of Persia, yet he was not even a Persian and his successes proved to be only temporary. After his death his many achievements were reversed.

Nadir Kuli was born in Khorasan of Turcoman stock at a time when Persia was in serious decline. He joined the imperial army and led a distinguished career. It took disaster to bring Nadir to the forefront of events. In 1722 the wild Ghilzai tribesmen swept down from Afghanistan and defeated Tahmasp II, Shah of Persia. The ruler of the Ghilzai assumed the title of Shah, and encouraged the Turcomans to throw off Persian control.

Nadir Kuli stepped forward at this crisis to lead the battered and defeated forces of Tahmasp II. Nadir reorganized the Persian forces, imbued them with fresh spirit and, in 1730, led them in a brilliant campaign against the Ghilzai. The Afghans were beaten back to their mountain home and Nadir placed Tahmasp II back on the throne of Persia. The Shah, however, was allowed little hand in government for Nadir used the army to keep power firmly in his own control.

After two years of ruling through Tahmasp, Nadir tired of the fiction. He quietly overthrew the Shah, placing the ex-monarch's infant son Abbas III on the throne. Nadir took the office of regent and began to rule unfettered by the need to refer to another. In 1736 Abbas died and Nadir took the title of Shah for himself. In the following years, Nadir continued his brilliant military career. He defeated Turkey, took territory from Russia, overran Afghanistan and plundered Delhi. In the latter campaign, Nadir captured the fabulous Koh-i-nor diamond and the richly bejewelled Peacock Throne. In 1747, in the midst of another successful campaign against Turkey, Nadir was assassinated.

— 👑 —

ELIZABETH Petrovna (1709–1762)

Usurped: Tsardom of Russia 1741
Social Origins: Royal Family

Few rulers in history have shown a greater change in character upon their accession than Elizabeth Petrovna. So sudden and marked is the break that it is sometimes difficult to see how Tsarina Elizabeth could be the same woman as the Princess.

While still a child Princess Elizabeth Petrovna, the daughter of Peter the Great, became known for her grace and education. As she grew older these qualities matured into intelligence and an almost dazzling beauty. At the age of 18, Elizabeth had her first love affair and quickly developed a taste for men and moved through a succession of lovers, at least two of whom were common soldiers of the guard. These activities were rather frowned upon by the Imperial family and Elizabeth tended to stay in the background at court.

In 1730 Peter II, grandson of Peter the Great, died without children. A bitter family feud broke out which resulted in Peter II's cousin Anna Ivanova securing the throne. Anna installed three German favourites in government and began overturning many of Peter the Great's reforms. She died in 1740, bequeathing the throne to her young nephew Ivan VI. The boy was in the hands of the German favourites and the regent Anna Leopoldovna, who continued to rule.

Eventually this rule by foreigners became too much for Elizabeth. She had admired her father and his reforms and could not bear to see them destroyed by outsiders. In December 1741 she organized a bloodless coup and declared herself Tsarina. Elizabeth dismissed all foreigners from high office, curbed the growing power of the boyars, or high nobles, and reintroduced the reforms of Peter the Great.

As Tsarina Elizabeth abandoned her love affairs and frivolous way of life, she dedicated herself to preserving the heritage of her father and to securing the smooth succession of power within the Imperial family. The hardworking Elizabeth of post-usurpation power was a very different woman from the flighty girl she had once been. The transformation seems to have surprised her contemporaries as much as had her usurpation.

HAIDAR ALI (c. 1720–1782)

Usurped: Sultanate of Mysore 1750
Social Origins: Obscure

Haidar Ali's career was one of spectacular conquests and dramatic battles in which he expanded his territories and created a fine state to be inherited by his son Tipu Sultan. In contrast to this brilliant adult career, Haidar Ali's birth and early life are obscure. He himself showed no willingness to discuss them; presumably they were very humble.

In 1749, at the age of around 30, Haidar Ali joined the army of the Raja of Mysore, a state of southern India on the lower slopes of the Western Ghats. All those who met Haidar Ali described him as a remarkable man, with a striking personality and terrific presence. These gifts brought him to the notice of more senior officers and he was soon given his own command. By 1763 Haidar was the commander of the entire army and was making war and peace on his own account.

Exactly when Haidar Ali dispensed with the authority of the Raja of Mysore is unclear, but in 1767 he made an alliance with the Nizam of Madras as the Sultan of Mysore. The new alliance promptly suffered severe defeat by the British at Chengam. Haidar Ali thereafter avoided the British, concentrating on building up his state by attacking neighbouring Indian princes. A raid on British territory in 1779 ended in another defeat, after which Haidar Ali retreated on Mysore. By the time of his death in December 1782, Haidar Ali was the ruler of a large and powerful state, able to resist British encroachment for many years to come.

ROBERT CLIVE (1725–1774)

Kingmaker in India 1751–1767
Social Origins: British Gentry

When Clive arrived in India in 1744 both he and the sub-continent were in a troubled state. India was at this time nominally under the control of the Mughal Emperor, but was in reality a patchwork of princely states each fighting for survival or for gain. Clive had been sent out as a clerk in the East India Company by a family exacerbated by his fiery temper and inability to settle down.

Clive soon gave up clerical work and gained a commission in the small army which the Company maintained to protect its trading stations. At this time the British held no lands in India, which was ruled entirely by native princes. In 1747 the Nizam of the Deccan died and his immensely rich inheritance was contested. The French Indian Company supported one pretender, the British company another. Both companies hoped to obtain trading concessions if their candidate was successful. In the fighting which followed the French placed their man on the throne and the British nominee, Muhammad Ali, was besieged at Trichinopoly.

The British almost gave up the struggle, but in August 1751 Clive suggested a scheme so unusual that his superiors allowed him to proceed. With 210 men Clive raced to the wealthy city of Arcot and captured it. Ten thousand French and Indian troops were diverted from the siege of Trichinopoly to deal with Clive. The British, however, held Arcot for 7 weeks and then launched a surprise attack which completely routed the enemy. Clive then led his force to Trichinopoly to relieve Muhammad Ali. The remaining French troops were routed and Muhammad Ali placed on the throne.

By 1756 Clive had been promoted to the command of the British troops in Madras. In that year Nawab Siraj of Calcutta executed 120 Britons in the infamous Black Hole. Clive set out with an army of around 2,000 men to punish the Nawab. Taking Calcutta in January 1757, Clive was approached by an elderly general named Mir Jafar, who was a pretender to the throne of Calcutta. Sensing great benefits to be gained by having a friendly ruler in Bengal, Clive agreed to support Mir Jafar.

On 23 June 1757 Clive with his small army met Nawab Siraj and his enormous force of over 50,000 men. Clive won a devastating victory, Siraj being killed in the rout. Mir Jafar was placed on the throne and immediately gave Clive a gift of £200,000. He later handed over financial control of his kingdom to the British. Clive became the master of Bengal and continued to amass his fortune.

In 1760 Clive retired to England with his riches, but in 1765 was asked to

Robert Clive
Clive is shown here in the uniform he wore as commander of the army of the British East India Company. The army was small and designed to protect British trading stations, but Clive used it to defeat the much larger armies of Indian princes and to control the succession in many states. The Company and its troops continued to control British interests in India until nearly a century after Clive's death.
(*Mary Evans*)

return to India to resume the government of the territories he had acquired. In India he used the power of Britain to coerce Indian princes and to influence the succession of various states. He finally returned to England in 1767 with a tremendous fortune, estimated at around a quarter of a million pounds, a truly enormous figure for the time. He died in 1774 as the result of an accident, though some think that he may have committed suicide.

— ♕ —

Sophia Augusta Frederica, CATHERINE the GREAT (1729–1796)

Usurped: Tsardom of Russia 1762
Social Origins: German Nobility

Catherine, Tsarina of Russia, has been given the epithet 'the Great' by history and her achievements were indeed mighty, but she was a cruel, immoral and utterly untrustworthy woman. A cynic might say that she was exactly the type of ruler which Russia needed at this time.

Catherine was born Sophia, daughter of Prince Christian of Anhalt-Zertbst, a minor German state. In 1744 Frederick the Great of Prussia organized her betrothal to Grand Duke Peter, heir to the Russian throne. Upon arrival, in Russia, Catherine, as she was now called, immediately fell ill. She called for an Orthodox priest and so established her popularity with the common people which she would never lose.

Following the death of Peter the Great in 1725 Russia passed through the hands of various ineffective rulers until the accession of Tsarina Elizabeth who attempted to reintroduce some form of order and strength. Grand Duke Peter, whom Catherine married in 1745, was weak-willed but brutal, and he ignored his wife in favour of various mistresses. Catherine, for her part, took a succession of lovers.

In 1762 Tsarina Elizabeth died and Peter ascended the throne as Peter III. He quickly installed foreigners in positions of power and made a humiliating peace with Prussia. In July 1762 the royal bodyguard rose in rebellion. It was strongly suspected at the time that Catherine had organized the coup, but if so she covered her tracks well and no proof has been found that she was responsible. The guard bustled Peter to the fortress of Ropsha where he was strangled, though Catherine's bulletins announced he had died of apoplexy.

At once Catherine began ruling in her own right. She was popular with the people and posed as the safeguard of Russian tradition against foreign influence. In fact she was nothing of the sort. She insisted upon French table manners and French dances, though she never allowed any Frenchman to occupy a position of influence. The ordinary people were ground down by a series of laws favouring landowners rights over those of the workers, who were reduced almost to the position of slaves.

Her foreign policy, however, was extremely successful. She defeated Turkey, gaining a Black Sea coast, and took part in a three-fold partition of Poland. Russia gained immeasurably from these actions, becoming for the first time an important European power. After ruling Russia for 34 years, Catherine died on 10 November 1796 and was followed by her son Paul, who was already showing signs of insanity.

AGA MOHAMMED (c. 1740–1797)

Usurped: Shah of Persia 1779
Social Origins: Tribal Chieftain

Aga Mohammed was born some time around 1740 as the son of Mohammed Hasan, a chieftain of the Kajar Turks. As son of such a chieftain, Aga became involved in the cruel politics of Persia at an early age. While still a boy he was castrated by the Shah Adil, who soon fell from power to be replaced by Kerim Khan, a Persian. Aga was kept as a prisoner by Kerim as a hostage for the good behaviour of the Kajar Turks.

In 1779 Kerim Khan died, Aga escaped and for the first time in his life tasted freedom. He at once assumed the leadership of the Kajar Turks and became a troublesome subject to Shah Lutf Ali Khan. In 1795 Aga felt confident enough of his power to attack Lutf Ali Khan. He led his troops into Kerman, the capital city, captured the Shah and put him to death. Aga at once announced his assumption of the title Shah and began an active series of campaigns. He brought the Zend tribesmen to heel and reconquered Khorassan, but was thrown southward by the Russians. In the wake of this defeat Aga was murdered by two of his slaves.

NAPOLEON BONAPARTE (1769–1821)

Usurped: Power in France 1799 and 1815
Social Origins: Army Officer

The Emperor Napoleon of France has been hailed as one of the greatest heroes of French history and is said to have had an effect on French society more profound than any other man. Yet he was not a Frenchman, a fact which makes his rise to power all the more remarkable.

Napoleon was born on 15 August 1769 in Ajaccio, Corsica, son of a lawyer, one of the few supporters of the French occupation of that island. In 1785 Napoleon was sent to school in France and then entered the army as an artillery officer. In 1793 Corsica rebelled against France and the Bonaparte family moved to Marseilles. After early successes, Napoleon fell from favour due to his political sympathies. He could no longer provide for his family and his mother was reduced to taking in washing to earn a living.

At midnight on 4 October 1795, Napoleon had the good fortune to be in Paris when a mob of around 40,000 threatened to overthrow the government. Napoleon took command of a battery of cannon and drove them through the streets to the seat of government. When the mob appeared at dawn, Napoleon opened fire quelling the revolt with what was termed a 'whiff of grapeshot'. Three hundred men died that day, but Napoleon was on his way to greatness. The grateful government appointed him General of French troops in Italy. With secure pay, Napoleon married Josephine de Beauharnais, a beautiful socialite widow, and set out for Italy.

In 1796 and 1797 Napoleon won a series of brilliant victories against the Austrians in Italy, including the Battles of Rivoli and Lodi, and imposed peace on that great empire. He returned to France with immense booty and even greater glory. In 1798 Napoleon set out for Egypt, capturing Malta en route, and evading the British fleet under Nelson. Napoleon conquered Egypt in a lightning campaign and then advanced into Syria and Palestine. When his lines of communication were cut by Nelson's victory at the Battle of the Nile, Napoleon abandoned his army and raced back to France.

He arrived in November 1799 to find France reeling from defeats in Italy and dispirited by internal discord. Napoleon acted at once, before news of his defeat in Syria became public. Working with his brother Lucien and a dashing young cavalry officer named Murat, Napoleon overthrew the constitution and established himself in power. Hiding behind a screen of Roman Republicanism, Napoleon assumed the title of First Consul while he imposed his dictatorship. He reformed the law into the *Code Napoleon*, centralized the administration and made an agreement with the Papacy regarding the status of the Church in France.

In 1802 Napoleon manipulated a public election to have himself pro-

1515

NAPOLEON BONAPARTE (1769-821)
ROBERT LEFÈVRE (1755-1830)
R.M.S.A.-1845

Napoleon
The French Emperor Napoleon is shown here in around 1806 when he was at the height of his power. He is dressed as the Colonel of Chasseurs à Cheval of the Imperial Guard, the regiment which formed his personal guard on campaign. The Imperial Guard originated as a central core of veterans numbering 9,000 men, but by the end of Napoleon's rule had grown to be a self-contained army of 126,000 men. (*Macdonald/Aldus*)

257

claimed First Consul for life. Two years later Napoleon bullied Pope Pius VII into coming to Rome to crown him Emperor of the French, echoing the coronation of Charlemagne as Emperor of the Franks. At the height of the ceremony, however, Napoleon snatched the crown from the startled Pope and placed it on his own head. Perhaps he did not want to owe his crown to anyone. Napoleon's usurpation of power was complete. He had overthrown a democratic government and replaced it first with a dictatorship and later with an hereditary Emperor.

In the following years Napoleon led France to great glory, defeating Austria and Russia at Austerlitz in 1805 and Prussia at Jena and Auerstadt in the following year. In 1809 Napoleon defeated Austria again and took the Emperor's daughter as his wife, divorcing Josephine to do so. In 1812, however, Napoleon led his incomparable army into Russia, to death and destruction. By 1814 Napoleon was powerless to halt the armies of a grand alliance of European states from invading France. Cannon could be heard in Paris before the Emperor accepted the inevitable and abdicated. He was exiled to the Mediterranean island of Elba where his enemies hoped he would live a quiet life as a petty prince. But Napoleon was not finished yet.

In France the allied nations installed King Louis XVIII, brother of the king toppled by the Revolution, on the throne. Louis was a moderate, but he allowed his government to be influenced by extreme right-wingers who despised the Revolution and its achievements. The people, and those who had gained during Napoleon's regime, were alienated by the new government. Napoloeon kept in touch with friends in France and was well aware of the unpopularity of the Royalist Regime. He decided that he stood a chance of regaining power and set sail for France.

Napoleon landed on the south coast on 1 March 1815. General Ney, sent to halt him, was an old comrade and at once switched loyalties to Napoleon. All along his route northwards, Napoleon was met by cheering crowds and eager soldiers. On 20 March Napoleon rode in triumph into Paris and Louis fled to Ghent.

However, Napoleon knew that the enthusiasm for his rule would evaporate unless he could achieve something spectacular. The nations of Europe rebuffed his offers of peace, so Napoleon prepared for war. He raised an army of 120,000 veterans and invaded Belgium to face the British and Prussians. On 18 June Napoleon met the British at Waterloo, failed to break their line and was defeated when the Prussians arrived late in the evening. Fleeing the battlefield, Napoleon abdicated on 22nd June and was later captured by the British. He lived the rest of his life as a prisoner on the remote Atlantic island of St Helena.

— ♛ —

THOMAS HORTON (1759–c. 1825)

Usurped: Sheikdom of Kishmah 1798
Social Origins: English Tailor

In his own lifetime, Horton was described as a 'renegade', a description with which few would argue. His life was one of high adventure, culminating in splendid success, but his morals and methods were base and disreputable.

He was born in Newcastle-on-Tyne in 1759 and apprenticed to a tailor at an early age. In 1778, however, Horton swindled a large sum of money from a bank and fled to Sweden. There he married a rich widow, but had to flee when he came under suspicion of various crimes. He moved to southern Russia where he and his wife set up an hotel. Under the cover of this Horton carried on a highly successful smuggling business. However, his wife discovered Horton committing adultery and threatened to inform the authorities of the smuggling activities. In a fit of anger Horton murdered her, and fled once again.

This time he travelled south to the Ottoman Empire, where he converted to Islam and engaged in trading activities of varying degrees of illegality. After some years, Horton bought a dhow and set himself up as a pirate in the Persian Gulf. He was staggeringly successful, becoming the captain of a fleet of ships and acquiring great wealth. The Sheik of Kishmah, whose lands bordered the Gulf, asked Horton to become admiral of the fleet. Horton eagerly accepted, adding the Sheik's ships to his own fleet on the next piratical voyage.

Horton, however, was far from content. By his own account Horton became ambitious and jealous of the Sheik. He bribed palace officials to join him and then led his pirates into the palace. The Sheik was murdered and Horton took his place. Horton took over the Sheik's harem together with his palace and power and settled down to a life of luxury and ease.

The last known reference to Horton comes in 1818 when the British sloop *Hope* called at Kishmah. Horton displayed a knowledge of the longings of sailors by sending 120 female slaves aboard 'for the pleasure of the crew'. The exact date of Horton's death is unknown.

DINGANE (?–1838)

Usurped: Kingdom of the Zulu
Social Origins: Royal Family

Shaka Zulu was one of the greatest men of African history. His brother, Dingane, was a lesser man but he followed his brother to greatness and killed him at the height of his power.

In origin the Zulu were a fairly small tribe among the many cattle-raising peoples who inhabited the grasslands of southeast Africa during the early 19th century. In 1816 Shaka inherited the leadership of the Zulu and at once set about reorganizing the tribe. He introduced new weapons and far more deadly tactics to the army and almost at once wiped out the Buthelezi, traditional enemies of the Zulu. Numerous other tribes were broken by force and assimilated. From an original homeland of 100 square miles, Shaka increased Zulu territory to cover over 200,000 square miles and enlarged his army to include 50,000 men.

Shaka's rise to power had been unstoppable and his judgement accurate in all things, but in 1827 his mother died. Shaka, the greatest man in his world, seems to have been sent mad by grief. He ordered the death of any who sneezed in his presence, began eating meals lying on his stomach so as to resemble a lion and began complaining of strange dreams. His actions became increasingly unpredictable. When a boy committed a crime and then hid among some other youngsters, Shaka had the whole group killed. Not long afterwards he pardoned a man of a serious crime because the man had a young child.

Dingane, the king's brother, became increasingly alarmed by Shaka's action. When Shaka began killing his wives on suspicion that one of them had caused the death of his mother, Dingane became convinced that he would be the next to die. He confided his fears to his brother Mhlangana, who shared them, and to a senior chieftain named Mbopa. Dingane persuaded the others to help him to murder Shaka before he killed them.

At dusk on 24 September 1828 Shaka came out of his hut to greet messengers from one of his armies. As the messengers left, Mbopa distracted the attention of the guards while Mhlangana leapt forwards and stabbed Shaka in the back. Dingane followed with a similar blow. Shaka turned and stared at his brothers. He had never meant them any harm and was staggered that they were trying to kill him.

'What have I done, Dingane?' he asked, before Mbopa stabbed him for a third time. Shaka stood still, gazing around him and then crashed to the ground. The conspirators fled to their homes for the night, only appearing in the morning to take control of the terrible panic which broke out on Shaka's death. Dingane took over the Zulu Empire, launching campaigns against neighbouring tribes and enlarging the army still further. But he made no new innovations and merely continued the work of his great brother Shaka.

MEHEMET ALI (1769–1849)
Usurped: Power in Egypt 1811
Social Origins: Christian Merchant

Born the son of a Christian Albanian, Mehemet Ali ended his life as the most powerful man in the Middle East and a rival to the Ottoman Sultan himself. His life was a remakable episode of skilful and daring acts which brought him to power.

Early in life Mehemet Ali 'took the turban' by becoming a Moslem. This opened up the prospects of a career in government, which was closed to Christians. In 1799 Mehemet was in Egypt when Napoleon invaded and he fought with a skill and determination which brought him to the notice of the Sultan. In 1805 Mehemet was appointed Pasha, or governor, of Egypt. Mehemet found his power constantly thwarted by the slave-soldiers, the Mamelukes, and by partisans of the previous Pasha.

In 1809 Sultan Mahmoud II ascended the Ottoman throne. Mehemet had no great regard for the new Sultan and felt little personal loyalty to him. In 1811 Mehemet Ali used his troops to massacre the Mamelukes, and all those he felt he could not trust. The slaughter marks the point at which Mehemet ceased obeying the Sultan and set himself up as independent ruler of Egypt. In 1816 he defeated the Wahhabis tribesmen of Arabia and two years later conquered the holy cities of Medina and Mecca. These Arabian territories were given to his son, Ibrahim, to govern.

Mehemet Ali set about consolidating his new power and improving the prosperity of his lands. The cotton industry was revived and canals and other irrigation projects constructed. In 1831 Mehemet Ali openly defied the Sultan by invading Syria and Palestine. Russia, Britain and Austria were alarmed by the rise of a new power in the Middle East. They forced Mehemet Ali to abandon Syria in return for recognition by the Sultan of his right to hold Egypt and pass it on to his son. Mehemet died on 2 August 1849.

ALEXANDER I (1777–1825)

Usurped: Tsar of Russia 1801
Social Origins: Royal Family

If Tsar Alexander I was a usurper, and many believe that he was, he covered his tracks very well indeed. At the time and ever since nobody could be quite certain to what extent he was involved in the overthrow of his father, Tsar Paul, nor whether his murder was in any way premeditated.

Tsar Paul was prone to bouts of insanity and even when sane was brutal and unpredictable. By the spring of 1801 the nobles of Russia were losing patience with their tsar's changeable foreign policy and dangerously inconsistent behaviour. A group of them decided to remove Paul and replace him with his eldest son, Alexander. It is almost certain that Alexander knew of this plot, though the extent of his involvement is unclear.

On the night of 11 March 1801 a group of 60 noblemen and army officers forced their way into the royal bedchamber, just as Paul was stepping into bed. According to the story broadcast next day, one of the generals stepped forward to arrest Paul 'in the name of Tsar Alexander', but another man could not resist slapping Paul's face in revenge for some earlier insult. Tsar Paul struck back and attacked the conspirators. In the ensuing struggle he was killed. However, many historians find it hard to believe that 60 grown men could not have subdued one man without kicking him to the ground and strangling him. Many believe that Alexander planned the coup, and the murder of his father, in advance.

Next day Alexander mounted the throne and at once altered his father's policy of co-operation with Napoleon, Emperor of France. He continued to rule Russia until 1825 when he died just as a conspiracy was being formed against his rule.

George Petrovitch, KARAGEORGE (1752–1817)

Usurped: Power in Serbia 1804
Social Origins: Peasant

Karageorge was born George Petrovitch in the little village of Topola, but he was universally known as George the Black, or Karageorge, because of his famous sulks and bouts of depression. At the time of his birth, Serbia was ruled by the Ottoman Empire, but Karageorge was to be instrumental in freeing his nation.

Like many young Serbian men of his time, Karageorge left his home to serve in the Austrian army against the Turks. In the wars Karageorge gained the reputation of being a brave and resourceful leader of men. The conclusion of peace between Turkey and Austria left Karageorge without a job, so in 1804 he returned home. He found Serbia in a forment following atrocities perpetrated by the Janissaries, household troops of the Sultan. Karageorge felt that the time had come for him to make a desperate gamble.

He announced that Serbia should be a free nation and that he was going to fight the Turks over the matter. Suddenly thousands of men came flocking to his banner, sickened by the behaviour of the Turkish troops. Within a matter of months the Turks found large areas of Serbia to be ungovernable. By 1808, Karageorge had the whole country under his control, and had driven the Turks south of the Nisava River. On 26 December he was proclaimed the hereditary chief of the Serbs, the first man to bear the title since the 14th century.

Karageorge ruled Serbia well, but firmly, for the following five years. He tried, and to large extent succeeded, in keeping order among the tough men of Serbia, and in setting up the institutions of a new state. In 1813 the Turks mustered a new army and invaded Serbia. Karageorge was defeated and fled to Austria. He was later killed in a squabble with a fellow Serb patriot leader (see Milosh Obrenovich below), but his descendents continued to rule Serbia, and later Yugoslavia, until the Communist revolution of the 1940s.

Jean Jacques DESSALINES (1758–1806)

Usurped: Power in Haiti 1804
Social Origins: Slave

Dessalines' status, or indeed his name, before he was captured by slave dealers on the Guinea Coast is unknown. It is probable that he was a prisoner captured in some wars between tribes of the interior who was then sold by his captors to European slave traders arriving off the coast in their ships. He was taken to the French colony of Haiti in the Caribbean and sold to a plantation owner.

When the French Revolution broke out with the storming of the Bastile and other events, the French overseas possessions were thrown into turmoil. Haiti was no exception and the slaves took advantage of the confusion to rebel. Slaughtering those masters and overseers who had treated them cruelly, the slaves embraced the ideals of freedom proposed by the French Revolutionaries. Dessalines took an active part in this uprising and, when order was restored, he was made Governor of southern Haiti. In 1804, Dessalines took advantage of a depletion of French troops on the island to declare himself an independent power with the title of Emperor Jean-Jacques I. His pretentions lasted only a little over 2 years before he was killed in a revolt.

— ♔ —

LOUIS BONAPARTE (1778–1846)
Usurped: Power in Holland 1806
Social Origins: Corsican Gentry

Louis Bonaparte was a man of no great capabilities, but rode to power on the back of his elder brother, Emperor Napoleon of France (see above). Eventually the dependence on his brother became too much for Louis, and he fled the position of power he had won for himself.

In the late 18th century Holland was split between those who favoured more autocratic rule by the Stadtholder, and those who emphasized the Republican limits placed on the Stadtholder's power. By 1795 the Stadtholder was losing the struggle and could only maintain his position with foreign troops. The Dutch were, therefore, only too happy to invite a French Revolutionary army in to drive out their ruler. At first the Dutch seemed to have got the better of the deal by gaining a truly Republican constitution and only a slight degree of interference from France.

However, as the years passed the French government interfered more and more in Dutch affairs. Finally, in 1806 Louis Bonaparte arrived in Holland with a large body of French troops. He was, he announced, removing the constitution and was making himself king. Any dissenters were quickly silenced by the French troops, and Louis ascended a throne which had never before existed.

For four years, Louis ruled Holland to the mutual benefit of himself and his elder brother. But gradually Napoleon began to interfere with Louis's government in Holland. Eventually, Louis became completely exasperated by the whole affair. He abdicated and retired to Italy with a sizeable fortune which he had acquired. He spent the rest of his life writing books and moving in Italian artistic circles. His son, Louis Napoleon, later seized power in France (see below).

FERDINAND VII (1784–1833)

Usurped: Kingdom of Spain 1808 and 1814
Social Origins: Royal Family

Ferdinand was a treacherous intriguer who hungered after power and seemed capable of any act which might win him the coveted crown. He was, however, a complete coward and refused to risk his life in pursuit of his claims. It was an unfortunate combination which plunged Spain into years of bloodshed and ruin.

Ferdinand grew up in the court of his father, King Charles IV, where he learnt the arts of political intrigue and subterfuge. Charles himself was little interested in politics and left affairs in the hands of his wife, Maria Luisa. In her turn Maria Luisa was heavily influenced by her lover, Manuel Godoy. Ferdinand believed that he should be king and plunged into the palace intrigues in the hope of outwitting Maria and Godoy.

After first fighting against Revolutionary France, Spain became an ally of Napoleon, leading to the disastrous defeat of the combined French and Spanish fleet at Trafalgar. In 1807 Godoy, expecting a Prussian victory against France mobilized the Spanish army. The Prussians, however, were defeated and French troops poured into Spain under the command of Marshal Murat. Riots broke out against Godoy and his government in Madrid, and the favourite was forced to resign.

Believing that his moment had come, Ferdinand launched his usurpation bid. He was successful in using the civil disorders to force his father to abdicate and mounted the throne himself. No sooner had Ferdinand seized power than he found himself faced by the army of Murat at the gates of Madrid. Murat refused to deal with Ferdinand but insisted on dealing with the deposed King Charles.

Ferdinand did not wish to anger the French Marshal who had so many troops at his command. Such a move might entail his own deposition and might possibly cost him his life. When Murat suggested that both Ferdinand and Charles should travel to Bayonne to meet Napoleon in order to decide who really was king, Ferdinand agreed. He believed that he could easily persuade the French Emperor to confirm his grip on power. Ferdinand, however, was mistaken. As soon as he reached Bayonne, he was placed under arrest and bundled off to detention in a comfortable home in France. His father suffered a similar fate and Joseph Bonaparte took the empty throne (see below). The Spanish people, however, refused to accept the new regime and began a long, bloody guerilla war against the French.

Released from captivity in 1814, the wily Ferdinand persuaded the statesmen of Europe to place him on the throne of Spain, assuring them that he was the only king who would be accepted by the people and that he could ensure peace and order after long years of war. The diplomats at the Congress of Vienna agreed and gave Ferdinand Spain, despite the fact that Charles was still alive and had likewise recently been released from French custody.

Ferdinand hurried south to his homeland where he imposed a regime of the utmost cruelty and autocracy. In 1823 a rebellion nearly robbed him of his throne, but he gained the help of a foreign army and put down the rising. His final act for Spain was to change the law of succession, thus ensuring the existence of two claimants to the throne who fought a bitter civil war after his death.

— 👑 —

JOSEPH BONAPARTE (1768–1844)

Usurped: Kingdom of Spain 1808
Social Origins: Corsican Gentry

Even more so than his brother Louis (see above), Joseph was a puppet of his brother Emperor Napoleon (see above). During the French Revolutionary period, Joseph occupied a variety of governmental posts, and as a diplomat represented France in the United States of America. As such he was able to help his younger brother Napoleon at different stages in his career.

In 1806 Napoleon gave Joseph the Kingdom of Naples, which had been confiscated from its king. Two years later, however, the Spanish played into Napoleon's hands (see Ferdinand VII above) and the Emperor needed to find a king. He chose Joseph as the new King of Spain, forcing him to relinquish the Kingdom of Naples.

Once in Spain, Joseph struggled to implement the orders of Napoleon, but the two brothers had completely failed to understand the Spanish. Joseph instituted a fairly liberal constitution, a device which had earned the support of large sections of the population in other occupied countries. The Spanish however, preferred firm government and viewed any attack on the Church as sacrilege and an insult to Spanish honour. Just 11 days after entering Madrid, Joseph was forced to flee. The rest of his reign was spent in a long, bloody struggle to put down rebellions and to drive out the British armies who were aiding the guerillas. In both he was unsuccessful and he abdicated in 1813. He later moved to America where he spent a comfortable retirement.

— 👑 —

JORGEN JORGENSON (1780–1845)
Usurped: Power in Iceland 1809
Social Origins: Privateer

The activities of Jorgen Jorgenson provided Europe with a piece of light, almost comic, relief in the midst of the long, grim Napoleonic wars. For the people involved in the six-week adventure in Iceland, however, there was nothing funny about the affair.

Jorgen Jorgenson was born in Copenhagen and took to a life at sea at an early age. In 1807 Jorgenson fitted out and became captain of a privateer ship. Privateers were ships owned by private men which were enrolled into a navy during wartime on the basis that they would not be paid but could keep any loot they captured. In practice privateers preyed on the merchant shipping of the enemy and avoided naval action whenever possible. Though such acts were basically piratical, the privateers were protected by their letters of marque, the enrolment papers, so long as they only attacked enemy ships and obeyed the rules of war. Jorgenson overstepped the conditions of his letters of marque in truly spectacular fashion.

On June 21 1809 Jorgenson sailed into Reykjavik Harbour and led his men ashore. Storming through the capital, which was little more than a large village, Jorgenson captured the state treasury and looted it of everything of value. Guessing that Europe was too preoccupied with its own affairs to bother with Iceland, Jorgenson set himself up as ruler of the island. He used his privateersmen to impose his instructions on the farmers and fishermen of Reykjavik, and he gave every impression of staying. However, a ship of the British Royal Navy then arrived off Iceland, learnt what was going on and put a landing party ashore. Jorgenson was captured and taken to England where he lived until 1820 when, convicted of another crime, he was transported to Australia for life.

Joachim MURAT (1767–1815)
Usurped: Kingdom of Naples 1808
Social Origins: French Innkeeper

Joachim Murat was dashing, handsome, brave and reliable in a crisis, but he had his faults and one of these was to prove his undoing. At the age of 20

Murat left his father's inn to join a cavalry regiment in the French army, obtaining a commission as an officer in 1792. As early as 1795 Murat had struck up a friendship with the young Napoleon Bonaparte (see above), helping him to quell a riot in Paris.

Over the following years Murat commanded the cavalry under Napoleon on several important campaigns and made a great contribution to the Emperor's victories. In 1808 Murat commanded an army sent into Spain to seize border fortresses and impose terms on the king Charles IV. He found, however, that Charles had recently been deposed by his son, Ferdinand VII (see above). By cunning strategem, Murat captured both kings and forced them to hand the throne over to Napoleon. Murat hoped to be made King of Spain, and was furious when Napoleon's brother was given the honour instead. Murat had to be content with being offered the Kingdom of Naples.

Perhaps surprisingly, Murat managed to maintain order in his turbulent new state, a feat few rulers had been able to achieve in recent years. After bravely commanding the rearguard during Napoleon's disastrous retreat from Moscow in 1812, Murat returned to Naples and began plotting for his own safety. He was convinced that Napoleon was doomed and made peace moves to the allies, who willingly responded. When Napoleon fell from power, Murat was allowed to keep his throne.

However, Napoleon landed in France in 1815 determined to stage a comeback. Murat responded by raising the Neapolitan army and marching north towards Austrian territory, despite the pleas of his wife, Napoleon's sister, to stay put. He felt that his earlier treachery could only be put right by such drastic action. Both Napoleon and Murat were defeated, however, and Murat fled to Cannes. He later tried to stage a coup in Naples against the newly re-instated Bourbon king. He failed, was captured and shot.

— 👑 —

HENRI CHRISTOPHE I (1767–1820)

Usurped: Power in Haiti 1811
Social Origins: Slave

Born into slavery, Christophe saved enough money to purchase his freedom by the time he was 40, a not altogether unusual feat. He joined the army of Jean Jacques Dessalines (see above), self-appointed Emperor of Haiti, and by 1804 had risen to be Commander-in-Chief under the Emperor. In 1806 Christophe was instrumental in organizing the revolt which ended in the death of Emperor Jean. He at once made himself President of what now became the Republic of Haiti.

Christophe worked hard at consolidating his rule over his troubled state, which was in the throes of liberating slaves and under constant danger of French attack. By 1811 he felt confident enough of his power to declare himself hereditary King of Haiti and to insist upon receiving the deference owed to royalty. Christophe quickly became a cruel despot, who killed his subjects out of hand for the slightest offence and imposed his rule with a tough soldiery. He built a magnificent palace for himself on a mountain peak near Milot, surrounded by stout walls and strong defences, from where he ruled his island kingdom. In 1819 a revolt broke out against his rule. His soldiers deserted in the face of the mob, leaving Christophe on his own. On 8 October, rather than be captured, Christophe shot himself.

— ♔ —

Arthur Wellesley, DUKE of WELLINGTON (1769–1852)

Kingmaker of France and Spain 1814
Social Origins: British Nobility

Arthur Wellesley, later created the Duke of Wellington, was born in Dublin as the fourth son of the Earl of Mornington, an Anglo-Irish nobleman. At the age of 18 he entered the army, having failed to show an aptitude for any other career and being described as 'cannon fodder' by his own mother. Throughout his military career, Wellesley showed a strong sense of duty and loyalty to the crown. It was as the loyal servant of the British Crown that he was to be instrumental in making Kings of both Spain and France.

In 1796 Wellesley was posted to India, where he won a series of spectacular victories. On his return to Britain in 1805 he became a Member of Parliament, but in 1808 he was given command of the British expeditionary force to Portugal. There Wellesley made contact with Spanish guerillas struggling against the French occupation of their country (see Joseph Bonaparte above). He made great efforts to help the guerillas, while persuading them to co-operate with his own operations against the French.

In 1809 Wellesley defeated a French army at Talavera and was created Viscount Wellington. For the next three years the Peninsular War, as it became known, swayed back and forth as first Wellington and then the French gained the upper hand. At Vittoria, in June 1813, however, Wellington inflicted a decisive defeat on the French and drove them over the Pyrenees. King Joseph was ousted from his throne by Wellington's troops and his magnificent art treasures captured. It was after this victory that Wellesley was created Duke of Wellington. After a final battle at Toulouse early in 1814 the French army collapsed. The withdrawal of the French opened the

Duke of Wellington
In 1812, when the British were fighting the French in Spain, the Spanish artist Goya made a quick sketch of the Duke of Wellington. Later, when Wellington had pushed the French from Spain and had won the Battle of Waterloo, Goya worked the drawing up into a series of nearly identical portraits, of which this is one, which he was able to sell to British and other dignitaries. (*Topham*)

way to the return of the Spanish King Ferdinand VII, whose line persisted until 1931, and has recently been restored to the throne in the person of King Juan Carlos.

Wellington was made the British ambassador in Paris, and he worked ceaselessly for the enthronement of Louis Bourbon, the legitimate heir to King Louis XVI who had been executed by the French Revolutionaries in 1793. Wellington knew Louis to be a moderate who could unite the disparate opinions in post-Revolutionary France. Wellington's influence proved decisive and Louis was crowned as Louis XVIII. Napoleon's brief return to power in 1815 was terminated by Wellington on the field of Waterloo. Once again Wellington hurried to Paris to engineer the return of Louis to power, before the Tsar of Russia could arrive and install his own candidate.

After the establishment of peace, Wellington became Commander-in-Chief and then entered politics. He was Prime Minister of Britain for a while in the 1820s and served in several governments until 1846, when he retired. The Bourbon line which he had helped to install in France survived until 1848.

PRINCE Clemens Weazel Lothar
METTERNICH-Winneburg (1773–1859)

Kingmaker of Europe 1815
Social Origins: Austrian Nobility

Prince Metternich was the Foreign Minister of the mighty Austrian Empire for forty years, and he dominated European diplomacy for many of these years. However, his greatest influence came in 1814 and 1815 when the fate of Europe lay, almost literally, in his hands.

Prince Metternich was born at Coblenz in 1773 as the son of a senior Austrian diplomat. As a child he followed his father to various courts, making contacts which would be invaluable in later life. While still in his teens, Metternich joined the diplomatic corps and made an advantageous marriage to an Austrian countess who had friends at court. After serving as ambassador to Saxony, Prussia and France, Metternich was appointed Foreign Minister of the Empire in 1809.

In 1814 Napoleon, Emperor of the French was defeated after nearly twenty years of continual warfare. In the turmoil of battle the old political map of Europe had been destroyed. Some countries had ceased to exist and new ones had come into being. Dukes had made themselves kings and kings had lost their thrones. Prince Metternich invited the representatives of the various nations to Vienna to sort out the future map of Europe. In all 216 representatives arrived, including many of the lesser nobility of Europe dispossessed by the war.

Metternich was supreme in his role as master diplomat of Europe. He arranged balls, dinners and parties to keep the diplomats amused, while organizing clandestine meetings to secure his aims. If the stories are to be believed he encouraged certain amorous adventures between Austrian ladies and foreign diplomats to divert attention from his political manoeuvring. In all this Metternich had two main aims. He wished to restrict any future French expansion, and stop Prussia and Russia gaining too much from their military victories. He was outstandingly successful.

Russia and Prussia were stopped from partitioning Poland and Saxony between them. Prussia was, however, given territory along the Rhine so as to contain French expansion. The 360 independent states which had made up the Holy Roman Empire before the French Revolutionary Wars were swept away to be replaced by just 39 countries. Among the many changes engineered by Metternich the rulers of Hanover, Bavaria, Wurtemberg, Saxony and Holland were made kings, whereas before they had been Dukes or Electors, and the Dukes of Oldenburg, Saxe-Weimer and Mecklenburg were created Grand Dukes.

In Italy the previous rulers, or their heirs, were reinstated on Metternich's insistence. This made Italy a patchwork of small states, and ensured a dominant role for Austria. Metternich had caused the creation of more Kings, Dukes and Grand Dukes than any other man in history, and had ensured the place of Austria in international affairs.

MILOSH OBRENOVICH (1780–1860)

Usurped: Principality of Serbia 1815 and 1858
Social Origins: Nobleman

While in his early twenties, Obrenovich joined the Serbian uprising under Karageorge (see above), which drove the Turks from the country. He was made Voivoide, or regional governor, of central Serbia. In 1813, however, the Turks invaded in force and crushed the Serbian army. Karageorge and other leaders fled, but Obrenovich refused to leave. Instead he approached the Turks, offering to rule Serbia on their behalf. He promised to guarantee peace in return for limited concessions to Serbian nationalism. The Turks agreed and Obrenovich became Pasha. This move infuriated Karageorge and his followers, living in exile.

Obrenovich began ruling Serbia strictly but justly and soon became very popular with his subjects. On Palm Sunday 1815 he ordered the massacre of the Turkish troops occupying the country and announced that he no longer recognized the Sultan's supremacy. The Turks fought back, but were unable to defeat Obrenovich. In 1816 they recognized Obrenovich as ruler of Serbia, although Obrenovich accepted the nominal authority of the Sultan. A few years later he took the title Prince of Serbia.

In 1817 Karageorge returned to Serbia, hoping to take over the government himself. Obrenovich had him murdered in his sleep, thus starting a feud between the two families which dominated Serbian history for the rest of the century. In 1839 Obrenovich abdicated in favour of his son, Milan, but after the latter's death the National Assembly invited Karageorge's son, Alexander, to be Prince in 1843. Obrenovich was furious, but he was powerless. In 1859, Obrenovich took advantage of dissatisfaction with Alexander's rule to lead a rising of noblemen, though he was almost 70 years old. Alexander was forced to flee into exile and Obrenovich once again became Prince. He died the following year, leaving the throne to his son Michael.

— ♔ —

DOST MAHOMED (1793–1863)

Usurped: Khanate of Afghans 1818
Social Origins: Royal Family

Dost Mahomed was born into one of the many powerful noble families of Afghanistan. Then, as in more recent times, much of the country was in the hands of wild hill tribesmen and central authority was weak. In 1818 Dost Mahomed's elder brother, Futteh Khan, was treacherously murdered by Mahomed Shah, Khan of Afghanistan. The move was probably an attempt by Mahomed Shah to impose his authority on the nobles. If so, it failed.

The outraged Dost Mahomed immediately raised his troops in rebellion and was quickly joined by other noblemen, eager to throw off the authority of the Khan. The combined forces proved too much for Mahomed Shah, whose army was crushed. The victorious rebels divided the nation amongst themselves, with Dost Mahomed securing the wealthy plains and city of Kabul.

After securing power in Kabul, Dost Mahomed set about conquering new territories. He defeated the Sikhs, and became an ally of the British. He later abandoned this alliance in favour of friendship with the Russians and in 1838 was removed from his throne by the British. Two years later during an uprising in Kabul, the entire British garrison was massacred. Dost Mahomed was allowed to return by the British on giving a promise to restore order and to shun the Russians.

273

Dost Mahomed remained true to his word. He brought peace to the area around Kabul and proved to be a staunch ally of Britain. Even during the Indian Mutiny, Dost Mahomed proved to be a friend of the British. He died in 1860, shortly after bringing the whole of Afghanistan under his control.

Augustin de ITURBIDE (1783–1824)

Usurped: Empire of Mexico 1822
Social Origins: Hidalgo (Lesser Nobility)

Iturbide was a proud and haughty member of the landowning class of the Spanish colonies, yet he was shrewd enough to take advantage of popular sentiment when it suited him to do so. He joined the Spanish colonial army at an early age, and soon gained senior positions through a combination of ability and family influence.

In 1810 a parish priest named Hidalgo raised a revolt against government from Spain. The revolt quickly became a widespread peasant uprising which formulated a constitution in 1812. Iturbide fought against the rebels, having little sympathy for their democratic ideals. By 1815 the rebellion had been put down and its leaders executed; only one, a man named Guerrero managing to escape.

Following the fall of Napoleon, Ferdinand VII was reinstated as King of Spain. Though Ferdinand was a believer in absolute monarchy it appeared, in 1820, that he was on the point of accepting democratic government and curtailing the privileges of the aristocracy. Iturbide and his fellow landowners were apalled at the prospect of losing their power and privileges. In 1821 Iturbide, now the acknowledged leader of the landowning classes, contacted Guerrero. The two men reached a compromise known as the Plan of Iguala, which called for complete independence for Mexico and gave the peasants some rights, while guaranteeing privileges to the aristocracy.

A popular rising immediately broke out, and on 24 August Iturbide marched on the residence of the Viceroy and forced him to sign over all power. Iturbide proclaimed himself Emperor Augustin I in May the following year. At first hailed as a liberator, Augustin soon revealed his despotic attitude, refusing to listen to the demands of the peasants. In March 1823 another rebellion forced him to abdicate and he fled to Europe. The following year he returned to Mexico, where he had been outlawed in his absence, and was executed by the new government.

SAMUEL HOUSTON (1793–1863)

Usurped: Power in Texas, 1835
Social Origins: Soldier

Texas is now one of the United States of America, but for centuries was an integral part of Mexico, first under Spanish colonial rule and later as an independent power. The present allegiance of Texas is largely due to the activities of Sam Houston.

During the 1820s and 1830s the Mexican government allowed citizens of the United States to settle in northern areas of Mexico. By the mid-1830s the immigrant Americans considerably outnumbered the native Mexicans. They began agitating for self-government. The Mexican President, Santa Anna (see below), was not prepared to grant an American-style constitution to Texas and was determined not to allow the Americans to keep slaves. Slavery had been banned in Mexico some years earlier as a barbaric and inhuman institution.

Houston and the other immigrants, however, were determined to keep their slaves, which they believed were vital to the economic running of their farms. Proclaiming that they wanted a return to the more liberal Mexican constitution of 1812, the American-Texans rose in rebellion in 1836. Sam Houston was a leading figure in the decision to announce a rebellion, and took command of the small army which the rebels could raise.

President Santa Anna marched north with an army of 5,000 men. He crushed one Texan force at the Alamo on 6 March and pushed on to confront the main Texan army. Houston, however, had laid hands on two cannon. While Santa Anna was fording the River San Jacinto, Houston opened fire with grapeshot, mowing down the Mexicans. Santa Anna was captured and forced to accede to Texan independence.

As the successful general who had gained independence for Texas, Houston had no difficulty in being elected President. He legalized slavery, allowing the importation of many negroes to work the farms, and introduced an American-style constitution. After Texas joined the United States in 1845, Houston sat as Congressman and later as Governor. He was finally deposed from office in 1861, on the eve of the American Civil War, for refusing to swear allegiance to the Confederate States and so take Texas out of the Union.

— ♔ —

Samuel Houston
This photograph shows Sam Houston in later life. His contribution to the independence of Texas was immense and he was named as first President and later Governor of the state. The city of Houston in Texas is named in his honour.
(*BBC Picture Library*)

Charles LOUIS NAPOLEON Bonaparte (1808–1873)

Usurped: Power in France 1851
Social Origins: Imperial Family

Born when his great-uncle, Emperor Napoleon I, was at the height of his powers, Louis Napoleon was brought up to believe in the destiny of the Bonaparte family. It was a belief which shaped his future life. In 1832 the death of Napoleon I's son made Louis Napoleon the head of the Bonaparte family. He began distributing leaflets and papers emphasizing the past glories of the Bonapartes and spreading his political ideas. In 1836 he organized a rebellion at Strasbourg, but it failed dismally and he fled to the USA. In 1840 he returned to France and was immediately arrested. He escaped to London in 1846.

In 1848 events played into Louis Napoleon's hands. In February of that year the French government banned a public meeting on the subject of electoral reform. Riots broke out and the mob erected barricades across the streets of Paris. The middle class National Guard joined the rioters and King Louis Phillipe abdicated. A Republic was proclaimed and elections organized for June.

Louis Napoleon hurried across the Channel to France where he successfully stood for election to the National Assembly. The new Assembly was dominated by moderates elected from the provinces. The Paris mob was far more left-wing in views and refused to accept the results of the election. They rioted again, and savage fighting broke out on the streets. More than 10,000 people were killed before the army put down the uprising.

In the wake of these riots the Presidential elections were held in December. Louis Napoleon was one of the candidates. His campaign was based largely on the glamour of his family and on the promise of firm government, such as had been carried out by his great-uncle. He won by a majority of 5 to 1.

The constitution gave the President wide-ranging powers, but demanded his resignation after 4 years. The President was not allowed to stand for re-election. Once having tasted power, Louis Napoleon did not want to relinquish it. He was cheered in the streets and he was hailed at military reviews with shouts of 'long live the Emperor', just as Napoleon I had been. Louis Napoleon asked the Assembly to change the constitution to allow him to stand for re-election. It refused.

On 2 December 1851, the anniversary of Napoleon I's great victory at the Battle of Austerlitz, Louis Napoleon led troops to the Assembly. He ejected the delegates at bayonet point and announced a new constitution which extended the franchise, but placed great powers in his own hands as First Consul of the Republic. A plebiscite was organized which produced a majority in favour of the new constitution by a majority of 14 to 1. Louis

Napoleon spent the following year consolidating his hold on government. On 1 December 1852 he proclaimed himself Emperor Napoleon III, and gathered all political power into his own hands.

Napoleon established a court of great magnificence which became famous throughout Europe for its art, splendour and decadence. He continued to rule France until 1870, when his armies were defeated by Prussia, and he was forced to abdicate.

Lajos KOSSUTH (1802–1894)

Usurped: Power in Hungary 1848
Social Origins: Lesser Nobility

Born the son of an Hungarian lawyer, Kossuth became a passionate believer in Hungarian nationalism at an early age. Hungary, at this time, was a major part of the Austrian Empire. In theory, Hungary was not amalgamated with Austria, but simply shared the same sovereign. Hungary had its own Diet, or parliament, and had its own nobility. However, since the 1780s, there had been a strong policy of integration by which the Emperors hoped to 'Germanise' the Hungarians. Under the leadership of Count Szechenyi the Hungarians had passively resisted, but to little effect.

In 1825 Kossuth was elected to the Diet, and became known for his passionate speeches on Hungarian issues. In the 1830s he spent a few years in prison because of his refusal to accept censorship of his writings. In 1847 a new Diet was elected which had a majority of nationalists. Early in 1848, Kossuth made a powerful speech demanding the establishment of a separate Hungarian cabinet responsible to the Diet, not the Emperor. The proposal was passed. At the time liberal uprisings were taking place in other parts of the Empire, so Emperor Ferdinand accepted the Hungarian demands. He appointed the respectable Count Batthyany as Prime Minister.

In March the new government passed a package of laws involving sweeping reforms. Such a move outraged Ferdinand, but he was powerless to intervene. In December Ferdinand abdicated in favour of his dashing, handsome nephew, Franz Joseph. The new Emperor quickly quelled rebellions throughout his Empire, but Hungary refused to accept him as sovereign. Franz Joseph sent an army to enforce his rule. Kossuth toured Hungary making a series of impassioned pleas to the Hungarians to defend their nation. Two hundred thousand men answered the call and in May 1849 the Austrian advance was halted.

Under Kossuth's influence, the Hungarian Diet abolished the monarchy, declaring the nation to be a republic with Kossuth as President. In reality the office of President involved the powers of an absolute dictator, a move Kossuth excused on the grounds that such powers were necessary in the emergency. The Tsar of Russia, worried about the effects a Hungarian victory might have on his own subject peoples, sent an army to help the Austrians. On August 9 a great battle was fought at Temesvar which resulted in total defeat for the Hungarians. The disaster was largely due to Kossuth's interference in military affairs, which he did not understand. Kossuth fled to Britain where he lived until moving to Italy in 1859.

Hungary, meanwhile, was totally subject to Austrian rule and came under the control of the Emperor Franz Joseph. In 1867, following the military defeat of the Austrian Empire by Prussia, Franz Joseph granted Hungary a democratic constitution and allowed many of the reforms of 1848. Although Kossuth was never permitted to return to Hungary, he was given a state funeral in 1894 and is still remembered as one of the heroic founders of Hungarian independence.

— 👑 —

Giuseppe GARIBALDI (1807–1882)

Kingmaker of Italy 1860
Social Origins: Fisherman

The present face of Italy, as one nation containing the Vatican as a Papal enclave, is largely the work of Garibaldi. His dashing military adventures and ardent belief in Italian nationhood carried his supporters through against overwhelming odds, and forced actions on the crowned heads of Europe.

Born in Nice, then part of the Italian kingdom of Piedmont, Garibaldi abandoned fishing when in his twenties and joined the navy. There he became involved with subversive liberal political groups and was forced to flee Piedmont. He travelled to South America where he became involved in various independence movements and proved himself to be a military leader of genius.

When liberal revolutions broke out in many Italian states in 1848, in common with many other parts of Europe, Garibaldi returned from South America. He commanded the heroic defence of Rome against the Papal and Austrian armies, but was finally forced to flee to the USA. In 1859 he joined the Piedmontese army in the war against Austria. When Piedmont was abandoned by her ally, France, King Victor Emmanuel was forced to make peace with Austria. Though much of northern Italy was united under

Garibaldi
After helping to free several South American colonies of Spanish rule, Garibaldi returned home to Italy to create a unified nation under King Victor Emmanuel. Idolized as a national hero in Italy, Garibaldi's international reputation was less certain. In liberal nations, such as Britain and the United States, he was considered to be a genius, but in the more autocratic Russian and Austrian Empires he was considered to be a dangerous subversive. (*Mary Evans*)

Piedmont, Venetia and the lands south of Siena remained under the control of autocratic rulers.

Garibaldi was disgusted by the peace arrangements and set about planning a stupendous adventure. At his estate outside Genoa, Garibaldi gathered together a thousand men committed to the ideal of a united Italy under King Victor Emmanuel of Piedmont. Garibaldi armed the men and, understanding the Italian love of show and glamour, dressed them in striking red shirts. In May 1860 Garibaldi and his 'Redshirts' left Genoa harbour on a ship bound for Sicily.

He landed at Marsala on 11 May. He was welcomed by local revolutionaries opposed to the despotic rule of King Francis II of Naples. Within a few weeks, Garibaldi had overrun the Neapolitan troops on the island and had been proclaimed Dictator of Sicily. Thousands of men flocked to his banner and in August he sailed across the Straits of Messina. Brushing aside 20,000 Neapolitans, Garibaldi entered Naples on 7 September. Three weeks later he crushed the 40,000 remaining Neapolitan troops.

Victor Emmanuel was delighted by these successes, but he knew that Garibaldi was determined to make Rome the capital of Italy. Such a move would involve stripping the Pope of his temporal power, which would not be tolerated by the Catholic powers of France, Spain and Austria. Knowing he had to stop Garibaldi, Victor Emmanuel led the Piedmontese army south, through the Papal States, smashing the Papal army on the way. In October, Victor Emmanuel entered Naples, which voted overwhelmingly to join Piedmont. Garibaldi had made Victor Emmanuel King of Italy.

After the momentous events of 1859–60 Garibaldi remained active. He led volunteer troops in the war with Austria in 1866, which resulted in the capture of Venice, and campaigned constantly for the inclusion of Rome within the Kingdom of Italy. This was finally achieved in 1870, when France removed her support for the Pope. Garibaldi enjoyed a pension of 2,000 per year from the King of Italy and died on his estate in 1882.

— 👑 —

ABDUL HAMID II (1842–1918)

Usurped: Ottoman Empire 1876
Social Origins: Royal Family

Abdul Hamid II was one of the most unfortuante sovereigns in history. During his reign the decaying Ottoman Empire staggered from one crisis to the next. Though Abdul Hamid's diplomatic skill and duplicity kept the Empire alive, he was incapable of solving its problems.

Born in 1842 as a younger son of Sultan Abdul Mejid, Abdul Hamid spent much of his early life in the shadow of other members of his family. In 1861 his father died and the throne was taken by his uncle Abdul Aziz. Abdul Hamid and his elder brother, Murad, were lucky not to be executed or murdered on the accession of the new Sultan, as was almost customary in the Ottoman Empire. Instead they were imprisoned.

Aziz proved himself to be an incompetent ruler, concerned mainly with gathering wealth and leading a life of outright hedonism. In May 1876 an uprising against Aziz was organized by the Young Turks, a secret society of Turks committed to modernizing the Empire. The rebels dethroned Aziz, who committed suicide five days later, and placed Murad on the throne. At the same time they released Abdul Hamid from imprisonment.

Disapproving of the modernizing sympathies of his elder brother, Abdul Hamid wasted little time in organizing his own party of support within the government. Less than three months after Murad was placed on the throne, Abdul Hamid launched a dramatic coup. The Sultan was hurried from the palace and once again placed in prison, where he remained until his death in 1904. Abdul Hamid, meanwhile, secured the throne and established himself as a despotic Sultan of the old style. In 1893, for instance, he attempted to stop the calls for self-government by the Armenians by simply massacring 200,000 of their more prominent citizens. In 1909 Abdul Hamid was removed from power by a rebellion led by the Young Turks and spent the rest of his life in prison.

Antonio Lopez de SANTA ANNA (1795–1876)

Usurped: Power in Mexico 1853
Social Origins: Soldier

Santa Anna was an unprincipled adventurer who held power in Mexico on no less than four occasions, though each time he was compelled to relinquish government. The confused conditions of these years were largely a result of the manner in which Mexico became independent.

In the early 19th century Mexico, in common with most of the Spanish colonies, gained its independence. However, accustomed to being ruled by professional administrators from Spain, the Mexicans were uncertain how to establish a government and political murders and violence became common. Santa Anna had taken part in the successful struggle with Spain and had gained a military reputation for himself. In 1833 he was elected to the Presidency, an office which carried almost dictatorial powers. Three years later he was captured by the rebellious Texans. In his absence, Santa Anna was deposed.

Two years later he recovered his reputation as a successful fighter by holding the port of Vera Cruz against a French fleet. In 1841 he seized the Presidency, but in 1844 he so bungled negotiations with the United States that he was overthrown by an insurrection and forced to flee abroad. Two years later war broke out with the United States and Santa Anna hurried to take command of the army. He was defeated at Cerro Gordo and went into hiding, thus evading the ignominy of surrendering Mexico City.

By 1853 the Mexican politicians had divided into a number of hostile factions which were entirely unable to agree on policy. They appealed to Santa Anna to return in the role of a strong man and mediator. On his return, Santa Anna overstepped his authority and astounded everyone by assuming the powers of despotic dictator and insisting that he be addressed as 'Serene Highness'. The army quickly deposed him and ejected him from the country. This time Santa Anna did not return, but spent the rest of his life in comfortable obscurity in South America.

— ♔ —

Juan Manuel ROSAS (1793–1877)
Usurped: Power in Argentina 1835
Social Origins: Landowner

It has been said of Rosas that he 'exercised a great influence for good and evil in the Argentine'. Much the same could be said of Argentina's effects on Rosas.

Born into the privileged Hidalgo, or landowning, class of the Spanish colonies, Rosas owned vast cattle ranches on the Pampas, inland from Buenos Aires. In the near-anarchic conditions which followed Argentina's independence in 1824, Rosas hired gangs of tough gauchos, or cowboys, to protect his herds and property. As Rosas became increasingly involved in politics, this private army grew and was directed against his rivals. He gradually came to assume the leadership of the Federalist Party and gained the Presidency in 1835.

Once in position, Rosas crushed the rival Unitarian Party, stripped the democratically elected council of power and made himself dictator of Argentina. The early years of his rule were beneficial to Argentina, for Rosas imposed peace and allowed the economic development of the country. As the years passed the anarchy Rosas had suppressed was forgotten and opposition to his rule grew. Rosas attempted to maintain power by bloodily subduing any movement against him. Eventually he was ousted by members of his own party and forced into exile. Stripped of his ranches and wealth, Rosas eked out an existence in England.

— ♔ —

Justo Rufino BARRIOS (1835–1885)
Usurped: Power in Guatemala 1873
Social Origins: Soldier

Barrios was born just four years before Guatemala freed itself from control by Mexico. His ambition to impose a similar control on other nations of Central America was to result in his death. Barrios joined the opposition to President Cernan which culminated in 1871 with the overthrow of Cernan and the installation of Granodos. As President, Granodos rewarded the loyal Barrios by making him Commander-in-Chief of the army. Just two years later, however, Barrios used his army to remove Granodos and install himself in power. Determined to remove the threat of a similar insurrection occurring again, Barrios redrew the constitution to give himself dictatorial powers.

He expelled the Jesuits, who had a great influence in politics, and seized the enormous wealth and lands of the Catholic Church. In the early 1880s he organized a federation of Guatemala, Salvador, Costa Rica and Nicaragua. When, in 1885, Salvador attempted to withdraw from the organisation, Barrios led the Guatemalan army into Salvador. On 2 April he was killed in battle, his death causing the disintegration of the federation.

— ♔ —

José Gaspar Rodriguez FRANCIA (1757–1840)
Usurped: Power in Paraguay 1816
Social Origins: Lawyer

Of Portuguese and French extraction, Francia was a scholar and an extremely learned man, but this did not stop him from being one of the most ambitious and ruthless men of South American history. When the revolution against Spanish colonial control broke out in Paraguay, Francia joined the rebels and proved himself to be one of the movement's ablest leaders. After the establishment of a republic under President Yegros, Francia began plotting and building up a network of supporters. To each group, were they peasant or noble, Francia promised to satisfy their demands.

In 1816 the government was dismissed and a congress called to formulate a constitution along the lines of ancient Rome, with a Senate and Consuls. A chair was placed in the hall inscribed 'Caesar'. It was intended that Yegros would occupy the chair and supervise the meeting. Instead, Francia strode into the hall and sat down in the chair. When Yegros entered he meekly joined the body of the delegates. In control of the meeting, Francia delayed voting and caused constant interruptions. Finally, Francia let it be known that as soon as he was elected Consul, he would conclude the meeting. The delegates, who all had businesses or farms to run, quickly voted Francia into office for the term of one year and hurried home.

Francia used his year to ensure he could not be ousted from power. He instituted a secret police and dismissed all senior officers in the army, replacing them with those loyal to himself. He handpicked the next Congress, which voted him the office of Dictator for three years, a term later extended to life. Francia's rule degenerated into tyranny with cruel punishments being meted out for the most trivial of offences, and Francia taking an active part in the torture of criminals. However, the firm government ensured stability and peace, which allowed Paraguay to develop rapidly.

The fear and terror with which Francia ruled eventually caused his death. On 20 September 1840, Francia fell down in a fit while conducting an interview. The man being interviewed rushed out to tell the guard to call a doctor. The guard refused to move without Francia's order to do so. The man protested that Francia was unconscious, but still the guard did not move. 'When he gets better he will punish me for acting without orders' the guard declared. Without medical help, Francia died.

JAMES BROOKE (1803–1868)
Usurped: Power in Sarawak 1841
Social Origins: British Merchant

James Brooke was one of those fortunate men who happened to be in the right place at the right time. If it had not been for the chances of fate, Brooke might have passed his life quietly and never come to the notice of history. Brooke was born in India of wealthy English parents and obtained a commission in the army of the East India Company at the age of 16. Wounded in fighting with the Burmese, Brooke was invalided back to India for convalescence.

Brooke soon became bored by the inactivity and invested much of his £30,000 fortune in a risky trading venture. Although pirates were common in the area, Brooke decided to chance trading with the Philippines. He bought a small vessel, armed it strongly and set off on his venture. He arrived off Borneo in 1839 to find that the Sultan of Sarawak, a state on the northern coast, was fighting a desperate civil war. Brooke offered his help, and that of his men and ship, to the Sultan. After two years of fighting, the rebellion had been put down and the Sultan was safe on his throne. The Sultan conferred the title of Rajah of Sarawak on Brooke.

Brooke gradually took over the whole business of government. He stamped out the head-hunting by Dyak tribesmen and reformed the government, so gaining more power for himself. In 1847 the British government made Brooke Governor of Labuan, a nearby island, and created him Knight Commander of the Bath. By this time Brooke was the virtual ruler of Sarawak, the Sultan having lost all authority. In 1857 Brooke handed control and the title of Rajah to his son, Sir Charles. The Brooke family remained hereditary rulers of Sarawak until the islands were captured by the Japanese during World War II.

— ♔ —

Ras Kassai, THEODORE (1816–1867)
Usurped: Empire of Abyssinia 1855
Social Origins: Bandit Chief

By the start of the 19th century the once powerful Christian state of Abyssinia was in ruins. Central authority had disappeared in the face of pagan invasions from the south and rebellions by provincial governors. It seemed that the ancient culture, which dated back to the 4th century, was doomed to extinction. Theodore turned the nation around, establishing it once more as a major power, though he probably had few motives other than personal ambition.

Ras Kassai, as the future Emperor was christened, was born in the northwest of the country and became a bandit at an early age. Preying on the trade caravans which traversed the Tigre region, Kassai built up a large personal army and great wealth. His authority gradually extended from bands of robbers to areas of territory from which he exacted tribute. An extremely competent military leader, Kassai organized his forces along modern lines and equipped them with the best weapons available.

In 1855 Kassai had himself crowned as Emperor Theodore at Axum. It was not unusual for local rulers to take this title, and there was often more than one 'emperor' in the country. Theodore, however, was able to impose his rule over the northern and central regions of the country, giving Abyssinia its first semblance of unity for many generations and laying the foundations of the present state. In 1867 Theodore imprisoned two British diplomats. He was defeated by the resulting British punitive raid, and committed suicide.

Otto Edwin Leopold von BISMARCK (1815–1898)

Kingmaker of Germany 1870
Social Origins: Landed Gentry

Bismarck was responsible for Wilhelm I of Prussia progressing from being the ruler of a middle-sized European country into becoming the monarch of a world power, changing the face of Europe for ever as he did so. Though he gained great power and influence for himself, Bismarck seems to have been genuinely inspired by the doctrine of obedience to the sovereign. When a new monarch dismissed him, Bismarck stepped aside.

Bismarck was born into the landed gentry, the traditional backbone of Prussian society, and engaged in the customary duels and military career of his class. In 1848 he entered the Prussian Diet, or parliament. During the agitation for liberal reforms of 1848 and 1849, Bismarck spoke forcefully in favour of royal power. In 1851 he was appointed Minister to the Frankfort Diet, a parliament of the German states. Later Bismarck obtained ambassadorial posts in Russia and Paris until, in 1862, he was appointed Minister President by King Wilhelm I.

Bismarck largely ignored the Diet and its democratic ideals. He aimed, instead, to gain internal support by foreign success. In 1864 he engineered an alliance with Austria against Denmark in a war which solved the long-running and complex Schelswig-Holstein question by force. Confident of the superiority of the Prussian army, Bismarck then pushed Austria into a war. At the Battle of Sadowa in 1866, the Austrian army was smashed. Bismarck had removed the one obstacle to Prussian domination of Germany.

Rather than inflict humiliating terms on Austria, Bismarck asked for practically nothing from the Empire. Instead he imposed a North German Confederation on the smaller states of that area and signed military treaties with the southern states. Such a move awakened fears in France of having a powerful neighbour, and Emperor Napoleon III (see Louis Napoleon above) made his displeasure clear. Bismarck was aiming at unifying Germany, a move which would inevitably involve war with France.

In 1870 Bismarck released an edited version of a telegram from Napoleon III, so putting him into an embarrassing position, and forcing the French to declare war. Once again the Prussian army defeated its opponents within a few weeks, and Napoleon III was himself captured at the Battle of Sedan. On 18th January 1871 the Prussians dictated peace terms in Versailles, and at the same time declared the establishment of a unified Germany under Wilhelm I, who took the title of Kaiser. The various kings and dukes of Germany kept their titles and lands, but surrendered most of their power to the Kaiser.

Bismarck remained in control of German foreign affairs for a further 19 years, formulating an anti-Russian alliance with Austria and gaining German colonies in Africa. In 1888 Kaiser Wilhelm died to be succeeded by his son, Wilhelm II. The new Kaiser was intent on ruling Germany for himself and dismissed Bismarck from office in 1890. Bismarck retired, but continued to voice his opinions on political matters until his death.

Antonio Guzman BLANCO (1828–1899)

Usurped: Power in Venezuela 1870
Social Origins: Politician

Venezuela was one of the first of the Spanish American colonies to rebel against rule from Europe. The colony declared independence in 1811, but did not drive out the last Spanish troops until 1821. The nation was relatively stable at first but under President Monagas, who held office 1849–1859, the country degenerated into near anarchy, rebellions became common and bandits flourished in the unstable conditions.

Amid this turmoil, Guzman Blanco clawed his way upward through politics. Government offices offered enormous scope for bribery and corruption, opportunites Guzman Blanco eagerly took. Passing through a succession of appointments, he amassed great wealth, but became greedy for more. In 1870 he organized a coup which swept away the entire government, placing himself in office as Dictator.

Guzman Blanco proceeded to establish a government almost unsurpassed for the level of greed and corruption. His main aim seems to have been to acquire wealth for himself. He found plenty of men who shared similar ambitions, and gave them posts in government. However, Guzman Blanco was astute enough to realize that he could squeeze more money from a rich nation than from a poor one. He therefore encouraged trade and industry, offering important concessions to successful men. In 1889, however, the corruption of the government had increased to an intolerable level and a rising of creoles, Venezuelans of European descent, forced his resignation. Guzman Blanco retired to Britain with his riches while Venezuela passed into the control of the military.

Porfirio DIAZ (1830–1915)
Usurped: Power in Mexico 1876
Social Origins: Soldier

Diaz came to power in Mexico after a period of instability and violence caused as much by foreign intervention as by Mexican rebellions. In 1855 the government proposed sweeping reforms of the Church, which held great power and wealth. An uprising led by the clergy plunged the nation into civil war. The reforming party was led by Benito Juarez, and Porfiro Diaz joined the Juarist army. Diaz showed himself to be a leader of ability and won many military engagements.

In 1860 French troops invaded Mexico to protect their interests, and soon combined with the clerical party. Together they installed the Austrian Archduke Maximillian as Emperor of Mexico. The Juarists continued the struggle against the new Emperor, and in 1867 captured and executed the hapless Austrian. Jaurez immediately became President and implemented the expected reforms. In 1871 Juarez offered himself for re-election to the Presidency. Diaz decided to stand against his leader, but was defeated. After this Juarez never trusted Diaz, who in his turn grew increasingly hostile to the government.

In 1872 Juarez died and was replaced by Lerdo, a man detested by Diaz and many others in Mexico. Diaz at once raised a rebellion. Many of his old soldiers rallied to his cause, together with opponents of Lerdo. At Tecoac in 1876 Diaz finally brought Lerdo's forces to battle and utterly defeated them. Diaz became President of Mexico. Although in theory subject to elections, the office of President was made into a self-perpetuating dictatorship by Diaz. He raised a secret police, the *rurales* from among the bandits and brigands which infested the country and used it to suppress all opposition.

Diaz ruled Mexico strictly, but in a fairly enlightened manner until 1910. In that year a split among his own supporters occurred, with many defecting to Francisco Madero (see below). Diaz resigned and fled to France, leaving Madero to take over as President. A fresh era of anarchy and civil war had begun.

Diaz

Porfirio Diaz brought peace to Mexico, but maintained his rule through a brutal dictatorship. Like many other usurpers, Diaz sought to secure his rule by taking on the outward show and regalia of legitimate authority, in this case, the wealth of stars, orders and ribbons with which Diaz appeared in public.

CETEWAYO (c. 1836–1884)

Usurped: Zulu Empire 1872
Social Origins: Royal Family

After the death of the ruler Dingane (see above) in 1838 the Zulu Empire was inherited by his brother Mpande. Unlike his predecessors Mpande was not a warlike man. The massive Zulu army was kept largely idle, although new regiments were raised. This caused great social problems for according to custom young men were not counted as mature, and were not allowed to marry, until they had 'washed their spears', that is taken part in a battle. As Cetewayo and his elder brother Mbuyazi grew to manhood the powerful Zulu nation seemed in danger of stagnation. Mbuyazi supported his father's policies, but Cetewayo did not.

As the years passed the pressures caused by peace built up to an intolerable level. The young men wanted war so as to become accepted into society, but Mpande kept them idle. Young Cetewayo became the hero of the young men, and many of the older warriors who yearned for a return to the days of Zulu supremacy. In 1856 the quarrel between Cetewayo and Mbuyazi came to blows. Both brothers raised regiments loyal to themselves and began a civil war. Far more men joined the cause of Cetewayo, and Mbuyazi's force was slaughtered. Mbuyazi was killed and all his supporters' relatives speared to death.

Cetewayo and his men moved on to confront Mpande. The old king knew that he could not restrain his army and gracefully handed over control of the kingdom to his warlike son. Cetewayo resumed the customary raids on neighbouring tribes, thus allowing his men to 'wash their spears'. Mpande died in 1872 and Cetewayo became King. Throughout his reign Cetewayo had been careful not to clash with the British, whose military force he respected, and who held lands bordering the southern edge of Zululand.

The British, however, were wary of the Zulu. They knew Cetewayo to be a blood-thirsty man and that he had an army of around 70,000 men at his command. The British believed that it was only a matter of time before the Zulu raided British territory. In July 1878 a force of Zulus, chasing a criminal, crossed the Tugela River into British territory. The British took this as a hostile act and invaded Zululand.

The first battle took place at Isandlwana on 22 January 1879. The main Zulu army fell on a British column of over a thousand men and annihilated it. A second British invasion later that year resulted in a devastating defeat for the Zulu at Ulundi. Cetewayo was captured and shipped to England. He later returned to Zululand but, harassed by rivals, he fled to British territory where he died. In 1952 his grandson, Bhekizulu, was recognized as Chief of

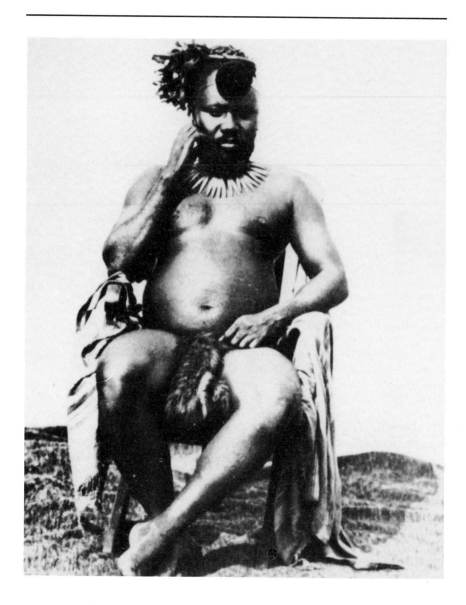

Cetewayo

A photograph of Cetewayo taken by British observers immediately after his installation as King of the Zulu. Misunderstandings between Cetewayo and the British began at the ceremony when the British believed they had gained certain promises, the significance of which Cetewayo appears not to have fully grasped. The later British–Zulu war arose largely from these and later confusions as much as from the threat of the Zulu army.

the Zulu by the South African government. It was a position of little power but immense prestige, and is still held by the family.

Mehemet Ahmed, The MAHDI (1844–1885)
Usurped: Power in Sudan 1881
Social Origins: Holy Man

Mehemet Ahmed, known to history as the Mahdi, was one of the most remarkable religious leaders of history. Proclaiming his divinity, the Mahdi attracted a fanatical following of Sudanese tribesmen with whom he smashed the Egyptian army, defied the British Empire and laid the foundations for the modern state of Sudan.

Born at Dongola, a town on the banks of the Nile, Mehemet followed his father into the profession of Islamic holyman. Such wandering ascetics studied the Koran and moved from village to village teaching children the basics of Islam, and holding more-learned conversations with adults. Mehemet Ahmed acquired a great reputation both for learning and holiness among the tribesmen.

In 1881 he announced that he was the long-awaited Mahdi, the new Prophet destined to follow Mohammed and spread Islam throughout the world. The wild tribesmen of the Sudanese desert believed the pronouncement and committed themselves fanatically to the new leader. Raising a massive army from the tribesmen, the Mahdi massacred two Egyptian armies and in 1883 threw back a fresh Egyptian invasion, led by British officers.

The whole of the Sudan fell under his sway, except the town of Khartoum, peopled by Egyptians. The British general Charles Gordon was sent by the Egyptian government to evacuate the city, but was besieged by the Mahdi. A British relief column was also attacked, and held up long enough for Khartoum to be captured in January 1885. Hearing that Gordon was dead, the British withdrew.

The Mahdi was supreme, ruling the Sudanese tribesmen as he wished and apparently vindicated in his claims to holiness. But five months later he died. Sudan passed to the spiritual successor of Mehemet Ahmed, was conquered by the British in 1898 and became independent in 1956.

MIDHAT PASHA (1822–1884)

Kingmaker of Turkey 1876

Social Origins: Politician

Born into the large class of Turks committed to administering the vast Ottoman Empire, Midhat Pasha entered the civil service at an early age. In the 1860s he served as Governor of Bulgaria, and it may have been here that he became convinced of the need to westernize Turkish society and technology.

In 1876 he was appointed Grand Vizier by the Sultan Abdul Aziz. Abdul Aziz was an extravagant and despotic Sultan of the type long traditional in Turkey. He was also a devout Moslem who refused to accept that Christian Europe had anything to offer the Turks. Midhat Pasha was sickened by the wasteful luxuries of the court and harem, and frustrated in his attempts to institute reforms. He turned to a secret society, the Young Turks, committed to modernizing Turkey.

On 30 May 1876, Midhat Pasha and the Young Turks launched a palace coup which ousted Abdul Aziz and replaced him with his nephew Murad. On 4 June Abdul Aziz was found dead in his room. It was announced that he had committed suicide, but many suspected Midhat Pasha of murder. On 31 August the traditional Moslems launched a counter-coup under Murad's brother Abdul Hamid (see below). Midhat Pasha was imprisoned, but was later released on condition that he left Turkey.

— 👑 —

Sir Henry BARTLE Edward FRERE (1815–1884)

Kingmaker of Zululand 1879

Social Origins: British Administrator

The activities of Sir Bartle Frere were in many ways typical of British administrators of the late 19th century. Placed hundreds of miles from Britain and out of touch with the home government, colonial officials had to act on their own judgement and responsibility. Some ruled areas at peace. Others, like Frere, were in charge of regions of high tension and frequent warfare.

In 1877 Frere was appointed High Commissioner of South Africa. He found his colony in a state of unrest. The settlers were terrified of the neighbouring mighty Zulu Empire, which had an army possibly 70,000 strong. The aggressive King Cetewayo had so far restricted his warfare to other tribes, but it was considered inevitable that he would one day attack the British. Frere became convinced of this fact, though it later transpired that Cetewayo had no immediate intention of attacking European settlers.

In 1878 a band of Zulu warriors crossed the border in pursuit of a criminal. Frere took this to be a scouting party for a full scale invasion and declared war. He sent a strong column into Zululand under Lord Chelmsford, but Cetewayo's troops massacred half the column and forced the rest to withdraw. Reinforcements from Britain arrived and were launched on a second invasion which successfully beat the Zulu army.

With Cetewayo captured, Frere had the responsibility for establishing a new government in Zululand. He decided to dismember the Empire into thirteen states, each ruled by a native chief under the watchful eye of a British resident. The result should have been foreseen. The Zulu were a proud and warlike people who could only be kept quiet by firm, central authority. Released from the tyranny of the king, the Zulu chiefs fell to bitter internecine warfare which the British residents were powerless to stop.

In 1880 Frere was recalled by the new government and dismissed. He wrote a spirited defence of his actions, but this was largely ignored. In 1889 Zululand was annexed by the British and the fighting suppressed.

— ♕ —

Shimazu Hisamitsu, Daimyo of SATSUMA (1817–1887)

Kingmaker of Japan 1868

Social Origins: Nobleman

The actions of Satsuma assured the development of Japan from a feudal, backward nation into the modern technologically-advanced state which it has become. His actions, however, were in the best traditions of the militaristic samurai.

In 1853, Japan was opened up to foreigners for the first time, and the Japanese became painfully aware of their industrial underdevelopment. Many noblemen saw the need for modernization, but the Tokugawa Shogun, who ruled Japan in the name of the Emperor, tried to maintain his power and that of his clan. Satsuma first entered the stage of politics in 1862 when an Englishman named Richardson refused to bow down before him. One of Satsuma's samurai casually killed Richardson for this slight. The resultant row between the British, the Shogun and Satsuma rocked the nation.

By 1867 several things were becoming clear in Japan. The first was the conflict between the rising tide of modernization and the autocratic power of the Shogun. The second was the opposition of Satsuma and other Daimyo, or provinical nobles, to the Shogun. In that year a new Shogun, Tokugawa Keiki succeeded to power. A new Emperor, the 14-year-old Mutsuhito, ascended the throne at about the same time. The fanatically xenophobic samurai faction known as shishi were now demanding that Japan develop so as to achieve equality with the foreign powers. Civil war between the Shogun and the reformers seemed inevitable.

It was then that Satsuma struck upon a solution to the problem. His plan was astoundingly novel, yet reached back to a centuries' old tradition. He decided to appeal to the Emperor to take over the government of Japan. For nearly a thousand years the Emperor had been a mere figurehead and had exercised no real power, yet the samurai always swore loyalty to the Emperor.

On 3 January 1868 a group of Satsuma samurai gained entry to the Imperial palace, guarding the gates and allowing admittance only to supporters of Satsuma. The young Emperor Mutsuhito then appeared and read a declaration stating that he was taking control of government. There was to be no Shogun and no Prime Minister, only the Emperor and his servants. The move cut away Keiki's support, for the nobles and samurai were honour-bound to serve the Emperor. Within a year the shogunate was a thing of the past. A new government was set up, initially under the control of Satsuma. Later, a constitution was introduced and Japan became a thoroughly modern country.

TZU HSI (1835–1908)

Usurped: Power in China 1861
Social Origins: Imperial Concubine

When Tzu Hsi was born the Chinese Celestial Empire was a confident power. The Chinese believed that they were the only civilized nation on earth and that all other nations were barbarians who should be brought under the sway of the Chinese Emperor. In reality, China was backward, desperately poor and militarily weak. Tzu Hsi was forced to cope with the realization of these facts.

At the early age of 15 the beautiful young Tzu Hsi entered the court of Emperor Hien Fung as his concubine. She seems to have exercised considerable influence over Hien Fung and secured the recognition of her son Tung Chih as heir to the Celestial Throne. Hien Fung died in 1861, when Tung Chih was just 6 years old. Tzu Hsi immediately stepped in to act as regent and imposed her rule on China. When, in 1875, Tung Chih died, Tsu Hsi organized the accession of Kwang-su, whom she could dominate.

Her personal control of affairs remained unchallenged until 1895 when Japan invaded Korea, then held by China. The crushing defeat suffered by China reflected badly on Tzu Hsi, but she saved her position by blaming and executing General Tso, who had surrendered to the Japanese, but her prestige had been damaged. In 1898 Kwang-su announced that he was going to rule for himself and dismissed Tzu Hsi. Her control of affairs seemed to be at an end, but Kwang-su made the mistake of introducing reforms and western technology. This angered the traditionally minded Chinese government and nobility. Tzu Hsi took advantage of this to return to court after just 100 days and to oust Kwang-su. She remained in power until her death eight years later. She is sometimes referred to in the West as the Empress Dowager.

— ♕ —

Stepan STAMBULOV (1854–1895)
Kingmaker of Bulgaria 1887
Social Origins: Innkeeper

Stambulov saw his dream of an independent Bulgaria come into being, but was cruelly assassinated soon after his plans came to fruition. Stambulov was born the son of an innkeeper at a time when Bulgaria was part of the Ottoman Empire. The Christian Bulgarians, however, resented control by a Islamic power.

Stambulov was sent to Odessa by his father to be educated. When, in 1877, war between Turkey and Russia broke out, Stambulov joined many other Bulgarians in a volunteer corps serving with the Russian army. The war resulted in defeat for Turkey and the formation of two new states, a completely independent northern Bulgaria and a semi-autonomous Roumelia, which covered the lands of southern Bulgaria.

Stambulov hurried to Bulgaria and was elected to the new Sobranje, or parliament. In 1879 the Sobranje invited a German prince, Alexander of Battenberg, to be their king. At first Alexander was dominated by Russian advisers and ministers. However, he gradually appointed native Bulgarians to positions of power, thus earning the enmity of Russia. In 1884 Stambulov became President of the Sobranje. The following year Roumelia threw off its nominal allegiance to the Sultan and voted to join Bulgaria.

The Russian government was disturbed by the emergence of a new power on its southern border and began plotting with pro-Russian Bulgarians. In the summer of 1886 Prince Alexander suddenly vanished. He had been

Stephan Stambolov
Stephan Stambolov acted as Bulgarian kingmaker after King Alexander was abducted by Russian-backed dissidents and forced to abdicate at gunpoint, as shown in this contemporary engraving. By supporting such violence Russia hoped to place her own candidate on the throne. Instead the Bulgarians turned against Russia in favour of friendship with Germany.

kidnapped by a gang of disaffected Bulgarians with Russian aid. On 21 August Prince Alexander, with a pistol held to his head, was forced to sign papers of abdication. After his signature he added 'God protect Bulgaria'.

After the abduction of the Prince, Stambulov organized a national government loyal to the absent prince in opposition to the pro-Russian faction which attempted to seize power. When news of the abdication was received, Stambulov put forward another German prince, Ferdinand of

Saxe-Coburg-Gotha as the new king. He persuaded the Sobranje to agree and Prince Ferdinand arrived to take his throne. Stambulov crushed the pro-Russian party with swift and brutal measures. By 1894 Bulgaria appeared a secure and peaceful country. Stambulov resigned from government. A few months later he was cut down in the street by a political opponent.

— ♛ —

ALEXANDER I Obrenovitch (1876–1903)

Usurped: Power in Serbia 1893
Social Origins: Royal Family

King Alexander of Serbia was the headstrong son of a headstrong monarch, whose rashness and determination in the face of strong opposition led to his tragically early death. He came to the throne in 1889 upon the abdication of his father, Milan Obrenovich.

It was Milan who, as an ally of Russia, had freed Serbia of Turkish suzerainty in 1878 and established the nation as a Kingdom. However, after 1882 Milan abandoned the traditional alliance with Russia, a fellow Slavonic state, in favour of friendship with Austria, an Empire which kept Slavs under suppression in the province of Bosnia. The move was unpopular in Serbia and hostility to Milan was heightened by his public arguments with his beautiful and popular wife, Queen Natalie, who supported the Russian alliance. At the height of his unpopularity Milan abdicated in favour of young Alexander.

The National Assembly took the opportunity to exercise their position as an advisory body to the new king. In effect, Serbia became a limited democracy with the Assembly appointing ministers and holding them responsible. In 1893, at the age of just 17, Alexander organized a coup. Carefully choosing his supporters in the Assembly and the army, Alexander planned well despite his age. The move was overwhelmingly successful, the government was dismissed and the regents excluded from all future state decisions. For six years Alexander ruled well, but autocratically, with the advice of his father and other noblemen.

In 1900 Alexander announced his choice of queen. The nation and his advisors were appalled. He had decided to marry Droga Mashin, a widow some years older than himself who had previously been his mother's lady-in-waiting. Not only was the lady socially unsuitable as a queen, but she was an unpopular character with a reputation for loose morals. Opposition formed which Alexander ruthlessly crushed. His father strongly advised against the match, and was banished from the kingdom, whereupon the entire cabinet resigned. The marriage went ahead, and Alexander lost even more popularity. The Austrians withdrew their support and relations with the Empire became decidedly chilly. Alexander next quarrelled with Russia.

Early in 1903 a group of army officers began plotting against Alexander. On 11 June they burst into the palace, having first ensured that the guards would not resist, and marched into the royal chambers. In the brief fight which followed both Alexander and Droga were killed. Their deaths had probably been planned beforehand. The Assembly received the news calmly and voted to hand the crown to Peter Karageorgevich. The long feud between the Karageorge family and the Obrenovich clan, which had begun nearly a century earlier (see Milosh Obrenovich above), had come to a bloody end.

— ♔ —

Abdul Aziz ibn Abdul-Rahman ibn Feisal IBN SAUD (c. 1880–1953)

Usurped: Sultanate of Nejd 1901
Social Origins: Tribal Chieftain

The great founder of the modern state of Saudi Arabia was born the son of a tribal chieftain and spent some years as a nomadic exile in the Arabian desert. It was only by sheer force of personality and outstanding military skill that he created a major power in the Middle East.

Ibn Saud was born some time around 1880 to a younger son of the Sultan of Nejd. The first few years of his life were spent at Riyadh, the centre of the desert state of Nejd, but in 1891 Nejd was overrun by the Rashid tribesmen. Young Ibn Saud and the rest of his family took to the desert accompanied by a loyal band of followers.

Ten years later Ibn Saud returned. With a small force of loyal tribesmen he launched a surprise night attack on the camp of the Rashid chieftain. The attack was successful, driving the Rashid from Nejd and establishing Ibn Saud on the throne. In 1906 he took over the lands of the Rashid and began reorganizing his sultanate. The traditional laws of the nomadic tribesmen were swept away to be replaced by a national legal code based firmly on the Koran, the holy book of Islam. He hoped, by converting his people to fundamental Islam to unite the Arabs and recreate the glories of early Islam.

During the First World War, Ibn Saud remained aloof from the fighting, but aided Lawrence (see below) and his Arab allies in the struggle against Turkey. In 1924 Ibn Saud invaded the Hejaz, displacing King Hussein and taking the holy cities of Medina and Mecca. By 1932 he had created the modern desert kingdom of Saudi Arabia. He made valiant efforts to modernize his nation, but was hampered by lack of money. In 1950 the first significant oil filds were discovered under the Arabian deserts, and by 1953 the nation was making $2.5 million a week from oil revenues. The sudden affluence did much to undermine the strictly fundamentalist nature of Ibn Saud's regime and he died a disappointed man.

JUAN Vicente GOMEZ (1859–1935)

Usurped: Power in Venezuela 1908
Social Origins: Rancher

The usurpation of Juan Gomez brought great benefits to Venezuela, although his motives were far from selfless, indeed Gomez seems to have been motivated largely by self-interest throughout his career.

Born of mixed European and Indian parentage, Gomez first worked on a ranch and later joined the army. In 1892, under the government of Guzman Blanco (see above) Gomez obtained a minor position in politics, but his rise to power began when the military took control of the country in 1895. His rise through the ranks was rapid and in 1908 he became Vice President to General Castro.

The Castro administration was financially inept and corrupt. Foreign debts escalated while members of the government, including Gomez, lined their own pockets. In 1908 a Dutch fleet began a blockade of Venezuelan ports in an attempt to force action on Castro. Under such conditions scandals and plots were common. In 1909 Gomez was implicated in one such plot, though his guilt remains in doubt, and was sentenced to death by Castro. Receiving warning of his fate, Gomez rallied his supporters and took over the government. Castro was absent on a state visit to Europe at the time, and was exiled in absence.

Once in power Gomez revealed an unexpected talent for tight fiscal control and sound government. Corruption was greatly reduced and the state finances overhauled. A wide-ranging system of roads, schools and universities was constructed and international trade encouraged. By 1930 Gomez had paid off the colossal foreign debt built up under Castro. Throughout these years Gomez continued to use his position to build up his enormous personal fortune. By the time of his death he was the richest man in South America.

AHMET ESSAD (c. 1864–1920)

Usurped: Power in Albania 1914
Social Origins: Nobleman

Ahmet Essad was born into one of the most distinguished families of Albania, being descended from the mediaeval monarchs who had once ruled the rugged mountain kingdom. At the time of his birth, however, Albania was a province of the Turkish Ottoman Empire. Early in life Essad joined the Ottoman army, loyally serving his Moslem masters in the 1897 war with Greece. He proved so efficient that he was created a Pasha of the Empire and transferred to the court at Constantinople.

In 1909 Essad joined the rebellion against Sultan Abdul Hamid II (see above) and was chosen as the man to inform the Sultan of his deposition. In 1912 Essad once again took the field in the war against Montenegro, Serbia and Greece. The following year Albania threw off Turkish control and became independent. Essad at once abandoned his position at the Turkish court and hurried to pledge allegiance to the new King William of Albania. He was appointed Minister of War and of the Interior by a king desperate for men with experience of government.

Albania proved a difficult country to rule, both because of its mountainous terrain and the independent spirit of its people who resented any governmental control. In 1914 Essad began plotting against King William and in October launched a coup which drove William from his throne. Albania was overrun by the Austrians and Essad fled to Greece where he set up a government in exile.

The Italians, who liberated Albania in 1918, refused to allow Essad to return after peace was declared and he moved to France. The National Assembly of Albania, however, elected Essad King of Albania and demanded his return. A few weeks later, on 13 June 1920, Essad was murdered on the streets of Paris by an Albanian student opposed to his rule.

— ♔ —

ELEUTHERIOS VENIZELOS (1864–1936)

Kingmaker of Greece 1917
Social Origins: Lawyer

Venizelos was born on the island of Crete, which remained under Turkish rule long after the Greek mainland had achieved independence. The young

Venizelos was a passionate believer in the right of the Cretans to join Greece. In 1886 he was elected to the Cretan Assembly, an advisory body concerned with local government, where he made his views known through outspoken comments. When an anti-Turkish rebellion broke out in 1889, Venizelos joined the insurgents, but the movement was crushed and he fled into exile.

Venizelos returned to Crete after a few years, and at once began organizing another rising. In 1896 Venizelos' plotting came to fruition when the Cretans rose in rebellion and, after a struggle, drove the Turks from the island. The peace arrangement made Crete autonomous within the Turkish Empire, but the island was to be governed by a local government and by Prince George, a younger son of King George of Greece. Venizelos became Minister of Justice in the new government. In 1906 Venizelos organized a coup which ejected Prince George, who had proved to be dictatorial and insensitive, in favour of an official appointed directly by King George. Soon afterwards Crete became part of Greece, and Venizelos joined in Greek national politics.

In 1910 Venizelos became Prime Minister of Greece and formed a close working relationship with King George. In 1913 King George died and was succeeded by his son Constantine. The following year the First World War broke out when Austria invaded Serbia. Venizelos favoured joining the war to help Serbia, but King Constantine preferred neutrality. In 1915, after a series of quarrels between the two men, Venizelos resigned. An election returned him to office with a sizeable majority and he ordered the mobilization of the Greek army. King Constantine immediately dismissed Venizelos, who left for Crete.

Frustrated of achieving his ends by normal means, Venizelos turned to subterfuge. He opened negotiations with Britain and France, promising them an alliance with Greece if he was returned to power. The ploy worked. A large allied force was already in Salonika and in June 1917 a joint move by the Allies and supporters of Venizelos forced King Constantine to abdicate.

Venizelos set up a government in Athens, declared war on Austria and ordered the coronation of Alexander, younger son of Constantine, rather than the heir Prince George. Greek troops joined the allied campaign in the Balkans and gained large territories for Greece. Venizelos was at the height of his influence.

In October 1925 King Alexander died after being bitten by his pet monkey. King George returned from exile, and swept Venizelos from power. The ousted prime minister remained in politics, but his support for an abortive coup in 1933 caused his forced retirement.

— ♕ —

MULAI Abd-el-Hafid (1875–1937)
Usurped: Sultanate of Morocco 1906
Social Origins: Royal Family

In the early years of this century Morocco was an underdeveloped Islamic nation ruled by its own Sultan. The towns and ports of the north coast were fairly prosperous, but the tribesmen of the southern deserts still lived the traditional nomadic lifestyle. The neighbouring state of Algeria had been ruled from France since the French invaded to suppress the Algerian pirates in the 1820s. All these factors were to play a part in the rise to power of Mulai and in his fall.

In 1894 Mulai's brother Abd-el-Aziz inherited the Sultanate. He had travelled through Europe and realized the benefits which could be brought to his nation if European ways were adopted. He therefore began introducing European technology and institutions. At first Mulai supported his brother, but he began to grow uneasy. Mulai saw the innovations as seriously affecting the traditional religious nature of Morocco. Fearing a debasement of Islamic ideals, Mulai abandoned his brother.

Searching for support Mulai travelled south to the nomadic desert tribes. There he found a willing audience for his tales of religious debasement and the growing influence of the infidels. The fiercely religious tribesmen were outraged by what they heard, and encouraged by promises of rich payments for helping Mulai. In 1906 hordes of wild tribesmen galloped down from the Atlas Mountains, with Mulai riding at their head shouting religious encouragement. The Sultan's army was brushed aside and Mulai rode into Fez at the head of his army. The tribesmen were paid off and returned to the hills, while Abd-el-Aziz was given a pension and a house.

For six years Mulai Hafid ruled Morocco in the traditional manner. However, opposition in the towns of the coast remained strong, and slowly gained in strength. Mulai appealed to the French for assistance. The French stepped in to prop up the regime, thus establishing their presence in the nation, but the opposition proved too strong. In August 1912 Mulai Hafid abdicated in favour of his brother Mulai Yusef.

FRANCISCO MADERO (1873–1913)

Usurped: Presidency of Mexico 1911
Social Origins: Politician

Growing to maturity in the years of peace which Mexico enjoyed under the rule of Porfiro Diaz (see above), Madero did not appreciate the great achievement of Diaz in bringing order and discipline. Instead Madero could only see the cruelty of the methods Diaz used to enforce that peace. Madero opposed the tyranny of Diaz and so opened the way for the anarchy and bloodshed which soon engulfed Mexico again.

Born in Coahuila, in the north of the country, Madero progressed from local politics to the national stage at an early age. He became the leader of the Independent Party, opposed to Diaz and continually attacked the president's cruelties. In 1910 Presidential elections were due to be held. Madero announced himself as a candidate, but was quickly arrested by Diaz's secret police and held until the elections were over and Diaz had been returned to office. Such tactics were commonly used by Diaz to ensure his power.

As soon as he was released the enraged Madero began plotting a rebellion. Diaz was, for once, outwitted and was caught unprepared. He fled to Europe, leaving Madero as President of Mexico. Madero began a series of reforms which were intended to liberate the country from the dictatorship imposed by Diaz. Instead, the relaxation of control meant that the nation degenerated into anarchy and civil war. On 23 February 1913 Madero was murdered by his opponents.

FRANCISCO Pancho VILLA (1877–1923)

Usurped: Power in Mexico 1914
Social Origins: Bandit

While still a teenager Villa left his home in the Mexican town of Las Nieves for the more adventurous life of a bandit. His daring raids and apparent immunity from arrest attracted many young men to him. Within a few years, Villa had a large force of bandits riding with him, and was able to launch attacks on heavily defended banks and other targets. President Diaz made determined efforts to catch Villa, but although the bandit's operations were curtailed he was not captured.

When, in 1910, Diaz was overthrown the new President Madero (see

Francisco Madero
The Mexican leader Francisco Madero overthrew a despotic government and brought liberal laws to a land not yet ready for them. He was overwhelmed by the forces he unleashed and was murdered in 1913.

above) pardoned Villa along with many others who had supposedly suffered unjustly under Diaz. Villa at once began operating on a large scale. His gang of bandits swelled to become a small army. In 1911 he captured Juarez and set himself up as an independent power in northern Mexico, paying little heed to central government. When Madero was murdered, Villa and fellow bandit Emiliano Zapata (see below) backed Venustiano Carranza in the succession dispute. The bandit army was instrumental in winning the Presidency for Carranza from Victoriano Huerta.

The new president refused to give Villa the rewards he demanded for his services. Villa raised his bandits in rebellion and in October 1914 crushed the Presidential army at Torreon. Riding into Mexico City, Villa set up a puppet president named Gutierrez, through whom he ruled. Carranza, however, was not finished. He eluded capture by Villa and in 1916 gained the recognition of the USA as the rightful President. He proscribed Villa as an outlaw and recaptured most of Mexico in a long campaign.

Villa retreated to his northern bases where he continued to rule as a separate power, waging a savage guerilla war with Carranza. In 1920 Carranza was murdered, and Villa was offered a massive bribe by the new government to cease his operations. Villa took the money and retired to a ranch. He was murdered by the government three years later.

EMILIANO ZAPATA (1879–1918)

Usurped: Power in Mexico 1915
Social Origins: Indian Peasant

Possibly the most powerful bandit ever to use a gun, Zapata made and unmade Presidents as he wished, but he still suffered the violent death met by most lawless men. He was born into the Guerrero tribe of Indians and early in life became their spokesman. At this time the majority of Mexico's Indians lived a life of grinding poverty. Tied to the land they suffered at the hands of unscrupulous bureaucrats and grasping landlords. The strict regime of President Diaz (see above) kept the Indians in subjection.

As soon as Diaz was overthrown, in 1911, Zapata raised a rebellion of over 1,000 Indians to enforce their claims for better conditions. Ranches were raided and bloody revenge exacted on those who had ignored the demands of the peons, or peasants. In the fighting which followed the murder of President Madero in 1913 Zapata joined with Villa (see above) in placing Carranza in power.

Carranza, however, failed to introduce reforms to help the peons. Zapata rose in rebellion once again. As champion of the Indians, Zapata had almost

Zapata
The Mexican Emiliano Zapata (right) together with his brother Eufemio. Zapata has been described as 'the most powerful bandit in history'. Leading disciplined gangs which at one time numbered 20,000 men, Zapata made and unmade Presidents at will and led a life of astounding extravagance and licentiousness.

limitless reserves of manpower on which to draw and commanded armies many thousands strong. With bitter grievances to avenge the peasant armies of Zapata rode the length and breadth of Mexico causing upheaval and destruction wherever they passed. However, Zapata employed able administrators to govern his conquests and he was able to impose law and order within his realm. At one point Zapata's men controlled three quarters of Mexico. He appointed two Presidents to office, dismissing them when they quarrelled with him.

In his short career, Zapata proved himself to be both cruel and devoted to luxury. He ordered the execution of 11,000 people, many of whom he killed himself, and his men caused an estimated $250 million worth of damage. The vast wealth which he gained through pillaging and extortion was spent on drink and women and on his notoriously licentious parties. He was, however, always ready for action and never allowed his pleasure to interrupt his activities as a bandit and leader. The rising might of Villa and Carranza slowly limited Zapata's power, though he still held on to extensive territories. He was finally gunned down by a supporter of Carranza in 1918.

REZA KHAN PAHLAVI (1877–1944)

Usurped: Peacock Throne of Persia 1921
Social Origins: Army Officer

The close of the 19th century saw the once-powerful country of Persia reduced to a sorry state. Her economic and political life was dominated by British and Russian influence and intrigue. It seemed that only the rivalry between the two great powers saved Persia from losing independence altogether. Partition seemed a very real threat. It was in this atmosphere of national decline that Reza grew to manhood.

As a young man Reza followed his father by becoming an officer in a regiment of cossacks in the Persian army. He showed himself to be an able soldier and gained rapid promotion to high command. In 1907 the British and Russians divided Persia into 'spheres of influence' without reference to Shah Muhammed. This involved officials of the two powers living in the respective spheres of influence and taking a part in local government and judicial procedures. The move was resented in Persia, especially by the army, but there seemed to be little that the degenerate nation could do. Two years later Shah Muhammed abdicated in favour of his son Ahmad.

During the First World war Ahmad resisted calls from the army to attack the British and Russians and remained passively in Tehran. Through all this Reza had been a supporter of the more militant faction which favoured resistance to the great powers. In 1921 he decided to act. Gathering the army behind him Reza marched on Tehran, entered the royal palace and confronted Shah Ahmad. He informed the Shah that he would have to accede to the demands of the army or face deposition. The Shah agreed and appointed Reza Premier.

The spheres of influence were repudiated and a vigorous overhaul of government began. Age-old practices were swept aside by the reforms of Reza as he set about restoring the fortunes of Persia. In 1926 the nobles proclaimed Reza to be Shah, exiling Ahmed to France, where he was recovering from an illness. The following year Reza was seated on the Peacock Throne and invested himself with the crown and sceptre of Persia. The reforms continued, but Reza was careful not to offend the religious sensibilities of his people. In 1941 the needs of war caused Britain and Russia to divide Iran, as Persia was known after 1935, between them. Reza abdicated in favour of his son, Mohammad, and retired to Cape Town. The dynasty Reza founded survived until the revolution of 1979 placed the Ayatollah Khomeni in power.

— 👑 —

BENITO MUSSOLINI (1883–1945)

Usurped: Power in Italy 1922
Social Origins: School Teacher

The usurpation of power by Mussolini was one of the most remarkable of recent history. Not only did he engineer his rise to power with consummate skill but he retained his popularity throughout. Once in power he used public display and private censorship to maintain his position. His famous achievement of making the trains run on time should not be taken lightly. In a country as naturally temperamental and anarchic as Italy punctuality is not a virtue much admired. The accurate time-keeping of the railways was indicative of the changes he brought throughout the land.

Mussolini qualified as a school teacher at the age of 19, but soon abandoned teaching for journalism. He worked on several socialist newspapers before becoming editor of *Avanti* in 1911, and his writings caused his arrest on several occasions and earned him five months' imprisonment. Mussolini was always far more patriotic than socialist in his leanings and the failure of a series of strikes in June 1914 caused him to abandon the socialist cause.

Mussolini volunteered for the army when Italy joined the First World War and served well before being wounded and invalided home in March 1917. After peace returned the Communists attempted to start a revolution on the

Russian model. Though unsuccessful the outbreaks were sufficiently serious to disturb the government and the people. It was at this time that Mussolini formed the *Fascio*, an organization of young men willing to stamp out Communism by force. The name 'Fascist' was taken from the bundles of sticks carried as badges of office by the police of ancient Rome.

The Fascist movement spread rapidly, becoming immensely popular with the young man of Italy. At the same time the ineffectual government was becoming increasingly unable to cope with the economic collapse and the political agitation of the Communists. In August 1922 the Fascists broke up a major Communist-inspired strike and in October the government fell. Mussolini sensed that his moment had come and acted with great speed.

The Fascist forces throughout Italy were mobilized and ordered to travel to Rome. Disembarking from trains on the outskirts of the city, thousands of Fascists marched into the centre on 27 October. Communists tried to halt the advance, as Mussolini knew they would, and savage street-fighting broke out. The Fascists won their way through to the city centre. Mussolini was now able to point out the weakness of the government, the violence of the Communists and the ability of the Fascists to deal with the problem. It was a well stage-managed operation. The King called for Mussolini to visit him that evening and made the Fascist leader Prime Minister.

In the months which followed, Mussolini stamped out all opposition. Political parties were banned and newspapers closed down. However the repression was accompanied by some drastic improvements. The taxation system was overhauled and improved together with government administration and the national finances. With his theatrical posturings and vibrant speeches Mussolini led Italy to a revival most had believed impossible. Yet Italy paid a heavy price for this success. Democracy was destroyed and, in 1939, Mussolini led Italy disastrously into the Second World War in support of Nazi Germany. He was finally overthrown and murdered by his fellow countrymen.

Miguel PRIMO DE RIVERA (1870–1930)

Usurped: Power in Spain 1923
Social Origins: Army Officer

Primo de Rivera, the Marquess de Estella, was a charming man but a rigid disciplinarian who seized power in a Spain which was rapidly sliding towards Civil War. Though he appeared to have restored peace, his actions only delayed the outbreak of civil strife.

Born in 1870 Primo de Rivera joined the army as an officer cadet and was soon promoted to captain for bravery on the field of battle during a skirmish in Morocco. He rose rapidly through the command structure of the Spanish army, becoming a general in 1915. During these years Primo de Rivera played a minor role in politics, making his views known in outspoken speeches which were resented by the government, but won favour with the army.

In 1921 Primo de Rivera was given the position of Captain General of Catalonia. This region of eastern Spain had long been a centre for seperatist movements and in the early years of the 20th century had descended into a state of near anarchy. By a combination of military force and gentle persuasion, Primo de Rivera reimposed order on Catalonia, winning great support from the ordinary people.

The central government in Madrid, meanwhile, was proving itself to be incapable of solving Spain's problems. Military operations in Morocco were a constant drain of resources while socialists at home were a continuing source of trouble. In September 1923 Primo de Rivera, encouraged by his recent successes in Catalonia, marched on Madrid. He was convinced that he could rule Spain far better than the ineffectual government. He cleared the parliament of members, suspended the constitution and imposed martial law on the nation. He quickly set up a new government in which he appointed himself to be minister of every department.

Once in power, Primo de Rivera pulled out of Morocco and embarked on large road-building projects and other civic schemes aimed at reducing unemployment and so easing the social tensions in Spain. In 1925 he announced a new constitution under which elections were held, but his position as dictator was assured. Under his rule, Spain prospered and the great social divides seemed to be healed over. However ill-health forced his retirement in 1929 and he died the following year. Democracy was restored but no steps were taken to halt the slide into political extremism. Within a few years the civil war Primo de Rivera had tried so hard to avoid had begun.

FENG YU-HSIANG (1880–1948)

Usurped: Power in China 1923
Social Origins: Army Officer

Efficient, honest but utterly ruthless, Feng Yu-Hsiang became first the power broker of China then set himself up as an independent power, until finally his influence collapsed in the face of the Japanese invasion. At a young age Feng Yu-Hsiang was converted to Christianity, a faith he adhered to throughout his career, and joined the army while still in his youth. He advanced rapidly in the ranks of the post-revolutionary regime and in 1921 was appointed Governor of the northwestern province of Shensi. There he put down the powerful bands of brigands and restored order.

In 1923 he returned to Peking to find the government of Li Yuan Hung losing its grip on affairs. Provincial governors were paying little attention to central authority and independent warlords were springing up across the nation. In Peking Feng Yu-Hsiang joined forces with Chang Tso-Lin, a notorious former bandit who had risen to high command, and plotted the fall of the administration. Together the two strong men of northern China were irresistible and Li Yuan Hung was ousted and replaced by a candidate acceptable to both Feng and Chang. However the new regime was no more capable of imposing order than the previous one and Feng fell out with Chang.

In 1926 Feng Yu-Hsiang retreated to his power base in the north and joined the Kuomintang movement or Nationalist Party, started earlier in the century, which held power in southern China. The following year Chang attempted to establish himself as dictator in Peking, but was quickly defeated and killed by the Kuomintang. Feng Yu-Hsiang became Minister for War under the new government, and angered the USSR by attacking Chinese Communists within the Kuomintang. In 1929 he made a bid for power by seizing Peking. The Kuomintang were driven from northern China and Feng Yu-Hsiang set himself up as a dictatorial warlord.

His power was shortlived, however, for an army under Chiang Kai-Shek, the new Kuomintang leader, defeated his forces and ousted him from power in 1930. Feng Yu-Hsiang was too able a man to be abandoned. When Japan invaded China in 1931 the Chinese resistance collapsed. In 1933 Feng Yu-Hsiang was recalled to organize defences in the province of Chahar but failed and fell from favour once again.

In 1947 Feng Yu-Hsiang seemed about to re-enter politics and embarked on a lecture tour of the USA. He died in what appeared to be an accidental fire on a Russian ship soon afterwards.

— ♛ —

Joseph Clemens PILSUDSKI (1867–1935)

Usurped: Power in Poland 1926
Social Origins: Middle Class

At the time Pilsudski was born Poland did not exist as a state. The majority of the lands inhabited by Poles formed part of the Russian Empire, while other Polish territory lay within Germany or the Austrian Empire. The Poles, however, had a proud history and as recently as 1848 an anti-Russian rising had taken place. Pilsudski threw himself into the resistance movement, editing nationalistic newspapers and taking part in political agitation. As a result he spent some time in Russian gaols.

In 1901 Pilsudski fled Russian Poland to settle in Cracow, then ruled by Austria. In 1914 Pilsudski took command of a regiment of Poles fighting on the side of Austria in return for promises of an independent Poland. The regiment fought well and, in 1916, Pilsudski was appointed to the Polish Council which ruled the areas of Poland taken from Russia under joint German and Austrian control. Pilsudski soon tired of the interference of his allies in what he considered Polish internal affairs and resigned. The following year he was accused of anti-German activities, after agitating for increased political control to be given to Poles, and was imprisoned.

Following the defeat of Germany in November 1918, Poland was proclaimed an independent republic. Pilsudski, newly released from prison, returned to Poland and was hailed as President of the new nation. In 1920 he led an army into the Ukraine with the aims of annexing territory which had belonged to Poland two centuries earlier and separating the southern steppes from Russian control. The enterprise was a failure, but Pilsudski managed to win some military glory for himself. In 1921 he resigned as President after disagreements with the government, but shrewdly kept his title of Marshal of Poland.

By 1926 the government was in serious trouble, unable to agree with its own members and faced by severe economic collapse. In May of that year Pilsudski donned his old uniform and strode into the military barracks in Warsaw. Declaring that he was better able to solve Poland's problems than an ineffective civilian government, Pilsudski raised a rebellion in the streets of the capital and was swept to power. Pilsudski then reformed the constitution giving greater and more effective powers to central government, while placing himself in supreme control of the administration. Pilsudski remained the unchallenged dictator of Poland until ill-health forced his resignation in 1928. Even in retirement the old warrior remained a powerful influence on Polish affairs. He realized the danger of Hitler's growing power and often urged rearmament, but to little avail.

— ♔ —

Ahmed bey Zogu, KING ZOG (1893–1961)

Usurped: Power in Albania 1928
Social Origins: Nobleman

Born Ahmed Zogu, Zog belonged to the powerful and influential Zogolli family which had extensive holdings in Albania. When Albania became

314

independent in 1913 Zog moved into politics, strongly backing the elevation of William of Wied to the throne. When the First World War broke out and engulfed the Balkans, Zog left Albania for Austria in whose army he fought throughout the conflict.

After the peace treaties, which left Albania largely untouched, Zog returned to take office as Minister of the Interior. He held a succession of offices, culminating in his premiership of 1922–1924. In June 1924 a sudden uprising of his enemies forced Zog to flee to Yugoslavia. Though in exile, Zog was determined to return and was in constant contact with his supporters.

In February 1925 Zog returned to Albania, taking office as President of the Albanian Republic. He introduced many liberalizing laws and measures which eased the conditions of the mountain peasants of Albania, but was careful not to jeopardize his grip on power. In 1928 he felt secure and popular enough to ascend the throne which had been vacant since 1914. In his later years Zog encouraged contacts with Italy and introduced Italian advisers to his government. The policy was highly unpopular among the fiercely independent Albanians and paved the way for Mussolini's takeover of the country in April 1939. Zog then fled but was not allowed to return to the country after the war. He abdicated in January 1946.

— ◡◡◡ —

Bacha Saquo, AMIR HABIBULLAH (?–1930)
Usurped: Kingdom of Afghanistan 1929
Social Origins: Brigand

In 1919 Afghanistan under its energetic ruler Amir Amanullah threw off British overlordship and became fully independent. The future for Amanullah looked rosy, but in the ranks of his own army was the man who would overthrow him. At this time young Bacha Saquo was an ordinary soldier in the Afghan army, though as a child an old mullah, or religious man, had foretold that Bacha would achieve greatness. The prophecy seems to have had a large influence on the young man.

In 1925, after striking an officer, Bacha Saquo fled to the hills of Kohistan with his friend Jamal to become a bandit. He quickly became rich through robbing caravans and soon attracted a large following. A chief obstacle to Bacha was the man Sharfuddin who controlled all brigandage in Kohistan and exacted protection money from the merchants to allow their caravans to move through the passes. Bacha dealt with Sharfuddin by creeping into his house one night and slitting his throat. Bacha took over the unofficial role as 'King of the Passes'. Government efforts to suppress Bacha and his bandits were ineffectual. In the rugged mountains and narrow defiles, more than one patrol of troops was ambushed and massacred.

Throughout his reign Amanullah had slowly introduced western ideas, such as schools and hospitals, which were greatly resented by the staunchly Moslem Afghans. The hill tribes in particular resented the fact that their children were being educated by German-speaking laymen instead of Afghan mullahs. The Amir had been forced to raise heavy taxes to pay for these unpopular reforms. The resentment this aroused accounts, in part, for the success of Bacha and other brigands. In 1928 Amanullah embarked on a long tour of Europe. The Afghans were worried that he would return with even more reforms and, in their eyes, sacriligious ideas. Their fears were justified for on his return Amanullah announced wide ranging reforms. Perhaps even worse Queen Suraya had stopped wearing the veil and bared her face to the common people.

Almost at once the Shinwari tribe rose in revolt, to be joined by other hill tribes. Bacha called his brigands to arms, amassing a force of 2,000 men. He marched down from the mountains into the valleys, where he met and defeated a government force, and was at once hailed as the leader of the revolting hill tribes. He moved on to Kabul, laying ambushes on all roads in and out of Kabul and maintaining a constant, if minor, barrage on the city itself.

Bacha sent spies and agents into the city who spread the word that Bacha was a devout Moslem who would sweep away the hated reforms of Amanullah. The people of Kabul welcomed the news, but remained wary of allowing a mountain brigand into their city. An attempt by the royal army to break the siege ended in a bloody, hand-to-hand struggle which Bacha won convincingly.

The next day, 14 January 1929, Amanullah abdicated in favour of his brother Inayatullah and fled from the city, over the Khyber Pass to India. Bacha stormed into the capital, captured Inayatullah and made himself King of Afghanistan with the title Amir Habibullah. His victory was short-lived, however. A few months later he was murdered by a tribesman pursuing an old family feud.

Jean Bedel BOKASSA (1921–)

Usurped: Power in Central African Republic 1966
Social Origins: Army Officer

Born in an obscure village named Berengo in what was then the French colony of Shari Ubangi, Bokassa joined the French Army while still a teenager. He was an efficient and competent soldier, rising through the ranks to captain and being decorated for gallantry several times, once by President de Gaulle himself.

When Shari Ubangi became independent as the Central African Republic in 1960, Bokassa was promoted to Colonel and given army command. Under President David Dacko, Bokassa established the army and its command structure. The government, however, was almost unimaginably corrupt with officials diverting massive amounts of state revenue into their own pockets. The ineffectual Dacko was unable to keep the problem under control. The new republic, already poor, began to slide into serious economic decline. Bokassa began to make his antagonistic feelings toward the government known, as did Jean Izamo, the chief of police.

In December 1965 Izamo invited Bokassa to a New Year's Eve party. Bokassa became convinced that Izamo was laying a trap and that he would be arrested. He therefore asked Izamo to come to sign some papers earlier that afternoon. When Izamo arrived he was pounced upon by Bokassa's troops and locked up. Bokassa and his men hurried to the Presidential Palace where Dacko was forced to resign at gunpoint. Bokassa eased himself into power as President, but he was not yet satisfied.

Bokassa acted as an absolute monarch and consciously styled himself on Napoleon I (see above) of France. His regime was brutal, but little more so than that of most African Presidents. What was so remarkable was his extravagence and love of opulence. He wore a uniform so bedecked with medals that special strengthening straps had to be inserted in the cloth. His military parades were magnificent shows and his 'court' became a byword for luxury.

In December 1976 he proclaimed himself to be Emperor of the republic, henceforth to be the Central African Empire. A magnificent coronation was arranged with a diamond-studded crown, 15-foot tall gilded throne, fireworks and the finest food and wine purchasable. The new Imperial Guard was decked out in glittering uniforms for the occasion and mounted on thoroughbreds. The ceremony was fantastic, but the contrast with the impoverished state of the Empire's two million inhabitants caused widespread criticism.

In 1979 protests against his extravagance and neglect of the country escalated into riots. After an affair in which schoolchildren pelted him with stones, Bokassa ordered the police to round up the culprits. Over 100 children were caught, and Bokassa ordered their immediate execution, wielding one of the guns himself. When the French learned of this they told Bokassa to abdicate, but he refused. On 29th September 1979 French troops were flown into the Empire, overthrew Bokassa and reinstalled Dacko as President. Bokassa fled to the Ivory Coast.

— ♕ —

IDI AMIN (c. 1924–)

Usurped: Power in Uganda 1971
Social Origins: Army Officer

Amin's coup was successful almost in spite of itself. Forced into precipitate action, Amin had the backing of only a small faction of the army. Yet he swept to power in a single night, established himself as the sole authority in the country and became the hero of Black Africa. His fall was as much of his own making as his rise.

Amin began his career in the army. He joined the King's African Rifles of the British colonial army in 1946 and rose rapidly to the rank of sergeant major. He was given a commission when Uganda became independent in 1962 and loyally served Prime Minister Obote, who made him Commander-in-Chief. When Obote removed the Kings of Uganda, Amin's troops were instrumental in the move and Amin became a member of the inner ring of government. However, a break in relations between the two men began in 1969.

In December, when an assassination attempt was made on Obote, Amin was not at home and could not be found. Obote felt Amin was involved in the plot, but could not prove it. For his part Amin became convinced that Obote was looking for an excuse for revenge. In January 1971 Obote was in Singapore attending a Commonwealth conference. He received news of a plot against him and ordered the immediate arrest of Amin on suspicion. The order was leaked to Amin before it could be implemented and on the night of 24 January Amin led a regiment of men and a column of armoured vehicles loyal to him into Kampala. The remaining troops made no move to oppose him, though they did nothing to help, and Amin proclaimed himself President of Uganda.

From the start Amin was aware that he was the leader of only a small faction and came from a minority tribe in the north of the country. He seems to have been continually frightened by the possiblity that larger tribes or factions would oust him. Whenever he felt a plot was hatching, Amin ordered immediate executions. Within two years several thousand soldiers and tribesmen had been killed. Yet Amin remained popular. His action in expelling the disliked Asian racial minority won him support in Uganda and neighbouring countries while his continuing flouting of European opinion made him appear to be standing up for the rights of Black Africa.

Within Uganda, factionalism in the army began to threaten Amin's rule as officers vied with each other for power and wealth. In an attempt to divert the army Amin resorted to the typical pre-colonial African practice of starting a war. He launched a raid into Tanzania in October 1978. The Tanzanians were caught by surprise, but by January had a massive army

Amin
President Idi Amin of Uganda, his chest bedecked with self-awarded honours, talks to
Kurt Waldheim, Secretary-General of the United Nations. By posing as the African
champion against post-imperial intervention Amin gained a great following in the
Third World and forced himself into prominence on the international stage. Only
after his fall was the true extent of the brutality of his regime revealed. (*United
Nations/Y. Nagata*)

operating on the shores of Lake Victoria. They pushed deep into Uganda,
reaching Kampala in April. The city was subjected to looting and plundering
before the Tanzanians moved on in search of Amin. Amin, however, had
escaped to Libya where he lived for some time before moving to Saudi
Arabia.

BIBLIOGRAPHY

Ady, Cecilia M. 'Materials for the History of the Bentivoglia Signoria in Bologna'. *Transactions of the Royal Historical Society*, vol. XVII, 1934

Alliborne, Finch. *In Pursuit of the Robber Baron, Robert Guiscard*. Lennard Books, 1988

Allmand, Christopher. *The Hundred Years War*. Cambridge University Press, 1988

Anonymous Officer on the Staff of Napoleon. *Relation of the Last Campaign of Buonaparte*. Translated by John Curling. Hitchin, 1858

Appleby, John. *The Troubled Reign of King Stephen*. G. Bell and Sons, 1969

Ashe, Geoffrey. *Kings and Queens of Early Britain*. Methuen, 1982

Basham, A. L. *The Wonder that was India*. Sidgwick and Jackson, 1956

Bede. *A History of the English Church and People*. Translated by Leo Sherley Price. Penguin, 1984

Beeler, John. *Warfare in Feudal Europe*. Cornell University Press, 1971

Billins, Malcolm. *The Cross and the Crescent, A History of the Crusades*. BBC Books, 1987

Bradford, Ernle. *Cleopatra*. Hodder and Stoughton, 1971

Bradford, Ernle. *The Sultan's Admiral Barbarossa*. Hodder and Stoughton, 1969

Bridge, A. *Sueliman the Magnificent*. Granada Publishing, 1983

Brooke, Christopher. *Europe in the Central Middle Ages 962–1154*. Longman, 1987

Brooke, Christopher. *The Saxon and Norman Kings*. Fontana, 1963

Bruce, George. *The Paladin Dictionary of Battles*. Paladin, 1986

Bruce, Marie Louise. *The Usurper King—Henry of Bolingbroke*. Rubicon Press

Burman, Edward. *The Assassins*. Crucible, 1987

Burn, A. R. *The Warring States of Greece*. Thames and Hudson, 1968

Butler, Denis. *1066 The Story of a Year*. Putnam, 1966

Byrne, Francis John. *Irish Kings and High Kings*. Batsford, 1973

Canning, John (Editor). *100 Great Kings, Queens and Rulers of the World*. Hamlyn, 1967

Canning, John (Editor). *100 Lives of Antiquity*. Century Books, 1985

Chamberlin, Russel. *Charlemagne*. Grafton Books, 1986

Chambers, James. *The Devil's Horsemen, The Mongols*. Weidenfeld and Nicolson, 1988

Cotterell, Arthur. *China, A Concise Cultural History*. John Murray, 1988

Cottrel, Leonard. *Queens of the Pharaohs*. Evans Brothers, 1966

Daiches, David. *Charles Edward Stuart*. Thames and Hudson, 1973

Davenport-Adams, W. H. *Warriors of the Crescent*. Hutchinson, 1893

Davis, R. H. C. *The Normans and their Myth*. Thames and Hudson, 1976

Donaldson, Gordon. *Scottish Kings*. Batsford, 1967

Dunan, Marcel (Editor). *Larousse Encyclopedia of Ancient and Medieval History.* Hamlyn, 1981

Dunan, Marcel (Editor). *Larousse Encyclopedia of Modern History.* Hamlyn, 1967

Ferril, Arthur. *The Fall of the Roman Empire, The Military Explanation.* Thames and Hudson, 1986

Finberg, H. P. R. *The Formation of England 550–1042.* Granada, 1976

Fitchett, W. H. *The Great Duke.* Smith, Elder and Sons, 1915

Forster, Margaret. *The Rash Adventurer, Rise and Fall of Charles Edward Stuart.* Panther, 1975

Fuller, Major General J. F. C. *Julius Caesar.* Eyre and Spottiswoode, 1965

Furneaux, Rupert. *The Zulu War.* Weidenfeld and Nicolson, 1963

Geoffrey of Monmouth. *Histories of the Kings of Britain*

Ghirsham, R. *Iran.* Penguin, 1954

Glover, Michael. *Warfare in the Age of Bonaparte.* Cassell, 1980

Grant, Michael. *Cleopatra, Queen of Kings.* Granada, 1974

Grant, Michael. *The Twelve Caesars.* Charles Scribner's Sons, 1975

Grinnell-Milne, Duncan. *The Killing of William Rufus.* David and Charles, 1968

Hallam, Elizabeth (Editor). *The Plantagenet Chronicles.* Weidenfeld and Nicolson, 1986

Holmes, George (Editor). *The Oxford History of Medieval Europe.* Oxford University Press, 1988

Jacob, E. F. *The 15th Century.* Oxford University Press, 1987

Johnson, Stephen. *Later Roman Britain.* Routledge and Kegan Paul, 1980

Kelly, J. N. D. *The Oxford Dictionary of Popes.* Oxford University Press, 1986

Lacey, Robert. *Robert, Earl of Essex—An Elizabethan Icarus.* Weidenfeld and Nicolson, 1971

Lamb, Harold. *The Flame of Islam.* Garden City Publishing. 1951

Lindsay, Philip. *Kings of Merry England.* Ivor Nicholson and Watson, 1936

Lissner, Ivar. *Power and Folly, the story of the Caesars.* Jonathan Cape, 1958

Longford, Elizabeth. *Wellington—The Years of the Sword.* Weidenfeld and Nicolson, 1969

Lot, Ferdinand. *The End of the Ancient World.* Routledge and Kegan Paul, 1966

Machiavelli, Niccolo. *The Prince*

Mackie, J. D. *The Earlier Tudors.* Oxford University Press, 1987

Magnusson, Magnus. *Vikings!.* Bodley Head, 1980

Meredith, Martin. *The First Dance of Freedom, Black Africa in the Postwar Era.* Hamish Hamilton, 1984

Morgan, David. *Medieval Persia.* Longman, 1988

Morgan, David. *The Mongols.* Blackwell, 1986

Morris, John. *The Age of Arthur.* Phillimore, 1973

Newark, Tim. *The Barbarians.* Blandford Press, 1985

Newark, Tim. *Celtic Warriors.* Blandford Press, 1986

Newark, Tim and McBride, Angus. *Medieval Warlords*. Blandford, 1987

Newby, P. H. *Saladin in his Time*. Faber, 1983

Norwich, John Julius. *Byzantium the Early Centuries*. Viking, 1988

Oliver, Roland and Fage, J. D. *A Short History of Africa*. Penguin, 1962

Oman, Charles. *England Before the Norman Conquest*. Methuen, 1910

Oman, Charles. *A History of Greece*. Longmans Green, 1921

Oman, Charles. *Warwick the Kingmaker*. Macmillan, 1903

Payne, Robert. *The Dream and the Tomb, a history of the crusades*. Robert Hale, 1986

Pehrson, Justine Davis Randers-. *Barbarians and Romans: The Birth Struggle of Europe AD 400–700*. Croom Helm, 1983

Platnick, Kenneth. *Great Mysteries of History*, David and Charles, 1972

Potter, Jeremy. *Pretenders*. Constable, 1986

Pryde, David. *Great Men of European History*. Nimmo, Hay and Mitchell, 1896

Radice, Betty (Editor). *Who's Who in the Ancient World*. Penguin, 1973

Ridley, J. *The Roundheads*. Constable, 1973

Riter, E. A. *Shaka Zulu*. Granada, 1971

Rodzinski, Witold. *The Walled Kingdom, A History of China*. Fontana, 1984

Ross, A.. *The Pagan Celts*, Batsford, 1986

Ross, C. *Edward IV*. Eyre Methuen, 1975

Ross, C. *Richard III*. University of California Press, 1981

Roux, Georges. *Ancient Iraq*. Penguin, 1964

Saggs, H. W. F. *Civilization before Greece and Rome*. Batsford, 1989

St Aubyn, Giles. *The Year of Three Kings 1483*. Atheneum, 1983

Salway, Peter. *Roman Britain*, Oxford University Press, 1981

Scott, Martin. *Medieval Europe*, Longman, 1964

Spear, Percival. *A History of India*. vol. 2. Penguin, 1965

Stenton, Sir Frank. *Anglo-Saxon England*. Oxford University Press. 1971

Thapar, Romila. *A History of India*. vol. 1. Penguin, 1966

Thorpe, Lewis (Translator). *Gesta Guillelmi Ducis Normannorum et Regis Anglorum by William of Poitiers*. Folio Society, 1973

Tranie, J. & Carmigniani, J.-C.. *Napoleon's War in Spain*. Arms and Armour Press, 1982

Turnbull, Stephen R. *The Book of the Samurai*. Magna Books, 1982

Turnbull, Stephen R. *Samurai Armies 1550–1615*. Osprey, 1979

Unstead, R. J. *A History of the World*. A & C Black, 1983

van der Zee, H. & B. *William and Mary*. Macmillan, 1973

Waley, Daniel *The Italian City Republics*. Longman, 1969

Warren, W. L. *Henry II*. University of California Press, 1973

Webster, Graham. *The Roman Imperial Army*. A & C Black, 1979

Wilson, David. *The Anglo-Saxons*. Penguin, 1972

Wood, Michael. *In Search of the Dark Ages*. BBC, 1981

Young, Col. G. F. *The Medici*. Random House, 1930

Index of Entries

Chao Kao *fl.* late 3rd century BC (China) 81

Charles I 1226–1285 (Naples) 179

Charles IX 1550–1611 (Sweden) 233

Charles Martel *c.* 690–741 (Franks) 116

Christopher I, Henri 1767–1820 (Haiti) 268

Christopher ?–770 (Papacy) 119

Claudius II ?–AD270 (Roman Empire) 93

Clement VII 1342–1394 (Papacy) 197

Cleopatra III ?–90 BC (Egypt) 50

Cleopatra VII 69–30 BC (Egypt) 61

Clive, Robert 1725–1774 (India) 252

Cola di Rienzi *c.* 1313–1354 (Rome) 188

Cortes 1485–1547 (Mexico) 219

Cromwell, Oliver 1599–1658 (England) 240

Cyneheard ?–786 (Wessex) 120

Cyrus the Great *c.* 600–529 BC (Persia and Babylon) 19

Darius I ?–485 BC (Persia) 21

Darius III ?–330 BC (Persia) 26

Decius AD201–251 (Roman Empire) 88

Demetrius Soter ?–150 BC (Seleucid Empire) 46

Dessalines 1758–1806 (Haiti) 263

Diaz 1830–1915 (Mexico) 289

Didda *fl.* mid-10th century (Kashmir) 177

Dingane ?–1838 (Zulu) 260

Diodotus the Younger ?–225 BC (Bactria) 44

Dion 408–353 BC (Syracuse) 24

Dionysius the Elder *c.* 432–367 BC (Syracuse) 23

Dost Mahomed 1793–1863 (Afghanistan) 273

Dracula *c.* 1430–1476 (Wallachia) 200

Edward IV 1442–1483 (England) 209

El Cid *c.* 1040–1099 (Valencia) 153

Elizabeth 1709–1762 (Russia) 250

Enrico II ?–1379 (Castile) 191

Eric Bloodaxe *c.* 925–954 (York) 133

Essad, Ahmet *c.* 1864–1920 (Albania) 302

Evagoras ?–374 BC (Salamis) 22

Felix V 1383–1451 (Papacy) 202

Feng Yu-Hsiang 1880–1948 (China) 312

Ferdinand VII 1784–1833 (Spain) 265

Francia 1757–1840 (Paraguay) 284

Fredegond ?–597 (Neustria) 107

Frere, Sir Bartle 1815–1884 (Zululand) 294

Galba 3 BC–AD 69 (Roman Empire) 67

Gao Yang ?–550 (China) 112

Garibaldi 1807–1882 (Italy) 279

Gaumata ?–521 BC (Persia) 20

Gelimer *fl.* early 6th century (Vandal) 106

Godunov, Boris *c.* 1550–1605 (Russia) 233

Godwin ?–1053 (England) 147

Gomez, Juan 1859–1935 (Venezuela) 301

Gonzaga, Luigi ?–*c.* 1340 (Mantua) 186

Gopala *fl.* mid-8th century (Bengal) 176

Gregory VIII *c.* 1070–*c.* 1140 (Papacy) 156

Gyges ?–*c.* 685 BC (Lydia) 15

Habibullah ?–1930 (Afghanistan) 315

Haidar Ali *c.* 1720–1782 (Mysore) 251

Hatshepsut ?–1480 BC (Egypt) 2

Hazael *fl.c.* 860 BC (Syria) 8

Hengist ?–488 (Kent) 100

Henry I 1068–1135 (England) 155

Henry IV 1367–1413 (England) 194

Heraclius 575–642 (Byzantine Empire) 110

Herod the Great 73–4 BC (Judaea) 56

Hiang Yu ?–202 BC (China) 37

Hiero II ?–216 BC (Syracuse) 41

Honorius II 1009–1072 (Papacy) 151

Horemheb ?–1320 BC (Egypt) 4

Horton, Thomas 1759–*c.* 1825 (Kishmah) 259

Hoshea *fl.c.* 720 BC (Israel) 14

Houston, Samuel 1793–1863 (Texas) 275

Huang Chao ?–*c.* 884 (China) 144

Huan Kung ?–642 BC (China) 80

Hugh Capet ?–996 (France) 140

Hulagu ?–1265 (Persia) 178

Hung Wu *c.* 1328–1396 (China) 192

Ibn Saud *c.* 1880–1953 (Nejd) 300

Idi Amin *c.* 1924– (Uganda) 318

Irene 752–803 (Byzantine Empire) 121

Isaac II Angelus ?–1204 (Byzantine Empire) 167

Isaac Comnenus ?–1061 (Byzantine Empire) 151

Iturbide 1783–1824 (Mexico) 274

Ivan the Terrible 1530–1584 (Russia) 228

Jehu *fl.c.* 840 BC (Israel) 9

Joan of Arc 1412–1432 (France) 198

John IV ?–1670 (Portugal) 243

John VI 1292–1383 (Byzantine Empire) 187

John of Gaunt 1340–1399 (Portugal) 189

John the Fearless 1371–1419 (France) 196

John Tzimisces 925–976 (Byzantine Empire) 138

Juba II ?–AD 20 (Numidia) 63

Jorgenson, Jorgen 1780–1845 (Iceland) 267

Jugurtha ?–104 BC (Numidia) 47